# ENERGY
## IN THE
# EXECUTIVE

ALSO BY TERRY EASTLAND

*Counting by Race: Equality from the
Founding Fathers to* Bakke *and* Weber
*(with William J. Bennett)*

*Ethics, Politics and the Independent
Counsel: Executive Power, Executive Vice
1789–1989*

# ENERGY
## IN THE
# EXECUTIVE

## THE CASE FOR THE
## STRONG PRESIDENCY

Terry Eastland

THE FREE PRESS
*A Division of Macmillan, Inc.*
NEW YORK

Maxwell Macmillan Canada
TORONTO

Maxwell Macmillan International
NEW YORK   OXFORD   SINGAPORE   SYDNEY

AMY 1416-7/3

## TO JILL AND KATIE

The Free Press
A Division of Macmillan, Inc.
866 Third Avenue, New York, N.Y. 10022

Maxwell Macmillan Canada, Inc.
1200 Eglinton Avenue East
Suite 200
Don Mills, Ontario M3C 3N1

Macmillan, Inc. is part of the Maxwell Communication
Group of Companies.

Printed in the United States of America

printing number
1  2  3  4  5  6  7  8  9  10

**Library of Congress Cataloging-in-Publication Data**

Eastland, Terry.
    Energy in the executive : the case for the strong presidency /
Terry Eastland.
        p.   cm.
    Includes bibliographical references and index.
    ISBN 0-02-908681-7
    1. Presidents—United States.  2. Executive power—United States.
3. United States—Politics and government—1981–1989.  4. United
States—Politics and government—1989–   I. Title.
JK516.E27   1992
353.03′13—dc20                                            92-14045
                                                          CIP

# CONTENTS

# CONTENTS

## TWO
## THE PRESIDENT AND THE EXECUTIVE BRANCH

## THREE
## THE PRESIDENT AND THE APPOINTMENT OF JUDGES

# CONTENTS

# CONSERVATIVES IN POWER AND THE STRONG PRESIDENCY

In the fall of 1961 a small group of political conservatives met at the Avenue Hotel in Chicago to dream some big dreams: capturing the Republican Party and ultimately winning the presidency. Barry Goldwater's candidacy as the Republican nominee in 1964 was the first major step toward that goal, finally reached in 1980 when Ronald Reagan was elected President. Reagan's most important legacy was a less ideologically defined but still conservative President, George Bush.

Electorally speaking, conservatives have enjoyed enormous success, having now held the presidency for three consecutive terms, the longest custody by either party since the twenty-year run of the two Democrats, Franklin Roosevelt and Harry Truman. As President, Reagan successfully advocated policies that contributed significantly to the longest period of economic growth since World War II and to the winning of the Cold War. And were Bush not President, Iraq might still have Kuwait in its criminal grip. Nonetheless, despite their achievements—indeed despite the generally recognized fact that Reagan's was the most successful presidency since Dwight Eisenhower's—conservatives in power, as especially their friends have argued, could have done, and could be doing, much better.

What makes for effective and proper presidential governance, whether by conservatives or anyone else, is not reducible to a simple formula. The person and character of the President matter, as do the ideas and politics that inform his many decisions. Congressional support, or its absence, obviously is relevant. But no presidency that is weak can expect to govern as well as it might. Only the strong presidency will do.

The idea of a strong presidency may be unappealing to conservatives taught by Ronald Reagan that "government is not the solution to the problem" but the problem itself. But Reagan ironically proved that government can be the solution; indeed, Reagan demonstrated that the strong presidency is necessary to effect ends sought by most conservatives. A strong presidency was on display when Reagan secured cuts in the marginal tax rates, argued for tax reform, and promoted the arms race that exhausted the Soviet economy, hastening the end of the Cold War (and indeed the Soviet Union). On the other hand, a weak presidency contributed to the Iran-Contra affair, the savings-and-loan mess, and the defeat of the Bork nomination. And it would have taken a strong presidency to have secured major reform of entitlement spending, among other still distant goals.

The experience of the past dozen years should have forced conservatives to rethink their views of government to a greater extent than they have. Evincing a concern that—curiously for conservatives—has deemphasized the past, obscuring the resources of earlier periods, conservative intellectuals are primarily interested in U.S. political history since the 1930s. That decade marked the advent of the big government we have today, and the conservatives of that era did not like it. They decried FDR's New Deal, which gave us the much bigger state, and they argued that Congress should be the

2

dominant branch of government. In his classic work, *Congress and the American Tradition,* published in 1959, James Burnham specifically identified belief in Congress rather than the executive as central to conservatism. Burnham worried that Congress, the "peer of the executive" in 1933 when FDR took office, had declined to a "mere junior partner."[1] Yale's Willmore Kendall saw the issues similarly, becoming a critic, as historian George Nash has put it, of the "imperial presidency."[2] Twelve years after Reagan, who voted four times for Roosevelt, was first elected President, few conservatives still speak of the elective branches in the same terms as Burnham and Kendall. Now conservatives complain about the "imperial Congress"[3] and worry about the condition of the congressionally "fettered" executive.[4] They embrace, it appears, a much stronger presidency than their ideological forebears did.[5] Cynics will be forgiven for thinking that conservatives have been attracted to a strong executive on purely instrumental grounds, for there have been few efforts on the part of conservatives to discuss the strong presidency in terms other than political self-interest.[6] But if the only explanation conservatives have for their new faith in the presidency is pragmatic, they will find themselves bereft of principle and thus in sync with those many liberals, journalists, and academics who are impatient with governing forms and procedures.

Conservatives definitely should embrace a strong executive, but for the best of reasons: the Constitution. For what the Constitution proposes to establish is limited government that can maintain the conditions of freedom against internal and external threat, administer the nation's laws, and encourage rational deliberation and choice on the part of a self-governing people. And the presidency it regards as necessary for achieving this government, which the framers saw as *good* government, is a strong one. Or, as Alexander Hamilton preferred to say in the vocabulary of his time, an energetic one. As Hamilton succinctly stated the matter in the *Federalist Papers,* "energy in the executive is a leading character[istic] of good government."[7]

The purpose of this book is to recover and restate the enduring case for energy in the executive, which is to say: the strong presidency. The argument that unfolds in this book proceeds from theory but is attentive to practice. The abiding focus is on how a President should think about his office, and act, during his tenure. Toward this end, I examine numerous events from the Reagan and Bush years, such as the enactment of tax reform (1986), the litigation over racial quotas (1981–89) and the legislative debate over quotas (1990–91), the Persian Gulf War (1990–91), and the Bork and Thomas confirmation battles (1987 and 1991, respectively). The various episodes teach, by way of both positive and negative example, the meaning of the strong presidency. The book thus contains within itself another book—a critique of the present conservative experience in power. So I should say explicitly: This book is written for conservatives serious about politics and governing. But it cannot be for conservatives only, for the simple reason that the strong presidency is the American presidency.

Candor compels acknowledgment, however, that if liberals still see the presidency the way some used to see it, their kind of strong President will likely prove a disaster. Liberalism from the first years of this century has argued against localism and for an ever more inclusive, more equal national community. Toward this end it has posited the need for a powerful federal government brought about by a visionary President who would mount the "bully pulpit" and lead the American people toward its special future. The liberal Presidents of this century made some undeniably great contributions to our public life, but in the Johnson presidency a liberalism ambitious to do so much finally did too much, exhausting the institutional capacities of the office and damaging it in the process. Joseph Califano, in his recent memoir of White House service as LBJ's domestic adviser, captured a central problem of the Johnson presidency: "Perpetually trying to get everyone—business, labor, churches, schools, cities, and states—working on every problem, Johnson failed to accept that he couldn't do it all. . . . [He] overestimate[d] the capacity of the government to administer and the nation to absorb so much so fast."[8] While liberals today are willing to criticize the Johnson presidency on many grounds (especially foreign policy), it is an open question whether they still subscribe to the liberal progressive idea of national community

4

and in particular to the kind of activist presidency it required (and which Johnson embodied), for that concept of the office still makes appearances in our politics. It was there in Walter Mondale's post-Watergate call for a President who is "the moral, spiritual leader of our country," and it was there in the actual person of Mondale, in his 1984 campaign for President. Mondale personified the enduring liberal belief that the President of the United States should insinuate himself into all aspects of our national life, indeed that, in respect to domestic issues at least, the nation should be presidential—a presidential nation.[9] But this concept of the presidency long ago hit its limits.

Many of the problems Johnson-style liberals have asked the nation to solve have proved to be quite stubborn; they are different in kind from the traditional tasks of government. Fighting the Persian Gulf war proved much easier than waging LBJ's Great Society war on poverty. But this is not the worst of the political problem for old-fashioned liberals. The big government their politics required has proved a field of dreams: built in Washington over the decades, it is now the vast arena in which special interests of all descriptions compete in mostly legal but often unseemly ways for their "share." Their presence has not only made it difficult for an overcommitted government to do its basic work but also contributed to government's continuing growth (and the ever greater national debt). The idea of national community that the federal government now reflects is hardly so noble; the nation's capital has become, as George F. Will has written, "an arena for entrepreneurship, engulfed in a feeding frenzy of people bending public power to private purposes."[10] There are reasons the American people are put off by politics and government, and unlikely to elect a liberal eager to read from the same cookbook that gave us modern Washington. And should someone like that ever be elected, he is asking, most likely, to become a weakened President, less able to be energetic where the Constitution positions him to be, and therefore less able to contribute to good government.

One place where the Constitution positions the President to act is as Commander in Chief of the nation's armed forces—to use military force when authorized and necessary,

5

and it will always, at some point, be necessary, given recalcitrant human nature. Here, too, liberalism has a problem in presidential politics. Many liberals do not mean by a strong foreign policy presidency the one that bombed Saddam Hussein out of Kuwait, except after the fact of that event.[11] In this downsizing of the presidency, modern liberals who cut their teeth on Vietnam and Watergate have overreacted to the sometimes too aggressive actions of the liberal Presidents of prior decades, who were quite willing to go to battle. For these modern liberals, a strong foreign policy presidency is one that wages war only tomorrow, and tomorrow never comes. There is a reason that the televised pictures of Michael Dukakis riding in a military tank during the 1988 campaign provoked derisive laughter and contributed to his electoral defeat: The American people sense that a liberal Democrat is the last person to turn to for a presidency willing to use *all* of the powers committed to it by the Constitution.

One reason for the continuing crisis of liberalism is its discontent with the presidency as it exists within the constitutional order. It is not surprising that over the past decade the proposals for reforming our system of separated powers so as to make it conform to a parliamentary model have come mainly from liberal Democrats. As James Q. Wilson has observed, the states in Western Europe in which the powers have been massed in the parliamentary system have grown larger and more expensive than ours.[12] And in general parliamentary systems allow for less vigor and efficiency in the execution of foreign affairs than ours does.[13] Conservatives have argued for certain changes affecting presidential power, such as strengthening the President's hand in budget battles with Congress through a line-item veto. But the structural modifications some conservatives tend to support are ones like this, of degree, not kind. Far more so than liberalism, conservatism is at home with the presidency as it currently exists.

This is not to say that a big-government style liberal cannot win the presidency, especially if he disguises himself, as Mondale did not. Still, unless there is considerable change within the Democratic Party, the Republicans will remain the more credible presidential party.

Conservatism faces not a crisis regarding the nature of

the presidency but the challenge of presidential governance. That challenge cannot be met when the presidential office is underemployed, as it often has been during George Bush's tenure, the striking exception of the Persian Gulf war duly noted. Nor can it be met when the office is *mis*employed. During the past dozen years, conservatives in power have chased down some futile roads, thinking them avenues to effective governance, implicitly (if not explicitly) equating them with the strong presidency. But that institution is not found—to name some prominent examples—in a bully pulpit merely satisfied with the sound of its own voice, or in the will-of-the-wisp of "cabinet government," or in rote defenses of aides accused of wrongdoing, or in "budget summits" that scant the hard work of public argument. The strong presidency rather is found in actions that further—or at least do not undermine—the great purposes of the Constitution. It therefore takes its cue from the Constitution. But here there is a problem.

The most influential teaching on the presidency over the past thirty years has invited Presidents and those who serve them to think about governance in terms tenuously—if at all—related to the Constitution. I refer to Richard E. Neustadt's *Presidential Power: The Politics of Leadership,* first published in 1960.[14] Neustadt addresses what he called "the power problem" faced by every President—that, namely, of how a President makes his powers "work for *him*." Neustadt's theme is "personal power and its politics: what it is, how to get it, how to keep it, how to use it."[15] While conceding that the power provided by the Constitution does enable a President to have "personal influence," Neustadt emphasizes as far more important the individual's personal skills and abilities. Obscured in his treatment of the presidency is the office itself, its powers and duties and structure, and how it might be executed from a constitutional perspective.

Some Presidents have read Neustadt's book, as have many presidential aides. And clearly there are many important things that students of government and politics, including Presidents and their aides, may learn from it. But the realist perspective of *Presidential Power* is in the final analysis unsatisfying; that approach needs to be more securely grounded in the Constitution than it is in *Presidential Power.*

7

In our form of government, the "power problem" cannot be mainly a matter of "personal power." The Constitution empowers the President, and the President should strive to understand his office and use it from the perspective of the Constitution, in behalf of its great ends. He may employ all of the realist teachings of *Presidential Power* as he might like in that effort, but his destination—and the means to it—must not be at odds with the Constitution.

This book may be read as a corrective to *Presidential Power,* a *constitutional* corrective, to be precise. A first step in this correction is to recognize the error of a fundamental assumption of that book. In the discussion that follows, I draw upon the insightful analysis made by Joseph M. Bessette of Claremont McKenna College at a 1991 conference on separation of powers at the Ashbrook Center for Public Affairs, Ashland University.

"The Constitutional Convention of 1787," Neustadt writes, "is supposed to have created a government of 'separated powers.' It did nothing of the sort. Rather, it created a government of separated institutions *sharing* powers."[16] As Bessette observes, in one sense, Neustadt is right: The Constitution of 1787 did create separated institutions, and it did provide for *some* sharing of powers. The President, for example, shares in the legislative power by virtue of his duty to recommend legislation and his authority to veto bills presented to him.[17] But by denying that the Constitution created a government of separated powers, Neustadt implicitly questions the framers' view that power is by nature of three quite different kinds—legislative, executive, and judicial—and that good government lies in the distribution of at least the *bulk* of each kind of power to each of the three branches. As Bessette points out, *Presidential Power* has encouraged the view so widely held today that governmental power is an "undifferentiated mass" over which "separated institutions . . . compete for control." This understanding—to cite just one example—is full-blown in Hedrick Smith's 1988 best-seller, *The Power Game: How Washington Works.* On page 15 Smith approvingly quotes Neustadt's (oft-quoted) remark about our government as one in which separated institutions share powers, never again to return directly to the subject.[18] Smith's book is dedicated to the proposition that all governmental power is alike (and something to be grabbed by those with the personal skills and abilities to do so); there is, one is invited to believe, nothing really distinctive about presidential power.

Neustadt and Smith are wrong. The Constitutional Convention of 1787 did indeed create a government of separated (albeit to some extent shared) powers—powers that at their core are different in nature. Article I, concerning Congress, begins: "All legislative powers herein granted shall be vested in a Congress. . . ." Article II, regarding the presidency, begins, "The executive power shall be vested in a President. . . ." And Article III, on the judiciary, begins, "The judicial power of the United States, shall be vested in one Supreme Court, and in such inferior courts as the Congress may from time to time ordain and establish." Reading these texts, Bessette observes that each time the Constitution vests power, it states the kind of power it is vesting. This, he says, reflects the framers' view that there was such a thing as legislative power and such things as the executive power and the judicial power. For them, the essence of legislative power was that of enacting laws—"prescrib[ing] rules for the regulation of the society," as Hamilton put it.[19] The essence of the executive power lay in administering the government—in the "execution of the laws and the employment of the common strength . . . for the common defense" (Hamilton, again).[20] And the essence of the judicial power consisted in interpreting and applying the written law in "cases and controversies."[21]

The presidency, not to mention the rest of the government, cannot be understood apart from what the Constitution says it is. Thus, at various points throughout this book I discuss the executive power vested at the beginning of Article II in the President and also many of the various powers and duties listed in Sections 2 and 3—what Alexander Hamilton called "particular cases of executive power."[22] These powers and duties include the President's authority as Commander in Chief of the armed forces, his power to make treaties, his power to appoint U.S. ambassadors and his duty to receive ambassadors from other nations, his authority to appoint executive officers and judges, his duty to recommend legislation, his duty to take care that the laws are faithfully executed, his power to pardon "for offenses against the United States," and his power to require written opinions from the heads of the executive departments.[23] The President also has the veto power, which is found in Article I, a placing that suggests its at least partial legislative character.

By focusing on the President's powers and duties, one sees more clearly not only what the presidency is but also where it is, in relation to the other two branches, and what it may and even should do. Consider, for example, that the President has duties that obligate him to speak to both Congress (by recommending legislation) and the judiciary (by defending challenges to laws and actions taken pursuant to the laws). Consider, too, that the President, through the exercise of his veto power, can induce second thoughts in Congress about its legislative handiwork. And it is through the veto that the President, as Hamilton put it, is able "to defend himself . . . [against] an immediate attack upon [his] constitutional rights."[24] It is testimony to the genius of the constitutional design that the President can through his legislative power defend against attacks upon any aspect of his power. He can, that is, and he should. Imposed by that design upon individual Presidents is a substantive public policy: vigilant defense of the office itself. The Constitution equips and asks Presidents to be strong, for their own sake but also that of good government.

Through consideration of the presidential powers and duties, and the structure of the office itself, one is also able to understand why the best, most comprehensive way to think about the presidency is as the framers conceived it: in terms of energy. Because that word comes to us from the late eighteenth century, some historical context is relevant.

The framers designed and empowered the presidency so that it would provide the energy that the government under the Articles of Confederation lacked. *The Federalist Papers,* the most authoritative exposition of the meaning of the Constitution, saw the presidency in just these terms. Energy, wrote Hamilton, "is essential to the protection of the community against foreign attacks; it is not less essential to the steady administration of the laws; to the protection of property against those irregular and high-handed combinations which sometimes interrupt the ordinary course of justice; to the security of liberty against the enterprises and assaults of ambition, of faction, and of anarchy."[25] Hamilton's *Federalist* collaborator, James Madison, put it most concisely: "Energy in government [and therefore in the executive] is essential to that security against external and internal danger and to that prompt and salutary execution of the laws which enter into the very definition of good government."[26]

Now, the government prior to 1787 could not have had an adequate supply of energy because the Articles of Confederation under which it operated did not even provide for an executive. Congress had tried to administer the government, with little success. And it had done a poor job handling foreign affairs. Thus did their experience at the national level teach the framers what they believed in theory: That a body best suited to deliberate over public policy, the legislative body, cannot be expected to provide what only an executive can. And their experience at the state level meanwhile reminded them of the illiberal impulses of legislatures. John Marshall, later Chief Justice, observed that the states lacked any principle "which could resist the wild projects of the moment, give the people an opportunity to reflect, and allow the good sense of the nation time for exertion."[27]

So it was that when the framers met in Philadelphia, they had to fashion an executive. What they did, of course, was create the presidency. Partaking of elements dating to Aristotle and Machiavelli, it was, in 1787, a new thing and indeed our thing—an American original.[28] Even so, as is well known, there was, in Hamilton's words, "hardly any part of the system which could have been attended with greater difficulty in the arrangement of it than [the executive]."[29] Eventually, the delegates agreed upon the need for an independent executive—that is, one who was not dependent on Congress for his election or reelection; "the executive," as Hamilton explained, "should be independent for his continuance in office on all but the people themselves."[30] And the framers wound up vesting the bulk of the executive power not in a council, as some desired, but a single person.[31]

This independent executive—the presidency—was absolutely critical to the success of the new government in which

11

fundamentally different powers had been separated and assigned to distinct institutions of careful design. (Note that in 1787 the presidency—itself government—was part of the solution to the problem of bad government under the Articles of Confederation.) Hamilton talked about the presidency as though he were holding test tubes in a physics lab. Noting that one person was to hold the office, not several, Hamilton said this "unity" was an "ingredient" of energy. Observing that the one person—the President—was to hold the office four years, Hamilton applauded this adequate "duration" as another "ingredient" of energy because it would provide time in which the President could undertake what he called "extensive and arduous enterprises" for the public benefit[32] and the people could judge their efficacy. Turning to the powers and duties of office found in the Constitution, Hamilton characterized all of these, including the veto power, as "ingredients" of energy.

A modern reader might conclude that Hamilton was overly energetic with his use of the word, but he made his point. And, notwithstanding the well-known changes in the presidency over the past two hundred years, it is still valid today.[33] For however one judges these changes, it remains the case that the presidency must be the source of energy in government. Neither of the other two branches can provide it, and neither should be expected to, because neither was designed for that purpose. The presidency is to be the source of energy in government so that things that need doing are done (such as recommending legislation and administering the law and appointing judges and prosecuting a war) and so that the government itself remains stable and has a means of survival. Energy in the executive is indeed a leading characteristic of good government.

This book is a study in energy in the executive, that is, the strong presidency of the Constitution. But, to repeat, the argument of the book concerns not only theory but also practice. The presidency in its structure and powers and duties is energy, but how does a President act so that his office is the source of energy, properly understood? While the Constitution obviously cannot guarantee energy, it does contain a realist teaching, inviting Presidents to act energetically. ("A latent teaching exists in the constitutional powers themselves that is discernible," observes Harvey C. Mansfield, Jr., "or at least presentable to politicians."[34]) Decision, activity, secrecy, dispatch, vigor, expedition, promptitude of decision, firmness. These are some of the nouns Hamilton used in *The Federalist* to explain the energetic executive; these are behavioral terms, characteristics of the energetic executive who acts for the sake of good government. The point of the case studies examined in this book is to enhance our understanding of how the strong President should act, especially today, in the context of a politics characterized by so-called "divided government" (only three times in the past thirty years has a national election given one party control of the White House and both houses of Congress) and influenced by the growing and influential class of political elites and entrepreneurs in the nation's capital.

While the presidency most emphatically is energy, this book does not ignore the important cognate teaching of the framers, who saw energy *and* responsibility as the two sides of the same coin of "unity." They vested the executive power in a single person not only to facilitate energy in government but also to ensure responsibility on the theory that "We the people" can more easily identify, and hold accountable for often controversial executive actions, a single person. Built into the presidency, then, is an ethic of energy *and* an ethic of responsibility. The President is to act on the basis of his powers and in accordance with the laws of Congress and the Constitution, and he is to be responsible to the people for his actions in a system of government that provides for quadrennial presidential elections, judicial review, and impeachment by Congress.

The President's oath of office suggests its nature as the unique source of energy in government whose occupant is to be held accountable. Consider that it is the only oath spelled out in the Constitution (in Article II).[35] And consider that in the oath the President, who along with the Vice-President is the only officer elected by a national vote, is the *only* officer obligated to execute a *particular* office. Everyone else in the federal establishment is bound only "to support this Constitution," as Article VI states. The Constitution clearly expects much from the President—leadership, in a word—even as it

13

expects that "We the people" through our constitutional system will keep an eye on him.

This book divides into three parts: "The President and Congress," "The President and the Executive Branch," and "The President and the Appointment of Judges." This structure is usefully constitutional, comprehending the presidency in its unique relations to the other two branches of government, and doing so in the order in which the Constitution itself discusses all three. It is, of course, common to speak of the President in terms of his various roles—as chief administrator, chief diplomat, commander in chief, and the like. This book does not so much disagree with that perspective as argue for a more precise, which is to say more constitutional, view. One advantage of this perspective is that it offers the opportunity to see the President in terms of judicial selection. The generalists who write on the presidency do not allocate much space to judicial appointments—none of the editions of Neustadt's classic work speaks to the subject—but no treatment of the presidency at this remarkable point in its history can ignore it. (Indeed, recent confirmation battles, notably those of Robert Bork and Clarence Thomas—emphatically demand it.) The judiciary has become more significant in our politics—which is to say more powerful—for two reasons. One is the growth of government itself through statutory law, a joint product of Congress and the executive; the more law there is, the more lawsuits there are (especially when law is written in vague terms, as much is today). The dockets become bigger and the federal courts, at one level or another, render more decisions. The other reason is the willingness of federal courts to intrude into often controversial matters, such as abortion, that judges once regarded as the preserve of the Congress and the President, or the states, or both. Over the years, Congress has increased the number of judgeships to deal with the increasing numbers of cases—there are now almost 1,000 federal judges—but it is the President, under the Constitution, who is positioned to influence the direction of the courts through his appointments. Hence the treatment of this subject in Part Three.

The claim of this book is not that the strong presidency will cure all that ails government today. That would be too simple. There is a growing literature on the problems of Congress. And, as noted earlier, effective presidential governance under the Constitution turns on a variety of factors, including the substantive merits of the policies a President pursues as well as the nature of his political convictions. For these reasons, the argument for a strong presidency presented in this book may be regarded as modest. But it also advances something bold, for the strong presidency of these pages is proud to speak its name around those conservatives who think any such notion must mean a Great Society–type presidency, even as it disagrees with instrumentalists (of all political persuasions) who believe in a strong presidency only when their candidate is elected President. Moreover, the strong presidency of this book implicitly accepts the necessity of governing and the importance of public life. Conservatives who have believed that they could fix government and then retire from the work of governing should have learned by now that there can be no end to an intelligently pursued public life—not if they intend to make an enduring difference.

Again it must be emphasized that the strong presidency of this book is available to whoever is elected President. And whoever is elected must bear in mind that the justification for such a presidency is found in the often abandoned territory of the Constitution. From there, leadership is possible—leadership in behalf of good government.

# PART ONE

# THE PRESIDENT AND CONGRESS

I n his memoir, former budget director David Stockman recalls his belief in 1981 that the constitutional prerogatives
of the legislative branch would have to be "suspended" in order
to enact the Reagan economic program.[1] Like many conservatives, Stockman thought that only a "roaring bully pulpit"—
starring Ronald Reagan—could achieve congressional passage
of the fiscal measures he (Stockman) thought necessary.[2]

Stockman held a popular view of how a President should
press his legislative views upon Congress. He envisioned what
he doubtless thought was a strong presidency. But such a
presidency is not found in a roaring bully pulpit that seeks to
suspend the constitutional prerogatives of Congress. Here as
elsewhere, the beginning of wisdom about the energetic executive lies in the Constitution itself.

In creating the presidency, the framers envisioned a chief
executive who would administer the laws and conduct foreign
policy, and who could stand as a check against Congress, the
most powerful branch. The framers gave less thought to—or
at least talked less about—the President's legislative role;
Alexander Hamilton barely mentions it in his treatment of
the executive's powers and duties in the *Federalist Papers*.
And certainly the framers did not expect the advent in our
century of presidential rhetoric. But the Constitution they
drafted and proposed and ratified plainly provides for a presidential role in legislation that is best described as potentially
very strong.

One of two relevant texts is Article II, Section 3, which
provides that the President "shall from time to time give to
the Congress information of the state of the Union and recommend to their consideration such measures as he shall
judge necessary and expedient." That the President gives a
State of the Union speech to Congress every January is an
event as well-known as any in our politics; unfortunately, the
second part of the Recommendation Clause, as it is called, is
less noticed by citizens and scholars alike.[3] It imposes a *duty*

upon the President, and the framers purposely chose language to this effect. They considered making the recommendation of legislation a matter of political prerogative by first proposing the construction, "he may," but turned to the language of duty apparently to foreclose objections to the very idea that the President might have legislative views.[4] Of course, the Constitution does not require Congress to introduce legislation, hold hearings, or even vote on the President's recommendations; it may do nothing, and often has. Still, the President has this duty, and it is a duty upon which the Constitution imposes limits notably consistent with deliberative democracy.[5] The measures the President recommends are ones he is to deem "necessary and expedient." "Expedient" in the late eighteenth century did not mean only "politic" or "opportunistic" but also "conducive to advantage in general, or to a definite purpose; fit, proper, or suitable to the circumstance of the case."[6] Before he recommends measures, then, the President is to think about them. He must be aware of relevant facts. He must analyze and judge.

The Recommendation Clause appears in the same section of Article III as the Take Care Clause, which obligates the President to "take care that the laws be faithfully executed." The textual proximity of these clauses has led the separation-of-powers scholar J. Gregory Sidak to observe that the framers saw the execution of a law and recommending ways to improve it as closely related tasks.[7] That seems right. The President is uniquely positioned by the Constitution to know about a given law's implementation; so it would make sense for the Constitution to capitalize upon his special knowledge by asking him to recommend "necessary and expedient" legislative changes.

Along these lines consider also the obligation to give "information of the state of the Union"—which is even more textually proximate to the duty to recommend measures; here it appears that the Constitution seeks to take advantage of the fact that the President is the only officer elected by the whole nation. He is apparently expected to inquire into, and think about, the state of the union, and on the basis of that exercise recommend "necessary and expedient" measures.[8]

The other relevant text, found not in Article II but Article I, concerns Congress. Article I, Section 7 discusses the destiny of every bill that has passed both houses of Congress.[9] Such a bill must be presented to the President if it is to become law. And: "If he approve he shall sign it, but if not he shall return it, with his objections to that House in which it shall have originated, who shall enter the objections at large on their journal, and proceed to reconsider it." The Constitution does not tell the President *what* to do with the bill: he may sign it or veto it (or refuse to take any action for ten days after "presentment," in which case it becomes law automatically.) But the Presentment Clause, containing as it does the veto power (although it is not explicitly called that), places the President at or near the end of the legislative process. The President is there whether he wants to be or not; and he is there whether he has recommended the particular measure now before him or not. Some of the genius of the constitutional design is seen in the Presentment Clause, and in particular in the provision of a qualified veto power; for through the veto the President can defend himself against legislation that threatens his own powers, and he can invite Congress to have second and third thoughts about a bill it has passed, and perhaps to pass a more well-considered version of it.[10] Observe that if the President casts a veto, he is under an obligation to send his objections in writing to Congress. A veto thus forces Congress to consider the President's view, on pain of losing to him, as two-thirds plus one of both houses must vote against a President if his veto is to be overridden.[11]

The Recommendation Clause and the Presentment Clause define the President's potentially substantial legislative role by asking his involvement in the lawmaking process, at both its start and finish, and inferentially throughout.[12] The practical issue for every President is how, in meeting his duty to recommend measures and to decide on the merits of

21

legislation at presentment, he should act from a constitutional perspective.

To rally popular support for their legislative recommendations, Presidents since Theodore Roosevelt have mounted bully pulpits. As I will show, the energetic executive today must speak publicly in behalf of his legislative goals; the non-rhetorical practices of most nineteenth century Presidents cannot be recommended. Even so, the presidential practice of rhetoric is not as easy as hiring speechwriters, press secretaries, and other communications wizards. Constitutionally speaking, it is a difficult endeavor that requires far more thought than either liberals (who invented the bully pulpit) or conservatives have often given it. The chapters in Part One seek to provide the necessary reflections by discussing the history of presidential rhetoric in behalf of legislation and then examining in detail some recent examples of rhetoric (both good and bad) by Presidents Reagan and Bush.

I also focus in Part One on the President's actions when legislation is presented to him. There is little appreciation in our political culture of some purposes of the veto power; the "self-defense" veto, so essential to maintaining a government of separated powers, draws far too little commentary. Nor is there much awareness of what else a President may or even should do at the moment of presentment; the use of presidential signing statements is a subject largely neglected, except when controversy flares. The Reagan and Bush presidencies contain certain episodes in governing at presentment—or the failure to govern—that deserve careful analysis.

The tax reform legislation of 1986, the budget accord of 1990, the civil rights legislation of 1990 and 1991, the Boland amendments addressing contra aid in the 1980s, the independent counsel reauthorizations of 1983 and 1987: these are among the legislative events I treat in Part One in an effort to elaborate the meaning of the strong presidency today. The very last chapter in Part One takes up another piece of legislation that was "ordinary" in the same sense the measures noted above were, namely, that it, too, was passed by both houses of Congress and presented to the President before becoming law. But the Iraq Resolution that the President signed on January 12, 1991, was in another sense hardly ordinary, for Congress infrequently declares war (only five times in our history) or otherwise authorizes the use of military force, as it did in that instance. I treat the President's role in respect to the Iraq Resolution because of the discussion on the war powers it affords as well as the remarkable window on the strong presidency it opens.

# 1

## SPEAKING FROM THE BULLY PULPIT
### The Rhetoric of Recommendation

Ronald Reagan, the most conservative President since Calvin Coolidge, was by no means the first President to speak from the bully pulpit in behalf of his legislative proposals. Yet his popular speechmaking in this respect would have been considered quite radical as late as a century ago. Nineteenth century Presidents delivered State of the Union messages and also gave patriotic speeches on ceremonial occasions. But rarely did they make popular appeals for their legislative proposals.[1] With the notable exception of President Andrew Johnson (notable because his speeches helped fuel the fires of impeachment that almost burned him), they made their communications in writing—for example in written messages to Congress—not (or not also) in popular remarks.[2] Indeed, they

24

tended to pass up occasions to speak on serious matters to the people.

Consider, for example, the view of popular rhetoric implied by Abraham Lincoln in remarks made to a Pittsburgh audience in 1861:

> And here, fellow citizens, I may remark that in every crowd through which I have passed of late some allusion has been made to the present distracted condition of the country. It is naturally expected that I should say something upon this subject, but to touch upon it at all would involve an elaborate discussion of a great many questions and circumstances, would require more time than I can at present command, and would perhaps, unnecessarily commit me upon matters which have not yet fully developed themselves.[3]

The newspaperman who reported that speech also said that it was followed by immense cheering and cries of "good!" and "that's right!" Remarks like Lincoln's by a modern President would no doubt be followed by lusty boos and indignant editorials.

The nonrhetorical practices of Lincoln and most other nineteenth century Presidents reflected the dominant political understanding that dated from the American founding. This understanding did not proscribe a strong executive or a strong national government. To the contrary, it embraced those ideas. What it did proscribe was popular leadership on the part of Presidents. The framers envisioned Presidents who would be constitutional officers—who understood that while their authority came ultimately from the people, it came immediately from the Constitution. Such Presidents would promote reason and deliberation in a system of separated powers which needed such behavior from a President—the only national officer, as Thomas Jefferson said, "who command[s] a view of the whole ground"—if it were to avoid capsizing under some wave of popular passion. "It is the reason, alone, of the public, that ought to control and regulate the government," wrote James Madison.[4] It is "the deliberate sense of the community [that] should govern," wrote his *Federalist* collaborator, Alexander Hamilton.[5] The political science of the framers had no place for popular appeals by a President. Rhetoric of that kind and reason could not coexist; to "go to the people" was necessarily to act the demagogue.

The framers' political science summons for judgment any popular appeal a President today might make. The merits of any particular speech to the side, however, one cannot accept a blanket prohibition against popular presidential rhetoric unless one is also prepared to accept a presidency *less able* to meet its constitutional *duty* to recommend legislation.[6]

The practical fact is that over the past century the political world has changed in ways the presidency today cannot ignore. This world now encompasses a professional political class (that includes academics, writers, and lobbyists, among others) and the news media. In this environment, if a President were simply to recommend legislation to Congress, perhaps posting a letter in its behalf, but saying little or nothing to the people, he would be even more likely to be ignored. (This is not to suggest, of course, that when he says a lot, Congress will listen and do his bidding.) Moreover, in today's political environment, a President recommending major legislation who refuses to make popular speeches in its behalf would probably be less able to fulfill an original expectation of the presidency as the institution uniquely able, as Alexander Hamilton put it, to undertake "extensive and arduous enterprises for the public benefit."[7] The very notion of presidential leadership in a legislative context thus would be compromised. Finally, a President who did not appeal to the people in favor of his legislative recommendations would appear to lack democratic legitimacy in an age when elected officials routinely make popular remarks. For better or worse, Lincoln's Pittsburgh audience is not the same audience Presidents today face; there is now an expectation that Presidents *will* speak to the people.

While, for these reasons, Presidents today cannot forgo popular rhetoric, why and how they speak remains critically important. The framers may have underestimated the people; while a popular address can become a flight from reason, it need not, and a President and his aides who sufficiently focus on his speechmaking and other public remarks can guard against this and related problems. The key point is that the deliberative democracy contemplated by the Constitution—defined as one in which there is reasoning on the merits of a given policy—remains today a worthy idea. A modern President's rhetorical strategies in recommending measures to Congress must therefore be conceived and executed in ways that at a minimum do not violate it.

The first instance of popular rhetoric by a President—also a successful one in terms of desired congressional action—appears to have posted few problems on this score. In 1904 President Theodore Roosevelt mounted a rhetorical campaign to overcome his own party's opposition to the Hepburn Act, a railroad regulation bill central to his "square deal."[8] In the end, both houses of Congress approved the legislation, part of the foundation of the modern administrative state. Jeffrey K. Tulis, a careful student of Roosevelt's activities in behalf of the Hepburn Act, concludes that, far from repudiating the framers' political science, Roosevelt embraced it at the deepest level. According to Tulis, Roosevelt took seriously the very problems that had concerned the framers—of demagoguery, policy by passion, and nondeliberative government. These negatives would characterize our politics, Roosevelt thought, if the American polity were to divide into a battle between rich and poor—the very kind of division that the framers had hoped their political science would forever prevent. Indeed, for Roosevelt, this division was occurring, as passions were flaring and demagogues arising. Roosevelt thus did not launch his rhetorical effort by accident, but deliberately. He thought the United States was in a crisis that could be described as fundamental, because it implicated the founding principles, and he concluded that only a President providing plebiscitary leadership could help the nation stay true to those original principles. In his speeches, according to Tulis, Roosevelt did not try to preempt congressional deliberation, and he honored the imperatives of reason by constructing principled arguments in support of his legislation. At the same time, however, he did employ appeals to passion, which he justified on grounds of the crisis that he believed threatened the nation.[9]

Roosevelt coined the term, "bully pulpit," meaning "first-rate" or "smashing," and it bears emphasis that the history of the bully pulpit begins with him, the first strong President since Lincoln. Since Reconstruction the nation had witnessed a parade of weak Presidents, including Grant, Hayes, Garfield, Arthur, Cleveland, and Harrison, all men who saw their jobs as narrowly administrative. Under the Whig theory of the presidency that dominated national politics during the second half of the nineteenth century, the President had little legislative influence. Moreover, Congress dominated the executive, using its committees to curb discretion in administering the law. Roosevelt's energetic tenure broke the pattern of weak presidencies since Lincoln, and his virtually unprecedented use of popular rhetoric reflected his view of the President, stated in his autobiography, as "a steward of the people bound to actively and affirmatively do all he could for the people, and not to content himself with keeping his talents undamaged in a napkin."[10] No one could say that Roosevelt had failed to engage the great issues of his time, chief among them the relationship of the national government to business, nor could anyone challenge his own estimate of his tenure, offered in a letter in 1908 shortly before he left office: "While President, I have *been* President, emphatically."[11]

Roosevelt, a Republican, also was the first of this century's progressive or liberal Presidents, who included, principally, Woodrow Wilson, Franklin Roosevelt, and Lyndon Johnson. Historians typically view each as a strong President, and each employed the bully pulpit.[12] Yet in an important sense, with implications for rhetoric (and much else besides), the first Roosevelt differed from his immediate successor, Woodrow Wilson. For while Theodore Roosevelt appeared to be satisfied with the original Constitution, Wilson, who taught at Princeton before becoming its President, clearly was not.

Wilson's formative intellectual period occurred during the late nineteenth century era of congressional dominance and executive subservience. *Congressional Government,* his first book, published in 1885, expressed his disagreement with the founding principle of separation of powers.[13] His entire career is appropriately understood, at one level, as an effort to overcome that principle in order to effect the progress that in his view history inevitably would bring about. Early on Wilson advocated reforms designed to increase the probability that one political party would control the two elective branches, and to make the leaders of the majority party in Congress part of the President's cabinet. Later, as he argued in his 1908 book, *Constitutional Government,* he turned to strong presidential leadership in which popular rhetoric would play a central role.[14]

As Charles R. Kesler has observed, however, what Wilson called "constitutional government" was not government according to the original Constitution. Rather it was government that, in overcoming the limitations imposed by the Constitution's separation of powers, "respects the right of the governed to strike whatever balance may suit them between [in Wilson's phrase] 'the power of the government and the privileges of the individual.' "[15] For Wilson, the task of the President in striking this balance was to articulate what was "in our hearts."[16] The President thus was to be a popular leader who "interpreted" the wishes of the people and manufactured them into legislative recommendations. At the same time the President was to "create" popular support for the necessary congressional action he would seek. For Wilson, only the President who could thus "mass opinion," which he called "the whole art and mastery of politics," could make our governmental system work as he thought it should work—in behalf of the people's inchoate desire for progress.[17]

From an early age Wilson saw himself destined for greatness, and in 1912 he was elected President, thus becoming the only presidential nominee ever to defeat two former Presidents, Theodore Roosevelt and his successor, the incumbent William Howard Taft. Wilson promised a New Freedom, arguing that federal power should be used to sweep away social, economic, and political privilege, and to restore business competition. Toward this end, Wilson practiced as President what he had preached as an academic. Succeeding in controlling the legislative agenda, he convened a special session of Congress in 1913, framed bills with the help of Democratic leaders in both houses, and, revising a custom that died with the Jefferson presidency, appeared in person before Congress to speak to the measure under consideration and urge its passage. And, of course, he spoke directly to the people in behalf of his proposals. Congress has rarely been so legislatively busy as between 1913 and 1916, when, among other things, it provided for banking reorganization and control through the Federal Reserve System, enacted tariff reduction, and imposed new regulations on business.

Putting to one side Wilson's view of separation of powers and his progressive politics, certain of his presidential practices must be regarded as fully constitutional and indeed a model for the energetic executive. Article II, Section 3 does require the President to recommend legislation he deems necessary and expedient, and in framing and speaking in behalf of his proposals—both to the Congress and the general public—Wilson was an appropriately strong President, regardless of how one views his discrete legislative proposals or the particular rhetorical formulations he used in pushing them. Like Theodore Roosevelt (and, later, his cousin Franklin), Wilson did not shy from engaging the major issues of his time.

But Wilson also is the source of problems that have plagued the presidency especially in more recent decades. Not surprisingly, these problems are related to his basic disagreement with the principle of separation of powers and his belief that Presidents are to lead the people ever onwards and upwards—to an unknown destination only history can reveal, but which, as the decades have passed, inevitably seems to have required larger and more costly government whose reach extends more deeply into the states and the private sector.

To begin with, the modern tendency of Presidents to "dumb" down their speeches can be traced to Wilson. Wilson said that Presidents should make arguments that are "broad and obvious," because "only a very gross substance of concrete conception can make any impression on the minds of the masses."[18] Wilson was a man before his time, for the technology of mass communications (and the democratization of the presidency) has encouraged "broad and obvious arguments"—not to mention nonarguments—in the popular speeches of modern Presidents. Wilson's theoretical impact shows up today in presidential speeches whose paragraphs are only sentence length. From the perspective of this book, Presidents do not have to rid their speeches of nuance and argument, and for the sake of deliberative democracy they should not.

More seriously, since Wilson, Presidents, trying to be popular political leaders, sometimes have failed to see themselves as constitutional officers. This helps explain why the administrative side of the presidency often receives little presidential attention, notwithstanding the President's constitutional duty to "take care that the laws are faithfully executed." A Congress eager to administer the executive in any event thus has been more able to do so, through oversight hearings and other means.[19] The attempt at popular leadership, meanwhile, has not often fared so well. Presidents have become so preoccupied with trying to anticipate what the people want and to effect change that they have become overly preoccupied with polling data[20] (see George Bush; the Wilson legacy is no respecter of political parties); or they have tried to do far more than government can accomplish or reality requires. A Wilson legacy is the refrain, "Let's get the country moving again"—it is considered impolite to ask exactly *where*—and nowadays Presidents are expected to try to get it moving regardless of the facts of the situation ostensibly calling for movement or the government's competence to perform whatever is to be done or its authority to do so in the first place. Ironically, some Presidents who have tried to be Wilsonian political leaders (whether consciously or not) have discovered they are ineffectual at that task, notwithstanding the employment of ambitious rhetorical strategies; it is doubly ironic when they discover that meanwhile Congress is in effect running much of the executive branch. So much for overcoming the separation of powers; so much for strong presidential leadership through popular speech; and so much, as well, for accountability. Garry Wills finds in Wilsonian theory and presidential practice, particularly in foreign policy, the origins of the "imperial presidency," but however one judges that, Wilson did plant seeds that have germinated weak presidencies.[21]

This did not occur immediately. Wilson's progressive successor, Franklin Roosevelt, was a strong President—legislatively *and* administratively (and in the appointment of judges). And, to be sure, Roosevelt saw himself following in Wilson's footsteps. In his 1932 acceptance speech at the Democratic Convention, Roosevelt called for the resumption of the nation's "interrupted march along the path of real progress"—

which would embrace greater economic security and a much wider prosperity. "Our indomitable leader in that march is no longer with us," said Roosevelt, but his spirit still survives, and "[we must] feel in everything we do ... the soul of our Commander in Chief, Woodrow Wilson." Roosevelt's frankly experimental presidency, aimed at overcoming the depression and reforming the economy, was carried out as though the nation were constantly at war. Thus, in his first inaugural, FDR said that as a last resort he was willing to ask Congress for "broad executive power to wage a war against the emergency as great as the power that would be given me if we were in fact invaded by a foreign foe." Roosevelt's early talk of warring against domestic emergency set the tone for what Robert S. Hirschfield has accurately described as "the consummate crisis presidency."[22] An irony of Roosevelt's tenure is that it took a real war (World War II) finally to revive the nation's economy, but modern Presidents since Roosevelt, both Democratic and Republican, have been fond of invoking crisis and asking the American people to declare war on this or that domestic problem.

Still, by 1945, writes the historian John Morton Blum, the progressive Presidents had established a legacy for American liberals—"a legacy of a strong chief executive, skilled in politics, engaged in promoting gradual social reform, and accomplished in managing international policy."[23] To liberals, this legacy did not seem problematic at the time. Harry Truman was heir to this tradition but unable to get his legislative program enacted, and John F. Kennedy, who spoke the tradition's language of getting the nation "moving again" after Eisenhower's two terms, died young from an assassin's bullet. Nothing had occurred since the end of World War II to make progressives question their tradition, and Kennedy's successor, Lyndon Johnson, brought excitement to many liberals. Franklin Roosevelt was Johnson's great inspiration, and in seeking to complete what Roosevelt had started, Johnson declared a "war on poverty" as part of his call for a Great Society, a place, as he put it, "where the city of man serves not only the needs of the body and the demands of commerce but the desire for beauty and the hunger for community." Johnson fashioned a legislative agenda of unprecedented ambition—

32

there was nothing, it seemed, that the national government, led by the President, could not do for the American people. And of course he mounted the bully pulpit in behalf of his legislative recommendations, some of which—such as the Voting Rights Act of 1965—were great in purpose and have proved successful in practice. But Johnson tried to do more than government could achieve at home even as he tried to fight an increasingly unpopular war abroad. His "grandiosity," as Blum writes, proved crippling.[24] It is with Johnson, who withdrew from the Democratic primary in 1968, that the series of strong liberal presidencies, as conventionally reckoned, comes to an end.

Johnson was not Jimmy Carter's inspiration, but adhering to the understandings of the presidency accumulated since Wilson, our last Democratic President gave his "malaise" speech to the nation. Carter said, in a Wilson-like statement, that the President should be "the leader of the people" rather than "the head of the government." Carter declared that the nation was facing "a crisis that strikes at the very heart and soul and spirit of our national will." In this Carter saw the nation as a sickly thing in need of resuscitation that only a President, apparently, could provide. His understanding of the central role of the President in curing a nation of its pathologies paralleled that of President Johnson, as captured by his speechwriter Harry McPherson:

> People were [seen to be] suffering from a sense of alienation from one another, of anomie, of powerlessness. This affected the well-to-do as much as it did the poor. Middle-class women, bored and friendless in the suburban afternoons; fathers, working at "meaningless" jobs, or slumped before the television set; sons and daughters desperate for "relevance"— all were in need of community, beauty, and purpose, all were guilty because so many others were deprived while they, rich beyond their ancestors' dreams, were depressed. What would change all this was a creative public effort. . . .[25]

Like Johnson before him, Carter engaged in that kind of effort. He gave inspirational speeches designed to create an

33

active public opinion that would be reflected—or so he and his aides thought—in higher opinion ratings and thus greater effective power for him as President.[26] But Carter's rhetoric represented an attempt to save not the nation but his presidency. It failed, in large part because the people sensed there was no crisis; reality could not be changed by presidential speechifying. His presidency, soundly rejected by the voters in 1980, is a reminder that under the Constitution the President is a constitutional officer, and that his popular leadership should be conditioned by that fact.[27]

Ronald Reagan accepted the bully pulpit passed down from the progressive era, and he used it more than any President ever, including his hero, Franklin Roosevelt, for whom he voted four times. But Reagan obviously did not propose to be a "visionary" of the Wilson, Roosevelt, Johnson, or even Carter variety. Reagan thus presents a paradox, for historians and political scientists alike have regarded the bully pulpit as essential to a strong presidency, and the strong presidency as essential to an ever larger, more powerful federal government, and such a government as essential to effecting, and maintaining, major social reforms. Reagan did see the bully pulpit as essential to his presidency, but he also saw the purpose of his presidency in terms of reducing the size and influence of government; Reagan wanted less of the public sector so that the private sector might increase and work its own social benefits. Thus, said Reagan in his first inaugural, "government is not the solution to our problem; government *is* the problem." Yet it would take government in the form of a strong presidency to solve the problem of government Reagan had identified; and in 1981 it would take the popular leadership of Reagan to help bring about passage of the tax-rate cuts that helped fuel the more than seven years of unbroken economic growth from 1982 to 1989. While Reagan was the most politically conservative President since Calvin Coolidge, a better comparison perhaps is with Andrew Jackson, who, like Reagan, sought less federal government; Jackson used the presidency to expand the power of the states at the expense of the national government. Not at all interested in recommending measures that would add to the size and reach of the federal government, and hardly one to see the people as suffering from anomie or malaise and in need of special presidential ministration that might enable them to glimpse new vistas of progress, Reagan did not deliver speeches infected with Johnsonian grandiosity. Nor did he feel obliged to declare crises in order to "get the country moving again." Reagan's political philosophy dramatically differed from Johnson's, of course, but by 1981 the nation had been exhausted by liberal ambition and rhetoric. The people could not be whipped rhetorically by Presidents into nonexistent crises or summoned to wartime domestic efforts and asked to sacrifice in ways that would increase the size of a government which many no longer could believe was a benign or effective instrument of social progress.

Even so, Reagan's popular rhetoric was not problem free. Indeed, both Reagan's and Bush's efforts in the bully pulpit demonstrate the kind of problems that can attend presidential rhetoric, especially in a media-driven era. Moreover, their efforts merit examination by not only conservatives but also those who are not; for the kind of problems found in the speeches of Reagan and Bush—problems that have as a common element their inconsistency with the idea of deliberative democracy—are likely to be no respecter of political parties.

Consider, to begin with, Reagan's 1981 speeches in behalf of his spending and tax proposals. These speeches helped inspire the popular outpouring that led to the legislative enactment of Reagan's fiscal policy. But the effort also in an important way undermined deliberation, even within the executive branch. In his memoir David Stockman relates the inadequate preparation that went into the fast-paced effort to produce a revised budget within Reagan's first six weeks in office. Stockman tells the specific story of how he thought he had managed to persuade Defense Secretary Caspar Weinberger to accept a 7 percent rate of increase in defense spending, consistent with the President's public promise to strengthen the nation's security. But Stockman later discovered that, as a result of a hasty calculation made during his short meeting with Weinberger, he had agreed to a base year that jacked up the rate of increase to 10 percent, thus mistakenly adding scores of billions to the spending side of the fed-

35

eral budget he was elsewhere trying to cut. Stockman made this error under pressure from Reagan's rhetorical needs—the President was about to give a speech unveiling his economic package and had to have numbers—and he was unable to get Weinberger to reconsider.[28] Reagan's popular leadership thus not only failed to force more careful consideration of federal spending, whose upward spiral in the 1980s has substantially contributed to the large budget deficits. It also actually contributed to overspending in the defense budget, and thus in a real sense to the greater national debt.

Also instructive is Reagan's campaign in behalf of the Strategic Defense Initiative, which the media dubbed "Star Wars."[29] According to Reagan's popular utterances, the defensive system he proposed would not supplement but supplant offensive weapons, thus providing the nation with absolute protection. Yet Reagan's advisers put the case differently: Defensive systems would enhance our deterrent capability, and they could be effective even if they did not work perfectly. Reagan's own speech appeared to have been influenced by the demands of popular rhetoric—that is, the need to make complex or technical issues intelligible and appealing to a lay audience—while the speech of his advisors clearly reflected their knowledge and expertise. These two views about the same policy—both coming from the administration—showed up in congressional debate and, ironically, contended against each other.

This example illustrates how popular rhetoric unfortunately can lead a President to use terms that may well be persuasive with the general public but are not with policymakers, who tend to be more familiar with the technical aspects of an issue. This is not to suggest that Reagan purposely intended exaggerated rhetoric; Reagan himself believed what he said in support of SDI. He thought, sincerely but incorrectly, that the new system would actually provide a protective shield for the entire nation—an antinuclear astrodome that would stretch from Maine to Florida to California to Hawaii and all the way back. To ask for rhetoric faithful to the technology is virtually to ask for a different President, and in any assessment of SDI, it is doubtful that any President but Reagan could have given birth to the project, which already has yielded important fruit.[30] Future Presidents, however, can learn from Reagan's rhetoric on SDI; rhetoric faithful to known facts is more conducive to generating an enlightened public opinion than rhetoric which is not.

One of Reagan's more visually memorable speeches is also instructive. First, some background: Under the 1974 Budget and Impoundment Control Act, Congress must pass thirteen separate appropriations bills before the start of the new fiscal year, which begins October 1; this is how the government is to be funded. Repeatedly during the 1980s, however, Congress failed to pass the necessary bills on time, instead enacting, close to the October 1 deadline when the government was about to run out of money, a "continuing resolution" that, in its most typical form, bunched together all thirteen spending bills. In late 1987 Reagan signed just such a last-minute continuing resolution for fiscal year 1988. In January of 1988, in his televised State of the Union message, Reagan carried to the podium as stage props three hefty tomes—"behemoths," he called them as he showed them to the viewing public. They were the continuing resolution he had signed that autumn, the reconciliation bill, and the conference report. Together, they weighed forty-three pounds, the continuing resolution itself about a third of that. Reagan said that to cope with this kind of bill he needed a "line-item" veto. This would allow him, he said, to "reach into massive appropriations bills, pare away the waste, and enforce budget discipline." The President cited as examples of waste the "millions" designated for "cranberry research, blueberry research, the study of crayfish, and the commercialization of wild flowers."

Seeking to drive home his point about the need for an item veto, Reagan then challenged Congress: "In thirty days, I will send back to you those items, as rescissions, which if I had the opportunity to line them out, I would do so." But Reagan didn't do that. Nor could he have, without violating an agreement the administration had made with Congressional leaders not to make a formal rescission request. A few weeks after this deadline, Reagan instead submitted an *informal* list of proposed rescissions. "These are the projects that, if I were able to exercise line-item veto authority, I would delete," he said. The amount came to $1.5 billion, but Congress ignored him.

With this speech Reagan hoped to educate the public

about the degree to which a continuing resolution forces a President into a corner where he must agree to it or else allow the government to shut down. He hoped to show how nondeliberative the budget process had become; after all, who could have read the three "behemoths" and then have made a considered judgment as rapidly as the Constitution requires, with the government about to shut down? As well, as a response to these problems, Reagan was asking for a device that Congress could enact—the line-item veto. Finally, he was issuing a veto threat, for in his address Reagan declared that he would not sign another continuing resolution in the fall of 1988. As it happened, Congress, whether under the influence of Reagan or the election campaign or both, was on better behavior that year, and did not deliver a continuing resolution to his desk at the midnight hour.

In these ways one may give the Reagan speech its due. On the other hand, it contained empty and even disingenuous rhetoric. Surely the members of Congress listening to him knew, if the national television audience did not, that his rescission talk was meaningless. And as for his ardent desire to "item veto" the millions involving cranberries, blueberries, crayfish, and wild flowers—those millions representing a bucket's worth of the ocean of federal spending—the fact is that Reagan could not have reached any of those "items" with a line-item veto. The fact is, none was in the continuing resolution. Instead, the items were found where most items are: in the conference report, which is not a bill. Constitutional scholar and budget expert Louis Fisher has observed: "The props used by Reagan were what some people in the theater industry call a 'flat': a front with nothing behind it."[31]

It may presume too much, however, to accuse Reagan of intentional misrepresentation. As with SDI, he probably believed what he was saying, that had he possessed the authority to "item veto," he could have cut out the assorted appropriations. His speech thus raises the possibility that a speechwriter or other aide came up with the budgetary items to plug into his address. If so, this is hardly the only time a speech a President has given was not his own.

On September 5, 1989, President George Bush gave his first nationally televised, prime-time address (he gave just two in 1989). This was a speech announcing his administration's drug enforcement policy and calling on Congress to enact drug-related legislation—a speech notably constitutional in its pairing of the Take Care Clause (the enforcement policy) and the Recommendation Clause (the legislation). During the speech, Bush had his own prop—a bag of crack cocaine. He told Americans that it had been seized across the street from the White House, in Lafayette Park. Bush's point was that the drug trade was so prevalent that it occurred even in his own neighborhood. Unfortunately for his speech (though fortunately for him), it didn't occur there. It turned out that a Drug Enforcement Administration official had lured a dealer *to* Lafayette Park to do his business (he sold the drug to an undercover agent) in order to produce for President Bush the needed prop. The man had never sold drugs there. Nor was the park a thriving drug market. Bush was said to be furious when these facts were reported, not because he did not want them known, but because he had not known them in the first place and did not think speeches should be written in this fashion. Bush's response, assuming its authenticity, was the correct one. But the fact that such a speech as his could have been composed and given illustrates the degree to which speechmaking can become the possession of the army of communications specialists inhabiting the modern White House. It also shows how the bully pulpit can be scripted for television, to the detriment of the office itself.

Presidents who employ popular rhetoric should strive to ensure that what they say is truly *theirs*. This is hardly to say they should write their own speeches; it is to say that they must invest enough time and effort in the process so as to be able to claim legitimate ownership of what they say.[32] When Presidents give speeches that are not their own, they have effectively divested themselves of power the Constitution gives them. Indeed, and ironically, they become the aides of those who compose and provide them with speeches. More, they renege on the oath of office that commits them not only to faithfully execute the office but also to preserve the Constitution, which vests the executive power in the President, not in their ghosts.

Reagan's 1988 State of the Union reveals another potential difficulty with popular speech: Words substituting for deeds. The fact is, Reagan could have vetoed the continuing resolution that instead he signed into law. He could have done that as the culminating act in a rhetorical campaign which would have begun much earlier in the year, indeed in his presidency; this would have been a campaign as to the wrong of putting the President in an almost impossible position, through the device of a last-minute continuing resolution. A Reagan veto threat would have been word serving deed; it might have worked to prevent the continuing resolution, and Reagan then could have delivered a much different State of the Union. And if Reagan had been forced to veto the continuing resolution, his deed might have led to lowered spending levels (as it did in 1981 when he did veto such a resolution) and multiple appropriation bills; it might have led to more vetoes of some of those bills, and thus a series of interactions between the White House and Congress that would have promoted second and third thoughts about spending policy. Certainly the casting of a veto would have represented an energetic effort to preserve the power of office that Reagan complained had been weakened by the budget process.

"The framers recognized," write Gordon Crovitz and Jeremy Rabkin, "that without a considerable amount of presidential assertiveness, no textual delineation of duties and powers could secure the conditions of 'energetic' government."[33] Nor, one might add, can any speech *alone* secure those conditions. Deeds matter. Presidents and their aides must not indulge the belief that speaking can replace governing, or its more common variant, that speaking is all there really is to governing. This point is worth stressing in an age of media politics that already has produced one pundit-politician in Patrick J. Buchanan, and emphasizing to conservatives who tout "communications skills" as though they were the sum of governing.

At the same time it should be noted that even those not accused of possessing communications skills have preferred speaking to governing. For three years President Bush said he might assert, on his own authority, a line-item veto. He never did so, and on March 20, 1992 he publicly gave up the idea; "some argue," he said in a White House speech, "that the

President already has . . . the line-item veto authority, but our able Attorney General . . . and my trusted White House Counsel backed up by . . . legal scholars, feel that I do not have [it]." Whatever one's view of the inherent line-item theory, a subject I discuss in Chapter 4, Bush preferred to flirt with a controversial idea in his public remarks—as though it could solve our spending woes—instead of taking actions lawfully available to him to address the problem. Through the first three years of his presidency, Bush did not cast a single veto on excessive spending grounds. And while discretionary spending under President Reagan declined for eight years, under Bush it remained constant. Congress in fact appropriated $14 billion less in discretionary categories—the ostensible target of a line-item veto—than Bush formally requested. The irony of Bush's finally ending his flirtation with the inherent line-item theory is that as he did so he announced his intention to employ a previously unused provision in the 1974 budget act to force Congress to vote on his proposed rescissions. Finally, Bush had decided to govern. It is a striking commentary on the twelve years in which conservatives have held the presidency that they did not before employ quite available statutory authority to bring about through the rescission process at least some of what the line-item veto might achieve.

For all the popular speeches Presidents have given in the twentieth century, few have actually worked as most Presidents hoped they would, by rallying the people to compel Congress to act in support of their legislative measures. Presidents and their aides doubtless will continue to think of popular speeches in this way; certainly Reagan and his aides did.[34] So will some presidential scholars. Richard Neustadt, whose first edition of *Presidential Power* had nothing to say about popular rhetoric, included it in later editions as one of the ways Presidents may seek personal influence.[35] His view of popular rhetoric only begs the question, however, of whether it will be disciplined rhetoric, at least consistent with the Constitution. Ultimately, that remains the key issue for every President who aspires to be energetic in a legislative capacity for the sake of good government.

41

# 2

# TAX REFORM
Reagan's Right Rhetoric

On May 28, 1985, President Reagan went on national tele-vision to unveil a major tax reform proposal. "My fellow citizens," he began, in a prime-time address, "I'd like to speak to you tonight about our future, about a great historic effort to give the words 'freedom,' 'fairness,' and 'hope' new meaning and power for every man and woman in America." Declaring that "unjust taxes are not "inevitable," Reagan re-called that the "first American Revolution" was "sparked by an unshakable conviction—taxation without representation is tyranny." Reagan called for a "second American revolu-tion for hope"—"a peaceful revolution, but born of popular resentment against a tax system that is unwise, unwanted, and unfair." Decrying "the special interest raids of the few" that can "rob us of all our dreams," Reagan declared that tax relief is in sight: "We can do it. And if you help we will do it this year."

But the people did not help. "The only constituents that lawmakers heard from," report Jeffrey Birnbaum and Alan Murray in *Showdown at Gucci Gulch,* "were those who complained about losing this or that tax break."[1] "I have found very little sentiment" for tax reform, said Speaker of the House Tip O'Neill, who thought the cause doomed unless Reagan proved able "to convert the nation's apathy to excitement."

Reagan continued to make that effort. In September 1985 he made popular appeals for tax reform, giving speeches in Independence, Missouri; Concord, New Hampshire; Raleigh, North Carolina; and Athens, Tennessee. The people still did not respond; polls showed the citizenry equally divided on the merits of the idea. Not until the summer of 1986, when enactment of tax reform seemed a foregone conclusion, did polls show a majority of Americans finally in support.

Reagan's popular rhetoric thus did not work the way he thought it should. It did not rally the people to compel Congress to act, although Congress eventually did, and in a way Reagan applauded. Still, Reagan's speechmaking in behalf of tax reform remains a model for the kind of popular rhetoric a President who aspires to act from a constitutional perspective should strive to emulate.

Reagan's rhetoric avoided the mistakes of popular appeals—indeed the very ones he committed at other times. First, it did not damage deliberation either within the executive branch or on Capitol Hill. Unlike some parts of Reagan's 1981 program for economic recovery, Reagan's tax reform proposal was not a rush job but just the opposite: It came out of a keenly deliberate process. Having endorsed in his 1984 State of the Union "an historic reform for fairness, simplicity, and incentives for growth," Reagan directed Treasury Secretary Donald Regan to study the issue and report to him by the end of the year. In his memoir, Regan observes that he had 310 days to devise a plan—no fewer.[2] Regan assembled a group of Treasury experts and focused their attention on the task. It proved an intellectual task that could not have been damaged by harmful presidential rhetoric if only because Reagan said little about the subject during this time. And as an intellectual endeavor, not incidentally, the Regan effort helped Reagan meet his constitutional duty not simply to recommend legislation, but to recommend legislation that the President judges "necessary and expedient." When Reagan unveiled his proposal to the nation on May 28, 1985, he said that now "a great debate" would begin, and he did not preempt that debate in Congress. "At critical junctures, but only at the behest of supporters from both parties," observes Jeffrey K. Tulis, "the President . . . entered the deliberative process."[3]

Second, Reagan's rhetoric was not schizophrenic. Examination of his speeches shows that he did not speak one way to the people and in another to Congress. He was consistent in his arguments, and nothing that he said publicly was at odds with the representations made on his behalf by the administration's lobbyists on Capitol Hill, James Baker and Richard Darman.

Third, the President's rhetoric did not rely on unfortunate props or make appeals only tenuously related to fact, nor could it be attributed simply to speechwriters or other aides. There was no doubt about where Reagan stood. Reagan's convictions on taxes and tax reform were well-known, having a long history dating to his days as an economics major at Eureka College and later as an actor in the late 1940s when the highest marginal rate for individuals (and he hit this level) was 90 percent.

Fourth, Reagan's rhetoric did not substitute for necessary action. A critical moment in the legislative journey occurred in the House, after the Ways and Means Committee had approved its version of tax reform. For ten days the White House had no comment on the committee action. Speculation grew that Reagan had abandoned tax reform, and House Republicans, who thought the Ways and Means bill set marginal rates too high, were ready to oppose it on the House floor. They had enough votes to defeat the rule by which the legislation would be considered, thus denying it a merits vote and leaving to the mercy of the Democratic leadership whether there would be a second vote on the rule, and thus a second chance for tax reform in the House. Had tax reform died in that chamber on account of the rule vote, that might have been the end of the effort during Reagan's second term, and Democrats credibly could have maintained that it was not their fault. The administration went to work, managing to get a second vote on the rule, which was approved, and then seeing the House bill through to final passage. The administration's campaign included skilled lobbying by Baker, Darman, and White House aides, but also a critical visit by President Reagan to Capitol Hill, where he met with the House Republican Conference. There the President asked House Republicans to support the bill in order to keep tax reform alive; acting pursuant to his constitutional power to "return" legislation, he specifically promised that he would veto any bill at odds with his tax reform principles, which included a top marginal rate for individuals of no higher than 35 percent. Subsequently, a number of House Republicans changed position on the rule and voted for legislation they opposed, hoping that the final bill would be one they could approve.

Fifth, Reagan's rhetoric made the case for tax reform. His speeches contained argument, and through it he influenced the deliberative process in Congress, setting the terms of debate in two important ways.

In the first place, he presented tax reform as an issue of fairness. Fairness was an argument he pursued from the moment he began his public effort. In his 1984 State of the Union address, in which he asked the Treasury to study tax reform, Reagan emphasized that what he wanted was "a plan for action for the entire tax code so all taxpayers, big and small, are treated more fairly." And note the language in his May 1985 speech, setting forth his plan: "Death and taxes may be inevitable, but unjust taxes are not." Reagan's focus on fairness had an obvious political impact on Capitol Hill. After Reagan gave his May 1985 speech, Dan Rostenkowski, selected by Democrats to give their televised response, felt obliged not to oppose but to join him. "Trying to tax people fairly," said Rostenkowski, "has been the historic Democratic commitment."[4] And when tax reform had finally passed both houses, Republican Senator Robert Packwood told reporters, "this bill is not about economics, it's about fairness."[5]

Also, Reagan just as successfully was able to present tax reform as an issue of growth, to be achieved through lower tax

45

burdens. Over and over he referred to the tax-rate cutting that was a key part of the reform as a further elaboration of a larger process of tax-rate reduction begun in 1981. In his May 1985 speech Reagan insisted on a top rate of no higher than 35 percent, and never wavered from that. The final legislation in fact contained a lower top rate—33 percent (for certain high incomes).

In these two ways Reagan's rhetoric helped advance his political goals without damaging the constitutional order. And his rhetoric indirectly enhanced the deliberative process on Capitol Hill. Al Hunt, the Washington bureau chief for the *Wall Street Journal,* has observed that Reagan's speechmaking skills "commanded such respect that they scared off a lot of potential opponents"—especially those representing the special interests.[6] The very possibility that Reagan might use popular speech against the special interests deterred them from the kind of lobbying they otherwise might have engaged in—lobbying born of the modern entitlement mentality in which many Americans, including those in the business community, believe they are equally entitled to some kind of "benefit" from the government. The result was an atmosphere that gave Congress more room in which to reason more freely, because more rationally, about the public interest. Reagan's rhetorical threat helped achieve what Woodrow Wilson's spoken remarks did in a similar context more than seventy years earlier. In a speech to the nation in behalf of his tariff reduction measure, Wilson urged public opinion "to check and destroy" the "intolerable burden" of "insidious lobbyists" working for special interests.[7] Wilson's appeal helped lessen the influence in the Senate of the interests who wanted tariff protection, thus paving the way for the bill's enactment.

Reagan believed that the point of his popular speech was to get the people on his side in a legislative battle.[8] Presidential rhetoric may have that effect, and there is no constitutional reason Presidents should not hold this belief and strive for majorities in Congress. Theory aside, of course, a President who did not want to "win" in Congress would be a bizarre political creature, hardly practical enough to be elected to his office in the first place. Still, the way in which a President wins remains important, and a President who understands the constitutional order will see to it that his popular rhetoric at least does not distort the deliberative process. While Reagan may not have contemplated this point—there is no evidence in his memoir or any of his other public statements that he did—his rhetoric in behalf of tax reform well served the constitutional order.

What Reagan did understand, at some level, was the nature of the contribution that the presidency can make to a major legislative undertaking—what Alexander Hamilton called an "extensive and arduous enterprise" for the public benefit. In essence, Reagan understood presidential leadership in regard to legislation. Since FDR's "first hundred days" in 1933, newly elected Presidents have been expected to hit the ground running, to have a fast legislative start, and in 1981 Reagan had a legendary fast start, using popular speech to help secure passage of his program for economic recovery. But Reagan's employment of the office in the first year of his *second* term, in behalf of tax reform, is the more interesting example of how the energetic executive can contribute to good government.

Because of the twenty-second amendment, which bars reelection to a third term, second-term Presidents are called "lame ducks," and in an important sense they are: Alexander Hamilton regarded reeligibility as an "ingredient" of executive energy, and the fact that today a second-term President is *not* eligible represents a diminution in presidential energy (a regrettable energy loss urged on the nation by conservative Republicans in the wake of the Roosevelt presidency). Lame ducks are not supposed to accomplish much legislatively, and yet Reagan was able to sign major tax reform legislation that most experts had given few chances of passing. Reagan showed that the office, even in a second term, can still be used to contribute to good government.

Nor is this all. Reagan did not run for reelection on a platform including tax reform. It was in his 1984 State of the Union address that Reagan asked Don Regan to devise a tax reform plan, but the Treasury Secretary was not to report "specific recommendations" until December—and therefore after Election Day. When Reagan mentioned the December reporting date, Democratic congressmen in the audience

47

laughed out loud, cynically. And the cynicism was bipartisan. Reagan chronicler Lou Cannon reports that speaking to a business group in Florida on the day after the election, Republican Senator Bob Dole waved a blank piece of paper at his audience and quipped, "I've just obtained a copy of President Reagan's secret tax plan."[9] Reagan's 1984 campaign was purposely devoid of tax reform and all other substantive proposals; the single idea of his campaign was to have no ideas. This is not the way to campaign, but the point here is that running on nothing very meaty in 1984, Reagan nonetheless was able to govern. That he did not seek a mandate did not prevent him from successfully pursuing, in a second term, such a major innovation in public policy as tax reform.

Whatever else it does, a presidential election at least confers an office, and it gives the occupant the legitimate authority, right, and indeed the opportunity to press through constitutional means for the adoption of his public policies. Even more: it gives the occupant the responsibility to do that. The mandate-less, lame-duck Reagan did not shrink from using the office to make the case for tax reform. Reagan in this instance became the strong President. Four years later, George Bush would have found it useful to study this Reagan example.

# 3

# "NO NEW TAXES"
## The "Processed" President

The budget agreement of 1990 proved the biggest mistake of the Bush presidency. The agreement failed by its own criteria to reduce either federal spending or the budget deficit, both of which, in the spring of 1992, stood at postwar highs as a percentage of gross domestic product. By raising taxes without truly solving any long-term structural problems in government spending, the agreement penalized the private sector in the short run and reduced Americans' long-term confidence in the health of the economy. It contributed to both the depth and the length of the 1991–1992 recession. These economic facts, plus the political one that the budget agreement was President Bush's idea, which he asked for despite a well-known promise to the American people not to accept new taxes, helped spawn the surprising primary challenge by Patrick J. Buchanan. With Buchanan collecting as much as a third of the vote in some states, Bush decided to confess error after the New Hampshire primary. "Total mistake," he called it, hoping to erase the agreement from public memory. But the budget accord is worth retrieving and analyzing for what it teaches—by way of negative example—about the legislative role of the President.

Under the Constitution, the presidency is the unique source of energy in government. In the legislative context the energetic executive will use his office to frame rational terms of political debate.

President Bush conspicuously failed to do this in 1990 when he sought a "deficit-reduction" package from Congress. Committing himself to what Washington calls the "process," Bush failed to clarify the political and economic choices available to the nation as he could have done by stating what those choices were, which ones he endorsed, and why. In sharp contrast to the President who pushed Saddam Hussein from Kuwait in 1991, this President did not cut a profile of energy in the executive.

In retrospect, the problems began in 1988.[1] Having repeatedly stated his opposition to tax increases, Bush used his acceptance speech at the Republican National Convention to say the now famous words, "The Congress will push me to raise taxes, and I'll say no, and they'll push, and I'll say no, and they'll push again, and I'll say to them, 'Read my lips: No new taxes.' "[2] Bush's promise helped him get elected, but it was not made in the context of a larger effort to frame a principled debate over the direction of the nation's fiscal policy. Nor did Bush, once elected, try to enlarge the discussion of fiscal policy, as he continued simply, and simplistically, to reiterate his campaign vow. Bush could have broadened and defined the public debate through speeches to Congress and the nation that would have advocated an economic growth policy focused on tax *and* spending policy. After all, if no-new-taxes was to stick, Congress—and the nation—eventually would have to make some hard spending choices, and the presidency was the office of government best positioned by the Constitution to make this point and to frame the terms of debate as to how and where and why the budget should be cut.

Having failed to employ his office in behalf of such an "arduous extensive enterprise," however, Bush found himself in the spring of 1990 faced with the prospect of a larger deficit for fiscal year 1991 than his budget office had only months earlier predicted. The focus of the President's fiscal policy suddenly switched from no-new-taxes to deficit reduction, which implies the possibility of some new taxes. Yet Bush did not try publicly to frame the debate over deficit reduction, either. At a press conference on May 3, 1990, the President merely said that he intended to "talk process" with congressional leaders from both parties, and that he would ask them to join him in a "budget summit" on which he would impose "no preconditions."

Bush thus committed his presidency to a method of seeking legislation that disdains public debate over important policy ends, relying instead on private meetings aimed at producing a Washington consensus. One problem with this method of governing is that, in the absence of a clearly defined public position, presidencies tend to resort to strategies of finesse that seldom lead to satisfying results, whether for the President, the "political process," or the nation. So it happened in this instance.

Not surprisingly, Bush's "no preconditions" remark was interpreted in the press and by Republican congressmen as a willingness on his part to accept some (as yet unspecified) tax increases. In a clumsy effort at "spin control," Chief of Staff John Sununu told reporters—on "background" as a senior administration official while flying with the First Lady to Costa Rica—that "no preconditions" meant that Democrats could propose tax increases but that the White House would veto them. Fearing a trap in which their party would be cast by the President as the one proposing new taxes, Democratic congressional leaders reacted by refusing to reach any kind of budget agreement until the President signaled a different position. Constrained by his unwillingness to use his office to frame a public debate and his commitment to "process," and with his budget office now forecasting a fiscal year 1991 deficit of close to $170 billion, Bush attempted to finesse Democrats back into the process huddle.

Meeting with the congressional leadership on June 26 for

a White House breakfast, Bush issued a statement through his press secretary:

> I met this morning with the bipartisan leadership—the speaker, the Senate majority leader, the Senate Republican leader, the House majority leader and the House Republican leader—to review the status of the deficit-reduction negotiations.
>
> It is clear to me that both the size of the deficit problem and the need for a package that can be enacted require all of the following: entitlement and mandatory program reform, *tax revenue increases,* growth incentives, discretionary spending reductions, orderly reductions in defense expenditures and budget process reform, to assure than any bipartisan agreement is enforceable and that the deficit problem is brought under responsible control. The bipartisan leadership agrees with me on these points.
>
> The budget negotiations will resume promptly with a view toward reaching substantive agreement as quickly as possible. [Emphasis added.]

That was it. "Tax revenue increases" can refer to revenues from ordinary economic growth or tax rate cuts (such as Bush had proposed on capital gains). But it can also mean higher tax levies: "some new taxes." There was no White House press conference, no elaboration of the meaning of the ambiguous phrase by the President or his aides. Asked about it in the White House Rose Garden, Bush only said, "I'll let the statement speak for itself."[3] Others—in the media and on Capitol Hill—filled the interpretive void. "Bush Abandons Campaign Pledge, Calls for New Taxes," ran the headline in the *Washington Post*. "Read his lips: New taxes after all," said the *Washington Times*. Lesley Stahl of CBS went further: Bush, she said, was "reversing ten years of Republican catechism on taxes."

Here was the single most important issue of domestic policy—the overall levels of federal taxing and spending—and Bush was hiding from his position instead of framing the debate. Bush tried to dance his way out of difficulty through his favorite means of communication—the press conference. But the President failed to explain why he had taken the position on taxes suggested in the statement. He simply asserted that "this deficit is bad," making no argument for that proposition. And he said that the people "know" the deficit is bad. Yet the people did not know that. The people could have drawn other conclusions from the available economic data; it was not obvious, for example, just why the budget deficit had to be reduced through higher taxes or lower spending at a time when the economy was stagnating.

The President said that he was motivated to accept tax increases by the threat of "Draconian cuts in defense, student grants and a wide array of other necessary domestic services"—cuts that would result (through the process known as "sequestration") if Congress failed to meet the budget targets in the Gramm-Rudman-Hollings budget act. Bush seemed horrified by the prospect of any such cuts, and he did not use the press conference to make the case for entitlement reform, discretionary spending reductions, or budget process reform—three of the items characterized in his statement just three days earlier as "required" in any agreement. His focus was taxes.

Bush's press conference amounted to a statement that the American people should simply believe him as to the desirability of reducing the deficit through some as yet unspecified new taxes, this after he had abandoned his long-held promise to oppose any new taxes. The press conference did little to allay his credibility problem, much less to advance the cause of deliberative government. This was hardly surprising, because press conferences are a poor means of presenting a legislative policy and offering a coherent argument in its behalf. The President must share time with reporters who ask questions that can bounce from one subject to another or who wish to "pin" him down on a matter he would not care, or is not prepared, to talk about. Also, in press conferences the President typically does not read from a prepared text that can reflect his well-considered (in the best of all worlds) views. Press conferences (and television talk shows, for that matter) can be useful in reiterating points or arguments previously made—preferably in prepared speeches, a superior means of engaging the public debate.

It is a measure of the frequent weakness of Bush's presidency that he prefers press conferences to speeches. During his first year in office, for example, he gave almost six times as many press conferences as Reagan annually averaged, and he made only two nationally televised speeches during evening hours, one of these (on Thanksgiving eve) largely ceremonial.[4] Although his June 30, 1990, press conference was not one of his better ones, he generally won high marks for his performances. But a President who so prefers press conferences that he neglects the public argument he can make through well-considered speeches is underemploying the presidential office.

With his press conference, Bush did manage to get the "process" moving again. Throughout the summer the administration maintained that the capital gains rate should be cut, while Democrats, emboldened by Bush's willingness to accept new taxes, began to press, in the name of "fairness," for higher marginal rates for taxpayers. Eventually the Democratic leadership agreed to a capital gains rate reduction if the Republicans would accept an increase in the highest marginal rate for individual taxpayers, to 32 percent from 28. When the White House refused the offer, the budget summiteers, with Bush's blessing, decided on a package that included neither capital gains reduction nor a higher marginal rate for top income earners. Instead, taxes on gasoline, cigarettes, wine, beer, and hard liquor were to be increased, and a new luxury tax on certain expensive items to be levied. There was to be an effective tax increase for those making more than $100,000 (as a result of a new way of itemizing deductions), and an increase in Medicare taxes for those earning more than $51,300. In all, taxes were to rise by roughly $134 billion over the five-year period. Meanwhile, defense spending was to be chopped by $170 billion. The $105 billion in projected savings for nonmilitary spending—mostly Medicare, student loans, farm subsidies, and certain federal employee benefits—were concentrated in fiscal years 1994 and 1995, and thus subject to repeal.

Throughout this period Bush maintained sealed lips; he did not address the nation on the shape of fiscal policy. On September 30 Bush went to the White House Rose Garden with congressional leaders of both parties at his elbows, to announce the budget agreement they had struck. If the "process" had worked to the President's satisfaction, it quickly proved not to have worked politically. Immediately it drew opposition in Congress from both liberal Democrats and conservative Republicans. Liberals thought the package hit the middle class and the elderly too hard while barely touching the wealthy, and conservatives were appalled at the prospect of the largest tax increase package in history. In response to these developments, on October 2, the President decided to appeal to the nation for help. Obviously, Bush's first popular speech on the central domestic issue of his first two years in office was no part of any strategic effort to frame the public debate. Like his press release of June 26 and the subsequent press conferences, this, too, was reactive in character.

The President told the nation that the budget deficit was a cancer gnawing away at our nation's health. Unless it was contained and cut back, the economy would be further weakened and thousands of jobs lost. Bush said "we can do something"—enact the budget agreement, which he presented as the product of a bipartisan process. The agreement wasn't perfect, he said, just "the best . . . that can be legislated now." He acknowledged that it contained tax increases, which he was not "a fan" of, but nonetheless these increases "should allow the economy to grow" by reducing the deficit and therefore lowering interest rates. Bush emphasized that the agreement would not raise income tax rates, personal or corporate. Ominously, he added that failure to enact the agreement would result in a faltering economy and even recession. He noted that the Democratic majority leader, Senator George Mitchell, speaking after him, would not assume the traditional role of opposition but one of support. Finally, the President talked directly to the viewer: "I ask you to understand how important and, for some, how difficult this vote is, for your congressmen and senators. Many worry about your reaction to one part or another. But I want you to know the importance of the whole. And so I ask you to take this initiative: Tell your congressmen and senators you support this deficit-reduction agreement. . . . Your senators and congressmen need to know that you want this deficit brought down."

The people did the opposite; a huge majority of citizens calling Capitol Hill said no to the budget accord. It would have been surprising had the reaction been otherwise. Last-minute popular appeals rarely "work" in the sense of rallying public opinion behind a President's legislative goals.[5] That Bush failed with his speech should be interpreted not as an indictment of presidential rhetoric, but rather as one of Bush's failure to understand it, and thus how it might be used to promote reason and deliberation about public policy. Bush's very language at the end of his October 2 speech—"This is the first time in my presidency that I have made an appeal like this to you, the American people"—revealed the desperation of a President who had not used rhetoric as he properly could have, beginning much earlier in his presidency, in order to meet his constitutional duty to recommend legislation. Had Bush employed popular speech earlier and properly, making a cogent argument for his fiscal policy, Congress might well have produced a package more reflective of the President's political goals and more appealing to more legislators.

Bush's rhetorical failure was related to his preference for the kind of process he entered in order to reach a budget agreement. Both seemed to stem from an aversion to, if not a disdain for, the kind of politics our system demands if it is to work, especially in an age of divided government. By joining forces with congressional leaders in a "budget summit" whose results were to be presented to Congress and the nation virtually as a fait accompli, the President, together with the bipartisan congressional leadership, effectively sought to blur party and institutional differences, thus deemphasizing principles and ideas. With such summits, there is no need for the President to advance a public case, or for the opposition party (here the Democrats) to actually be in opposition, or for the two houses of Congress to deliberate in accord with procedures established in the Constitution. For that matter, with inter-branch, bipartisan, closed-door summits, there is no need to assign responsibility and hold anyone accountable.

The swift rejection by the House of the budget accord demonstrated the futility of trying to govern in the absence of politics. "What this vote proved was that closed-door sessions don't work," said Congressman Bill Thomas, a California Republican, who added that "the whole process should begin and end with full public debate." Vice President Dan Quayle's advice in mid-October that the President should take his case for economic policy to the voters reflected a similar belief that politics and governing should be related. Both Thomas and Quayle were right. The nation needs more politics, not less, more public argument and debate from its political figures about economic policy if it is to reach consensus during a time of deep philosophical division about the direction of that policy. As the *Wall Street Journal* put it on October 4, 1990, "What the United States dearly needs right now is a large national debate over its priorities. . . . [T]here are deep philosophical differences between the political ideologies in this country. The purpose of a functioning democratic system is to clarify and resolve those differences, ultimately with elections in which the voters choose between two positions."

In 1990, the real crisis in governing did not stem from the budget deficit but a deficit of politics to which Bush was the principal contributor; put differently, there was a deficit of energy in the executive. Bush's own view was never more clearly articulated than in answering a question during—as one could have expected—a press conference. Asked whether it would have been better to have engaged in a public debate over an increase in gasoline taxes instead of pursuing such a policy in a closed "process" with congressional leaders, Bush replied: "Well, I don't know that any person who is opposed to raising gasoline taxes would have been more inclined to accept them if the negotiations between Democrats and Republicans on these committees had been done in public." This is the comment of a President unwilling to use his office for the sake of good government.

The vote in the House rejecting the budget agreement was 254 to 179, with Republicans voting 105 to 71 against. With Bush now unable to count on House Republicans as allies, liberal Democrats in Congress began pressing for a new package that would increase the top personal tax rate without any cut in the capital gains rate; they also stepped up the attack on Bush's proposal to cut capital gains, characterizing it as welfare for the wealthy. Bush himself took a series of contradictory positions on whether he would accept a higher

57

marginal rate for "the rich." On October 9, at a press conference, Bush said that he would, if it could "be worked out in the
proper balance between the capital gains rate and the income
tax changes." Later that same day, after a meeting he and
sixteen Senate Republicans had with the President, Senator
Bob Packwood of Oregon said, "The President agreed, our
unified position is we will not go up on the rate, not one percent, not two percent, not one penny. . . . And we will leave the
rates where they are, drop capital gains and do nothing about
the rates." The following morning Senator Robert Dole remarked on the floor of the Senate, "[President Bush] did not
make any decision yesterday, even though that was reported.
He listened to us. He did not announce his position at all. He
did not acquiesce in what we said." Meanwhile, the President,
asked to clear up the confusion, said while on a campaign
swing in North Carolina and Florida that Congress should
clear it up. Later in the day, while jogging in Florida, Bush
was asked whether he was ready to give up cutting capital
gains. "Read my hips," he said, mocking himself. The next day
House Republicans met with President Bush. One of them,
Rep. Bill Archer, said, "He [Bush] is willing—and I think he'll
speak to you today about this—to equalize or level the rate at
31 percent . . . in exchange for a 15 percent capital gains
rate. . . . I'm telling you that he told us today that he has been
consistently for this all the way through." Later that same
day White House Press Secretary Marlin Fitzwater quoted
the President as saying: "I do not believe such a compromise
is now possible. Indeed, I'm quite concerned that pursuing it
in the current context may not only fail; it may legitimize
something farther to the left that we cannot accept."[6] Such
confusion can be expected when a President is attracted to
process-governing.

Bush staggered toward and finally got his package. The
five-year deal called for cutting spending by $320 billion while
hiking taxes by at least $170 billion. Specifically, it included
an increase in the top personal tax rate from 28 to 32 percent,
with certain very affluent taxpayers taxed an additional two
percentage points. Also in the package were increases in Medicare taxes (for middle- to higher-income earners) and gasoline
taxes. There were cuts amounting to $101 billion in benefit

programs ranging from Medicare and Medicaid to farm subsidies and veterans benefits, and reductions totalling $67 bil-
lion in defense. The remaining budget-reduction "savings"—
some $115 billion—were to be determined by House and
Senate appropriations committees, but not until the fourth
and fifth years of the budget accord.

It is an understatement to say that in 1990 Bush wanted
a deficit-reduction agreement. Yet the White House only quietly put out word that the President supported the overall
package ultimately enacted. And "a senior White House aide,"
as the story in the *New York Times* put it, "tried to regain the
political offensive by calling reporters into the Roosevelt Room
to issue a broadside against Democrats for having forced the
President to raise taxes."[7] When asked by reporters what he
was going to do with the new package, the President himself
commented, "I'm going to say, look, I've reluctantly signed
this." Campaigning for congressional Republicans, Bush
talked about how wonderful it was to be out campaigning
among "real people" who had nothing to do with Washington,
making little effort to explain and defend the budget agreement. Thus had campaigning ("no-new-taxes") been disjoined
from governing (the budget accord), and then the governing
disjoined from the new campaigning (amid "real people").

What a remarkable end to the story. Unlike President
Reagan upon passage of the Tax Reform Act of 1986, President Bush wanted as little as possible to do with what he
helped bring about. Having distanced himself from his no-
new-taxes vow, he now wanted to sprint away from his budget
agreement. After the 1990 elections, in which the GOP lost
nine House seats and which revealed strong sentiment in the
electorate against new taxes, especially at the state level,
Bush, ever the tactician, tried to put the budget package behind him by resurrecting an old theme: that he was against
new taxes.

Bush's "no-new-taxes" rhetoric did affect governance in a
way consistent with what was, for eighteen months or so, his
political identity: It was, in effect, a veto threat against any
tax increases. The force of this threat cannot be denied;
against all odds, a Congress more Democratic than ever (until
the Congress elected in 1990) did not raise taxes in 1989.

Significantly, Bush's governing success in this respect strengthened his political identity and even encouraged more Americans to believe that higher taxes could be avoided. According to the Gallup Poll, when Bush took office, some 24 percent of Americans thought Bush could avoid raising taxes. By February 1990 the figure was up 30 points, to 54 percent. But Bush did not twin his influential veto threat with rhetoric that intelligently and consistently made the case for the necessary fiscal policy. Bush would have been in position to maintain his solid anti-tax position more firmly than he did had he publicly elaborated a more comprehensive economic policy, if not in the campaign, certainly in the early months of his presidency. Bush did have views in this area; he and his aides had indicated from time to time their interest in major spending and budget reforms. But Bush never gave this intention the public play he accorded his anti-tax position.

For Bush, rhetoric was useful primarily while running for office, not for executing it once there. And the campaign rhetoric he used on taxes, while serving his short-term interest of getting elected, fell far short of the kind of sustained policy argument an aspiring President could have attempted and which the presidency is uniquely positioned to offer.[8] After all, if a President does not raise the question of how much government we need and how much we can afford, then who, especially in an age in which special interests clog the halls of Congress, can be counted upon to do so?

Bush put his faith in the wrong place when he organized a budget summit. A 1990 report by the Tax Foundation found that "ironically the fiscal years that were not preceded by budget summits actually resulted in the most real deficit reduction."[9] In fiscal year 1984—a nonsummit year—the deficit went down by $23 billion as spending was allowed to grow only half as much as revenues. In fiscal year 1987, another nonsummit year, a near budget freeze cut $71.5 billion in spending from the budget, reducing the deficit to $149.7 billion, from $221.2 billion. On the other hand, in fiscal years 1988 and 1989—summit years both—the deficits, which according to budget agreements between the Reagan administration and Congress were to be $93.1 billion and $66.9 billion respectively, were instead $155.1 billion and $152.1 billion.

There are reasons related to summits for this poor track record, chief among them that summits tend to produce real tax increases but only artificial spending cuts. This is so because many spending cuts are nothing more than "promises" to cut spending. The budget agreement the Bush administration embraced in 1990 included a sizeable portion of "promised" reductions in spending (some $115 billion in all). And by the end of 1991 it was evident that, if the purpose of the accord was to reduce the deficit, it was failing. The deficit for fiscal year 1991 was roughly $70 billion more than the administration forecast when the President signed the agreement into law in October 1990. And by the spring of 1992, the deficit for fiscal year 1992 was projected to reach almost $400 billion, some $170 billion more than the administration forecast at the time of the budget accord.

Like the previous budget summits, the 1990 budget summit focused on the "deficit," not on spending. Economists dispute both the definition and the economic significance of the deficit. Yet however it is defined, it is a product of a variety of factors, some of which are beyond the control of Congress. One reason Bush and the congressional leadership entered into a "deficit-reduction" process involved less what the deficit might do to the economy than what it might do to them politically; they feared the large spending cuts ($84 billion in all) that would have been mandated by the Gramm-Rudman-Hollings budget law in fiscal year 1991. Such cuts would have included, for example, $2.6 billion from NASA's budget, $1.4 billion from the Federal Aviation Administration, $769 million from highway building, $325 million from the National Science Foundation, $359 million from the National Bureau of Prisons, $86 million from education funds for the handicapped, and $453 million from energy assistance payments to low-income families. In an election year, few in Congress were eager to face the electorate with those reductions taking effect. The budget deal struck between Bush and Congress managed to avoid the Gramm-Rudman-Hollings sequester by legislating it out of existence—until 1993. And meanwhile the actual deficit reduction achieved by that deal for 1991 would be roughly $42 billion—about half what would have resulted from the sequester.

Spending would have been a better target for the President and Congress to address if for no other reason than it is more controllable than the deficit. Needed is the political will to focus on it. The office of President is best situated in our constitutional system to provide the necessary leadership. Here it bears noting that the very Congress that worked with the President to "reduce" the deficit also, in its final days, authorized costly new health and welfare programs, poured billions of dollars into pork-barrel projects, and approved a whopping 12 percent increase in domestic spending (excluding Social Security).

Beyond spending, the larger issue is economic growth, and specifically how federal policies advance or retard it. Within a year of the budget agreement, as the economy continued on its stagnant course, it was evident that the accord had asked the wrong question. Whether Bush understood this was an open question. In the early months of 1992, Bush seemed interested only in finding which position might play best politically in the campaign; apparently, he did not appear to have learned the lesson of his mistaken budget agreement, which is that it falls to Presidents to use their office to make a public case for their policy views. Quite in character, Bush did not use his State of the Union opportunity in late January as the opening paragraph in an ongoing argument about how we might generate real economic growth. It was a tactical speech, designed to get him through the event and into the campaign. Especially remarkable was the speech's disdain for ideas and argument—and its imperial attitude toward Congress. The President employed the imperative mood on several occasions, as though Congress were Saddam Hussein: "Congress, pass my bill." While the imperative is the mood appropriate for a Commander in Chief, it is not for a President seeking legislation from a coequal branch of government. (The President's lawyers do not argue in the Supreme Court by saying: "Court, accept our position.") Different governing tasks require verbs of different moods—and different kinds of presidential leadership. In 1992, as in 1990, what was missing in this President was a willingness to frame rational terms of political debate.

As future administrations assess the worth of budget

summits, including Bush's in 1990, equal consideration should be given the kind of alternative available to the President then: a refusal to convene a budget summit and a willingness to veto any tax increase and also abide by the automatic sequester (under the Gramm-Rudman-Hollings budget law) that would have cut a substantial amount of spending. Even better would have been this course of action *plus* a constant prosecution of the case for true economic growth measures, including cuts in the capital gains rate. Taking this route, of course, would have required a President willing to be political, in the best sense of the word, a President willing to use available power to focus the political system on spending and economic growth. Had Bush pursued this route, he might well have achieved the major budget reforms that were notably missing from the agreement produced via the budget summit. At a minimum he would have performed a public service by clarifying the economic choices Congress must eventually make.

The most important domestic policy issue facing the country remains what it was before the budget summit of 1990. It is the issue of how much taxation and how much government we as a people really want. And, relatedly, which government policies best contribute to economic growth. This remains an issue for presidential leadership, for a President who does not scorn politics in the best sense of that word, and who is willing to fully use the office he holds.

# 4

# VETOES AND SIGNING STATEMENTS

## The President at "Presentment"

Two errors commonly burden scholarly and popular discussion of the President's power to veto legislation. One is to say, as Charles L. Black, Jr., of the Yale Law School has, that the President should exercise the power only rarely and not for policy reasons.[1] The other is to overlook (as Black to his credit does not) the President's use of the veto as an instrument of self-defense. Thus, in a 1990 article reporting President Bush's successful use of the policy veto during his first two years, the *U.S. News & World Report* failed to observe that a large number of Bush vetoes were in fact cast to defend the constitutional rights of the executive.[2] Needed in any modern treatment of the presidency is a comprehensive consideration of the veto power, the only presidential power found in Article I of the Constitution.

That the veto enables the President to engage matters formally decided upon by Congress through its lawmaking power (i.e., a bill or a resolution) is of course well-known. But less appreciated is the fact that the veto is the only such enabling instrument found in the Constitution. Although the President does have the power to recommend measures to Congress and thus meet his constitutional duty in that respect, Congress is under no obligation to listen to him. As a practical matter, that is not the case with the veto. And because it takes a two-thirds vote by both houses of Congress to override, or nullify, a veto, this power is the most powerful weapon a President has in relating to Congress over legislation.

Article I, Section 7, clause 2 of the Constitution states: "Every Bill which shall have passed the House of Representatives and the Senate, shall, before it become a law, be presented to the President of the United States; if he approve he shall sign it, but if not he shall return it, with his objections to that House in which it shall have originated, who shall enter the objections at large on their journal and proceed to reconsider it." This, the "Presentment Clause," includes the veto power, although the text does not call it that.[3] "Return" is the verb used here for "veto," which from the Latin means "I forbid."

The records of the Federal Convention indicate that the word "veto" was rarely used by the framers. During the ratifying debates, the same held true. The word appears only once in the four essays of *The Federalist* in which the veto is mentioned or discussed (Nos. 51, 66, 69, 73). "[T]his semantic ploy," Robert J. Spitzer reminds us, "was no accident."[4] The dominant view at the American founding was that in a republican government the legislative branch should predominate, yet the veto had, as Spitzer observes, "monarchical roots." And in the hands of monarchs, the veto was *absolute*. While the veto in the Constitution is a "qualified" one, because it can be overridden, the framers were aware that the power, given its monarchical roots, might be misunderstood. So they used more palatable language to describe a power considered essential to the executive in the new system of separated powers.

The Constitution makes vetoing a public act, what Alexis de Tocqueville called "a sort of appeal to the people."[5] As the constitutional text indicates, the President is not simply asked but *obligated* to state his reasons for the negative when he returns the legislation.[6] When exercised, the power to veto thus triggers a constitutional duty. Federal courts commonly give reasons for their decisions, but unlike the President in vetoing legislation, they are under no constitutional obligation to do so; they could issue opinions that simply say, for example, "decision for the plaintiff" and, at the appellate level, "affirmed." The text providing for the veto thus contemplates, quite explicitly, a presidential contribution to deliberative democracy. It regards the President's views as worthwhile, not because of any special wisdom he might have, but rather because of his position within the constitutional order as the only national officer elected by the nation as a whole, and as the only individual in whom is vested the executive power. The theory of the veto is not that it will produce superior thinking about the law each time the power is used—Presidents obviously can veto for better or worse reasons, not worthy of consideration—but that a system in which the executive possesses the qualified veto power will tend over time to enact laws that better comport with reason and the Constitution.

The arithmetic of the veto is such that the President controls, in effect, one-sixth of the law-making power. That is the difference between an ordinary majority and the two-thirds majority in both houses required to override the President's veto.[7] Rarely are vetoes successfully challenged by Congress; of the 1,367 regular vetoes cast by American Presidents through 1976, only 92, or 6.7 percent, had been overridden.[8] In many cases, the veto has not led to an attempted override but to new legislation that to some degree accommodates the President's views.

The framers of the Constitution gave specific reasons for the veto's provision in the Constitution, beginning with the often neglected but absolutely critical one of "self-defense." The framers regarded power as inherently of an "encroaching nature." They did not believe the people should simply trust, as James Madison put it, in the "parchment barriers" of the Constitution.[9] "[E]ach department should have a will of its own," he wrote, explaining that "those who administer each department" must have "the necessary constitutional means and personal motives to resist encroachments [by] the others."[10] Otherwise separation of powers is an abstraction.

In power struggles among the branches, the framers thought the strongest branch—Congress—was to be feared most; it is, wrote Madison, "everywhere extending the sphere of its activity and drawing all power into its impetuous vortex."[11] The framers decided to fortify the President in his relations with Congress by giving him the veto power, for otherwise the President would be unable to force second thoughts about legislation that threatened his own power, much less stop it. Without the veto, the presidency might become enfeebled, drained of the very energy that the office was created to provide. And a government without energy would not be worthy of the name.

Thus, Hamilton wrote, "The primary inducement to conferring the power in question [the veto] upon the executive is to enable him to defend himself" against "an immediate attack upon the constitutional rights of the executive."[12] He added, "If even no propensity had ever discovered itself in the legislative body to invade the rights of the executive, the rules of just reasoning and theoretic propriety would of themselves teach us that the one ought not to be left to the mercy of the other but ought to possess a constitutional and effectual power of self-defense."[13]

Self-defense is the President's defense of the office. That self-defense vetoes may serve a President's self-interest is to be expected, for the theory of the Constitution in respect to the veto (and much else) is to rely on self-interest for the sake of the public interest. That such vetoes may assert constitutional interpretations that have not been reached by the Supreme Court, or even ones that differ from the Court's, is no argument against them. The President is sworn to defend the Constitution. He must interpret it if he is to defend it, and he is to defend not a Constitution that omits references to his own powers and duties but all of it.

The most common congressional threats to presidential power are aimed at the President's authority to administer the laws and to conduct foreign policy. In the next two chapters, I examine instances in which President Reagan should have cast vetoes in defense of his constitutional prerogatives in both of these areas. Suffice to say here, the strong President must be alert to congressional threats upon his rights and act accordingly. Hamilton and his colleagues were right to give the President the veto "chiefly," as he said, for this reason; for if the President does not act in his own defense, who will act for him? Moreover, it is often the case, as Madison observed, that neither Congress nor the President "can pretend to an exclusive or superior right of settling the boundaries between their respective powers." If Congress acts by passing law that crosses the President's boundaries, the Constitution does not guarantee him victory but neither does it leave him defenseless. He has the veto; he has an institutional source of executive energy. The question in any particular context is whether he has the personal energy—the will—to use it.

Given the importance of the self-defense veto to the constitutional order, no commentator on a particular President's vetoes should neglect it. In failing to notice President Bush's self-defense vetoes, *U.S. News,* for example, missed what they indicate about his presidency, namely a willingness to be energetic for the sake of executive energy. In the 1989–90 congressional term that drew the magazine's attention, Bush vetoed no fewer than six bills for reasons of self-defense. These included the bill regulating joint production of the FS-X fighter with Japan (Bush said it would "tie my hands in the exercise of my constitutional responsibilities"); the appropriations bill for foreign operations and expert financing (it would "interfere with my constitutional authority to conduct the foreign relations of the United States"); and the foreign relations authorization bill for 1990 and 1991 (it "threatens to subject to criminal investigation a wide range of entirely legitimate diplomatic activity, the authority and responsibility for which is vested in the executive branch by the Constitution").

Perhaps Bush's most significant self-defense veto in the 1989–90 term was cast against the Intelligence Authorization Act for 1991. In his veto message he zeroed in on a section of the bill defining "covert action" as any "request" by the United States to a foreign government or a private citizen to conduct a covert action on behalf of the United States. This provision, said Bush, "purports to regulate diplomacy by the President and other members of the executive branch" and could "seriously impair the effective conduct of our Nation's foreign relations." Bush also took aim at the provision that conditioned specific presidential actions on prior approval by congressional committees. "This language," he said, "is clearly unconstitutional under the Presentment Clause of the Constitution." Tired of efforts by Congress to enact "legislative vetoes," which the Supreme Court struck down in 1983 in *INS* v. *Chadha*,[14] Bush added: "I again urge the Congress to cease including such unconstitutional provisions in bills presented to me for signature."

The legislative veto, a feature of legislation since the 1930s, is a means by which Congress seeks to nullify decisions made by the executive branch pursuant to broad grants of policy-making authority. As written into a statute, the legislative veto has been exercised by both houses of Congress or just one, or one or more committees. Whatever its form, the legislative veto is unconstitutional because its exercise concludes the issue; even in the case of a two-house veto, there is no presentment of the matter to the President, as there must be if a congressional decision is to become law, a point the Supreme Court recognized in voiding the legislative veto in the *Chadha* case. In formally objecting to legislative veto provisions, President Bush evinced an understanding of his office to which he consistently held (save for his unfortunate agreement to a legislative veto in the so-called Bipartisan Accord on Central America, negotiated very early in his presidency[15]). In casting self-defense vetoes, President Bush did better by his office than President Reagan, who failed not once but twice to veto legislation clearly aimed at the executive. As discussed in Chapter 5, in 1983 and then again in 1987 Reagan approved when he should have vetoed reauthorization of the independent counsel statute.

A self-defense veto is a veto cast for constitutional reasons involving the presidency. But the veto power also may be used against laws of general applicability for constitutional reasons based on provisions that do not involve the presidency (such as, say, the First or Fourteenth Amendment) or for purely policy reasons. Thus Hamilton, after discussing the self-defense veto, wrote that the veto power

> has a further use. It not only serves as a shield to the executive, but it furnishes an additional security against the enaction of improper laws. It establishes a salutary check upon the legislative body, calculated to guard the community against the effects of faction, precipitancy, or of any impulse unfriendly to the public good, which may happen to influence a majority of that body.[16]

Hamilton hoped that this use of the veto power would "increase the chances in favor of the community against the passing of bad laws, through haste, inadvertence, or design."[17] He went on:

> The oftener the measure is brought under examination, the greater the diversity in the situations of those who are to examine it, and less must be the danger of those errors which flow from want of due deliberation, or of those missteps which proceed from the contagion of some common passion or interest. It is far less probable that culpable views of any kind should infect all the parts of the government at the same moment and in relation to the same object than that they should by turns govern and mislead every one of them.[18]

Perhaps the most famous example of an objection to a bill based on non-presidential constitutional grounds was President Jackson's veto in 1832 of the bill rechartering the national bank. Jackson argued that under the Constitution Congress did not have the authority to establish a bank of the United States. This example is especially instructive because in taking this action Jackson departed from the judgment sustaining the bank's constitutionality made by previous Presidents and Congresses, as well as the Supreme Court thirteen years earlier in *McCulloch* v. *Maryland*.[19] Rejecting advice based on those precedents that he had no choice but to sign the bill, Jackson correctly observed in his veto message that he had taken an oath of office to support the Constitution "as he understands it, and not as it is understood by others."

While Presidents may and do veto for a mix of constitutional and policy reasons, the great majority of vetoes today are cast for policy reasons only. In his short tenure, for example, President Ford cast sixty-six vetoes, most of them for policy reasons (especially excessive spending).[20] It was Ford's use of the policy veto that Yale's Charles L. Black specifically objected to, leading him to remark that the veto power should be applied "only rarely, and certainly not as a means of systematic policy control over the legislative branch, on matters constitutionally indifferent and not menacing the President's independence."[21] The Constitution, however, sets no limits on the frequency or the circumstances of veto. Black's argument necessarily draws upon the veto's infrequent use during most of the nineteenth and early twentieth centuries. But that is explained in large part by the infrequency of the opportunity to veto. Congress passes many more laws now than in the periods when the veto was seldom used; through the first thirty months of the Bush presidency, for example, Congress had passed more than seven hundred bills. With so much law being passed, the policy veto actually becomes even more important. It may be the only way a President can force a (too) busy Congress to rethink what it has done (assuming it has thought that much in the first place). Furthermore, in an era of divided government—in which one party controls Congress and the other the White House—the policy veto is a compelling tool of governance because it can clarify the differences between the parties that control the respective elected branches; such clarity is often necessary before a political resolution can be achieved. For a President to take Charles Black's advice and to sheath his policy veto when the other party dominates Congress would amount to a denial of the important political side of his presidency and acceptance of a purely administrative, perhaps even a clerk-like, role. To say no worse of this view of the presidency, it diminishes the energy needed to make the difference expected of the office in our form of government, especially today.

At the end of the 1989–90 congressional term, Ruti Teitel of the New York Law School criticized President Bush's use of the veto from a perspective similar to Black's.[22] Bush vetoed twenty bills during the term; for Teitel, this was far too many.

According to Teitel, Bush had made "activist" use of the veto power, undermining the popular will, and this activism was a departure from the "original intent" of the framers. But on key points Teitel was wrong. Again, the Constitution does not limit the number of times a President casts the veto. And in any event Bush's veto per year average—ten—was far less than that of some recent Presidents. President Kennedy's was 10.5, President Eisenhower's 22.6, and Harry Truman's 31.2. Teitel's criticism cannot turn upon Bush's alleged activism but upon the writer's own political differences with the President.[23]

There are at least three different kinds of policy vetoes. A President may differ with Congress as a matter of kind (he wants to kill the legislation) or in degree (he accepts or is open to the idea of the legislation but not its present incarnation) or in part (he wants not all but some part of a bill). The Bush presidency provides good examples of all three. In 1989 Bush wanted to kill the family leave bill "absolutely," as White House Press Secretary Marlin Fitzwater put it, and he did. On the other hand, agreeing with the general idea of raising the minimum wage but not with the amount Congress had legislated, Bush in 1989 cast a veto that forced the legislators then to revise the wage downward by the four dimes he had insisted upon. Finally, also in 1989, Bush vetoed four bills otherwise to his satisfaction because of their inclusion of provisions supporting abortion. The provisions never became law. In vetoing the civil rights legislation in 1990—the subject of Chapter 7—Bush also used a policy veto to help define the terms of a critical public policy debate. (By contrast, through the spring of 1992 he had not used the veto to force a debate on spending; none of his twenty-six vetoes had been cast as a protest against excessive appropriations.)

What Hamilton saw as an institutional aspect of energy in the executive, the veto when cast is a legislative force that may also have consequences for the administration of the laws and the conduct of foreign policy. Yet the impact of the veto upon Congress does not lie only in its exercise, as Hamilton recognized. The mere possibility that it might be cast, he wrote, could have a "silent and unperceived, though forcible, operation." As he explained, when members of Congress "are aware that obstructions may come from a quarter which they cannot control, they will often be restrained by the bare apprehension of opposition from doing what they would with eagerness rush into if no such external impediments were to be feared."[24] For the veto to be seen as such a possibility, for it to have any chance of shaping legislation, it must be credibly threatened. The factors that make a veto threat credible are for the most part specific to each situation; but one factor is plainly necessary: the willingness on a President's part to follow through and cast the veto every time his warnings have not resulted in change he can accept. A President who threatens vetoes but instead signs legislation containing provisions he said he would oppose will be ignored in Congress, and his veto power weakened.

In 1986 Reagan had veto credibility with House Republicans when he promised a veto at one stage of the tax reform effort. But, in general, Reagan did not have as much veto credibility as Bush. For unlike Reagan, Bush used the veto in every instance in which his warnings did not result in change he could accept. House Republican Vin Weber says that Reagan injudiciously threatened vetoes without casting them, while Bush judicially threatened and then deployed the negative.[25] Bush's veto power was respected on Capitol Hill, and his threats were influential. As a case in point, when, in the spring of 1990, Bush threatened to veto an aid package for Nicaragua and Panama on account of an abortion-funding provision, Congress stripped it out, aware that just months earlier he had vetoed four bills in a row with similar abortion-funding provisions.

Presidents not only veto but also approve bills presented to them (or allow them to become law by doing nothing). *How* a President approves legislation might seem a far less interesting subject than how he vetoes a bill, but on reflection it is not.

The President who signs a bill is not only a participant in the legislative process but also a constitutional officer of multiple responsibilities. One is taking care that the laws, including the one he is now approving, are faithfully executed. Statutes are not self-enforcing; they must be interpreted. At some point the constitutionally responsible President must provide direction to the executive branch as to how it should understand and enforce new law, especially a statute that is vaguely worded and open to interpretation. And there is no better time for a President to provide this direction than when he signs a bill into law. The President can do this through a carefully crafted signing statement.

The practice of presidential signing statements dates to at least 1830, when President Andrew Jackson used one to give his interpretation of a road appropriation measure. The later Reagan and Bush presidencies employed this device more systematically and meticulously than virtually any previous one. A measure of the importance the Reagan presidency correctly attached to signing statements lies in its successful effort in 1986 to persuade the West Publishing Company to include them in the *U.S. Code Congressional and Administrative News*.

Other uses of signing statements track the President's constitutional responsibilities. To return specifically to his legislative role, a President may use a signing statement to communicate to Congress his understanding of the law he is approving or to reiterate ongoing policy differences.[26] Thus, President Bush advised in one of his statements that the language employed in reporting a bill, because it was not part of the statute he was approving, had "no legal force or effect." And in signing the Military Construction Appropriations Act of 1991, Bush expressed his policy concern that Congress was underfunding the nation's NATO commitment. It is in a signing statement, too, that the President, also in his legislative capacity, can meet his constitutional duty to recommend legislation. Thus, in signing the Great Lakes Critical Programs Act of 1990, Bush advised Congress that he would be recommending legislation to correct a constitutional problem raised by the new law.[27]

The constitutionally responsible President will not use a signing statement to add new terms to the bill before him or advance an interpretation at odds with what it plainly says. Among the laws that the President must execute is the Constitution, which does not enable the President to, in effect, write his own statute. When the President's policy differences are sufficiently strong, he should use the veto power.

A different issue is posed when the President regards the legislation as sound from the standpoint of policy but questionable or even flatly objectionable from the perspective of the Constitution. Again, because the President must enforce the Constitution, he cannot be indifferent to constitutional problems in a bill presented to him even though he believes it is in the nation's best interest. Moreover, the President must recognize that his approval of a bill with unconstitutional parts cannot make those parts constitutional. Not every aspect of a bill passed by both houses necessarily becomes law when approved by a President; strictly speaking, only those aspects that are constitutional become law. The energetic and responsible President will use signing statements when approving necessary measures containing serious constitutional infirmities in order to point out such problems. Thus, when President Reagan approved the Gramm-Rudman legislation in 1985 because of his concern that "deficits have threatened our economic well-being for too long," he nonetheless observed that the new law unconstitutionally assigned executive functions to agents of Congress. The next year, the President through his Solicitor General successfully argued this position before the Supreme Court in *Bowsher* v. *Synar*.[28]

President Bush has often used signing statements to meet his duty to enforce the Constitution. Some of his concerns or objections are based on constitutional provisions that do not implicate his own powers; on a number of occasions Bush has objected to statutory language authorizing racial or gender preferences in violation of the Fourteenth Amendment's Equal Protection Clause. Most often, his constitutional comments reflect an effort to defend the "constitutional rights of the executive," as Hamilton would say. Thus, Bush objected to provisions attempting to regulate his power to conduct negotiations with foreign nations, to interfere with his authority to supervise the executive branch, to compromise his authority to preserve the confidentiality of diplomatic, military, or intelligence information, to regulate his power as Commander in Chief of the military forces, and to undermine his ability to carry out his duty to recommend legislation to Congress. Bush even objected to a provision that would interfere with his power to receive foreign ambassadors. And he emphatically objected to legislative vetoes: Every one that Congress legislated Bush damned as not having the force of law.

Relying on his constitutional duty to enforce the laws,

including the Constitution, Bush invariably treated a legislative veto provision as "severable" from the rest of the bill. When his constitutional objection was not so strong, he indicated that he would construe the provision in question as "advisory" or "precatory" only. Sometimes his complaint was milder yet, with the President simply indicating that he would interpret a provision in light of his constitutional responsibilities.

While there is much a strong President may and should do at the moment of presentment, there are also certain things he should not do, consistent with the Constitution. Specifically, he should not reach into a bill presented to him and attempt to veto some part of it. The Presentment Clause of the Constitution does not contain a so-called "item veto."

In addition to aggregating numerous spending items in a single appropriations bill, as in the so-called "continuing resolutions," Congress also has continued a practice dating to the last century by attaching substantive provisions as "riders" to appropriations bills, as in the well-known Boland amendments enacted during the Reagan years (discussed in Chapter 6). And it sometimes combines unrelated substantive provisions in a single bill. The argument for an already existing constitutional power of the President to edit out excessive spending items or objectionable substantive riders or, indeed, any objectionable provision is based on the notion that "a bill" may not contain more than one spending item or one substantive provision. But the Constitution does not define the term "bill" or place any restriction on the form of the legislation Congress may pass and send to the President. What the Constitution does say is that Congress cannot circumvent the President's veto power by passing legislation in some form other than a bill. Article I, Section 7, clause 2, the Presentment Clause, is immediately followed by Article I, Section 7, clause 3, which has been called the "residual presentment clause." The first provides that "every bill" that has passed both houses must be presented to the President before it becomes law. The second provides that "every order, resolution or vote" to which the concurrence of both houses is necessary must be presented to the President before it takes effect. Together, the two clauses mean that in the making of a law

76

"presentment" cannot be avoided; the President cannot be cut out of the constitutional process. But they do not enable the President to be so involved in the process that he is more powerful than either the House or the Senate, able to exercise an absolute veto on policy grounds. According to Article 1, Section 7, "if [the President] approve he shall sign *it,* but if not he shall return *it*" (emphasis added). Every bill, order resolution, and the like is an *it,* constitutionally speaking, save for any part that is constitutionally infirm (which cannot be law whether the President approves it or not).[29]

Conservatives especially have been attracted to the idea that the Constitution already provides the President with an item veto. The initial argument for such a power was advanced on the op-ed page of the *Wall Street Journal* in late 1987 by a New York securities lawyer, Stephen Glazier, and the *Journal's* Gordon Crovitz has vigorously prosecuted the argument over the years.[30] Their argument is not persuasive, and there is another, clearly lawful, way to achieve the same end, at least in terms of attacking discretionary spending— that which must be approved annually. On March 20, 1992, in a speech indicating he now accepted the view that he did not have inherent line-item veto authority, President Bush also announced a new rescission policy that comports with the 1974 budget act.[31] Under that act, the President must spend appropriated monies unless Congress approves his rescission proposals. The burden is thus on Congress to act, and often it hasn't. But the budget act also provides that 20 percent of the members of the House can in effect force a vote on the President's rescission proposals; unused and apparently unnoticed for eighteen years, this is the mechanism Bush proposed to employ, with 20 percent of the House members as allies, in order to cut approximately $4 billion in spending.

Conservatives proposed the inherent item-veto authority of the President in part because of their concern that Congress, especially through continuing resolutions, has "effectively vitiated the veto power," as Gordon Crovitz has written, "by creating a Hobson's choice of signing for all spending or vetoing all spending."[32] But the Hobson's choice cannot be avoided unless an item veto (with some kind of override provision included) is added to the Constitution through the amendment process set forth in Article V. And perhaps, on balance, it should not be avoided. A President who uses his already existing veto power to oppose continuing resolutions, or appropriations that come to him with substantive riders attached, or bills that include unrelated substantive measures—a President who wields his veto against these measures, dispatching veto messages that argue against the forms of these bills, might succeed in changing current congressional lawmaking practices. In any event, it is worth a try, and plainly it will have to made by an executive of palpable energy.

# 5

# SELF-DEFENSE, PLEASE
## The Independent Counsel Mess

During the Reagan presidency, the future of the special-prosecutor law, originally enacted in 1978 as part of the Ethics in Government Act, was in doubt. Scheduled by its own terms to expire in 1983, the statute, which establishes a system of court-appointed counsels to investigate charges of malfeasance on the part of the President, the Vice President, and other top executive officers, was reauthorized by Congress in January 1983 and extended five years. In December 1987, it was reauthorized a second time and given another five years of life in the U.S. Code. Neither time did President Reagan cast a veto. He should have, on the high ground of self-defense. While seemingly well-intentioned, a product of the "government ethics" ideology that pervaded Washington in the wake of Watergate, the law threatened—and will threaten, as long

79

as it is still on the books—what Alexander Hamilton called "the constitutional rights of the executive."[1]

The Reagan administration did offer some opposition to the law through its congressional testimony during the respective reauthorization processes. And it argued, albeit unsuccessfully, against the statute on constitutional grounds in the landmark case of *Morrison* v. *Olson*.[2] President Reagan himself was correct to speak out against this law. Congress was "apparently convinced that it is empowered to divest the President of his constitutional authority to enforce our nation's laws," he said on December 15, 1987—in a statement made, alas, while signing the second reauthorization bill. Reagan's words did not have the impact a veto could and probably would have had: initiating an interbranch fight over the law and its future. The veto power can do at least this much, and when the presidency itself is threatened, this much can be very important.

The special prosecutor law stemmed from an infamous presidential action that itself weakened the office—President Nixon's firing of Archibald Cox in the middle of his investigation of Watergate.[3] Past Presidents either on their own motion or through their Attorneys General had named outside special prosecutors; such was the case in Cox's appointment. But because of the Cox firing, Congress decided that in the future leaving such arrangements to executive discretion gave no assurance that special prosecutors would be able to conduct their inquiries free of executive-branch interference. For Congress, the only way to guarantee that outside counsels were truly "independent" of the executive was to change the method of a special prosecutor's appointment and limit the President's power to remove him.

Title VI of the Ethics in Government Act of 1978 filled the bill. It created a special panel—sitting on it would be judges from the federal court of appeals in the District of Columbia—and lodged in the panel the power to appoint a special prosecutor.[4] For his part, the Attorney General was required to open "a preliminary investigation" whenever he received "specific information" that certain high-ranking officials—the President, the Vice President, all cabinet officers—had violated federal criminal laws. During the preliminary investigation, lasting no more than ninety days, the Attorney General could not use the compulsory powers ordinarily available to him—that is, he could not convene a grand jury, subpoena witnesses, grant immunity, or enter into plea-bargaining agreements. The law thus reduced his discretion—and therefore the President's—in this special class of cases. Under the law, the Attorney General could close the investigation if he found that the allegation in question was—as the statute put it—"so unsubstantiated that no further investigation or prosecution is warranted." Otherwise, he had to apply to the court for appointment of a special prosecutor. The "so unsubstantiated" standard was a very low one, but it fit the statutory aim of sharply reducing the ability of the Justice Department to make traditional law enforcement judgments when reviewing allegations involving officials covered by the law.

Once the special court named a special prosecutor, he wore the shoes of the Attorney General insofar as his case was concerned. In fact, he had more power than the Attorney General. Special prosecutors were empowered, as Attorneys General were not, to contest in court any claim of privilege or attempt to withhold evidence on grounds of national security. And special prosecutors were required to comply with Justice Department policies only to the extent *they* thought appropriate. In other words, they were on their own. The statute required that the Attorney General could not remove a special prosecutor unless he committed some "extraordinary impropriety."

As originally enacted, the special prosecutor law was unprecedented in the annals of federal law enforcement, not to mention the presidency itself. Never before had the President been excluded from the process of appointing a government prosecutor.[5] And as for the removal provision in Title VII, the Reconstruction Congress, the most anti-executive Congress in U.S. history, had passed the Tenure of Office Act of 1867, which restricted the President's power to remove key cabinet officers, including the Attorney General.[6] The special prosecutor law was the first since that discredited statute to restrict the President's authority to remove for any reason individuals wielding powers that reasonably could be described as purely executive in nature.

Significantly, the method of appointment and the restriction of the President's removal power meant that federal criminal law enforcement authority could be given to individuals who were not clearly in the executive chain of command that finds the President at the top. Special prosecutors would be largely independent of the President. For all practical purposes, they were not answerable to him for their exercises of the law enforcement power.

The statutory reduction in the Attorney General's—and therefore the President's—traditional law enforcement discretion was unprecedented. The law obligated the Attorney General to conduct preliminary investigations even of allegations from unreliable sources and to refer them to the special court for appointment of a special prosecutor unless he could conclude that they were "so unsubstantiated" that they did not merit further investigation.

In sum, the special prosecutor law was the product of a startling new idea: that criminal investigation of the executive branch should have some independent place in a government of three separated powers. This idea does not fit easily within the framers' original design, nor is it commendable today. The framers did not design a government blind to the possibility of malfeasance in the executive branch (or the other branches). They provided not only for impeachment of the President and top executive officers through a constitutional process, but they also expected that these officials would be, as Hamilton put it, "liable to prosecution and punishment in the ordinary course of law."[7] The framers, however, made impeachment so difficult that it would be an extraordinary event, and they did not make prosecution of executive officers any easier than it is in all other cases. The special prosecutor law altered these arrangements in such a way as to encourage a very aggressive pursuit of alleged executive malfeasance. Whatever its consequences in terms of indictments and convictions, the statute thus promised as no "ethics" law ever had before to weaken the executive branch.

Those who had prophesied that the new law would require investigations that ordinarily would not occur were quickly proved right. In the late 1970s, theory became fact as a special prosecutor investigated Hamilton Jordan, Jimmy

Carter's former chief of staff, for allegedly using cocaine. Another special prosecutor named under the new law investigated a different Carter aide, Tim Kraft, on similar charges. Costing the taxpayers some $200,000 for their labors, both outside attorneys declined to prosecute; one later said that if he had been a regular prosecutor, he would have thrown his case out. But for the law, neither case would have been regarded as worth even the slightest investigation. At that time the Justice Department seldom, if ever, investigated or prosecuted cases of personal drug use unless they also involved large-scale drug trafficking—as neither the Jordan nor Kraft case did.

Notwithstanding the anti-executive character of the law, and its outrageous first applications, the Reagan administration did not attempt a frontal assault on the statute. During the twenty months in which Congress worked on reauthorization legislation, the Justice Department tried to persuade Congress to return to the Attorney General the prosecutorial function the statute had carved out for special prosecutors.[8] The Department's chief spokesman on the issue, Rudolph Giuliani, the associate attorney general, did urge Congress to consider repeal, declaring that Justice could not support an extension of the law. But—the first sign that the executive would not use available power to defend itself—Giuliani did not promise or even raise the possibility of a presidential veto. Congress eventually revised the law in ways that somewhat increased the Attorney General's discretion at the initial screening stage and recognized more of the President's constitutional power to remove an independent counsel. But, the law's infirmities were such that it still constituted an invasion of executive prerogative. When the bill was presented to the President for his signature, Justice held back from counseling a veto.

From early 1983 through early 1987 the Justice Department reviewed more and more allegations against high-ranking administration officials—thirty-eight in all. More cases went to the court for appointment of independent counsels. In early 1984, Attorney General William French Smith, having announced his resignation, found himself instead having to refer the man nominated to succeed him, Edwin Meese

III, the White House Counselor, for investigation by an independent counsel. Precisely because he had been the subject of such an inquiry, Meese was hardly a credible figure to enlist in any effective fight against a statute aimed at the President's "constitutional rights." That Reagan picked Meese to be his Attorney General, and stuck with that choice despite the independence counsel inquiry, was an indication of his lack of any strategy to oppose the law.[9]

A central theme of Meese's tenure as Attorney General concerned independent counsels. In early 1986 he asked the special court to appoint an independent counsel to investigate a first-term Reagan Justice Department official, Theodore B. Olson, on charges that Olson had obstructed justice and given false testimony to Congress. Later that year came the appointment of an independent counsel to look into charges that former Reagan aide Michael K. Deaver had violated post-government lobbying restrictions. And at the end of 1986 came the appointment of an independent counsel to investigate the Iran-contra affair. In early 1987, another independent counsel was named to investigate allegedly illegal lobbying by another former Reagan aide, Franklyn C. Nofziger. Soon thereafter yet another individual was referred for independent counsel investigation—Meese himself, this time on charges involving the scandal-ridden Wedtech Corporation. This investigation forced Meese to remove himself from all issues involving the independent counsel statute. These included the legislative reauthorization as well as implementations of the current statute and litigation based on it. Ultimate authority for these matters fell to the next in rank, Deputy Attorney General Arnold I. Burns.

On Capitol Hill, the Justice Department took a more forceful position against the law than it had in 1981 and 1982. The Department had previously argued that "extraordinary circumstances" might justify a restriction on the President's removal power of an independent counsel; now it maintained that *nothing* could.[10] As before, Justice objected to the method of appointment as an unconstitutional usurpation of presidential prerogative. The Department also raised other constitutional concerns (such as the judiciary's involvement in appointing independent counsels and carrying out other nonjudicial functions under the law), and various policy concerns (such as the sheer cost of independent counsels, which had sharply increased). But Justice mainly stressed the law's infringement on presidential authority and the resulting lack of accountability on the part of independent counsels. Justice urged Congress to make the law constitutional by vesting the appointment power in the executive branch and dropping the limitation on the President's power to remove a counsel.

But the reauthorization legislation changed neither the method of appointment nor the limitation on the removal power, and it reduced the Attorney General's already limited discretion in the initial screening period. Having joined a constitutional challenge to the statute in the U.S. Court of Appeals for the D.C. Circuit (the *Morrison* case), Justice counseled the President to veto the bill on both policy and constitutional grounds.[11] Declining the advice, Reagan signed the bill in order, as he put it in his December 16 signing statement, "to ensure that public confidence in government not be eroded while the courts are in the process of deciding these questions." The Supreme Court upheld the statute by a seven-to-one vote, with Chief Justice William Rehnquist writing the Court's opinion, and Associate Justice Antonin Scalia alone in dissent.[12] No, said the Court, the independent counsel statute does not violate the Appointments Clause; no, it does not give a federal court duties it shouldn't have under the Constitution; and no, the limitation on the removal power does not violate executive prerogative or the principle of separated powers. In effect, Reagan had relied upon the Court to protect the office; he should have relied upon himself.

Reagan should have vetoed the legislation, although this was not the only avenue of self-defense available to him. After all, upon taking office in 1981, the President could have instructed his Attorney General *not* to enforce the statute. That is, he could have told the Attorney General not to refer individuals for investigation by special prosecutors. Such an action, premised as it would have been upon the President's constitutional duty to take care that the laws are faithfully executed, would have required a willingness to engage the issue politically. As Paul W. Kahn of the Yale Law School has imagined the scenario, "[Reagan] could have gone before Congress and the nation and said that his oath of office required him to obey the Constitution as he understood it."[13] This would have been an extraordinary executive exertion, but not an impermissible one. President Thomas Jefferson refused to enforce the infamous Alien and Sedition Acts, duly enacted in 1798 (and thus before he took office). Those laws did not deny the constitutional rights of the executive, but Jefferson thought they were unconstitutional for First Amendment reasons. There are those who dispute the validity of Jefferson's right to do as he did, but far less disputable is the decision by a President to refuse to enforce a law he believes infringes on presidential prerogative, especially if he has inherited the law and not been a party to its enactment. Had Reagan pondered such a nonenforcement strategy, the important considerations would have been practical ones. While a successful lawsuit against the President would have been most unlikely, a political battle between the elective branches might well have erupted, harming the President's ability to win legislative approval for his economic package.[14] Prudence thus would have counseled against a strategy of nonenforcement, especially since the statute was scheduled to expire, had to be reauthorized, and therefore had to be presented to him—at which point the veto power could have been brought into powerful play.

Simple arithmetic demonstrates the importance of the veto. While a President who will not veto a bill he opposes in its current form must hope that majorities in both houses of Congress will accept his legislative views, a President who does veto such a bill needs one third of a quorum of a single chamber to defeat an override attempt. As we saw in Chapter 4, that is a steep hill for Congress to climb; only a very small percentage of vetoes have ever been overridden.

A successful veto strategy would have required a President willing to make a public case—a President willing to twin appropriate rhetoric and action. In 1983, such a case could have put to effective use the discredited Jordan and Kraft cases, the *only* special prosecutor cases then concluded. And such a case would have been heard by a Republican-controlled Senate and presented by a Republican President who had seen only one of his subordinates—Labor Secretary

86

Ray Donovan—become the subject of a special prosecutor investigation (which focused on activities occurring *before* Donovan joined the administration). Had Reagan mustered the votes necessary to sustain a veto, as seems likely, the law probably would have been changed to fit his views. Possibly it might have been allowed to expire. In either event, there would not have been a *Morrison* case, and so there would not be the *Morrison* jurisprudence, which provides a basis for future Congresses to attack the rights of Presidents.

Neither a nonenforcement nor a veto strategy was contemplated in 1981–82. During the transition in 1980–81 no one close to Reagan raised a concern about the special prosecutor law or about protecting presidential prerogatives in general.[15] Preoccupying the President-elect and his transition team was the substantive political agenda that focused on reviving the economy and rebuilding the national defense. The White House left separation of powers concerns to the Justice Department, then focused on other matters—staffing, reforming immigration policy, reviewing policy toward violent crimes.

Attorney General Smith was as aware of executive power issues as anyone in the administration. Indeed, it was Smith who took on a different threat to presidential authority. A suit had been brought by an alien threatened with deportation as a result of a so-called legislative veto; the question for the Supreme Court in *INS* v. *Chadha* was the constitutionality of such measures, which date to the 1930s.[16] The legislative veto was a product of the executive's desire to have broad discretionary authority and Congress's insistence on some means of control—short of having to enact new law—over the exercise of the granted discretion. The executive thus could make policy subject to a simple resolution of either House (a one-House legislative veto) or by concurrent resolution (a two-House veto).[17] A one-House veto was specifically at issue in *Chadha*. Smith thought legislative vetoes were unconstitutional, but the President himself had supported them on the campaign trail, on the political ground—for many conservatives the correct political ground—that the "liberal" executive must be reined in by the branch closest to the people. Smith not only won the President's approval for the position he advanced in the Supreme Court, but in the process helped educate conservatives to the more correct view of the presidency within the constitutional order. The Court adopted the administration's argument in *Chadha,* ruling that the legislative veto at issue violated the Presentment Clause of the Constitution as well as the requirement of "bicameralism" (found in the Presentment Clause).[18]

Smith also counseled the President to veto bills including legislative-veto devices. And the President in fact vetoed H.R. 7336, a package of education amendments. "The Attorney General has advised me, and I agree," said Reagan in his memorandum disapproving H.R. 7336, "that two Houses of Congress cannot bind the Executive branch by passing a concurrent resolution that is not presented to me for approval or veto." The President successfully vetoed this bill containing a two-house legislative veto—just nine days after he signed the independent counsel reauthorization. So there was a defense of the presidency here—but it was not part of any grand design. Such defenses proved ad hoc. As Smith observed in his memoir, "If there was one area in which the White House was deficient during my years in office, it was in the protection of presidential power. Decisions there were made on the basis of the substance of individual issues. There was no effective concern or review of the impact that issue or the position taken with respect to it would have on presidential power. Nor was there any effort to identify governmental activities elsewhere that, if developed, would adversely affect the province of the executive. Nor, to be candid, was the bully pulpit used to provide leadership or defense of that vital institution."[19]

In retrospect it is clear that 1983 provided Reagan his better opportunity to veto the statute. To be sure, Reagan could have vetoed the second reauthorization bill even though he had signed the first one. That previous signature did not require him to accept the law a second time. And the fact that a case challenging the statute's constitutionality was in the courts did not constrain him either. Reagan was free to veto. But the politics would have been difficult. The Senate was now controlled by Democrats. Congress was more willing to take on Reagan than at any previous time in the 1980s. Iran-contra, under investigation by an independent counsel, had politically weakened Reagan both in Congress and at the bar of public opinion. So had other independent counsel investigations, including the inquiry into Edwin Meese's involvement with the Wedtech Corporation. It would have taken a very strong effort on Reagan's part to win the needed votes to defeat an override attempt.

Still, if Reagan had been truly serious about protecting his office, he would have used the veto power. After all, the experience under the independent counsel law since 1983 had provided more damning evidence against the law. Estranged from the institutional environment that constrains all other criminal prosecutors, who, working with limited resources, have not one but many possible cases to consider, independent counsels had acted unreasonably. In his investigation of former Reagan aide Michael Deaver, for example, Whitney North Seymour tried to subpoena the Canadian ambassador to the United States, injuring relations with Canada.[20] (A federal district court ruled that the subpoenas violated diplomatic immunity.) A lawyer representing Lawrence Walsh, the Iran-contra independent counsel, told a federal appeals court that not the President but the independent counsel would have the *last* word in case of a disagreement over foreign policy and its implications for prosecution. Walsh himself told the American Bar Association in 1987 that if an investigation finds "probable cause that a crime has been committed, it is the duty of the independent counsel to prosecute"—a statement expressing a *lower* standard than that found in the prosecution manual of the Justice Department, which says that fundamental fairness requires that an indictment be issued only if the prosecutor believes that an unbiased jury would *convict*.[21] Alexia Morrison, the independent counsel named to investigate Ted Olson, worked a deed against him that no ordinary prosecutor would have: Upon finding that he probably had not violated the law, she nonetheless sought to expand her jurisdiction in order to see whether he might be implicated in a conspiracy with others—even though she had no evidence of that.[22]

Meanwhile, the independent counsels had worked a negative effect *within* the executive branch. Olson, who headed the Office of Legal Counsel in the Smith Justice Department, was investigated for actions that did not involve any element of personal gain or which went beyond the scope of duty. In fact, he was investigated for work that prior to the 1980s would never have been "criminalized." Early in the first Reagan term, House committees headed by two influential Democrats—Peter Rodino and John Dingell—objected to the Environmental Protection Agency's enforcement of environmental laws. When certain documents regarding open criminal investigations were sought, EPA Administrator Anne Burford claimed executive privilege, as directed by the President, who had been duly advised by Justice's Olson. Rodino and Dingell were upset that Olson had asked (unsuccessfully; the issue wasn't ripe) a federal court to put its imprimatur on this claim of privilege, thus heading off a contempt citation against Burford. Olson was summoned to Congress to testify, and there made statements regarding the advice he had given the President. Led by Rodino, the Democratic majority of the House Judiciary Committee used certain provisions in the independent counsel statute to force the appointment of a counsel to investigate Olson for misleading Congress. Thus Olson, departed from Justice in 1984, became in 1986 a defendant, not because the President or his aides thought his investigation was a justified use of scarce prosecutorial resources, worth the cost in money and in possible damage to other governmental interests, but merely because the Attorney General was unable to disprove the allegations made against him by House Democrats. It appeared that Democrats wanted a prosecutor who would investigate not a crime but a man, and to find some offense to pin on him; this is manifestly not what our criminal justice system is supposed to be about. The Olson case, eventually lasting three years, sent a message of caution to high-ranking executive officers. The thought that "this could happen to you, too" drained energy from the executive.

Having observed these cases, Deputy Attorney General Burns urged the President to veto the 1987 reauthorization.[23] And this time William French Smith, now retired to Los Angeles, also advised the President to cast a veto. In his signing statement, Reagan said the law was unconstitutional. So why didn't he veto it? A veto would not have disrupted indepen-

90

dent counsel investigations already in progress. And leaving the issue of constitutionality to the courts was dubious; few observers thought the Court would strike down the law. The most plausible explanation for the veto not cast is this: that Reagan shrank from the task for short-term political reasons, that he was unwilling to take action that would have provoked negative political and media reactions. In sum, Reagan lacked the courage of his stated conviction that the law was unconstitutional. On a matter of fundamental principle, he was unable to take a stand.[24]

The veto statement recommended by the Department of Justice in 1987 closed on this note: "In fulfillment of my own solemn obligation to uphold the Constitution, I believe I have no choice but to disapprove this legislation. I understand that this action may not be politically popular, but in carrying out my constitutional duty I simply cannot be moved by popular sentiment or considerations of political expediency."[25] In this the Justice Department was echoing essential Hamiltonian wisdom, worth quoting at length:

> When occasions present themselves in which the interests of the people are at variance with their inclinations, it is the duty of the persons whom they have appointed to be the guardians of those interests to withstand the temporary delusion in order to give them time and opportunity for more cool and sedate reflection. . . . [A] conduct of this kind has saved the people from very fatal consequences of their own mistakes, and has procured lasting monuments of their gratitude to the men who had courage and magnanimity enough to serve them at the peril of their displeasure.[26]

James Madison once observed that the constitutional powers of Congress were such that it could "with the greater facility, mask, under complicated and indirect measures, the encroachments which it makes on the co-ordinate departments."[27] The independent counsel statute represented, and still represents, a complicated but perhaps not so indirect measure. Prosecution of crime is and should remain an executive branch function, in the final analysis under presidential control. When, as here through the independent counsel law, Congress takes part of the President's authority away and locates it elsewhere, it increases the number of executive entities that it can effectively control. This is a recipe for the reduction of the President to, as Charles Fried has stated so well, "a ceremonial head of state."[28] It is the route to a government without energy.

The Reagan failure to veto independent counsel legislation invites future Presidents to absorb a basic lesson: Although the occasions for a "self-defense" veto may be few, they are most important; for it was precisely with these situations in mind that the framers, as Hamilton put it, "chiefly designed" the veto power. A President who understands this lesson will not rely, as Reagan in effect did in the independent counsel case, exclusively upon Justice Department argument either in Congress or in the Supreme Court in order to protect his office. In vain did the President hope for an anti-independent counsel majority to form in those quarters; and in the Court Reagan risked what he got—jurisprudence that may tempt Congress further to splinter the executive and usurp its authority.[29] (In this regard it is remarkable that Stephen Ross, the General Counsel for the House of Representatives, told a federal court reviewing the constitutionality of the independent counsel statute in 1987 that it would be constitutional for Congress to vest in the Attorney General the appointment of the Solicitor General; such are the anti-executive ideas found in today's Congress.)

A President who understands he should not rely on the Court to protect the office he holds must be as willing as any Justice to address questions of constitutionality. The Court is not the only arbiter of disputes involving the Constitution. The Constitution vests in the judiciary the power to decide "cases and controversies." The power to interpret the Constitution is a consequence of that power. Similarly, the other two branches of government have their respective jobs to do, and in doing them, they also interpret the Constitution. Or at least they should. Unfortunately, legislators today often abdicate their responsibility to think about the Constitution as they draft legislation; too often their attitude is, "we'll let the Supreme Court decide." The same is true of the executive branch. During the first reauthorization process, for example, Associate Attorney General Giuliani said that the constitutional questions involved "are difficult and not readily answered, given the lack of authoritative Supreme Court rulings on the relevant points." While it is one thing—a proper thing—for the executive branch to review Court rulings in order to reach its own determination of constitutionality, it is quite another effectively to cede to the Court the executive's duty to interpret the Constitution. On important occasions, Giuliani's testimony seemed such an act of cession. "Only a ruling by the Supreme Court would definitely resolve the constitutional issues," he said at one point, notwithstanding that the President himself could have moved toward resolving the constitutional issues *in his favor* by vetoing the law. The President did not have to wait for "authoritative" or "definitive" rulings from the Supreme Court.

Nor do future Presidents. Indeed, even when the Court has spoken, they still may act. Neither George Bush nor any of his successors is bound by the Court's decision in *Morrison* to sign legislation reauthorizing the independent counsel statute. Presidents worried about such judicial precedent should ponder the presidential precedent—handed down by Andrew Jackson. In 1819, in *McCulloch* v. *Maryland,* the Court upheld the constitutionality of a national bank.[30] One could say *McCulloch* "settled" the issue. But in 1832 President Jackson reopened the question when he vetoed legislation rechartering the bank. In his veto statement, he discounted the significance of *McCulloch* by arguing that the political branches were not bound by the judiciary's reading of the Constitution. "The opinion of the judges has no more authority over Congress than the opinion of Congress has over the judges," said Jackson in his veto message, "and on that point the President is independent of both. The authority of the Supreme Court must not, therefore, be permitted to control the Congress or the Executive when acting in their legislative capacities, but to have only such influence as the force of their reasoning may deserve."[31] Jackson prevailed in his fight with Congress; the idea of a national bank died. And, thus, by the way, did a strong presidency defeat bigger government.

Andrew Johnson was in many ways an undistinguished

President. But to his credit he vetoed the infamous Tenure of Office Act, precisely because it infringed on the rights of the executive. In part because of that act of self-defense, Johnson was impeached in the House and missed by a single vote being convicted by the Senate. But in casting that veto Johnson showed courage.

Having the courage to take responsibility for the office as Johnson did will be especially difficult in our time. Indeed, it is hard to overstate just how difficult. Multiple presidential primaries, incessant opinion polling, and insistent media attention upon the presidency have worked to encourage Presidents to be "men of the people" more than occupants of a constitutional office. (The very democratization of the presidency begun by Jackson in the 1830s and hastened in our century has, as Joseph Bessette observes, reshaped the "calculus of presidential ambition" in such a way that few Presidents will battle for the rights of office, unless their position is also the popular one, as was Jackson's, in opposition to the national bank.[32]) The desire to maintain popularity, and the belief that presidential power is simply a function of popularity, as measured in polling data, are attitudes found not only on the part of would-be Presidents but also their cadres of advisors. For a President to resist the counsel of the moment that cites opinion polls and to take what might be an unpopular action, such as a veto cast in defense of his own powers, thus may become an undertaking of enormous proportion. But in the long run the office of the President will not be worth having if Presidents and their advisers are not prepared to act in its defense.

This chapter has examined the self-defense veto in a particular governing context. But as indicated by the brief discussion in this chapter of a nonenforcement strategy, the veto is not the only means of self-defense. Consider also that a President who had administered the executive branch in a way that successfully discouraged criminal or unethical or imprudent behavior would have been better situated politically than Reagan was to cast a veto in 1987; this is a subject I discuss in Chapter 14. Here it is worth noting that, perversely, the independent counsel law encourages presidential irresponsibility. For instead of taking it upon himself to inquire into alleged misconduct of aides and deal with it accordingly—which might include standing behind an aide, or prosecuting and removing him—the President, as Reagan routinely did, can slough off his obligation onto the all-too-willing shoulders of an independent counsel.[33] A President who does not assume the responsibility for office by using available power to defend it may find at the end of the day, as Reagan did, that he and his successors possess fewer rights.

In its origins as well as its persistence through the years, the independent counsel statute is a monument to executive weakness. And that weakness has proved costly to our politics generally. The independent counsel law is a central piece of a post-Watergate Washington culture that has elevated the pursuit of malfeasance to such a high priority that the whole point of our political system, it sometimes seems, is to root out official wrongdoing, even to turn innocence into sin. Scandal substitutes for, and crowds out, ordinary politics. If this is one reason Americans hate politics, to borrow from the title of E. J. Dionne's 1991 book, it is also a reason more and more politicians hate politics, as witness the large number of retirements of incumbent Congressmen in recent years. The messy ethics environment is not likely to change until a strong President, who insists on his constitutional rights and on high standards of conduct as well, determines that it should.

# 6

# CONGRESS AGAINST THE PRESIDENT

## Reagan, Nicaragua, and the Boland Amendments

In the fall of 1986 Congress passed—and President Reagan signed without objection into law—the Continuing Appropriations Act for fiscal year 1985. Attached to the bill was an amendment providing that "no funds available to the Central Intelligence Agency, the Department of Defense, or any other agency or entity of the United States involved in intelligence activities may be obligated or expended for the purpose of which would have the effect of supporting, directly or indirectly, military or paramilitary operations in Nicaragua by any nation, group, organization, movement, or individual." The Boland amendment, so named after its chief draftsman, Representative Edward Boland, Democrat of Massachusetts, constituted the latest statement of what had been and would continue to be a vacillating congressional view of U.S. foreign policy in Central America. In time, of course, the amendment became an essential element of the Iran-contra scandal, serving as the basis for criminal indictments of National Security Adviser John Poindexter and his deputy, Oliver North. That scandal, the major foreign policy disaster of the Reagan years, stemmed ultimately from the President's general failure to provide the kind of strategic leadership on foreign policy that the Constitution positions him uniquely to provide—a role discussed in Part Two of this book. The focus of this chapter is Reagan's specific failure to frame the legislative debate over the Boland amendment in the fall of 1984. Reagan could have done that through a veto strategy.

The story of Reagan's failure to oppose the Boland amendment in 1984 must be told in a larger context dating back to 1981, when the President considered new policy to meet the challenge to the nation's security he believed was posed by the Sandinistas who had taken control of Nicaragua in 1979 and whose leaders were Marxist-Leninists allied with the Soviet Union. Reagan feared an expansionist communist enemy that could destabilize Central America. His options included (1) containment (i.e., letting the Sandinistas be while preventing them from getting their hands on other countries); (2) direct intervention (i.e., sending in U.S. troops to overthrow the regime); and (3) indirect intervention (i.e., using other means short of committing U.S. troops). In opting for the third, Reagan decided to organize and equip anti-Sandinista Nicaraguans—contras, as they were called. Reagan hoped not only to prevent the export of communism into Central America—in El Salvador to begin with—but also to effect a shift to democracy within Nicaragua itself, even if that meant overthrowing the Sandinista government—an unstated and even publicly denied goal.

The new policy—later seen as an instance of a more general policy called the "Reagan Doctrine" by columnist Charles Krauthammer—was pursued initially in secret. The administration, as required by law, kept the Intelligence Committees in both houses of Congress advised about certain aspects of the CIA's activities with respect to Nicaragua. It was in late 1982 that the administration's effort—its so-called secret war—first came to the attention of the American people through press accounts. Over the next four years Congress used appropriations bills as the means for debating, and regulating, the President's Nicaraguan policy.

During this period the two chambers divided along party lines on contra aid.[1] The Republican-controlled Senate consistently if narrowly voted to support the President's policy, while the Democratically controlled House sometimes supported and sometimes opposed it. The Boland amendment tacked onto the continuing appropriations resolution for fiscal year 1985 was actually the third, chronologically speaking, of five amendments addressing contra aid between late 1982 and 1986. All named for Representative Boland, they represented negotiated compromises between congressional liberals who sought an absolute ban on contra aid, on the one hand, and, on the other, the President and his congressional allies who wanted to keep the contras alive until a majority in Congress would agree to resume funding.

Boland I—amending the Defense Appropriations Act for 1983—provided that none of the funds in the act could be used by the CIA or the Department of Defense to aid militarily any group intent on "overthrowing the government of Nicaragua or provoking a military exchange between Nicaragua and Honduras." The executive branch took a more permissive view of the amendment than Boland and other congressional liberals did; thus, for the administration, so long as the U.S. government itself did not intend to overthrow the Sandinistas, the purposes of the contras themselves were irrelevant.

In 1983 House liberals sought to curtail all covert support for the contras, but proved unable to persuade the Senate. Boland II, enacted in December 1983 as part of not only the Defense Appropriations Act for fiscal year 1984 but also the Intelligence Authorization Act, placed a cap of $24 million on military aid to the contras. This amount was just enough to keep the contras going for half a year, at most—precisely what Boland and his colleagues intended.

Thus, crunch time for the administration's policy—and the contras themselves—was to arrive in the spring or summer of 1984. Everyone—from the contras to the Sandinistas to the Congress and the President—knew this. In an effort to force the Sandinistas to bargain for peace in Central America, the CIA assisted in early 1984 in the mining of Nicaragua's Corinto harbor. When, in April 1984, this event was publicly reported (thanks to leaks from Capitol Hill), congressional liberals expressed outrage. Congress, it was said, had not been informed. This happened not to be true—starting in January 1984 CIA Director William Casey had briefed Congress on numerous occasions.[2] But using the mining incident to public-relations advantage—even former President Richard Nixon described the operation as "Mickey Mouse"—opponents of the President's policy managed to enact Boland III, the most constraining of all of the kindred amendments.[3] As noted at the beginning of this chapter, Boland III, in effect from October 1984 to December 1985, prohibited the CIA, the Defense Department, or "any other agency or entity of the United States involved in intelligence activities" from using funds appropriated to them to aid the contras.

Through the Boland amendments Congress fairly confirmed the framers' point that foreign policy is more coherently conducted by one person than 535. But instead of opposing Boland III, the amendment that most of all demanded his response—on policy or constitutional grounds—Reagan acquiesced in it. What *then* happened is well-known. The National Security Council, already deeply involved in supporting the contras, took further charge: Proceeds from the covert sale of arms to Iran were channeled to the contras (about which diversion the President later said he was ignorant); private and foreign government contributions to the contras were successfully solicited; a private air resupply operation was established. When congressional committees investigated the Iran-contra affair, administration officials claimed that Boland III did not cover the National Security Council. But the time to have made that argument (and others) was at the moment of presentment in a veto message or at least in a signing statement; as it happened, in congressional testimony NSC officials seemed to agree that the amendment did apply to the agency.

Thus, in August 1985, National Security Adviser Bud McFarlane told three different committees of Congress that the NSC was complying with the letter and spirit of the law. In the summer of 1986, when Congress was again considering issues of contra aid, McFarlane's successor—Admiral John Poindexter—in effect reiterated McFarlane's "letter-and-spirit-of-the-law" statement in response to an inquiry from the House Intelligence Committee. Furthermore, although Boland III did not specifically address third-country solicitation, it was a matter of intense concern to Congress during 1984 and 1985, and both State Department and NSC officials told Congress that it did bar the administration from making such solicitations. Thus, for the sake of keeping the contras alive in the short term, Congress was deceived.

Commentary on the Iran-contra scandal has often focused on the representations made by McFarlane, Poindexter, North (and others) to Congress, and the cases brought by Independent Counsel Lawrence Walsh, which charged them with violations of statutes ostensibly covering what they told Congress. Chapter 16 of this book discusses the ultimate responsibility Reagan himself must bear as President for what happened in both halves of Iran-contra. Here I address what the President should have done in his legislative capacity.

Faced with Boland III, Reagan had three options. The first: veto the continuing appropriations resolution and explain why by taking on Boland III on both policy and constitutional grounds. The second: approve the resolution but do so in a signing statement indicating his interpretation of Boland III's coverage. That would probably have provoked even more restrictive legislation, in which case the President might have had to wield a veto. The third: approve the resolution, without comment. This, alas, is what Reagan did, thus managing to avoid partisan confrontation between the branches in the short run but doing himself—and the presidential office—no favors in the long run.

In a veto message (or a signing statement) Reagan could have made clear that the Boland amendment did not cover the NSC and that it could not be read to undermine the President's constitutional authority to conduct foreign policy, specifically that it could not be read to restrict his or his agents' ability under the Constitution to seek third-country and private donations to the contras. The majority report of the congressional committees investigating the Iran-contra affair did not think the amendment an unconstitutional invasion of the

President's foreign policy prerogatives. But as we saw in the previous chapter, it is up to the President to assert his constitutional rights when there is a dispute about them between the branches, and the veto as originally envisioned is just the instrument for doing that.[4] A lesson for future Presidents was put well enough by the majority report: "If the President believes that a law has provisions that are unconstitutional, he must either veto it or put Congress on notice of his position. . . . The one option the executive branch does not have is to pretend that it is executing the law when it is, in fact, evading it."[5]

A veto would have forced an institutional showdown over an important foreign policy issue. It would have furthered the cause of deliberative government because the policy and constitutional arguments would have been publicly joined in a way that would have forced a better debate. Of course, a public confrontation also would have posed an obvious risk: clear defeat of the President's foreign policy. But, for the sake of good government, which requires a strong President able to conduct foreign policy, that risk should have been taken. Reagan's acquiescence in Boland III created the circumstance in which his subordinates circumvented the law and then misled Congress about their efforts; their deception, when it was found out, undermined Reagan's capacity to govern and, more important, the political support the presidency needs—no matter its occupant—to conduct foreign policy in general.

When Congress opposes a President's foreign policy through legislation, the President must engage the issue from the position of institutional strength afforded him by the Constitution; he must use the veto power. Such an exercise of institutional muscle by Reagan would have strengthened the executive in its ability to conduct foreign policy—no matter the final legislative outcome of Boland III.

The matter of protecting presidential power in the context of Boland-type amendments has been usefully discussed by Michael Malbin, professor of politics at the State University of New York at Albany.[6] The Boland amendments represented what he calls "procedural warfare" against the President's foreign policy toward Nicaragua. Reagan was at a disadvantage in this contest, as all Presidents necessarily will be. As Malbin explains, members of Congress opposed to the Reagan policy pressed for "maximalist" interpretations of the Boland amendments even as the administration implemented a "minimalist" interpretation of the same language without telling Congress what it was doing. From the anti-Reagan congressional perspective, the fact that the several Boland amendments amounted to an on-again, off-again policy did not matter, for the amendments, taken as a whole, furthered their goal of preventing a sustained program of U.S. military support for the contras. Given the President's desire to maintain such a program, and given his institutional status as the one who actually has to conduct foreign policy in any event, his position was more complicated. For as Malbin puts it, "the short-term steps [i.e., acquiesce in Boland, but then pursue policies inconsistent with Boland that are concealed from Congress] needed to sustain specific program objectives one fiscal year at a time were not the best ones for maintaining the long-term political powers of the office."[7] Those short-term steps might have served what the President regarded as the strategic interest of the nation—but only in the short term. And given their consequences—the Iran-contra affair—they weakened political support for the powers of office necessary for any President to protect that very same interest in the long run. As Malbin generalizes, "[A] strong presidency—one that builds public support for the exercise of discretionary power—may well be a prerequisite for defending against foreign policy threats over the long term."[8]

If, as Malbin argues, congressional opponents of a President will generally be able to achieve consistency between their policy goals and their desire for institutional power—that is, they will be able to pass Boland-style amendments—the only option for a strong President is to lay down what he will do far in advance of the passage of any particular piece of legislation. "[H]e needs to make it clear, through his actions, that he will respond predictably and effectively to any congressional action that he considers a usurpation of presidential power."[9] Only in this way can a President avoid being forced to weigh policies and institutional power against each other.

Had Reagan proceeded in this no-nonsense fashion, he

would have taken his institutional stand early on—in 1981. At the same time, he could have taken his specific foreign policy case to the Congress and the general public, giving reasons for the kind of support necessary to sustain his program. Thus, Reagan could have explained the interconnected nature of Central America—that what happens in Nicaragua necessarily affects what happens in neighboring countries. He could have discussed the geopolitical factors, such as the Soviet aid pouring into Nicaragua since 1979, and pointed to the Sandinistas' allies—Cuba, East Germany, Bulgaria, and Libya, among others. He could have directly argued the case for U.S. aid to the contras.[10]

As it happened, it was not the "Great Communicator" who first discussed his own Nicaraguan policy with the people of the United States, but that policy's most vociferous opponents. Indeed, Reagan did not even give a nationally televised address in behalf of the contras—his first was in May 1984, just after the mining of Nicaragua's Corinto harbor became news—until public opinion had solidly congealed in opposition to administration policy.[11] In his account of the Reagan presidency, Lou Cannon argues that had Reagan gone to Congress and the public early on in his presidency in behalf of the contras, "he almost certainly would have won."[12] But whether Reagan would have won or not, on that particular issue, the presidency—and the nation—would certainly have been better off having had a principled, public confrontation that established a clear line of responsibility for the outcomes in Central America.

The Continuing Appropriations Act for fiscal year 1985 was a mere 1,200 pages long. It bundled together nine of the thirteen appropriations bills for that year. On top of this massive legislation rode the paragraphs of Boland III. The continuing resolution thus reflected two congressional trends since Watergate—the failure to pass single appropriations bills on time (which failure has led to huge, last-minute omnibus appropriations, such as the one here); and the willingness to use the Appropriations Clause of the Constitution to deny the President's constitutional rights. Besides objecting to congressional use of the Appropriations Clause to attempt to limit his foreign policy authority, Reagan could and should have taken special aim at the very form in which the legislation was presented to him. In his veto message, Reagan could have insisted that Congress pass *separate* appropriations bills, as in fact the 1974 budget act requires, and that it refrain from attaching substantive riders to appropriations bills. Reagan could have argued that otherwise neither the Congress nor the President can reason as well as it should about the merits of federal spending or new public policy. Deliberative government is ill served when continuing resolutions or other omnibus appropriations bills, especially when they come to the President with substantive riders attached, become routine.

President Rutherford B. Hayes faced appropriations bills containing Boland-like provisions. With the demise of Reconstruction in 1877, Congress began exercising its power of the purse to prevent using federal troops as in the South to maintain peace and prevent fraud at polling places in compliance with the Fifteenth Amendment; former slaves had been subjected to violence and intimidation when they tried to vote. No fewer than five times (in 1879–80) did Hayes veto separate appropriations bills that included riders prohibiting the use of any appropriated monies to deploy troops in this fashion.[13] Hayes recognized that as President of the United States he could not accept these riders—and therefore the bills that contained them. The Fifteenth Amendment provides that no citizen shall be denied his right to vote on the basis of race. Elsewhere the Constitution guarantees to each state a republican form of government and protection against domestic violence. If voting rights were infringed on the basis of race, the guarantee of republican government would be undermined; and depending on how those rights were infringed, states might need protection against domestic violence. But who is to ensure the rule of these parts of the law of the Constitution? Only the President, and the President is obligated by that very Constitution to do so. He has a constitutional duty to take care that the laws, including the Constitution, are faithfully executed, and he swears to an oath spelled out in the Constitution that obligates him to defend the Constitution. Moreover, the President is commander in chief of the very troops he might have to order to quell violence within a state.

If President Hayes had accepted the defunding riders by signing the appropriation bills, he would have been an irresponsible President. More than a half century later, in 1933, Attorney General William Mitchell succinctly stated the rule that should govern every President as he considers legislation presented to him: "Congress may not, by conditions attached to appropriations, provide for a discharge of the functions of Government in a manner not authorized by the Constitution."[14]

Through his repeated use of the veto, President Hayes succeeded in persuading Congress on each occasion to excise the rider from the appropriations bill. Hayes in this episode remains an enduring example of how a President should act, consistent with the constitutional order and indeed in its behalf.

# 7

# THE POLICY POWER OF THE VETO POWER

## Bush and the "Quota" Bill

Especially in an era of divided government, the veto of the energetic executive can protect administrative successes even as it changes the terms of public policy debate and creates the opportunity for the President to promote deliberation and even to forge a new politics. In October 1990 President Bush cast a veto that—more than any other veto in recent years—deserves analysis from this perspective. For in vetoing the Civil Rights Act of 1990, Bush was, in part, the energetic executive: He defended administrative success achieved by the Reagan presidency even as he managed to define the terms of public debate over civil rights, although not as effectively as he could have. That the President did not fully seize the governing opportunity available to him—among other things, he could have used popular rhetoric to promote a new civil rights politics—is a lesson for future Presidents, if not for Bush himself.

The Civil Rights Act of 1964 created a right to equal employment opportunity free of discrimination, but in subsequent years federal agencies devised racial quotas and other programs of minority preference. In 1980 the Republican Party and its presidential candidate promised to challenge these policies, which had been sanctioned by federal courts. The GOP platform said that "quotas, ratios, and numerical requirements" which "exclude some individuals in favor of others" were "inherently discriminatory." And candidate Ronald Reagan stated that "we must not allow the noble concept of equal opportunity to be distorted into federal guidelines or quotas."

While the Reagan presidency's effort against "numerical requirements" often stumbled for lack of an overall strategy, it did yield notable success, especially in the Supreme Court, where the Reagan Justice Department argued against certain features of the legal system that promoted and even required quotas.[1] In 1989 the Supreme Court—with four Justices appointed by Reagan now sitting—decided a series of cases in which it altered pro-quota doctrines to reflect neutral legal principles. The most important of these was *Wards Cove* v. *Atonio,* in which the Court addressed important litigation issues involving Title VII of the Civil Rights Act of 1964.[2] Upset with the 1989 decisions, especially *Wards Cove,* congressional liberals quickly moved to propose corrective legislation. The Kennedy-Hawkins bill passed both houses of Congress in the fall of 1990. This was the legislation Bush successfully vetoed on grounds that it was a "quota bill."

This brief review provides context for understanding the considerable power of the presidency, even when the other party controls Congress. Under the Constitution, the President has the duty to see that the laws are faithfully executed. The President thus may change the status quo in the execution of certain laws, consistent with the Constitution, assuming sufficient discretion to do so. In this task he may have occasion to argue through the Justice Department his legal positions in federal court. Precisely because the President meanwhile is selecting federal judges as he is authorized to do under the Constitution, a President who attends carefully to judicial philosophy in those choices can affect the kind of reception his legal arguments receive in court. Through litigation *and* court appointments, then, the President is uniquely positioned to seek his kind of decisional law. If the judicial rulings are to the administration's liking, but if there is a majority in Congress that strongly disagrees with them, there likely will be a legislative showdown in which the President's veto power may come into play. And that power trumps simple majorities in Congress, given the two-thirds of both houses needed for an override.

In the case at hand, the Reagan presidency's litigation in respect to civil rights won certain decisions from a Supreme Court whose composition it had changed through new appointments in a conservative direction. And the Democratic majority in Congress responded to the Court's rulings legislatively by passing Kennedy-Hawkins, thus setting the stage for the 1990 legislative battle in which the veto cast by Reagan's Republican successor, George Bush, proved decisive.

The bill Bush vetoed was the first ever passed by both houses of Congress that could reasonably be characterized as employment quota legislation. While the bill did not explicitly require quotas, in its most relevant parts it proposed technical legal doctrines that would have forced employers to resort to preferences or else face expensive Title VII litigation. As the President stated when vetoing the bill on October 23, 1990, "despite the use of the term 'civil rights,' " the legislation "actually employs a maze of highly legalistic language to introduce the destructive force of quotas" in the workplace.

Bush's veto, which the Senate failed by the single vote to override, defended the litigated success achieved by the Reagan administration against quotas.[3] Had the President failed to cast a veto, he would have not only repealed the complicated labor of his predecessor, but also compromised the Republican Party's long-standing political opposition to quotas and similar numerical requirements.

Bush's veto also defined the terms of an important debate. The Kennedy-Hawkins bill was introduced in Congress in February 1990. On May 17, at a Rose Garden ceremony to honor the U.S. Civil Rights Commission, Bush for the first time issued a veto threat. "No one here today," he said, "would want me to sign a bill whose unintended consequences are quotas. . . . [Q]uotas are wrong, and they violate the most basic principles of our civil rights tradition and the most basic principles of the promise of democracy. . . . I want to sign a civil rights bill, but I will not sign a quota bill." Until Bush said this, supporters of Kennedy-Hawkins had not been challenged about its pro-quota implications; they had freely advertised their legislation as a civil rights bill, without significant opposition. While the Bush Justice Department had commented in bill reports that Kennedy-Hawkins would foster quotas, only the President, given his position in the constitutional order, could have made this point in such a way as to command public attention and serious response. Throughout the summer and fall of 1990, Bush reiterated that he would not sign a quota bill.[4] During this period, the most important public question on the matter was not, as the civil rights lobby put it (and had always been able to put it), "Are you for or against civil rights?" but, "Is this a civil rights bill or a quota bill?"

Media coverage and commentary after Bush spoke on May 17 testify to his success in influencing the public debate. Such previously reliable supporters of positions taken by the civil rights lobbies as *The Christian Science Monitor* weighed the Bush argument and decided to oppose Kennedy-Hawkins. The Bush position was reflected in *The New Republic,* which commented: "[I]t gives employers a strong incentive to adopt [quotas]—or else face lawsuits alleging discrimination that would be costly to defend and difficult to win."[5]

As successful as Bush was in focusing public attention on the quota issue, he failed to take full advantage of the governing opportunity available to him in this high-profile legislative battle. His rhetoric went only so far—so far as his immediate political needs demanded, it appeared. Unfortunately for the nation, the President shied from the important leadership task of cogently explaining *why* quotas are wrong. For at stake in the Kennedy-Hawkins legislation was something far more important than pacifying conservatives upset with him for agreeing to a budget accord that included higher taxes, and far more important than gaining political advantage in the 1990 congressional elections (and beyond) over Democrats, whose failure to win the presidency in recent years is in part explained by its commitment to racially preferential goals and timetables and other such numerical devices.[6] At issue is a matter of fundamental importance—whether race should be a source of power or entitlement in the pursuit of equal opportunity. Bush could and should have argued, repeatedly, that it should not be, because race is dumb: By itself it cannot tell us anything morally important about a particular person. What makes a quota or a goal or any other similar device wrong, he could have said, is that it makes distinctions among citizens and confers benefits to certain ones on the basis of a characteristic that, standing alone, cannot supply a moral basis for such action.

The resources in American law and history with which the President could have prosecuted this case through popular but thoughtful rhetoric are rich indeed, beginning with the Declaration of Independence and Lincoln's reflections on the principle of equality it expressed. The resources include the post-Civil War amendments and federal statutes, and also the modern civil rights laws, especially Title VII of the Civil Rights Act of 1964, the very statute from which came the issues in legislative dispute.[7]

Elevating the public and congressional debate, Bush could have focused discussion of Title VII on not only the principle of equality that animated it but also its subsequent fate in the federal bureaucracy and the courts. Bush's public remarks to Congress and the nation could have been informed by the following points:[8]

First, Title VII, as enacted, outlawed employment discrimination based on race, color, religion, sex, or national origin. The Congress that passed Title VII defined the prohibited discrimination as that of the "intentional" variety, rejecting the competing notion of racial balance or "disparate impact." The decision in a 1964 Illinois case, *Myart* v. *Motorola,* had worried some members of Congress. Under that state's fair employment practices act, a racially neutral test had been invalidated on grounds that it had a disparate impact upon blacks; the employer was told he could not use it until he showed that it did not cause a racial imbalance within

110

his work force. Senator Clifford Case, one of the leading authorities on Title VII, assured his colleagues that the new federal law would not permit *Motorola*-type cases; a federal court, he said, could not read Title VII to require an employer "to lower or change the occupational qualifications he sets for his employees simply because fewer [blacks] than whites are able to meet them." An authoritative Senate memorandum maintained that bona fide qualifications tests would *not* have to be abandoned where, "because of differences" in background and education, members of some groups are able to perform better on the tests than members of other groups." An employer "may set his qualifications as high as he likes, he may test to determine which applicants have these qualifications, and he may hire, assign, and promote on the basis of test performance."[9] To guard against uses of the statute that might lead to quotas, the 1964 Congress added a provision saying that nothing in it "shall be interpreted to require any employer . . . to grant preferential treatment to any individual or to any group" on account of racial imbalance in the workplace.

Second, contradicting the original meaning of the statute, the newly created Equal Employment Opportunity Commission, in 1966 guidelines purporting to interpret Title VII, defined discrimination in statistical terms, to the effect that employment practices having a disparate impact upon minorities—including job testing—were suspect, and maintained that these practices had to be validated or else modified or eliminated. According to the EEOC guidelines, Title VII permitted only the use of *job-related* tests and held that employers using such tests must have available data "demonstrating that the test is predictive or significantly correlated with important elements of work behavior which comprise or are relevant to the job or jobs for which candidates are being evaluated."

Third, while the EEOC knew that its own approach to discrimination was at odds with Title VII and was concerned that either its interpretation of the law or the law itself would have to be changed, neither had to occur because of the Supreme Court's landmark 1971 ruling in *Griggs* v. *Duke Power Co.*[10] In its first significant interpretation of Title VII, the

Court sided with the EEOC (even going so far as to cite its guidelines as an authoritative rendering of the statute) by reading disparate impact theory into Title VII. In an opinion written by Chief Justice Warren Burger, the Court held in striking down tests for hiring and promotions that Title VII "proscribes not only overt discrimination but also [employment] practices that are fair in form, but discriminatory in operation." Only a practice justified by "business necessity"—a term found nowhere in Title VII or in previous Court opinions—could pass muster under Title VII. According to the Court, if an employment practice that operates to exclude blacks "cannot be shown to be related to job performance, the practice is prohibited." The Court maintained that when Congress wrote Title VII, it was concerned about not simply the motivation of employment requirements but also their consequences, and that for this reason Congress had placed "on the employer the burden of showing that any given requirement must have a manifest relationship to the employment in question." "What Congress has commanded," the Court said, "is that any tests used must measure the person for the job and not the person in the abstract."

Fourth, *Griggs* not only ratified the enforcement policy adopted by the EEOC but also provided policy direction for the rest of the government, including the Justice Department in its enforcement of Title VII against public employers. It also paved the way for private disparate impact cases. During the 1970s the Supreme Court and lower courts developed the disparate impact law first articulated in *Griggs*. Title VII became a plaintiffs' statute, with virtually no employment practice having a "disparate impact" immune from legal attack based on *Griggs:* A wide range of recruitment, hiring, assignment, testing, seniority, promotion, discharge, and supervisory selection practices were successfully challenged.[11]

Fifth, *Griggs* encouraged private and public employers to resort to preferential treatment of minorities and women in order to avoid litigation and liability under Title VII. Indeed, the theory of *Griggs* helped promote the trend toward race-norming, in which scores on officially validated ability tests (and therefore supposedly free of cultural bias) are "adjusted" for differences among whites, blacks, Hispanics, and other groups. In 1973, E. F. Wonderlic & Associates, a major marketer of cognitive-ability tests, promoted an "Ethnic Conversion Table" by which employers could ensure racially proportionate scores by those taking its test. Wonderlic sent employers information on how to race-norm, with this advice: "No further validation evidence is necessary nor will be accepted by Federal, state or local regulatory agencies for no disparate effect will exist which would trigger the need for individual validation. . . . The approved usage of the Wonderlic Personnel Test eliminates the possibility of adverse impact, allows you to administer the test to all job applicants regardless of job sought or minority statutes and becomes the one element of your selection procedure that you may use and act upon with full confidence in meeting [equal employment opportunity] requirements." To the end of the letter was appended this P.S.: "Select to fill proper ratios and quotas. Select the best-suited individuals by ethnic class."[12] Race-norming takes place as follows: Four job applicants take a standardized test of cognitive skills administered by a government job-referral service. All score the same. But when reported to prospective employers, the first gets an 83 because she is black; the second a 67, because she is Hispanic, and the third and fourth each get a 45, because they are white and Asian, respectively. Although the test-takers do not know this fact, the reported scores have been "converted" by race so as to give each racial group a proportionate share of the highest scores.[13] This is a quota practice, however, and as such is contrary to Title VII as originally enacted.

Sixth, in 1989 a Supreme Court concerned about the nature of the judge-made law since *Griggs* sensibly acted to reform it in *Wards Cove*. The case involved Alaskan salmon canneries that employed a mainly white work force in skilled jobs and a mainly nonwhite work force in unskilled jobs. The U.S. Court of Appeals for the Ninth Circuit had ruled that this "imbalance" created a *prima facie* case of disparate impact against the company, thus obligating it to show that its hiring and employment practices were justified by business necessity. The Supreme Court disagreed, relying on a 1977 ruling in which it had held that the proper comparison in a disparate impact case is between "the racial composition of the qualified person in the labor market and the persons holding at-issue jobs." The Court then went on to say (1) that a *prima facie* case of disparate impact cannot be made *without* attributing the imbalance to one or more employment practices; (2) that once such a case of disparate impact is established, the burden of producing evidence of a legitimate business justification for that practice shifts to the employer; and (3) that the burden of persuasion nonetheless remains with the plaintiff, who must disprove an employer's evidence that his practice has a legitimate business justification.[14] The Court said that what is at issue is whether a challenged practice "serves, in a significant way, the legitimate employment goals of the employer."

Bush's public rhetoric, shaped by these points, would have sought to convey the kind of issue facing Congress and the country since the *Wards Cove* decision in 1989. That issue was this: Do we now wish, for the first time, to codify disparate impact theory in respect to employment discrimination, and if so, how do we want to do that?[15] In a way that fosters quotas, or reduces their possibility? If we are to be true to our principles as a country and fair to all the many peoples of this earth who can equally be Americans, according to the principles of the Declaration of Independence, we must legislate, Bush could have said, in a way that strenuously seeks to avoid quotas and other numerical devices that confer and deny benefits on the morally irrelevant basis of mere race.

Had Bush taken this approach early on, he would have positioned himself not just to use the veto power but to meet his duty to recommend legislation. Thus, he could have proposed a codification of disparate impact theory that did *not* promise to encourage quotas and sought its alignment with the original terms of Title VII; in other words he could have proposed genuine reform of disparate impact law.[16] At the same time he could have threatened the use of his veto power to block any legislation that did not meet his standard. Taking this position, Bush could have directed congressional attention to the difficulties that disparate impact theory, as supporters of Kennedy-Hawkins defined it, has created for minorities in particular. Thus, Bush could have argued, as he in fact did come to argue in 1991, that the theory works against the setting of reasonable standards not simply for

114

getting a job but for achievement in life. For if an employer may test only for what is "essential"—as Kennedy-Hawkins advocates argued—and thus is effectively forbidden to test in ways that might demonstrate relative qualifications, then why test at all? And why should those who take tests have any incentive to do well on them? Or to study in school? Whatever the merits of disparate impact theory at the time the EEOC imposed it upon Title VII, the nation, Bush could have said, cannot afford to be saddled with a theory of discrimination that works against genuine achievement, especially on the part of minorities. All forecasts indicate that by the year 2000 the majority of new entrants in the American work force will be minorities. If America is to compete effectively in today's international economy, testing must no longer be regarded as synonymous with racial discrimination. The anti-high standards mentality fostered by *Griggs* and its progency, Bush could have continued, must come to an end. For otherwise the nation will not be able to prepare its students for, as Bush eventually did put it in 1991, "productive employment in our modern economy."

As it happened, Bush did not use the presidential office to frame a legislative response to *Wards Cove*. Instead, he reacted to what others in Congress did. In early 1989 the Bush Justice Department agreed that legislation was needed to modify two employment discrimination decisions—*Lorance* v. *AT&T Technologies* and *Patterson* v. *McLean Credit Union*.[17] But disagreeing with Kennedy-Hawkins, Justice denied any need to modify *Wards Cove*. That bill proposed, in disparate impact litigation, to place the burden of proof on employers with a racially (or sexually) imbalanced work force to prove that all of their employment practices are justified by business necessity, defined as "essential to effective job performance." Over the summer of 1990, the administration sought compromise.[18] The administration finally did agree to shift the burden of proof to the employer. But no agreement could be reached over the degree to which employees should be forced to identify specific employment practices when alleging discrimination, nor on the definition of "business necessity."[19]

With Bush now presented a bill he could not accept, consistent with his veto threat, Chief of Staff John Sununu argued internally that the President should take his substantive proposals and turn them into amendments that he would then ask Congress to pass. In the Sununu scheme, the President would promise to sign both Kennedy-Hawkins *and* the amendments. Because the President had veto strength, Sununu thought this approach might appeal to those in Congress who wanted a civil rights bill passed. At the same time, Sununu wanted to avoid the political problems that might result from the President's veto of a civil rights bill. The Sununu idea was rejected, as it should have been. The idea was too clever by half. The President's substantive proposals already had met defeat in Congress, and the ten-day clock triggered by the Presentment Clause had begun to tick. How the President was supposed to collect the necessary majorities as quickly as he would need them was unclear, especially since House Republicans who had voted against Kennedy-Hawkins and believed the President's veto threat were now upset with him. The Sununu idea got reworked: The President vetoed Kennedy-Hawkins *and* then recommended new legislation that included his approach to the disparate impact issues. But his bill was not significantly different in that respect; it, too, would have encouraged employers to resort to quotas. Bush was fortunate that Congress did not pass his bill, which would have provoked debate in Congress and the media over whether it was also a quota bill. Bush's veto protected him against himself, although this point drew no press attention at the time.

The moment Bush cast his veto was not the time for him to recommend legislation, and the defensive position he had occupied since the beginning of the year led him to endorse a bill that was not importantly different from the one he signed. Bush would have been in a far stronger legislative position if early in 1990 he had recommended to Congress an alternative that was truly consistent with his popular rhetoric against quotas.[20]

Here as in other contexts we see the importance of using the presidential office as energetically as it can be used, consistent with the constitutional order. Indeed, it is possible to imagine an even more energetic course than the one I have argued Bush should have taken. This course would have pursued a new politics of civil rights. It would have sought to redirect the search for equality from Title VII litigation to other, more promising means. Bush actually made a stab at this in his May 17 address, in which he first issued a veto threat against Kennedy-Hawkins. Toward the end of his remarks he endorsed "empowerment"—an agenda of "choice." Empowerment encompasses such policies as enterprise zones, educational vouchers, and urban homesteading. Empowerment aims to entice those on lower economic rungs, whom quotas are unlikely to help, to help themselves by choosing, for example, where their children should be schooled. This agenda is radically different from that of Kennedy-Hawkins, which contemplates litigation as the primary means to equal opportunity. But Bush did not effectively prosecute the case for this agenda championed by his Housing and Urban Development Secretary Jack Kemp, or even the larger one available to him.

Bush also could have announced a review of government policies to determine which ones help keep poor people poor. Poor families pay more than their share of the cost of many current subsidies—such as farm support—than does the middle class, which such subsidies typically benefit. That is one of several good arguments for their reduction, if not elimination. The President also could have committed his administration and his party to an understanding of criminal law enforcement that makes safety in the streets a central political issue.[21] The means toward safety are politically complicated, involving reform of certain Supreme Court rulings and also of federal and state statutes. But Bush could have established the general policy direction.

The empowerment agenda was the only alternative Bush had, but he hid this light under a bushel. Bush did not use speeches and press conferences to make the case for empowerment. Admittedly, Congress would have been under no obligation to consider his legislative views; but had Bush undertaken a popular effort to forge a new politics of civil rights he could have done so in ways that strengthened his legislative position in respect to the *Wards Cove* issues. For the President then would have been offering a comprehensive equal opportunity agenda as an alternative to the traditional, litigation approach favored by civil rights lobbies.

Had the President pursued a new politics of civil rights in 1989 and 1990, he would have been asking the nation to join him in one of those "extensive arduous enterprises" that Alexander Hamilton said the presidency is uniquely positioned to embark upon. While Bush and Congress eventually agreed on civil rights legislation in November 1991,[22] the need for a new politics of civil rights remained, as did the need for an energetic executive willing to provide the necessary leadership. That these were critical needs became all the more evident in the wake of the April 1992 rioting in South-Central Los Angeles that claimed more than fifty lives.

# 8

# THE POWERS OF
# PERSUASION

Bush *and* Congress v. Saddam Hussein

The President, through the Internal Revenue Service, may
not collect taxes unless Congress levies them. But may
the President, whom Article II makes "the Commander in
Chief" of the armed forces, use them without congressional
authorization? Never, sometimes, any time? If he may do so at
will, does his power in effect encompass what Article I vests in
Congress—power "to declare war"?

As the nation prepared in 1990 and early 1991 to do battle against Saddam Hussein, President Bush acted as though
presidential power does indeed include *all* of the war powers,
or at least all he felt was needed for him to go to war in the
Gulf. True, on January 8 Bush formally asked Congress to
adopt a resolution on the use of U.S. military force in the Gulf.
But the measure Bush sought would have only *supported*, not

authorized, the use of force. This very minimal request was made for reasons of prudence, not legality; indeed, on January 9 Bush told reporters: "I don't think I need [a resolution from Congress]." On January 12 Congress did adopt a joint resolution *authorizing* (not merely supporting) the use of American military force against Iraq. But Bush did not have a change of view about what he legally needed or didn't need. In signing the resolution, the President wrote, "As I made clear to congressional leaders at the outset, my request for congressional support did not, and my signing this statement does not, constitute any change in the longstanding positions of the executive branch of either the President's constitutional authority to use the armed forces to defend vital U.S. interests or the constitutionality of the War Powers Resolution." There can be no doubt that Bush was ready to drop bombs on Baghdad, regardless of how or even whether Congress voted.[1]

Bush probably did need a law before he could have acted militarily against Iraq. But there is little point in faulting Bush for not believing that he needed congressional authorization. Not only did he sign the Iraq Resolution—an important precedent for future Congresses and Presidents—he also made the most compelling case for passing it. And he did so not through popular speeches, but actions premised on his constitutional powers. The Constitution makes the President dominant in foreign affairs, and from August through December, 1990, Bush acted pursuant to his formal powers of office—freezing assets, deploying troops, negotiating with officials in the Middle East and in the United Nations, to cite three of the most salient examples. Bush's actions created the circumstance by early January in which Congress felt compelled to side with him against Iraq.

Alexander Hamilton would have understood this unusual dynamic, virtually unnoticed by commentary on the U.S. war effort. Writing in 1793 under the pseudonym Pacificus, in defense of Washington's Proclamation of Neutrality in the war between France and Britain, Hamilton observed that there is "the right of the executive, in certain cases, to determine the condition of the nation," and that "the consequences" of his doing so may affect "the exercise of the power of the legislature to declare war." While observing that "the executive cannot thereby control the exercise of that power" and that the legislature is "still free to perform its duties, according to its own sense of them," Hamilton wrote that the executive's "exercise of its constitutional powers . . . may establish an antecedent state of things, which ought to weigh in the legislative decision."[2] Bush established "an antecedent state of things," and verily it weighed in the legislative decision of January 12.[3]

While it is obvious that no two wars are alike, the Persian Gulf war, our most recent, affords an excellent opportunity to reflect upon not only the war powers provided for in the Constitution but also their exercise in a political era influenced by the War Powers Resolution of 1973 and characterized by divided government in which Democrats, many of whom are averse to using military force, control both chambers of Congress. Like the previous chapters in Part One, this chapter treats the President in his relations with Congress in regard to particular legislation (admittedly of a rare kind). Like Chapters 5 and 6, but at greater length, this chapter discusses the President in terms of actions taken pursuant to his non-legislative powers and duties. This chapter, placed as it is at the end of Part One, serves as a reminder that there are regions of presidential territory other than those mapped by the President's duty to recommend and his power to approve or veto legislation. Part Two explores more of that territory under the rubric, "The President and the Executive Branch."

Article I of the Constitution gives Congress power to provide for the armed forces and power to declare war. This represented a departure from the English system, in which such powers lay with the crown.[4] The King also directed the military—power that the Constitution explicitly gives the President as "the Commander in Chief." Since the founding but especially in recent years there has been debate over what this distribution of authority means: Must Congress always pass law that declares war or otherwise authorizes the use of force before the President can order troops into hostilities? Are there not occasions on which the President may act without a declaration of war or other law approving the use of force? If there are, are these occasions so inclusive of the possibilities as to make the War Clause ("To declare war") a nullity?[5] As a practical matter, is it the President who decides about and makes war? Are we back to the English King?

Only five times has Congress formally declared war—the War of 1812, the Mexican War, the Spanish-American War, World War I, and World War II. According to Louis Fisher, only in the case of the War of 1812 did Congress actually debate the merits of going to war; in the other cases, he writes, "members simply acknowledged that a state of war did in fact exist."[6] But of course those are not the only times the U.S. military has been ordered abroad. In its hearings on the War Powers Resolution in 1973, a House subcommittee published a list of 199 instances in which U.S. forces had been deployed without a declaration of war. By one estimate, only 81 of these "could be said under any stretch of the imagination to have been initiated under prior legislative authority."[7] The majority of the 81 were undertaken pursuant to treaty obligations, not all of them explicit in their commands, and the rest had vague statutory authority. The remainder—some 118, almost 60 percent—occurred without any kind of congressional authorization; some even took place in the face of seemingly contrary law.[8] For example, in 1818, the U.S.S. *Ontario* landed at the Columbia River and took possession of Oregon, then also claimed by Russia and Spain. In 1869, President Grant sent a naval force to the Dominican Republic to protect it from invasion while the Senate considered a treaty of annexation (which it rejected, yet the sailors remained in place). And on July 7, 1941, U.S. troops occupied Iceland, notwithstanding the Reserves Act of 1940 and the Selective Service Act of 1940, both of which provided that American forces could not be used outside the Western Hemisphere.

This history revealed a presidency dominant in foreign affairs, including the use of armed force. Determined to assert itself against what Senator Jacob Javits of New York derided as "the doctrine of executive war powers," Congress in 1973 passed, over President Nixon's veto, the War Powers Resolution. According to its statement of purpose, the resolution seeks "to fulfill the intent of the Framers of the Constitution"—or at least what *it* regards as that intent. Thus, the President may introduce U.S. military forces into hostilities or situations where imminent involvement in hostilities "is clearly indicated" by the circumstances—when Congress has declared war or provided specific statutory authorization, or when there is "a national emergency" created by an attack upon the United States, its territories or possessions, or its armed forces.

There are many problems with the War Powers Resolution, but in one respect, at least, it cannot be faulted: It does not attempt to deny what the Constitution provides—namely that the President may act on his own to meet attacks on the United States or its armed forces. (If the President is to defend against attacks, he must have the means of defense; thus he must be able to defend against attacks on the military itself.) It is well-known that in the early draft of the Constitution presented to the Convention by its Committee of Detail, the empowering infinitive phrase of what became the War Clause was "to make war." The framers changed "make" to "declare" at least to ensure that the President could repel sudden attacks without having to wait for Congress to act.[9]

To credit the War Powers Resolution in this respect, however, is to fall well short of understanding the authority the President has under the Constitution to use force without congressional approval. Consider that Article I also states: "No State shall, without the consent of the Congress, . . . engage in war, unless actually invaded, or in such imminent danger as will not admit of delay." While this provision concerns relations between Congress and the states, it would be implausible to argue that the Commander in Chief has less power than a state; he should be able, without the consent of Congress, to "engage in war" not only when the United States is invaded but also when the nation is in imminent danger that will not allow delay.[10] No attack is needed to create the kind of "national emergency" that the President may legitimately respond to. Moreover, the United States would obviously be facing "imminent danger" that won't admit of delay if a nation were to declare war against us. Under the Constitution and international law (both at the time of the founding and today), the President may indeed respond militarily, without waiting for Congress to act. He may wage preemptive war in the nation's defense, and he cannot be limited to waging a strictly defensive war in that effort. He is the "Commander in

Chief," and he has the power to do what he judges must be done to defend the nation.

The War Powers Resolution also does not recognize the President's right to employ the armed forces in hostilities short of war or in situations marked by armed confrontation. As Robert Scigliano has explained, "The resolution would, if followed, impair a President's ability to take forceful measures to protect or rescue American citizens abroad when their lives are endangered, or even to deploy American power in the service of American diplomacy."[11] No President should understand the resolution as limiting his authority in these instances, and fortunately none has. Thus, acting on his constitutional authority and considering himself not bound by the resolution, President Ford ordered American forces to free the U.S. merchant ship *Mayaguez*, which en route from Hong Kong to Thailand had been seized by Cambodians. Likewise did President Carter undertake the unsuccessful military effort to rescue American hostages in Iran.

The fundamental issue raised by the War Powers Resolution is whether the war powers are mostly legislative in character. The resolution wrongly assumes that they are. The framers of the Constitution understood the executive power as including the power of war and peace and, more generally, the power to conduct foreign affairs.[12] And they vested all of the executive power of the United States, subject to some exceptions, in the President. The most notable exceptions are found in the provisions giving the Senate authority to consent to treaties and Congress power "To declare war." But, having acknowledged the exclusive authority of the President to initiate the use of military force in a variety of circumstances, what kind of war is left for Congress to declare? Surveying historical practice since 1789, Professor James Grafton Rogers concluded in 1945 that the kind of "war" Congress is to declare is "a special use of force, apparently confined to cases of great effort, to major contests designed to crush and conquer another nation."[13] This has been described more succinctly by Eugene Rostow as "unlimited general war."[14] But it would also seem that there are other situations in which Congress should be involved in the decision to use force. These would be cases of "great effort" between those in which the

United States makes war to "crush and conquer another nation" and those in which it makes war because it has been thrust on the defensive. The situation in the Persian Gulf presented one such case.

Given that the Commander in Chief does not make war when he orders the armed forces into other nations at their request or into international waters, Bush would not have needed a law of Congress to maintain troops for purely defensive reasons in Saudi Arabia, nor to turn them loose in an offensive manner had they been attacked. (Nor, strictly speaking, would he have needed a law had Iraq declared war against the United States; nor if American hostages had not been released by Saddam Hussein.) Nor would Bush have needed a law had he decided only to strike the chemical, nuclear, and biological warfare facilities inside Iraq. But the sheer magnitude of the offensive operation he came to believe was necessary, as indicated by the more than 400,000 U.S. troops massed in eastern Saudi Arabia, and the overwhelming firepower they possessed, suggested "a great effort." The decision to go to war, raising the question of whether Americans would be willing to sacrifice blood and treasure in order to push Iraq from Kuwait and restore the Kuwaiti emirate, and secure peace and stability in a region vital to American interests, deserved consideration by Congress. A law was necessary as the nation went to *this* war, and the Iraq Resolution, in effect, declared war.[15]

In the end, President Bush, who throughout the fall said he wanted Congress as "a partner," was wise to go to Congress before he made war, notwithstanding his erroneous view of the legal necessity of congressional action. Better to have Congress on board from the start of war than to risk having it complain about and fight the effort once underway; better to have the two elective branches united, and to be seen as united both at home and abroad.

But it was even wiser for Bush to ask for the resolution *when* he did—when it appeared that Congress would finally agree with his judgment that military force was necessary. No amount of even the best rhetoric, that is, rhetoric that advances the most powerful reasons, could have moved to his side a Congress controlled by Democrats, many of whom were (and still may be) extremely reluctant to use military force. What did move such a Congress to side with him on January 12 against Saddam was the President's very powerful exercise of executive power, itself a rebuke to the unconstitutional assumption of the War Powers Resolution that the entire domain of foreign policy may be managed by the legislative branch.

A brief review of the chronology enables us to understand the strength of the formal powers of the presidential office.

On August 1, 1990, at approximately 8:45 P.M., the President learned from his National Security Adviser that Iraq was invading Kuwait. At 11:20 P.M. Bush issued a statement strongly condemning the invasion and calling for "the immediate and unconditional withdrawal of all Iraqi forces."[16] On August 2, Bush (1) froze Iraqi assets in the United States and prohibited any transactions with Iraq and (2) froze Kuwaiti assets so that Saddam Hussein would be unable to touch the $100 billion in investments held abroad by Kuwaitis. Also on August 2, Bush commenced his diplomatic effort within the United Nations. That day the U.N. Security Council approved Resolution 660, the first of twelve in all, condemning the invasion of Kuwait and demanding Iraq's unconditional and immediate withdrawal; four days later, it approved the second, Resolution 661, which imposed economic sanctions on Iraq. On August 4, Bush began work on another diplomatic front, sending to Saudi Arabia no lesser a delegation than the trio of Defense Secretary Richard Cheney, Deputy National Security Adviser Robert Gates, and General Colin Powell, the chairman of the Joint Chiefs of Staff; their mission: to persuade King Fahd to accept a large deployment of U.S. forces. On the way home Cheney, Gates, and Powell stopped off in Egypt and Morocco to recruit the participation of those Arab countries in what would become the multinational force (twenty-eight states in all), which battled Iraq. Bush meanwhile stated to the world that the Iraqi invasion of Kuwait "will not stand."

By August 8, Bush had ordered the first batch of U.S. troops to Saudi Arabia, invited there by King Fahd. (While the administration declined to say how many, the number of this initial deployment, which required more than three months to effect, was 250,000.) Advising the nation of his action, Bush explained that "the mission of our troops is wholly defensive. . . . They will not initiate hostilities, but they will defend themselves, the Kingdom of Saudi Arabia, and other friends in the Persian Gulf." The President meanwhile continued his diplomatic efforts. On August 17, Cheney, per Bush's instruction, left for Saudi Arabia and four other Arab states (Bahrain, Oman, the United Arab Emirates, and Egypt) to obtain more support for a war effort. Specifically, he sought landing and staging rights for U.S. forces, including Air Force fighters, bombers, and cargo planes. On August 22, Bush authorized the call-up of 50,000 reservists. He meanwhile declined to order boarding by the U.S. Navy of Iraqi vessels to enforce the U.N.'s economic sanctions against Iraq, waiting until August 25 to do so, when the U.N. Security Council voted to give the navies of the United States and other nations the right to use force to stop trade with Iraq. This, wrote Bob Woodward in *The Commanders*, "was the first time in the U.N.'s 45-year history that individual countries outside an umbrella U.N. command were authorized to enforce an international blockade, an extraordinary diplomatic victory for the administration."[17]

In early September, some thirty members of Congress, back from their August recess, met with Bush. According to Woodward, "Every senator and congressman who spoke at the meeting praised Bush's handling of the crisis, and expressed support for the military and diplomatic moves."[18] But Republican Senator William Cohen of Maine told Bush he should convene a special session of Congress so "that we deal with the law of the land in the War Powers Act." Cohen advised Bush to "resist the calls that are being made for an offensive action."[19]

In early October, the President, having decided that economic sanctions would not force Saddam from Kuwait, sought and received from Cheney a briefing on a potential offensive military operation designed to extract the Iraqi forces from Kuwait.[20] Persuaded that the U.S. military lacked the strength for an offensive operation, Bush prepared to deploy more troops. On October 30, he authorized a virtual doubling of the number, a fact announced on November 8. "I have today directed the Secretary of Defense to increase the size of the U.S. forces committed to Desert Shield to ensure that the coalition has an adequate offensive military option should that be necessary to achieve our common goals." Bush declined to explain why an offensive force might be necessary, but Vietnam apparently influenced his thinking. "The guiding principle" behind the decision, Woodward has reported, was the "maximization of firepower and troops."[21]

In response to the additional deployment, some fifty-four members of Congress—almost all of them Democrats—filed a lawsuit asking that the President be preliminarily enjoined from ordering U.S. armed forces to make war on Iraq "absent meaningful consultation with and genuine approval by Congress." Some Congressional leaders, including Republican Senators Robert J. Dole and Richard G. Lugar, called for a special session of Congress to debate war in the Gulf. Bush said he opposed such a session unless Congress would support what he had done. Democratic leaders decided against a special session to vote on war, instead opting for hearings. On November 28, two former JCS Chairmen, Admiral William Crowe and General David C. Jones, testified against war and in favor of staying with economic sanctions. Many in Congress held this same view; House Majority Leader Richard A. Gephardt in fact urged Bush to give economic sanctions far more time—up to eighteen months—before resorting to military force.

Bush meanwhile continued his diplomatic efforts within the U.N. Security Council. Spending ten weeks traveling 100,000 miles and holding more than two hundred meetings with foreign ministers and heads of state, Secretary of State James Baker succeeded in getting the council to pass, on November 29, the last of its resolutions. Resolution 678 demanded Iraq's unconditional withdrawal from Kuwait by January 15, 1991, and authorized "all necessary means"—and thus military force—to achieve compliance with the eleven other resolutions passed since August 2.

On November 30, Bush, appearing on national television, said that in order "to go the extra mile for peace," he would receive Iraqi Foreign Minister Tariq Aziz in Washington and send Baker to Baghdad to see Saddam Hussein "at a mutually convenient time between December 15th and January 15 of next year." This was done in an effort to demonstrate to Congress, the nation, and the world that the President was pursuing every diplomatic alternative to war. Later that same day, in a meeting with members of Congress, Bush said, "If the Congress wants to come back and endorse the U.N. resolution, let's go. But let's not have a hung jury. If you can't support [it], frankly, I'd be wary. So I'd welcome your support."[22] According to Woodward, Senator Lugar counted no fewer than seven times that Bush appealed for the support of Congress during this meeting, and each time he was told Congress would not give it.[23]

In late December Bush secretly approved a war plan that would have Schwarzkopf order the take-off of fighter bombers at 7:00 P.M. January 16, Washington time. On January 2, Bush, having been rebuffed by Saddam on a meeting with Baker, decided to send his Secretary of State to meet Iraq's Foreign Minister Aziz in order to issue (in the form of a letter from Bush) an ultimatum to Saddam to get out of Kuwait, or else. On January 4, Senate Majority Leader George Mitchell told the *Wall Street Journal* that a resolution authorizing the use of force and modeled on the one approved by the U.N. might now be conceivable. On January 6, Bush decided to ask Congress to support the use of force. He did so on January 8 in a letter. With the Baker-Aziz meeting proving futile, Congress passed on January 12 the joint resolution authorizing the use of American military force against Iraq after January 15, once the President had determined that all diplomatic avenues had been exhausted. After another last-minute diplomatic failure—this between Saddam Hussein and U.N. Secretary General Javier Perez de Cuellar—the United States began Operation Desert Storm on January 16, with 1,400 sorties against Iraqi military targets. The rest is history.

What Bush did starting on August 1 is evidence of the framers' wisdom in deciding to make provision for energy in government by creating the presidency. Bush was able to act swiftly, denouncing the invasion at 11:20 that night. He then took actions pursuant to his powers—freezing assets (the President has the duty to take care that the laws are faithfully executed), conducting diplomacy of various kinds (the President is the nation's chief diplomat), deploying troops (the President is the Commander in Chief), calling up the reserves (ditto), and doubling the deployment of troops (ditto).

But this is not all. Most remarkable is that only Bush, empowered as he is by the Constitution, could have moved Congress so that it finally authorized the use of U.S. military force. Thus, the exercise of formal presidential power—and specifically of power that is executive in character—had a powerful impact upon the congressional exercise of its own power, executive in character, to authorize war. Congress, a plural body, is slow to act in any event, but in this event it was bound to be even slower because of the ghosts of Vietnam, alive and well in the War Powers Resolution. Absent the energetic executive that was George Bush, Congress probably would not have voted for war, and Saddam Hussein might still be in Kuwait.

Consider again the Congress at crucial points. After its August recess, its leaders praised Bush but wanted him to convene a special session of Congress so that it might debate war in the Gulf. Throughout the fall leaders of both parties put the burden on Bush to convene a special session, but they could not promise majority support for the President's effort against Iraq; some members even went to court trying to get what would have been (they failed) a first ever injunction blocking a President from launching a military attack without congressional approval. Not until early January did it appear conceivable, according to Senator Mitchell, that Congress might approve a resolution authorizing force.

Article II explicitly provides that the President may "on extraordinary occasions" convene both houses. President Bush never used this power of office. Instead, he let his use of other formal powers do the work within Congress. The twenty-eight-member international coalition united against Saddam Hussein; the January 15 deadline imposed by the U.N. for Iraq's withdrawal from Kuwait; the coalition poised to use military force in the event Iraq remained in Kuwait past the deadline: these were facts that Bush himself largely created through the use of his powers. They proved persuasive in Congress.

Thus, it is a mistake to focus on Bush's clearly skillful

legislative work from January 8 to 12 to the exclusion of all he had done before. As earlier noted, Bush was wise to recommend legislation. And Bush and his legislative affairs team lobbied hard, their intelligent strategy focusing on six Democratic senators from three key states—John Breaux and Bennett Johnston of Louisiana; Howell Heflin and Richard Shelby of Alabama; and Richard Bryan and Harry Reid of Nevada— all of whom voted for the resolution. Their votes were the key to the 52–47 win in the Senate. But it was the cumulative impact of Bush's previous actions that created the circumstance in which majorities in both houses were ready to side with him. Bush asked Congress to join him at the last second. It was probably the only time he could have got what he wanted, but it was also a second largely of his creation. To employ Hamilton's language, Bush, through the exercise of his constitutional powers, established "an antecedent state of things" that weighed in the legislative decision to go to war in the Gulf.

In taking the nation to war, Bush had to contend, of course, with the War Powers Resolution.[24] How he did so is instructive. The resolution requires that troops be introduced only when there has been a declaration of war or specific statutory authorization, or when there is a "national emergency" defined in defensive terms. None of these bases existed, but Bush sent troops anyway. He sent them to a nation (Saudi Arabia) to which they had been invited—thanks to his diplomacy. Thus, Bush was not intimidated by the resolution but rose, on the strength of the exercise of his power, to act as a President may, under the Constitution.

The War Powers Resolution also provides that the President must withdraw all U.S. forces from any situation of actual or imminent hostilities within sixty days (extendable to ninety in certain circumstances) unless Congress specifically authorizes continued deployment. August and September passed without any such act of Congress; so did October and November. To be sure, Congress could be said to have expressed approval of what the President was doing through other means—such as it did by passing vague resolutions of support. But it did not stick to the ludicrous framework imposed by the resolution; how, after all, does one time a military operation? Bush treated the resolution as an irrelevance on this point—as he should have.[25]

Under the War Powers Resolution, the President is required to consult with Congress "in every possible instance" before introducing armed forces into actual or imminent hostilities. This requirement is unconstitutional if read as requiring consultation before using military force to repel a sudden attack upon the United States or its armed forces or, in this instance, to defend Saudi Arabia at its invitation. President Bush maintained that he was not bound by the consulting requirement, arguing that hostilities were neither actual nor imminent, and indeed that the presence of American troops in the Persian Gulf would reduce hostilities. But acting in behalf of interbranch comity, believing rightly that consultation with Congress can be a valuable means of ensuring unity in any war effort, Bush consulted with members of Congress anyway.

The resolution also requires that, in the absence of a declaration of war, the President report within forty-eight hours of introducing American forces into hostilities or imminent hostilities; or (in most cases) into a foreign territory "while equipped for combat"; or in numbers that "substantially enlarge" a previous deployment of U.S. troops "equipped for combat [and] already located in a foreign nation." Bush submitted a report to Congress within forty-eight hours of deploying the troops in early August, but he did not say it was required by the War Powers Resolution, but merely "consistent with it." In his report, moreover, Bush did not accept the resolution's premise, namely that he had introduced U.S. forces into a hostile situation. Here, again, Bush operated from an understanding of what may be called "constitutional policy," not on the basis of the War Powers Resolution.

In the wake of the Persian Gulf war, the *Economist* observed that there were "fewer questions about the power of the commander-in-chief" and "less talk of the War Powers Act." Whether that will be so in the future will depend on the President. The challenge, should equivalent circumstances arise, will be to deal as skillfully as Bush did in meeting his constitutional duties without allowing the War Powers Resolution to become a drag on executive energy.

There remains the role of rhetoric in Bush's effort to take the nation to war. Bush was often criticized on this score, especially by the *Washington Post*. Thus, on November 4, Jim Hoagland of the *Post*, whose columns on the war won a Pulitzer Prize, wrote that the United States had the right Gulf policy but "the wrong President" because Bush, who has "limitations" in speechmaking, had not made "a clear and ideally inspirational statement to the nation to explain the goals of the potentially bloody conflict we may be approaching." On November 15 the *Post* reminded its readers that Bush was no Great Communicator in a story headlined: "President Struggles to Articulate Goals." On December 2, another of the paper's correspondents, George Wilson, sang the same chorus: Bush was "still groping for a rallying cry to get teenagers and their parents to believe it is worth risking their lives to free Kuwait, save gulf oil, or topple Saddam." The premise of this journalism was that Bush's rhetorical performance would be *a* if not *the* critical factor in his success or failure as a war President.

While Bush could have done a better job making the case for what he was doing—he did not even try to explain why he had doubled the deployment in early November—it is not true that he failed to provide reasons for the general effort against Iraq; they may not have been reasons some in the press or Congress found compelling, but they were certainly worthy of debate. Still, how does one account for the fact that Bush never gave that "ideally inspirational" speech, and yet proved able to take the nation to a war that had the overwhelming approval of the American people, and to achieve his goal of evicting Iraq from Kuwait? Again, the explanation lies in what Bush did. The actions he took beginning on August 1 not only constituted an argument that persuaded Congress to act on January 12, by passing the Iraq Resolution; they also shaped public opinion in favor of the war effort, during both that period and the prosecution of the war itself. Columnist Charles Krauthammer has pointed out that many of the actions Bush took were not simply bold but "generally unpopular at the time. Yet each action reshaped the debate and *in time came to be seen* [emphasis added] as necessary if not inevitable—and correct."[26] One example: Three days before

Bush deployed the troops in August, the Gallup Poll reported that 56 percent of Americans opposed such a move; after he gave the order, 81 percent approved. A second example: Ten days before the ground war, a CBS/*New York Times* poll found just 11 percent favored starting one; the day after it was launched, some 75 percent approved. "As a shaper of public opinion," Krauthammer wrote, "the bully pulpit is overrated. The powers of the presidency, if skillfully deployed, are enough to move the nation. . . . Government schools will be studying Bush's march through Washington."[27] One is tempted to add that certainly they should be studying it.

Bush's performance also invites reflection on Richard Neustadt's influential theory of presidential power. For Neustadt, the President must acquire and use personal power in order to secure the formal power of office; the latter, which is the power to compel, is not central to the President's work, although it may be useful, in a subordinate way, to what Neustadt calls "the persuasive process." Of this, Professor Harvey C. Mansfield Jr. has rightly asked: "[I]s it not more reasonable and realistic to suppose, on the contrary, that persuasion is incidental or instrumental to compulsion?"[28] Bush's protection of the Persian Gulf war was a case in point; formal power was clearly central to what he did, working its own persuasive effects.

To recognize the centrality of formal power in taking the nation to a successful war in the Persian Gulf is not, of course, to imply agreement with every action Bush took pursuant to his power. The President was criticized for some of his diplomatic moves (such as buddying up to the notorious butcher, Syrian President Hafez el-Assad, relying too heavily upon the United Nations, trying to work a last-minute deal through Baker with Aziz) and, in November, for deciding to send additional troops. Criticism of the President on these counts faded during late January and February as the war proved successful, with so many fewer casualties than most every expert predicted, and with Iraq surrendering in late February on the terms demanded by the U.N. But suppose the effort had not gone so well. Would Congress have been justified in trying to create some "framework" legislation—say by amending the War Powers Resolution—in an effort to limit the President's ability to decide and act as Bush did? The answer is no. It is a mistake to think that wrong decisions on the part of a President constitute an argument for denying him—or future Presidents—the ability to make decisions of this kind in the first place. To go down this trail is to reduce the energy that the framers correctly believed must be provided for in any government worthy of the name.[29]

There is, of course, another trail that Congress might pursue in the case of a President whose actions it disagrees with—impeachment. But that is the proper trail because it is case-specific: directed at a particular President, on account of what he has done. To make this point is to recognize the great personal and institutional risk that attended Bush's effort against Saddam Hussein. That he was willing to accept the risk suggested the nature of his character and his leadership in this episode. So did the way in which he proceeded. Bush was not so foolish as to provoke a war—say in November—by sending his troops intentionally into harm's way. President Polk did precisely this in 1846 when he sent U.S. troops into disputed territory along the Texas-Mexico border, his exercise of executive power leading to the congressional declaration of war. In 1848, the House of Representatives censured him for "unnecessarily and unconstitutionally" starting a war.

While there is nothing in the institutional nature of the presidency that forces its occupants to use the powers available to them, or to use those powers in the most prudent way, those who vote on aspirants to the office will for good reason be interested in their character, including their ability to lead the nation in just such a situation as was created when Iraq invaded Kuwait. George Bush saw more clearly and earlier than anyone else in the U.S. government what the United States had to do, and he skillfully bent Congress and the nation to the task, refusing to wait on economic sanctions and pulling the trigger of war.

That Bush did not see clearly enough, and earlier, is one of two principal marks against him, the other being that he stopped too soon, failing to finish off Saddam Hussein. During the 1980s, the United States became a silent ally of Iraq's. In 1988 the Reagan administration rejected a change in policy toward Iraq that would have recognized its threat to U.S. strategic interests. In 1989 President Bush signed a national security directive that implemented a period of detente toward Iraq. Notwithstanding increasing evidence of Iraq's hostile intentions in the Middle East, and toward the United States, the Bush administration did not alter this position, refusing to "draw a line" in the sand lest the "good relations" between the two nations be undermined—good relations it thought necessary to achieving a comprehensive Middle East settlement. It was on July 25, 1991, that the U.S. Ambassador to Iraq, April Glaspie, made her remarkable statement to Saddam: "We have no opinion on the Arab-Arab conflicts, like your border disagreement with Kuwait." Just after Glaspie said this, or course, Iraqi troops massed on the Kuwait border. Had Bush adopted a different policy toward Iraq, perhaps the war that had to be waged could have been avoided.[30] The President rightly can be charged with failing to provide better strategic leadership through his national security bureaucracy, a subject generally discussed in Chapter 13.

The main purpose of Part One has been to show how the President should think about and act on the duty to recommend legislation, and how he should regard and exercise the veto power. Several of the chapters in Part One have directed attention to the fact that legislation presented to the President for his approval or disapproval may raise not only questions of appropriate public policy but also those of constitutionality, including ones involving the President's duties and powers. The various ways in which the President relates to Congress legislatively suggest how the energetic executive may contribute to "good government," as the framers understood it. For that term must encompass not only the enactment of general legislation for the public good—such as the Tax Reform Act of 1986—but also the blockage of legislation that might threaten the presidency and thus weaken the system of separated powers.

Facing Congress, then, the President has governing opportunities as well as duties. To borrow a sports metaphor, he must ponder offense and defense both. And he must do so while administering the executive branch, the subject of Part Two.

# THE PRESIDENT AND THE EXECUTIVE BRANCH

Once a year President Reagan assembled all of his political appointees in Constitution Hall, a long stone's throw from the White House, for what amounted to a Reagan Revolution pep rally. Cynics might dismiss such an exercise, but through it Reagan respected some essential facts about the presidency. For however any given President governs, whether legislatively or administratively, whether in terms of foreign policy or domestic policy, or in any other constitutional endeavor, he must govern through the executive branch, and his success depends in large measure on the commitment of political appointees placed throughout the executive.

The origins of the executive branch and the presidency are closely and instructively related. In the nation's beginning—in the late 1770s, to be exact—the need for something like an executive branch became apparent to the Continental Congress. Discovering (not surprisingly) that its own members, sitting in various committees, could not administer the domestic and foreign affairs of government, the Congress created "hybrid" committees—made up of members and nonmembers, such as the board of war and ordinance.[1] This didn't work so well either, so in 1781 the Congress decided to go totally outside itself by establishing a department of foreign affairs under the leadership of a congressional secretary. Soon Congress created similar departments of war, marine, and treasury. All the while, however, the Congress regarded this fledgling executive branch as inferior to it. According to Charles C. Thach, Jr., the Congress continued "to act as an administrative body," busying itself with details and issuing frequent orders.[2] Those who assembled to write the Constitution in Philadelphia regarded this organizational state of affairs as unacceptable: There had to be some sort of superintending administrative agency standing between Congress and the departments, and it could not be subordinate to Congress. In the Constitution that agency appears as the presidency itself. The broadest definition of the executive branch thus includes the presidency and the executive departments and agencies, although it is important to emphasize that the presidency is a creation of the Constitution, while the departments and agencies are creations of Congress.

Until the Civil War the very few departments that Congress established (such as State and Treasury) were charged with carrying out the traditional, core functions of government. After the war Congress created new departments reflecting the growing needs and interests of a diversified economy, such as Justice and Agriculture. In 1877, with the establishment of the Interstate Commerce Commission, the government commenced a new period in its growth. The ICC was, as Geoffrey P. Miller of the University of Chicago Law School has written, something new: "a strange amalgam of executive, legislative, and judicial powers, combining functions of all three branches yet the creature of none."[3] The nation's first independent regulatory commission (independent because the President's power to remove agency heads is limited), it was the cornerstone of the modern administrative state. Other independent agencies created since 1887 include the Board of Governors of the Federal Reserve, the Federal Trade Commission, the Securities and Exchange Commission, the Federal Communications Commission, the National Labor Relations Board, and the Federal Energy Regulatory Commission. Also in the twentieth century, Congress has increased the number of traditionally organized executive departments, adding, in recent years, the Energy, Education, and Veterans departments. And it has asked the presidency to take on duties it did not have in the nineteenth century, such as preparing a federal budget.

Over the past fifty years most of the rules governing the nation as a whole have been made by the executive branch. Congress has often written legislation in general terms, leaving the details to be filled in by the departments and agencies through what is known as the rule-making process. Hundreds of rules are written every year. And, of course, thousands upon thousands of decisions, pursuant to all of the laws the executive branch must enforce, are made. Some degree of discretion necessarily exists in the implementation of law, whatever its formal nature, for as Alexander Hamilton recognized, "He who is to execute the laws must first *judge for himself* of their meaning."[4]

The Constitution speaks directly, although by no means exhaustively, to the relationship of the President and the congressionally established executive departments. The President has the power to appoint principal executive officers, subject to Senate confirmation, and the President has the authority to require "the opinion, in writing of the principal officer" in each department "upon any subject relating to the duties of their respective offices." The Constitution also requires that the President keep the government running: Article II, Section 2 empowers him to fill vacancies that occur during Senate recess. And the President has the constitutional duty to take care that the laws are faithfully executed (the Take Care Clause).

That the Constitution thus empowers the President with respect to the executive branch is not to say that he lacks competition in directing its work. Consider, for example, that in approving presidential nominees, the Senate has often expressed and even imposed its views upon the President as to how it wants something done; it was a condition of Elliot Richardson's confirmation as Attorney General that he name an outside lawyer (Archibald Cox) to investigate Watergate. Meanwhile, notwithstanding the fact, as Jeremy Rabkin has observed, that the framers of the Constitution did not expect Congress to play a significant role in overseeing the conduct of executive operations, as they made the President formally accountable to the public and not to Congress, congressional committees since the Washington presidency have pried and probed into the day-to-day-work of the executive branch.[5] Today, as anyone even vaguely familiar with Washington knows, congressional oversight of the executive hugely occupies both houses of Congress. As was true in the 1780s, Congress often fancies itself as an administrative body that "plays the executive," in Hamilton's phrase.[6]

In managing the very large, organizationally varied, and

powerful executive conglomerate—obviously quite beyond the kind of personal supervision President Washington gave it (he read every bit of outgoing executive branch correspondence)—Presidents beginning with FDR have increased the size of their White House staffs. Today the Executive Office of the President employs 1,889 individuals.

The bulk of the day-to-day work of the executive departments and agencies concerns the administration of laws Congress has passed; this is one reason for the familiar designation of a presidency as an "administration." But as those Constitution Hall rallies recognized, it is through the executive branch that the President governs, however he governs. His appointees in the White House, and in the departments and agencies, assist him not only in faithfully executing statutes of Congress, for example, but also in recommending legislation to Congress, in selecting judges, in negotiating treaties—in sum, in every action he takes, or must take, under the Constitution.

Given the critical importance of presidential personnel, I treat this subject in the first chapter of this part of the book. By presidential personnel, I mean all individuals who owe their positions, in the final analysis, to the incumbent President. These include those he directly appoints, both in the White House and to the departments and agencies. (Most of the statutorily created positions require Senate confirmation). It also includes all of those whom the President's appointees name to subordinate "political," as opposed to career, positions, both in the White House and the departments and agencies. The total number of individuals is roughly 5,000. At the end of this chapter I argue, along lines similar to Richard Nathan's, for what he has called "an administrative presidency"—a presidency that through its personnel pushes its policies wherever lawful and prudent into administrative processes.[7] This is done by altering procedures, reorganizing parts of the executive branch, and coordinating activities. Chapter 10 discusses this trio of means by considering instances of them drawn mainly from the Justice Department under Reagan. Chapter 11 takes up the important but oft-neglected role that litigation can play in presidential governance. These two chapters indicate the kind of opposition a strong presidency can provoke from Congress. The president and his executive officers should understand the dynamics of the constitutional order in this respect and not be frightened into inaction by the possibility or reality of congressionally negative responses.

Chapters 12 and 13 illustrate the kind of problems that can arise when the President does not devise a strong White House system to help him shape and implement administration policy. Presidents do best when they combine good appointments to the executive departments and agencies with effective White House systems of policy development and implementation; "cabinet government," of which Ronald Reagan spoke so well and so often, can never be enough, not even when the cabinet choices share the President's political views and are generally competent. Chapter 12 is an analysis of Reagan's often messy administrative effort against racial quotas, which could have benefited from a White House council or group dedicated to formulating civil rights policy and seeing to its government-wide execution. Chapter 13 discusses the very clear need that existed in the Reagan White House for a stronger National Security Adviser and staff—one that could have served that President better than the Iran-Contra crew did.

Chapters 14 and 15 return to the subject of personnel. Wherever placed, in domestic agencies or those focused on foreign affairs, the President's subordinates are extensions of him. This fact imposes certain behavioral obligations on them—and him. As the Reagan presidency showed, indifference to this responsibility can weaken a President's ability to govern.

Chapter 16, which draws upon points developed in previous chapters in both Parts One and Two, briefly discuss Iran-contra, exhibit A-1 in any discussion of what a strong presidency should *not* look like. Iran-contra shows what can happen when the President is not the source of energy. It also teaches, by negative example, the meaning of presidential responsibility.

# 9

# PICKING THE INSTRUMENTS OF EXECUTION

## The President and Personnel

The President takes an oath to execute his *office*, which encompasses all of his constitutional powers and duties, from the command of the armed services to the issuance of pardons, to the negotiation of treaties, to the recommendation of legislation, to the selection of judges, and, of course, to the faithful execution of the laws. All that a President does may be classified as, in James Madison's useful phrase, the "executive business." Obviously, no President could tend to all of that business by himself; he must have help.[1] Madison provided a good way of classifying those engaged in the executive business when he called them "the eyes and arms of the principal Magistrate, the instruments of execution."[2]

Where Presidents should take the greatest care in picking instruments of execution—at the White House, department,

144

and agency levels—they often have followed regrettable selection practices. Presidents often have named a cabinet "balanced" in terms of political views (within a certain range) and geographical regions.[3] Often they have chosen advocates of the interests that stand to benefit from an agency's work, many of which have representatives in Washington. But a cabinet whose members are selected for these reasons is not a cabinet likely to help the President pursue the public interest as he sees it, especially if the President is a political conservative intent on changing the governing status quo. A President so committed must select for cabinet and other top positions individuals who share his political views, are dedicated to his programs (and, it goes without saying, are knowledgeable in the field) and who understand that public office is a public trust. In sum, such a President must seek out capable, publicly minded individuals who are effective advocates of his policies.

Introducing his first agriculture secretary, Clifford Hardin, President Nixon described him as "a man who could speak eloquently *for* farmers, *for* rural America and agriculture *to* the President."[4] This is exactly the wrong way to think about the selection of cabinet and other top-ranking officials, much less to announce a nominee. Nixon thus communicated to Hardin what was expected of him in the job. And on the job, of course, every cabinet head experiences three powerful groups that typically work, often in concert, to make sure he or she speaks not *for* but *to* the President. These are the department or agency he is placed in charge of, the interest groups that regard that department as "theirs," and the relevant congressional oversight committees.

The speed with which these forces converge on a nominee is remarkable. William Bennett recalls that almost as soon as President Reagan had selected him in 1982 to head the National Endowment for the Humanities, his predecessor during the Carter administration, Joseph Duffy, offered to set up a lunch for him with "constituent groups." Bennett refused; he reasoned that such a lunch would send the wrong message about what he intended to do, which was to loosen the grip of those groups upon the endowment so that it might operate in behalf of the larger public interest as determined by the new administration.[5]

145

As for the department and agency heads, so it should be for every other job in the executive branch that is a political position. Those selected should be able, publicly minded individuals committed to the President and his policies. The selection of subcabinet officers who head discrete offices within departments and agencies is especially critical.

Presidents often have allowed their chosen department and agency heads to select individuals for the offices under them, both those requiring Senate confirmation and those not. In theory this practice presents fewer problems for a President when the department heads have been selected with political compatibility in mind, the presumption being that they will pick subordinates of similar views. But an energetic executive will not cede so important an issue as political personnel exclusively to his principal officers.

Again, Nixon provides an example of precisely how not to proceed. As related by Rowland Evans and Robert Novak, Nixon used one of his first cabinet meetings in 1969 to delegate to cabinet members the responsibility for filling all appointive positions in their departments. He said to select on the basic of ability first and loyalty second. Evans and Novak report that after the meeting Nixon turned to an aide and said, "I just made a big mistake."[6]

A similar kind of mistake is made when the President simply defers to what his cabinet officers recommend as to choices for other positions within the executive branch. James Q. Wilson observes that President Ford spoke out against the "overzealous" and "nit-picking" regulations issued by the Occupational Safety and Health Administration, only to see his choice to head OSHA, Morton Corn, behave even more zealously than his predecessor. Ford chose Corn on the advice of his Secretary of Labor, John Dunlop, whose interests differed from the President's. "By contrast," Wilson writes, "Ford's successor, Jimmy Carter," deferred to no one in naming Eula Bingham as head of OSHA, "whom he knew would be, as he wished, a zealous regulator."[7]

The goal of the energetic executive, then, must be the selection of capable appointees at all levels who are committed to his programs and policies. That an appointee passes muster on this score is no guarantee, however, that the person will actually prove effective on the job. James Watt, Reagan's first Secretary of Interior, was politically compatible with the President, but Reagan could have achieved more through a more competent appointee. The same observation applies to the choice of Anne Burford, Reagan's first director of the Environmental Protection Agency.[8] And Sam Pierce, while philosophically in agreement with Reagan, miserably failed to manage Housing and Urban Development, his detached style at least in part responsible for the criminal wrongdoing and influence peddling that occurred on his eight-year watch.

These examples suggest that Presidents must be concerned about not only the politics of their cabinet and subcabinet heads but also their governing and administrative skills. Presidents, however, must look for more than knowledge of relevant subject matter and more than what is often called "managerial experience." Ideally they must look for men and women whose background suggests that they will attempt to "govern strategically."

The term is William Kristol's, formerly a Harvard government professor who served in Reagan's Education Department and is now Vice President Dan Quayle's Chief of Staff. Kristol has applied the term in a discussion of appointees assigned to domestic policies. Reviewing the work of three subcabinet agency officials in the first Reagan administration—William J. Bennett, chairman of the National Endowment for the Humanities from 1981 to 1985, James C. Miller III, chairman of the Federal Trade Commission, and Thomas W. Pauken, director of ACTION—Kristol found that they were able to translate the President's views into fundamental policy changes at their agencies.[9] Bennett shifted the NEH away from funding such political organizations as the National Organization for Women and restored the agency's traditional support of the core humanities disciplines. Miller redirected the FTC toward the promotion of free markets. And Pauken quit ACTION's dalliance with left-wing politics and focused it instead on programs of voluntarism and self-help. In each case, as Kristol points out, the key to "strategic governance" was the development of a clear agenda and its effective communication both inside the agency and to Congress and the public. Each of the three appointees also concerned himself with the details of administration—of personnel and program matters. Traditional client groups and committees of Congress sometimes opposed what these agencies did under their new leaders. But Bennett, Miller, and Pauken managed to succeed at their agencies on terms that clearly reflected the President's views.

That Miller was able to Reaganize the FTC teaches its own lesson. The FTC is an independent agency; the President's power to remove commissioners is limited by statute. Miller's success shows that the model of strategic governance is no respecter of an agency's statutory organization. Through his appointment power a President can insinuate his views even into an independent agency.

Whether the model of strategic governance can be fully transported to agencies larger than the NEH, say, and especially to the biggest executive departments, is a fair question. The smaller the agency and the narrower its mission, it would seem, the likelier the success of "strategic governance." Health and Human Services is a huge conglomerate of big-budget agencies that have vague and even contradictory missions. Still, the qualities that enabled Messrs. Bennett, Miller, and Pauken to succeed in their jobs are plainly desirable in a cabinet or subcabinet head and would assist in the pursuit of narrowly defined goals that require the work of part, if not all, of an agency. It bears noting that Bennett used the model of strategic governance at the Education Department, which he headed after his stint at NEH.[10]

From the standpoint of the Constitution, some appointments are more important than others. One of these deserves special mention: the position of National Security Adviser.

The adviser heads the staff of the National Security Council, established by statute in 1947. President Reagan intentionally downgraded the NSC apparatus in favor of the State and Defense departments and wound up choosing as his National Security Adviser several individuals of inferior ability. The Iran-contra affair, as well as other foreign policy mishaps and misadventures, was in part a consequence of the reduced authority of the NSC and its poor leadership. Reagan's example is not one to copy. The President should not deemphasize the NSC or even view it merely as one among many national security agencies (like the State or Defense departments); the President must see it as an extension of him. As Carnes Lord, who served from 1981 to 1984 on the NSC, has written, "The NSC is not simply a part of the bureaucracy, yet it is surely a part of the bureaucracy in some sense. The NSC has a critical function to perform in managing the national security decision process for the bureaucracy as a whole."[11] Obviously critical to the effective operation of the NSC is the National Security Adviser. Especially in light of his responsibility for national security that he is uniquely given under the Constitution, the President must choose wisely. In addition to sharing the President's political outlook and view of the world, the National Security Adviser must be able to think strategically and must possess bureaucratic skills that can enable him to work effectively with the government as a whole.

Two hundred years ago the President needed very few instruments of execution. Today he must fill not only the top White House, cabinet and subcabinet positions, but many below those levels. In 1933, there were 51 executive branch positions requiring Senate confirmation. Today there are ten times that many. In all, the President today must fill 5,200 executive branch positions.[12] While every President will select his closest aides, including some of those in the Cabinet, obviously no President can attend to the administrative acts involved in reviewing and choosing most of the one percent of the federal work force through which he hopes to meet his constitutional duties. A White House office of presidential personnel, run by political appointees, is a necessity for any President today. Obviously, an office of this kind must itself be carefully organized and staffed.

The Reagan administration's personnel office was headed initially by E. Pendleton James, who directed a staff of one hundred. The office considered individuals recommended for positions by Cabinet officers and other Reagan appointees, but it also actively recruited on its own. Critically, it retained for the President his authority to veto persons who did not share the President's substantive goals. While no process for picking political appointees can ever be perfect, Reagan's effort, according to one study, enabled him to enjoy far more success than either Richard Nixon or Jimmy Carter did in staffing the executive branch with individuals of compatible political views.[13]

First among the five selection criteria James listed at the beginning of the first Reagan term was "commitment to Reagan's objectives." The others were integrity, competence, teamwork, and toughness, with a sixth later being added, that of commitment to change. The requirement of political commitment seems to have been enforced with very few exceptions. Reports one study of Reagan personnel practices: "Few Democrats or Independents were selected to satisfy program constituencies or even to provide specialized expertise."[14] How an individual voted in the 1980 election and, beyond that, evidence of the person's support during the campaign for Ronald Reagan or a candidate for other office who supported Reagan, were among the factors considered in determining political commitment.

Of course, it would be foolish to predict effective job performance on the basis of whether or not a person voted for the President or otherwise demonstrated political support at some time in the past. And too often individuals have been named to even fairly high positions who satisfy this criterion only, which in itself says little about an individual's substantive political views or his commitment to the President's policy goals. That the presidential personnel office must select for as many positions as possible individuals who understand and are committed to the President's goals and have relevant knowledge and governing skills is obvious enough; the challenge, given constraints of time and necessity, is doing so.

Presidents intent on finding effective instruments of execution at all levels of government will make sure that their personnel office does not become "a stepchild" in the ranks of White House offices. James's deputy, Becky Norton Dunlop, wrote that this is a danger, given that the office is not seen as "part of the policy-making apparatus, the legislative apparatus, or the political apparatus." To avoid the danger, Reagan gave James the high rank of Assistant to the President and placed him in the West Wing of the White House to demonstrate the importance of presidential personnel. "This recognition," Dunlop writes, "is essential for any administration that believes . . . personnel is policy."[15]

The Reagan personnel experience shows that it is possible to pack the executive branch with political appointees, for Reagan pushed the limits of discretionary appointments allowed by law. As explained by Bert A. Rockman, the Civil Service Reform Act of 1978, which established the Senior Executive Service atop the federal bureaucracy, provides that 10 percent of the total SES appointments may be held by noncareer personnel, and in any given department this figure may climb to 25 percent. "Between 1980 and 1986," writes Rockman, "the total percentage of career SES officials declined by 5.3 percent, whereas the total percentage of noncareer SES officials increased by 13.1 percent. In addition, discretionary Schedule C appointments also rose by 12.8 percent."[16] Rockman also notes that the agencies experiencing the sharpest increases in noncareer executives and decreases in career executives were the core central management agencies such as the Office of Management and Budget and also the line departments of greatest importance to advancing the Reagan agenda—such as Justice and Education.

The Reagan personnel experience also teaches a special lesson for incoming Presidents. What helped facilitate Reagan's fast start in office was his decision to establish his personnel operation well in advance of Election Day in 1980. In April of that year, Reagan asked Pendleton James to begin the work. In his memoir Martin Anderson, a top Reagan aide who also had worked in the Nixon administration, writes that the impetus for this early effort was the Nixon experience in which the departments were "staffed primarily with people with an agenda different from that of the White House."[17] James's labor over the next seven months enabled the Reagan administration to undertake, according to one analysis, a "transition personnel selection with more forethought, with a larger commitment of resources, and with more attention to detail than any other administration in the postwar period, perhaps more than any administration ever."[18]

According to Richard P. Nathan, the idea of an "administrative presidency" can be traced to the Budget and Accounting Act of 1921, the Brownlow Committee of 1936–37, and a succession of presidential committees and task forces on executive management.[19] An administrative presidency seeks to push the President's views, wherever it is lawful and wise to do so, into the day-to-day management of the government. Such a presidency is most effectively pursued by means of strong White House systems authorized to shape and implement presidential policy. Elsewhere in Part Two, I discuss such systems. Here the subject is personnel, the "instruments of execution," from the White House to the departments and agencies. For only subordinates committed to the President's perspectives can be expected to have success in kneading the President's perspectives into the management of the government. As Nathan puts it, "Only with such persons can the President hope to get a handle on running the government. [Otherwise] the normal politics of Washington militate strongly against even a semblance of managerial cohesion in government."[20] In a typical description of those "normal politics," a Lyndon Johnson task force on governmental organization described the President and cabinet secretaries as presiding "[o]ver agencies which they never own and only rarely command. Their managerial authority is constantly challenged by powerful legislative committees, well-organized interest groups, entrenched bureau chiefs with narrow program mandates, and the career civil service."[21] Today's "normal politics," mostly liberal, are more difficult for a conservative President to overcome in pursuing an administrative presidency. This fact of Washington life puts even more emphasis on the need for a conservative President to select and appoint to positions throughout the government capable individuals who are committed to his views. Especially important are the subcabinet positions. The roles of those individuals are less general than cabinet secretaries and therefore more operational. It is here, "down below," that a President's policies become the government's policies. For this reason, the Reagan presidency especially emphasized careful subcabinet selection.

An administrative presidency is equally available to conservatives and liberals alike. Moreover, whoever is elected President is fairly asked by the Constitution to pursue such a presidency. Otherwise, the point of having an elected President, who is accountable to the people for the execution of the laws, and thus for making what necessarily will be disputable decisions, is nullified. Because of the presidency's constitutional organization—the executive power being vested in a single person—it is also, as a practical matter, far more able to impart cohesive policy guidance to executive branch departments and agencies than Congress, a plural body.

While an energetic executive will attempt to govern both legislatively and administratively, as Reagan did in 1981–82 in behalf of his program for economic recovery, the particular circumstance in which a majority of the party opposite the President controls Congress makes an administrative presidency especially attractive. For if a President is unable because of divided government to secure passage of his legislative preferences, he can still govern administratively through the executive departments and agencies. As will be seen in the examples in subsequent chapters, there is room, especially in a government of the sheer size and complexity of ours, parts of which, moreover, are effectively delegated to the executive, for lawful and effective maneuver for the strong President who seeks it.

Such a President cannot expect a Congress especially of the opposite party to stand by idly as he governs administratively; there will be congressional challenge. But an energetic executive will not be intimidated by that prospect. He is elected to govern, not to avoid the task.

# 10

# CHANGING THE STATUS QUO
## Rules, Reorganization, Coordination

A President may attempt through his aides to change the administrative status quo by altering procedures, reorganizing parts of the executive branch, and coordinating activities.[1] This subject is best approached by considering examples of each. The ones in this chapter—successful in the administration's own terms—are taken mainly from the Justice Department during the Reagan years.

That the Justice Department, established by statute in 1870, is today the world's "largest law firm" is well known. It has six litigating divisions—Criminal, Civil, Tax, Civil Rights, Environment and Antitrust—and it is home to the Office of Solicitor General, which represents the United States in the Supreme Court. But Justice does more than litigate. Reporting to the Attorney General, whose office was created by Congress in 1789, are five law enforcement agencies—the Federal Bureau of Investigation, the Drug Enforcement Administration, the Immigration and Naturalization Service, the Bureau of Prisons, and the Marshals Service—as well as the ninety-three U.S. attorneys. Unlike most departments and agencies, Justice dispenses very few grants but is labor-intensive, employing in its various pursuits of justice more than 70,000 persons (in 1988) supported by a budget of slightly more than six billion dollars. There can be no question that the work of the Justice Department lies at the heart of what government, stripped to its basics, must be about.

During the Reagan years, the administration of the Justice Department obviously had to be important to a conservative presidency.[2] Equally, by the way, it would have been important to a liberal presidency; many of the issues that Justice engages—consider crime and civil rights, for just two examples—arouse sharp controversy between the two political parties. President Reagan consistently named to key positions in the department individuals committed to his political objectives. At different times and in different ways they effected important changes in the status quo that illustrate how an administrative presidency is effectively pursued through a particular department.

Previous Justice Departments had sought busing as a remedy for school segregation. But there were many good practical arguments against busing, among them its failure to integrate schools and its ability to distract school districts from their primary purpose of educating students. And the extent to which the courts—let alone the Constitution—required busing was unclear. Here was an opportunity for the Justice Department to replace an inherited law enforcement practice with one reflecting the new President's views. As William French Smith, Reagan's first Attorney General, explained in his memoir, "We believed that no child should be assigned to a particular school solely because of race, and that no child should receive less of an educational opportunity because of race."[3] Smith redirected the change in which the Civil Rights Division no longer asked for busing but instead sought alternative remedies, including voluntary participation in magnet schools, outreach programs, and restructured school-district zoning. New plans were implemented in Odessa, Texas; Chicago, Illinois; Baton Rouge, Louisiana; and Bakersfield, California.

The Civil Rights Division in the 1980s also performed an about-face on the issue of the appropriate remedies for the wrong of public employment discrimination under Title VII of the Civil Rights Act of 1964.[4] Previous Justice Departments had sought hiring and promotion goals as a remedy for such discrimination. In May 1981 Attorney General Smith said in a speech that the department would no longer seek them in Title VII enforcement. Instead, the department would insist on make-whole relief for actual, identifiable victims of discrimination, including back pay, and demand that employers guilty of discrimination quit that practice and instead adopt fair recruitment procedures that ensured minorities and women knew about and could apply for job opportunities. This law enforcement change was possible because Title VII as written did not require numerical goals and reasonably could be read—as the Reagan Justice Department in fact read it—to proscribe such devices. Under the direction of William Bradford Reynolds, appointed by Reagan in the summer of 1981, the Civil Rights Division implemented the new approach in case after case. Guiding the new enforcement effort was the principled idea that government should not favor or disfavor someone merely on the basis of race or gender.

The Civil Rights Division was not the only site of major change at Justice. The Antitrust Division had ample discretion under the statutes it was charged with enforcing to effect a significant law enforcement shift. In the decades prior to Reagan's election, enforcement of the Sherman Act of 1890 and other antitrust laws had become preoccupied with the size of companies. Simply put, bigness was equated with badness and regarded as a sufficient reason for government intervention. Reagan antitrust (at not only Justice but also the Federal Trade Commission) refused to make size the dominant enforcement concern. Instead, it focused on economic efficiency and, more particularly, the consumer welfare thereby produced. In 1982, the Antitrust Division under the leadership of William Baxter, formerly a law professor at Stanford, issued the Merger Guidelines—a statement of the new law enforcement policy in this area—expressing the view that most mergers do not threaten competition and many can benefit consumers. Consistent with the new policy, the division dismissed the huge case brought thirteen years earlier, mainly on account of its size, against IBM, thus enabling it to compete more freely and efficiently in domestic and international markets. In another change, the division recognized that some joint efforts among competitors may enhance productive activity to the benefit of consumers. The division also established an altogether new process—a competition-advocacy program—through which it made its views known to federal regulatory agencies (and sometimes state and local bodies). Here the division sought to emphasize that the purpose of economic regulation is consumer welfare, not the market position of current incumbents, and that government regulation is often responsible for erecting the most enduring barriers to competition.

Nor was this all. The Antitrust Division made criminal prosecution of price fixing and bid rigging a top priority. This did not require a change in procedures but a reallocation of resources—in effect, a reorganization. In directing attention to criminal cases, the division sought to recover the original thrust of the antitrust law, theorizing that economic practices that have no justification and which plainly have the intent and effect of harming consumers should be vigorously prosecuted. In the 1980s, the Antitrust Division obtained record numbers of price-fixing and bid-rigging convictions, pursuing cases in the road building and electrical contracting industries, the soft-drink industry, the dairy business, and, eventually, in federal government procurements. Indicative of its effort in this area, the division obtained the largest fine ever assessed against a corporation for a single violation of the antitrust laws—$1.25 million.

The Criminal Division was another site of policy change. Prior to Reagan's election, federal laws against obscenity had rarely been enforced. This continued to be true under Reagan, as the number of individuals indicted on federal obscenity charges totaled two, seven, none, six, nineteen, and ten for the years 1981 through 1986, respectively. In 1987, however, the number jumped to eighty. Also in 1987, the number of child pornography indictments rose from 147 to 244. The reason for the much higher numbers was a policy change reflecting the President's concerns. The Attorney General's Commission on Pornography, empaneled under William French Smith in 1984, reported to Edwin Meese III in 1986, advising (among other things) that the department should simply enforce existing laws. Under Assistant Attorney General William Weld, the Criminal Division established a new unit and charged it with overseeing obscenity cases. Thus did a reallocation of resources—a reorganization—take place.

The FBI was also a site of important change—actually two changes. First, Attorney General Smith directed the FBI to make terrorism one of its four national priorities. More funds were allocated and more agents assigned to terrorism investigations. More agents conducted undercover investigations; there was more electronic surveillance as wiretap authorizations, rarely sought in the past, were used more frequently. All of this represented a reallocation of resources. While causation is impossible to establish, it bears noting that terrorism incidents within the United States steadily declined during the Reagan years, from fifty-one in 1982 to seven in 1985, blipping up to seventeen in 1986 before falling back to seven in 1987.

Second, as part of a comprehensive effort to increase the federal law enforcement effort against drug trafficking and violent crime, the DEA was in effect placed under the control of the FBI. Thus, for the first time ever, the FBI had the authority to work drug cases. This reorganization had been preceded by others intended to improve the federal drug enforcement effort, but none enjoyed nearly the success of this one, according to James Q. Wilson. While there was an initial period in which the one agency experienced a "culture shock" of sorts in working at close quarters with the other, in time "real changes occurred," writes Wilson.[6] Even the DEA admitted that the FBI training programs produced drug enforcement agents of better quality, while the FBI itself learned from the street-level skills of the DEA.

Another way of changing the status quo, mentioned at the beginning of this chapter is through coordination of activities. Thus, in 1982, as part of a new initiative against drug trafficking, Attorney General Smith established law enforcement task forces in geographical regions throughout the country. These task forces managed the investigation and prosecution of major drug cases by coordinating the efforts of U.S. Attorneys, the FBI, the DEA, the Customs Service, and other parts of the law enforcement establishment. The department achieved success in the terms sought. It chalked up record numbers of indictments and convictions, seized ever higher amounts of drugs at the borders, and stripped drug criminals of more and more assets associated with their illegal trade (such as boats, planes, and cars, even golf courses and country clubs).

Often, an administrative status quo is changed through a combination of altered procedures, reorganization, and coordination. The anti-obscenity effort, for example, involved both a reallocation of resources and a coordination of activities, as the Criminal Division's new anti-obscenity unit managed a nationwide effort involving the FBI, the Internal Revenue Service, the Customs Service, the Postal Service, the Organized Crime Strike Forces (another interagency law enforcement unit), and the United States Attorneys. And the intensified effort against terrorism involved both a reorganization and altered procedures, as Smith issued new domestic security guidelines designed to prevent abuses by the government while better enabling it to investigate terrorism.

Of the various means of changing the status quo discussed in this chapter, altering procedures may hold the most promise. Wilson reports that the success rate of most executive-branch reorganizations has not been high, and that efforts to coordinate executive labors are rarely effective. If Wilson is right, the examples in this chapter—all of which worked—are exceptions. The reasons for their effectiveness are instructive. The reorganizations substantially increased the amount of resources dedicated to the new law enforcement goals, and the efforts at coordination were initiated and monitored by the department head, the Attorney General.

Procedural change can occur in several well-known ways. The shifts in civil rights enforcement discussed above were accomplished simply by executive decision. The shift in antitrust enforcement took the form of written guidelines. Procedural change can be more formal, occurring in regulations issued by the departments and agencies and in executive orders issued by the President.

The opportunities for change through rule-making are numerous. In 1988—to cite one of the most controversial recent examples of rule-making—the Department of Health and Human Services issued revised regulations based on Title X of the Public Health Service Act of 1970. That statute authorizes the HHS Secretary to make grants "to assist in the establishment and operation of voluntary family planning projects which shall offer a broad range of acceptable and effective family planning methods and services." A section of the statute provides that "[n]one of the funds appropriated under this subchapter shall be used in programs where abortion is a method of family planning." Previous regulations had construed this section as prohibiting grantees from providing abortions as a method of family planning but failed to address abortion counseling. Investigations of the program by the General Services Administration revealed that many grantees were using federal funds to underwrite that activity. The Reagan administration therefore revised the regulations to prohibit abortion counseling, referral, or advocacy in Title X projects. In 1991, the Supreme Court sustained the legality of the regulations in *Rust* v. *Sullivan*.[7]

Perhaps the most well-known modern example of an executive order is Executive Order 11246, issued by President Johnson in 1965 (and amended by a second order of his in 1967). The order obligates government contractors not to discriminate against minorities and to take "affirmative action" in their employment practices. Since 1978 the Labor Department, through its Office of Federal Contract Compliance Programs, has enforced the order. Presidents have used executive orders to direct the executive branch in fulfilling a particular program, but the impact of an order—and so it has been with E.O. 11246—may reach into the private sector. Presidents typically have based their orders on any combination of constitutional and statutory authority thought to be available, and the orders have generally survived court challenges.[8] Precisely because they originate with the President, they are wholly within his discretion. What one President orders another can eliminate or modify; as President Reagan considered doing in respect to E.O. 11246, a subject discussed in Chapter 12, note 12, a President can change the order or the regulations implementing it.

The executive branch that takes advantage of opportunities to alter procedures, effect reorganizations, and coordinate activities may proceed as it will—prudently, one must hope, for good reasons, and under the Constitution. Of course, there may be political reaction to what is done. The more aggressive the executive branch is in pursuit of its policy objectives, especially in an era of divided government, the more it can expect negative response from Congress and affected interest groups and in the media. Congress may attempt to cut an agency's budget or otherwise express its displeasure. Disagreement over the anti-quota enforcement of Title VII no doubt figured in the Senate's 1985 rejection of the nomination of William Bradford Reynolds, the assistant attorney general in charge of civil rights, to become associate attorney general, the third-ranking position in the Justice Department. And the Justice Department appropriations act for 1984 was passed by a Congress upset with the new direction in antitrust policy; the act prohibited the expenditure of funds for "any activity, the purpose of which is to overturn or alter the *per se* prohibition on resale price maintenance in effect under Federal antitrust laws." More recently, after the Supreme Court sustained the Reagan administration's Title X regulations in *Rust*, promulgated in 1988, Congress passed a law designed to prevent their implementation by the Bush administration; President Bush successfully vetoed the bill.

The mere possibility of negative reaction from Congress or elsewhere should not deter the energetic executive from administrative governance. Neither should negative results, such as a rejected nomination. Again, the President is elected to govern, and mere maintenance of the status quo is not to be confused with energetic government.

Critical to any effort to pursue an administrative presidency is the executive's willingness to affirm its right to interpret the law it is charged with enforcing. Justice was willing to do that, even in the face of outside criticism. The Lawyers Committee for Civil Rights, for example, said in 1982 that Justice's anti-quota interpretation of Title VII was not compelled by any Supreme Court decisions. The Lawyers Committee was right, in small part: By 1982 the Supreme Court had not yet spoken to the question of whether federal courts may impose quotas as a remedy for proven job discrimination under Title VII. Even if it had done so, however, and even if it had permitted quotas, the Justice Department would not have been required by its decision to impose quotas in Title VII. Nor, in any event, would the Justice Department have been obligated by what lower federal courts had ruled. Law professor Norman Amaker actually has suggested that Justice was obligated to seek quotas in Title VII cases because lower federal courts had approved them.[9] But the only force these rulings could have had was persuasive in character.

Under the Constitution, the executive branch is legally obligated to abide by court decisions in the cases to which it has been a party, but it is under no obligation, except those of prudence, to fashion general law enforcement policy in accord with judicial opinion. When Drew Days, head of the Civil Rights Division during the Carter administration, said that "courts have held and we conclude that numerical hiring and promotional goals are a lawful . . . remedy," he could not properly be understood as saying, "we conclude as we do because courts have obligated us to conclude," but rather, "we conclude as we do because we think the policy, which courts have approved, is the right one." The energetic executive will resist such arguments as the Lawyers Committee's and Norman Amaker's that attempt to subordinate the executive branch to the judiciary; each as a coequal place within the constitutional order. The President has an independent obligation, arising from the Constitution, to interpret the law he enforces.[10]

The examples of changing the status quo discussed in this chapter have either exclusively or mainly involved an executive department, the Justice Department. An administrative presidency thus may be pursued—through the right instruments of execution—department by department, agency by agency. It would be a mistake, however, to conclude that such a presidency may not be pursued across departments and agencies in a manner coordinated by the White House. Indeed, as will be seen in Chapter 12, strong White House systems are necessary in any presidency that aims to shape and implement a policy that affects more than one department or agency, as is often the case.

Perhaps the best example of the kind of White House mechanism that can assist an administrative presidency comes from the Reagan presidency. I refer to Reagan's regulatory review effort, commenced in 1981 and building on the efforts of Presidents Nixon, Ford, and Carter. Through Executive Order 12291, issued within a month of his taking office, Reagan sought to ensure that regulations issued by the departments and agencies (which in themselves represented examples of altered procedures) were consistent with each other and with administration policies and priorities.[11] The order authorized the Office of Management and Budget to review all proposed and final regulations (and thus engage in a coordinating effort) before issuance and to resolve any disagreements, if necessary by a cabinet-level review group or by the President himself, before being published. Between 1981 and 1986, a new OMB unit—the Office of Information and Regulatory Affairs (OIRA)—reviewed almost 12,000 proposed and final rules under a cost-benefit standard by which new regulations would be issued only if the social benefits exceeded the social costs. OIRA objected to roughly a fifth, most of which were then revised by the agencies to OMB's satisfaction.

Reagan's regulatory review program was not simply an example of how the administrative presidency may be pursued; it is a must for any presidency that wishes to govern the modern administrative state. Until the 1930s, federal law typically was decided by Congress or inferred from past enforcement actions. Beginning with the New Deal, Congress extended the reach of the national government into many areas previously within the authority of state governments or the sole control of the private sector. But Congress could not make law at the speed or on the scale demanded by its new commitments, so it delegated lawmaking authority to the executive branch. The agencies thus would have to make—and have made—the law, mainly through rule-making. Under the Constitution, the President is responsible for this body of administrative law and its consequences for the nation. He therefore is duty-bound to review the rule-making to achieve consistency both among the rules and between the rules and his policy goals. If he neglects this duty, agency rules are likely to benefit special interests at the expense of the general public.[12]

In 1986, Christopher C. DeMuth and Douglas H. Ginsburg—the first two administrators of Reagan's regulatory review program—wrote in the *Harvard Law Review* that they were confident "no future President will disestablish the processes of regulatory review and regulatory planning."[13] Unfortunately, a future President acquiesced in what proved, in effect, a disestablishment of those processes. Facing a Congress opposed to the White House regulation "cop," and advised by a budget director lukewarm about the OIRA's work, President Bush failed to use the office to discipline rule-making by the executive branch.[14] When Bush learned in late 1991 that the number of new regulations had substantially increased since he took office, he complained to his staff, "surely we're not reregulating." But Bush had only himself to blame. The lesson is that a President who does not administer the government will find that the government administers itself—in ways he may not approve, yet for which he is ultimately responsible.

# 11

# LITIGATING THE AGENDA
## Argument in the Courts

For the most part the government's lawyers work at the Justice Department, repository of most federal litigating authority. Those lawyers appear in federal court for three purposes. First, to defend a law enforcement action; second, to sue to enforce the laws; and third, to articulate legal views as a friend of the court (the oft-used Latin term is "amicus curiae") in a case of interest to the government. While a pervasive concern of the United States in litigation is the integrity of the law, including the Constitution, many of the cases in which the government participates are occasions on which it may defend, if not advance, the President's policy objectives.

As a defendant, the government will often have the opportunity to defend policy objectives the executive already has achieved through, for example, an altered procedure. A recent example, noted in the last chapter, is the Justice Department's successful defense in the Supreme Court of the regulations barring family planning service grantees under Title X of the Public Health Service Act from providing abortion counseling. In *Rust* v. *Sullivan*, the Court held that the new regulations were a reasonable interpretation of Title X and did not violate either the First or the Fifth Amendments.[1]

When the government is a plaintiff in a case, and even more so when it has entered as a friend of the court, its lawyers have fewer institutional considerations to consider and can more freely pursue the President's interests. Consider the Justice Department's friend-of-the-court involvement in probably the most important school desegregation case of the 1980s, from Norfolk, Virginia. In the late 1960s Norfolk had been judged guilty of school segregation and ordered to bus its students for racial balance. In 1975 the federal courts declared the school system "unitary"—meaning that it had fully eliminated its segregated system. In 1982, acting on the assumption that because the system was unitary it could run its own affairs, and concerned about the flight of white and black students from its schools, the Norfolk school board decided to "debus" at the elementary school level and return to a neighborhood attendance plan, concentrating resources on strengthening the education offered in each school. Predictably, the city encountered opposition and a lawsuit was filed, charging in effect that Norfolk could not run its own affairs and had to continue busing. The Civil Rights Division saw the Norfolk case as an opportunity to advance the argument that a system which had been deemed unitary by a federal court was therefore free to manage its schools as it saw best; the division entered the case as an amicus curiae. In *Riddick* v. *School Board of Norfolk*, the U.S. Court of Appeals for the Fourth Circuit ruled in a manner reflecting the government's position.[2] (The Supreme Court declined to review the decision.) *Riddick* encouraged other school systems in similar legal situations to act as Norfolk did to end forced busing and its negative consequences. Thus advanced through litigation was a policy objective fully consistent with the specific law enforcement position Justice had taken with respect to remedies for school segregation.

A friend of the court gets in court because he first asks to be there. That decision involves multiple considerations that vary from case to case. It is seldom a simple matter, and no rule can be stated which applies in every case. What can be said is that an executive branch that lacks a litigating strategy designed to further the President's policy objectives will not be as alert to amicus opportunities. Obviously it is better to be in court as a matter of well-considered choice than haphazardly.

The role that litigation can play in pursuing policy objectives over time is best understood by example, and perhaps the most instructive in recent years is the Reagan Justice Department's long-term litigating effort against employment quotas.[3] As discussed in the previous chapter, Reagan as a candidate for President in 1980 had campaigned against quotas. Early in the first Reagan term, the Justice Department began to oppose them in litigation. Justice initially employed the argument that the law—whether statutory (Title VII) or constitutional (the Fourteenth Amendment's Equal Protection Clause)—is color-blind. Justice participated in quota cases both as a plaintiff in Title VII enforcement and as a friend of the court in Title VII and other cases.

The first effort came in late 1982, when Justice, acting as a friend of the court, asked the Supreme Court to review a layoff quota adopted by the Boston Fire Department. The Court took the case but then vacated it, as each of those claiming their rights had been violated were eventually back on the job.[4] Later that year Justice succeeded in gaining intervenor status in *Williams* v. *New Orleans*, a case involving a promotions quota for the New Orleans Police Department.[5] (An "intervenor" becomes a party to a lawsuit; in this case Justice was admitted to the case because under federal rules the government has the right to intervene whenever someone claims a denial of the Fourteenth Amendment's equal protection guarantee.) The U.S. Court of Appeals for the Fifth Circuit did not accept Justice's substantive arguments, here presented for the first time in a federal court, that the remedial authority of judges under Title VII extends only to making whole the actual victims of discrimination [the statutory argument] and that the quota violated the Equal Protection

Clause because it requires that racial classifications be "precisely tailored to advance a compelling government interest" [the constitutional argument]. Still, the court ruled against the promotions quota, giving Justice its first litigated triumph. *Williams* was not appealed to the Supreme Court.

In late 1983 Justice, again as a friend of the court, asked the Supreme Court to review a promotions quota in a case involving a Detroit plan for promoting black and white police officers in equal numbers. The Department was prepared to make its by now familiar statutory and constitutional arguments, but the Court declined to take the case.[6] Justice persevered, persuading the Court to review a court-ordered quota in *Firefighters Local Union No. 1784* v. *Stotts*.[7] The Court held that Title VII barred the quota under which white firefighters with greater seniority were required to be laid off before black firefighters with lesser seniority. Justice Byron White, in his opinion for the Court, seemed to accept Justice's statutory argument, writing that it was the policy of Title VII "to provide make-whole relief only to those who have been actual victims of illegal discrimination."

*Stotts* was decided in the summer of 1984. A year later Justice filed as a friend of the court in an employment quota case, *Wygant* v. *Jackson Board of Education*.[8] A school board had replaced its seniority-based layoff system with one based on race: The ratio of minority teachers to minority students must be maintained. There was no history of racial discrimination on the part of the school authorities. The question before the Supreme Court did not involve Title VII but the Constitution: Had the Jackson school board deprived Wendy Wygant of the equal protection of the laws when it fired her because she lacked the race needed to maintain the requisite ratio? In May 1986, the Court struck down the layoff quota, although the plurality opinion did not embrace Justice's brief for a color-blind Constitution.

A month after *Wygant* was decided, the Supreme Court supported quotas in two additional cases in which the Department had also participated, the first as a party, the second as a friend of the court. In *Local 28, Sheet Metal Workers* v. *EEOC*, the Court upheld a rigid remedial quota imposed by a court upon a union that had discriminated against nonwhites in recruiting, selection, training, and admission.[9] And in *Local No. 93, International Ass'n of Firefighters* v. *City of Cleveland*, the Court suggested that a race-conscious promotions program approved as part of a consent decree in Title VII litigation might survive legal challenge even though the same program might fail if entered as part of a court order.[10]

Forced—at least as a tactical matter—to drop its color-blind argument in favor of less sweeping ones, the Department continued to argue in the Supreme Court against quotas and to lose. In 1987, in *United States* v. *Paradise*, the Supreme Court upheld a promotions quota imposed by a district court upon the Alabama State Troopers, which had been found guilty of systematically excluding blacks from positions of every kind.[11] That same year, rejecting the arguments of Justice as a friend of the court, the Court in *Johnson* v. *Transportation Agency* upheld an affirmative action plan voluntarily adopted by a county government never accused of discrimination of any kind. The plan was designed to attain a work force whose composition in every job category reflected the proportion of minorities and women in the area labor market.[12]

With the setbacks in 1986 and 1987, the Justice Department clearly had seen the rejection of its broad argument that Title VII and the Constitution are color-blind legal instruments that permit relief only for identifiable victims of discrimination. But Justice persisted, continuing to argue in the Supreme Court against quotas and the legal culture that promoted them. The effort paid off. In the last term of the Court in which the Reagan Justice Department could participate, the Court handed down three decisions sharply restricting racial preferences. In *City of Richmond* v. *Croson*, the Court, maintaining that the Constitution equally protects all persons as individuals, and not as members of racial groups, held that a city ordinance setting aside 30 percent of public-works funds for construction firms owned by blacks or other minorities violated the Fourteenth Amendment.[13] In *Wards Cove Packing Co.* v. *Atonio*, the Court reformed the law of disparate impact under Title VII in such a way as to lessen its tendency to foster employment quotas.[14] Finally, in *Martin* v. *Wilks*, the Court ruled that a judicially approved promotions quota favoring blacks (in this instance they were firefighters in Birmingham, Alabama) might later be challenged by individuals who were not a party to the original case or willing participants in its resolution.[15] In the first two of these cases, the Justice Department participated as a friend of the court, and in the third (involving a consent decree agreed to by the Carter administration) as an intervenor.

These, then, were the dozen cases that describe the litigating effort against employment quotas. No one could have prophesied which cases the Court would accept, or which legal issues it would decide in which order. The Reagan Justice Department was fortunate that the first case in which the Court addressed the authority of courts to order quotas under Title VII concerned neither hiring nor promotions but layoffs, and thus seniority rights, perhaps the most sympathetic context for considering the injury caused by a quota, especially since Title VII contains a provision that explicitly speaks to this context. On the other hand, the cases in which the Court did eventually address promotions and hiring had, as the lawyers say, "bad facts": There were records of egregious discrimination against minorities in both *Local 28* (a case the union was determined to take to the Supreme Court) and in *Paradise*.

A litigating strategy also cannot confidently predict what judges will do. Justice Byron White, the author of the Court's opinion in *Stotts* and a Justice generally opposed to quotas, voted for a minority set-aside policy in 1990 in a case involving the Federal Communications Commission. Thus did Justice William Brennan, on the eve of his retirement from the Court, find a fifth vote to make a majority.[16]

Such considerations as these do not counsel timidity but intelligence on the part of lawyers and other litigating strategists within the executive branch. A President and his legal advisers must understand the rocky road litigation can be and prepare for loss as well as victory.

It is also necessary to recognize what success and failure in court can mean. A Supreme Court decision often has impact beyond the case at hand. Consider *Croson*, in which the Court struck down a 30 percent business set-aside. Some thirty-six states and 190 local governments lent their names to a brief in support of the City of Richmond; they did so because they, too, administered similar programs of racial preference. The

Court's decision forced these public employers to review their programs to bring them into conformity with the new law. On the other hand, the administration's losses in *Local 28* and *Paradise* meant that employers in similar positions as the defendants in those cases might be forced to adopt racial preferences. The outcome in the *Johnson* case also was a green light to public employers desiring to adopt affirmative action plans that hire and promote on the basis of race and sex.

It is also important to understand that Supreme Court decisions are not always the final word. Constitutional decisions, which can be changed only through constitutional amendment, are much harder to correct than those interpreting statutes of Congress. *Croson* was a constitutional case, and Congress passed on the very hard job it would have been to change it. But it did not pass on the less institutionally formidable task of amending *Wards Cove* and overturning *Wilks*. The Civil Rights Act of 1991 erased one part of *Wards Cove* (by shifting the burden of proof from the plaintiff, where the Court had said it must lie, to the defendant) while effectively asking the federal courts to reconsider another part of its decision (concerning the definition of "business necessity").[17] In cutting back much of *Wilks*, the act negated a large part of the five-year effort by the Civil Rights Division that led to the decisional law it finally obtained from the Court.[18]

Litigation, then, must be understood within a larger governing context that may result in a legislative battle. Yet even after such a battle, important litigated success may remain. Consider again the Reagan litigating effort against employment quotas, in which Reagan-Bush "losses" were eventually taken in Congress, in the form of the Civil Rights Act of 1991. In the final—that is, post-legislative—analysis, this is what endured:

First, in the context of proven discrimination under Title VII, court-ordered remedies in the form of layoff preferences are now unlawful, while remedies in the form of hiring or promotion quotas are confined to instances where the discrimination has been long-standing, has persisted despite efforts to end it, and has remained largely indifferent to other remedial efforts. Victim-specific remedies, while not required as a matter of law, are now seen as at least preferable.

Second, in a Title VII disparate impact case, the plaintiff

may not rely on just any kind of statistics; the proper statistical comparison is between the racial composition of the persons in the relevant labor market and the persons holding the jobs at issue. Further, the plaintiff, as a matter of both decisional and statutory law, must identify the specific practice said to cause the disparate impact.

Third, in the context of constitutional law, racial discrimination is now subject to the same high standard of strict scrutiny regardless of the form it might take, whether of the invidious kind of segregation or the so-called benign kind associated with racial preferences. Moreover, any quota remedy for a constitutional violation must be a "last resort" and "narrowly tailored" so as to least injure the rights of innocent third parties.

Thus, as a result of the Reagan litigating effort, and even after the passage of the Civil Rights Act of 1991, racial preferences faced a much more problematic future than they did in 1980. Only in certain, carefully defined circumstances are they permissible. An employer, for example, may voluntarily adopt a preference to break through a barrier of wholesale racial exclusion in certain jobs. But he may not do that just to maintain "racial balance" in his work force. Federal courts may order public employers to adopt racial preferences, but only to remedy long-standing discrimination that has obstinately persisted despite other remedial efforts—and only if the quota is a "last resort" and "narrowly tailored." Finally, a public employer may voluntarily adopt a preference, but only if it has a firm basis for doing so, and only if it does so as a "last resort," and only if the preference is "narrowly tailored."

The Reagan presidency's effort in court against quotas also teaches another important characteristic about litigation—its clarifying and educational effects. In 1981, the law of affirmative action and quotas, as determined in the courts, was, to say no worse of it, ill-defined. The Reagan administration's persistent arguments gradually helped clarify in the courts the meaning of both Title VII and the Fourteenth Amendment's Equal Protection Clause. And they had an impact outside the court room, for they became part of a needed public debate on not only the legality but the policy wisdom of programs of preferential treatment.

In sum, litigating an agenda is worth it. A presidency willing to litigate an agenda must be united in its purposes, and it must have lawyers committed to the enterprise.

In *Williams* v. *New Orleans*, the 1983 case, the Equal Employment Opportunity Commission voted to file a friend-of-the-court brief supporting the quota. Attorney General Smith told the EEOC it lacked authority to do that; the EEOC eventually voted not to submit its brief (although it did leak it to the news media). Had the EEOC made its argument in court, the government would have been officially speaking with two voices; executive energy in the form of legal argument would have been weakened, precisely because "unity" in the litigating executive would have been fractured.[19] Although today there are some agencies that by statute have independent litigating authority, the EEOC is not one of them; Smith was correct in his judgment. From the standpoint of executive unity, and therefore institutional energy, the fewer agencies that have such independent authority, the better. But an energetic executive at least must make sure, as Smith did, that an agency not empowered by statute with independent authority does not speak to a court. Wherever possible, the administration must speak with one voice.

And the administration must also have capable Justice Department lawyers—especially the lawyer who serves as Solicitor General—who understand that they work for the President. The S.G. is the fourth-ranking officer in the Justice Department. He is appointed by the President, subject to Senate confirmation, and his immediate supervisor is the Attorney General. The Judiciary Act of 1789 authorized the Attorney General to "prosecute and conduct all suits in the Supreme Court in which the United States might be concerned." The first Attorneys General regularly appeared in the Supreme Court; today they rarely do—there is now a department, and a very big one at that, to manage. The Solicitor General, whose office was created by statute (when the Justice Department was) in 1870, has the Supreme Court portfolio. He and the lawyers in his office (twenty or so) are the ones who regularly appear before the Supreme Court in cases "in which the United States might be concerned." Depending on inclination, a Solicitor General will appear once a month or so in the Court to argue a case. And he must manage the arguments by his lawyers in the Court. He also influences the shape of the positions taken in the federal appeals court by other Justice Department lawyers (who work in the litigating divisions), for he has authority to supervise and control the types of arguments they make.

The Solicitor General will be central to any effort to litigate a presidential agenda. And so it was during the Reagan years, in respect to the anti-quota effort (not to mention some others). Solicitors General Rex Lee and Charles Fried played key roles in pursuing legal policy goals largely determined by Attorney General William French Smith and the Assistant Attorney General in charge of the Civil Rights Division, William Bradford Reynolds.

An energetic President who aims to litigate an agenda will reject out of hand the argument of the political left that the Solicitor General must be independent of him and a sort of "Tenth Justice" of the Supreme Court. A 1987 book by that title, by Lincoln Caplan of *The New Yorker*, expresses this wrongheaded view.[20] Caplan argues that the Solicitor General was, until recently in our history, largely "independent" of the administration he served in; that the S.G. should be less an advocate of the President's positions before the Supreme Court than a servant of it, basically advising the Court of its precedents; and that should the Soliciter General fail to fulfill this role by attacking precedents, he flouts the "rule of law."

Caplan's arguments, provoked by the Reagan administration's efforts to litigate an agenda, including the anti-quota agenda elaborated above, are historically and constitutionally flawed.[21] Caplan exaggerates the "independence" from his administration the S.G. had in the past—President Eisenhower wrote part of the government's brief in *Brown* v. *Board of Education*; President Carter, Vice-President Mondale, the White House staff, and other Cabinet officers intervened with the Attorney General against the proposed S.G. filing in the well-known *Bakke* case—even as he understates it during the Reagan years. One of Caplan's anonymous sources in fact admits that he could not think of a case in which the Solicitor General had been overruled by the Attorney General, his direct supervisor, much less the President, who appointed him.

Even if some overruling had occurred, however, that would not be cause for alarm.[22] The S.G. does work for the President. He is not a Tenth Justice. This does not mean that he should slavishly translate the President's policy goals into legal argument; the S.G. owes the Attorney General and the President his conscientious, well-considered judgment, and if his legal views are not what the President wants, the Solicitor General has options—recusal or resignation. This is as it should be, for it is the President who is the elected official. The Solicitor General is one of his "instruments of execution," like the Attorney General of great importance to the President.

Implicit in Caplan's treatment of the Solicitor General is Richard Neustadt's perspective on separation of powers, which maintains that ours is a government not of separated powers but separated institutions sharing power. Apparently for Caplan, there must be a sharing of the executive and judicial powers every time the Solicitor General makes an argument in court. The S.G. is an officer of the Court (as is the Attorney General), but he reports to the President, and it is the President, not the Court, who has the total authority to remove him from office.

If the President has a view of the law at odds with the Supreme Court's, he has every right under the Constitution to a Solicitor General able and willing to press that understanding in the Court. If that means asking the Court to overrule one of its precedents, particularly a constitutional one, a Solicitor General surely may do that. "[T]he ultimate touchstone of constitutionality," Justice Felix Frankfurter once remarked, "is the Constitution itself and not what [the Supreme Court] ha[s] said about it."[23] It is possible that the Court gets the Constitution wrong; the Court in fact has said or implied it has been wrong, having reversed (through 1989) more than 260 of its prior decisions. It would be a denial of reason—and of the ability to get the rule of law right—to foreclose dialogue between the executive and the judiciary over the meaning of law.[24] And, as we have seen in other contexts, the executive does have an independent right to interpret the Constitution; the executive may disagree with the Court over its meaning.

In the aforementioned *Brown* case, President Eisenhower asked the High Court through his Solicitor General to over-

175

rule *Plessy* v. *Ferguson*, the 1896 case which had legalized segregation. Presidents Reagan and Bush both have asked the Court through their Solicitors General to overrule *Roe* v. *Wade*, in which the Court extended the right of privacy to encompass a woman's decision to have an abortion. In a widely publicized recent case, Attorney General Richard Thornburgh himself appeared in the Supreme Court in the administration's behalf to argue that so-called victim-impact evidence of a crime may be introduced by the prosecutor at the sentencing stage of a criminal trial. To make this argument, Thornburgh necessarily had to ask the Court to overrule two contrary cases decided just two and four years earlier. The Court did so, of course, extruding several opinions discoursing on *stare decisis*—the doctrine that the Court's precedents should govern the decision of like cases by later Courts.[25]

The executive branch has no guarantee, of course, that the Court will accept its view of the law. But prudently fashioned executive-branch arguments asking the Court to reconsider its precedents are entirely appropriate; they do honor to the principles of separation of powers and the rule of the law.

If the Solicitors General during the Reagan years had simply operated as a "Tenth Justice," it is doubtful whether any effort, much less the persistent effort, to challenge employment quotas would have taken place, much less borne the fruit it did. Energy in the executive requires a Justice Department willing to litigate the President's policy agenda wherever it is prudently possible and legally sound to do so. It also requires a Justice Department willing to litigate what Alexander Hamilton called the constitutional rights of the executive. While the Justice Department historically has been willing to stand with the President in behalf of his rights, every President should make sure that his Solicitor General is on the executive's side.

In this matter, no President could ask for more vigorous self-defense than Reagan's Solicitors General provided in a line of cases during the 1980s in which the constitutional rights of the executive were very plainly at stake. (Indeed, as we saw in Chapter 5, Reagan's Justice Department lawyers did better in his defense than he did.) These included the legislative veto case (*INS* v. *Chadha*) and the independent counsel case (*Morrison* v. *Olson*), both of which were discussed in Chapter 5. The defense of executive rights met with success early on but crushing defeat in *Morrison*.

In his memoir, Charles Fried, the Solicitor General who argued the government's position in *Morrison*, is doubtful that the ground the executive lost in the 1980s "can be retrieved in this Court."[26] Perhaps not. But it is most doubtful that it will be retrieved unless there are lawyers for the President willing and able to litigate the constitutional rights of the office. Defending those rights—in court as well as in other contexts—must be part of every strong President's agenda.

# 12

# POLICY MUDDLE
## Reagan and Quotas

A President who wishes to govern administratively in behalf of certain political goals must (1) frame and articulate a coherent public policy, and (2) take care that the laws in his charge are executed in ways that advance, or at least do not compromise, that policy. Of course, no President can give equal time to every issue; the President must choose where he will govern administratively. But one issue no modern President can avoid is race; whether a President wills it or not, he will have a domestic policy on race. The idea of equality is as old as the Declaration of Independence and at the heart of what America is about, and today issues of race are insistently, and controversially, with us. The Reagan presidency shows what can happen when a president does not make race a first-order issue. Consider, in particular, Reagan's governance in respect to quotas.

In 1980 Ronald Reagan campaigned against employment quotas based on race. The GOP platform maintained that "equal opportunity should not be jeopardized by bureaucratic regulations and decisions which rely on quotas, ratios, and numerical requirements to exclude some individuals in favor of others, thereby rendering such regulations and decisions inherently discriminatory." Reagan himself said: "We must not allow the noble concept of equal opportunity to be distorted into federal guidelines or quotas" which require race or ethnicity to be "the principal factor in hiring."

In 1980 three agencies were mainly responsible for most of the "bureaucratic regulations and decisions which rely on quotas, ratios, and numerical requirements." These were the Justice Department, the Equal Employment Opportunity Commission, and the Labor Department. Meanwhile, a number of agencies followed rules setting aside a portion of government contracts for certain racial and ethnic minorities.

As discussed in Chapter 10, the Reagan Justice Department quickly eliminated quotas from its Title VII enforcement. As discussed in Chapter 11, Justice's Title VII policy was part of a larger goal pursued through litigation, that of color-blind law. "Our goal," said William French Smith in a May 1981 speech, "must always be genuinely color-blind state action. . . . [R]ace or color or national origin must for purposes of government decision-making ultimately become irrelevant." In congressional testimony in September 1981, William Bradford Reynolds, head of the Civil Rights Division, noted that the legislative history behind Title VII established "a principle of 'color-blindness in employment.' "[1] He further argued that there was no moral justification for quotas: "Separate treatment of people in the field of employment, based on nothing more than personal characteristics of race or gender, is as offensive to standards of human decency today as it was some eighty-four years ago when countenanced under *Plessy* v. *Ferguson* [which legalized segregation]." Reynolds stated:

> This administration is firmly committed to the view
> that the Constitution and laws of the United States

protect the rights of every person—whether black or white, male or female—to pursue his or her goals in an environment of racial and sexual neutrality. The color-blind ideal of equal opportunity for all that guided the framers of the Constitution and the drafters of Title VII holds the great promise of lifting the incubus of race, national origin and sex discrimination from the Nation, and of realizing the proclamation of equality in the Declaration of Independence.

Although Reynolds did not specify what other action the Justice Department might take in pursuit of color blindness, his position could be construed as opposing racial preferences in any context and thus implying disagreement with *United Steelworkers of America* v. *Weber*.[2] In *Weber*, the Supreme Court ruled that Title VII did not prohibit private employers from adopting racial quotas in job training and apprenticeship programs. In December of 1981, Reynolds publicly commented upon *Weber*. "My own view," he told the *Wall Street Journal*, "is that *Weber* was wrongly decided and that the Court should take another look at it."[3] Reynolds was out in front of the President, who had no idea who or what *Weber* was when he was later asked about Reynolds's remark. The Reagan campaign formulations against quotas did not necessarily imply the color-blind goal that Justice in early 1981 so unequivocally endorsed. During the Reagan presidency, few others in the executive branch would join its campaign for color-blind law and policy.

Justice enforces Title VII against public employers, the EEOC against the private sector.[4] In 1980 the commission's enforcement policy called for goals and timetables in resolving both complaints brought by individuals against their employers and systemic charges initiated by the commissioners (five, all appointed by the President). This policy remained in force during the first Reagan administration. The policy changed in 1985: Under Clarence Thomas, the agency's chairman, the EEOC quit asking for quotas and instead sought make-whole relief, especially back pay, for identified victims of discrimination.[5] The new policy was amended in 1987, in accord with recent Supreme Court decisions, to accept the possibility of using remedial goals and timetables. But goals were rarely sought.[6] Thus, by the second half of the Reagan presidency, the EEOC enforcement conformed to the stated intention of the 1980 campaign.

At Labor, the story was much different. Through its Office of Federal Contract Compliance Programs, the Labor Department enforces Executive Order 11246, which, as amended, obligates federal contractors not to discriminate against minorities and to take "affirmative action" in hiring and promotions.[7] For years Labor had imposed affirmative action goals and timetables upon federal contractors. The Reagan administration was free to alter the enforcement regime, which affected some 325,000 companies and other organizations (including colleges and universities) and a total of 26 million workers—more than a third of the American work force. The Reagan transition team targeted the executive order enforcement for reform, proposing (among other things) an end to goals and timetables and a reform of affirmative action along race-neutral lines.[8] But this proposal was never realized. Early on Labor sought regulatory changes designed to make the compliance process voluntary and less burdensome.[9] The proposed change clearly relevant to the issue of racial quotas involved the point at which goals and timetables were to be established. During the Carter administration, contractors were obligated to adopt goals when the "availability analysis" showed any difference at all between the percentage of minority workers "available" and the percentage of such workers actually "utilized." Reagan officials instead proposed goals that did not have to be adopted unless the utilization was below 80 percent of the availability. Although this represented a proposal to reduce the numbers, the Labor enforcement of the executive order still was to be a matter of percentage goals. This was acknowledged by the Labor Undersecretary, Malcolm Lovell, who testified in Congress that the "mission of OFCCP is to insure . . . that the employment of protected groups does not vary to a major degree from the availability of their qualified, willing members in the work force."[10] Although Labor dropped its proposed revisions, their substance was effected through informal policy making— internal directives, orders, and notices.[11] Civil rights groups criticized the OFCCP throughout the Reagan presidency for relaxing civil rights enforcement, but the office did not significantly depart from the understanding of its mission as articulated by Undersecretary Lovell, as it continued to require goals and timetables. In the second Reagan term, the Labor Department under William Brock strengthened the regulatory regime by rebuffing a Justice-led effort premised on color blindness to eliminate the OFCCP goals and timetables.[12]

Also at odds with the Reagan campaign statements on quotas was the President's consistent support and expansion of the programs that "set aside" a certain percentage of government contracts for members of certain officially designated minority groups. Set-asides date back to the Nixon administration and have been supported by Democratic and Republican Presidents alike. The set-aside is perhaps the most egregious form of racial entitlement, however, and clearly qualifies as the kind of "numerical requirement" Reagan sharply criticized during the 1980 campaign.

These, then, were the varied results of what might be called Reagan's anti-quota administrative presidency. Reagan seldom involved himself in civil rights policy. His White House aides did not map an overall strategy against quotas, much less execute one through a mechanism by which policy in the various agencies could be developed, reviewed, and coordinated. Whatever happened under Reagan—whether consistent with his campaign or not, whether the best policy, on reflection, or not—tended largely to issue from the agencies and departments and at least in a nominal sense from the political appointees placed therein. The evidence shows that Reagan did not often pick these particular "instruments of execution" with policy change in mind. Neither of his Labor secretaries (Ray Donovan and William Brock) nor those directly responsible for the OFCCP—all of whom the President has the power to appoint—shared his opposition to racial quotas. As for the EEOC, when Reagan first tried to name a chairman in 1981, he picked William Bell, who had run a small Detroit employment agency that was unable to place any clients the year before. Not conspicuously qualified for the job, the man was black and a Republican; Reagan seemed to view the appointment as a matter of patronage for black supporters instead of as a means of policy change. (Minority set-asides were likewise a form of Reagan administration patronage for black supporters.) Clarence Thomas, then an Education Department official, privately protested the Bell appointment, which eventually was withdrawn—and given to Thomas. Yet the Thomas appointment—which proved Reagan's most important to the EEOC—was not made with a sense of purpose but more from desperation; the job had to be filled. As was true with others appointed to positions enforcing civil rights laws, Thomas was given no sense of how he was expected to do the job.[13] Reagan was not able until 1985 to appoint a majority of commissioners who shared his opposition to quotas.

For his first Attorney General, Reagan chose William French Smith, his personal lawyer. While Reagan did not select Smith on the narrow ground that he expected his Attorney General to challenge quotas, Reagan did know that Smith shared his politics and felt he could be relied upon to carry them out, consistent with the law. Smith's most important decision with respect to quotas proved to be his recommendation to the President that he appoint William Bradford Reynolds as assistant attorney general for civil rights. Smith, a partner in the firm of Gibson, Dunn & Crutcher, wanted someone in charge of civil rights who fit his firm's high standards of excellence. Reynolds was regarded as such. But he had no particular political reputation, having sought a job, in fact, in the Carter Justice Department. And he knew little about civil rights law, having originally been interviewed by Smith for heading up the Civil Division. "I was much more interested in the civil job," Reynolds says.[14] During his confirmation hearing, Reynolds actually drew criticism from conservatives who worried that as a relative newcomer to civil rights the nominee would soon find himself captured by a pro-quota bureaucracy.[15] But Smith thought Reynolds's lack of knowledge regarding civil rights law an advantage—Smith thought the law needed rethinking. And Smith already had established the Department's color-blind direction in a May 1981 speech. Reynolds, who agreed with Smith's view of his mission, recalls that the Attorney General left the actual means of doing the job to him.

Smith and Reynolds were the two appointments Reagan made early in his presidency that definitely reflected an anti-quota intention on his part. There is no reason that his other appointments—to the OFCCP throughout his tenure and to the EEOC early on—could not have been equally intentional. While the actual performance by a President's subordinate is more important than the intention behind an appointment, it is elementary that a President who does not use his appointment power to effect policy change is unlikely to achieve it.

To say that Reagan could have used his appointment power more strategically is to imply the existence of a more clearly defined agenda in this area. Fashioning a coherent agenda would have forced Reagan to decide among competing constituencies, including corporate America (which had become used to Labor's pro-quota enforcement of E.O. 11246) and some black Republicans (who, often for reasons of self-interest, supported federal set-asides). It would also have forced him to resolve the apparent contradiction between his own support of minority set-asides and his own opposition to quotas. Ultimately, it would have forced him to decide whether, in fact, he wished his presidency to pursue color-blind law and policy, as his Justice Department in fact did through 1986, and to determine the important means toward whichever end he eventually chose, as well as the public rhetoric in which he and members of the administration would discuss these matters. Had Reagan truly wished to govern administratively in accord with a carefully developed strategy, he could not have done so merely through his appointees at Justice, the EEOC, and Labor. Needed would have been a White House mechanism, a council or group, an institutional means for discussing, implementing, and coordinating the policy.

A coherent administrative strategy managed from the White House would have helped Reagan in other circumstances bearing on his ability to pursue an anti-quota agenda. Consider, for example, the matter that came to be known simply as "Bob Jones." On January 8, 1982, administration officials at the Treasury and Justice Departments announced an end to President Nixon's 1970 decision to deny tax-exempt status to racially discriminatory private schools. Their argument, relying on the principle of separation of powers and representing an extraordinary willingness to admit an executive power grab, was that the Internal Revenue Service, which is part of the Treasury, lacked the necessary statutory authority. At the same time, and consistent with this policy change, the administration said that it was asking the Supreme Court to render moot the appeals of Bob Jones University (in South Carolina) and Goldsboro Christian Schools (in Goldsboro, North Carolina). Pursuant to the Nixon policy, the tax-exempt status of Bob Jones had been revoked by the IRS in 1970, that of Goldsboro Christian in 1974. Both schools had lost their legal challenges to the IRS revocations in federal appeals court, and in October of 1981 the Supreme Court had decided to review the cases. In its September certiorari filing, the Justice Department had said that the appeals court rulings upholding the IRS actions were correct. The January 8 announcement thus included two reversals—one of IRS enforcement policy, the other of a Justice Department position in litigation. The administration found it very hard to articulate the merits of the new position, however, because it appeared to many that the Reagan presidency was guilty of reneging on the federal government's long-standing commitment to school desegregation. The public reaction by civil rights activists and in the press was overwhelmingly negative. The President himself was portrayed as favoring segregation, even as a racist. Four days later panicky White House officials persuaded the President to say: "I am unalterably opposed to racial discrimination in any form. I am also opposed to administrative agencies exercising powers that the Constitution assigns to the Congress." And, what was new, "I believe the right thing to do on this issue is to enact legislation which will prohibit tax exemptions for organizations that discriminate on the basis of race. Therefore I will submit legislation and will work with the Congress to accomplish this purpose." That legislative purpose was never accomplished; Congress decided to abide the event. In May 1983 the Supreme Court, with only one dissenting vote, rejected the administration's legal argument in *Bob Jones University* v. *United States*.[16]

The best account of the Bob Jones story, written by David Whitman for the Kennedy School of Government at Harvard University, contains no evidence to indicate that anyone at the White House understood the political downsides of the position taken in *Bob Jones* for a civil rights policy aimed at the demise of racial quotas or the recovery in law and policy of the principle of nondiscrimination.[17] When briefed on *Bob Jones*, Reagan saw the matter as procedural, unrelated to race. And none of his White House aides considered proposing legislation that would have given the IRS the authority the Justice brief said it lacked.[18] Ironically, Justice and Treasury officials working on the issue prior to the January 8 announcements generally agreed that allowing tax exemptions to racially discriminatory schools was bad public policy.[19] Some of those officials thought that a legislative "fix" was in order. But their noses were buried in the legal brief.

A President wanting to retain his political ability to eliminate federal quotas and to pursue policies of nondiscrimination did not have to play the cards dealt him by his aides. Reagan could have decided not to change the government's position in the Supreme Court or its enforcement policy at Treasury, on grounds that in the larger scheme of things (namely, the anti-quota battle to come) this particular fight was not worth it. Or, while pursuing the positions urged by Treasury and Justice, he could have opted to announce the "corrective" legislation on the day Justice filed its brief, if not well beforehand. That would have enabled Reagan not only to make the principled distinction between what the law commands and what is good policy but also to demonstrate moral leadership in behalf of nondiscrimination. And by indicating that he would not tolerate racially discriminatory policies on the part of private schools favorably treated for tax purposes, Reagan also could have earned the right to be heard whenever he insisted on adherence to nondiscrimination in other contexts, including those involving racial quotas.

As the administration's debut in the civil rights field, Bob Jones revealed a total lack of strategic insight.[20] The whole experience, moreover, seemed to inhibit the President in this area of policy; thereafter the President shied away from public discussion of race and effectively left policies involving race to his aides.[21] In consequence, the divisions between the color-blind advocates (such as Reynolds), the merely anti-quota advocates (such as Thomas), and those lukewarm about the entire business (such as Brock) only became more apparent as the years passed. Clarence Pendleton, whom Reagan named as chairman of the Civil Rights Commission, and William Bradford Reynolds at Justice filled the rhetorical and leadership vacuum.[22] Ironically, their emphatic denunciations of quotas and support for color blindness served to spotlight the administration's incoherence. In these circumstances, it was not surprising that the 1985 nomination of Reynolds to become associate attorney general, the third-ranking position in the Justice Department, was defeated by the Senate. When particular policies can be construed as perhaps not the President's, those pushing the policies are more vulnerable to political attack than they otherwise might be. Although Reagan delivered a radio address in Reynolds's behalf, his last-hour support could not change an outcome effectively determined by the dynamic of disunity in the executive branch in which Reynolds was seen as more conservative than Reagan.

Reagan was not the first (see Nixon) or the last (see Bush) President to administer a muddled civil rights policy.[23] The nation has yet to experience from any President the kind of intelligent, sophisticated leadership on race that could put an end to racial entitlements while forging a new politics of equal opportunity that emphasizes character and achievement.

A President aiming to provide that kind of leadership would do well to learn from Reagan's administrative (mis-)governance in respect to quotas. First of all, whatever the subject matter, a President must fashion a coherent policy, and then he must enforce that policy through the available means.[24] Obviously, he must make effective use of his appointment power. But he cannot rely upon good appointments alone. He must also see to it that the relevant laws are administered in ways that advance his policy, and to do that he needs the institutional assistance of a White House group he assigns to the task.

It is useful to think more about the kind of central White House mechanism Reagan so badly needed. Such a unit could have been organized along the lines of the office Reagan established in 1981 for regulatory review. It could have reviewed proposals for altered law enforcement at Justice, the EEOC, and elsewhere, both in terms of consistency with the President's policy and with each other, with disagreements forwarded to the cabinet or the President himself for final decision. It could have taken the initiative in reviewing Labor's executive-order enforcement. It could have ordered a review of all federal set-aside policies in order to conform those policies to the principles governing Title VII and Executive Order 11246 enforcement. And it could have kept an eye on the quota cases Justice litigated, both in terms of the arguments made in the cases and the implications for policy of the decisions rendered by the courts.[25] Additionally, it could have advised on related issues, such as what to do about the IRS policy denying tax exemptions to racially discriminatory schools. And it could have counseled on the government's governing of itself in regard to the ubiquitous quota issue.

On this last, consider the chaotic episode involving the EEOC and the National Endowment for the Humanities. Continuing a policy begun at the end of the Carter administration, the EEOC under Reagan asked all federal departments and agencies not only to supply data as to the racial composition of their work forces, but also to set goals and timetables for increasing the numbers of minorities hired and promoted. In 1983 and 1984 a few of these departments and agencies—the Justice and Education Departments and the Federal Trade Commission—quietly decided not to provide the EEOC with goals and timetables. The NEH joined them. Its chairman, William J. Bennett, informed Clarence Thomas of his position in a letter that NEH simultaneously gave to the press. Some members in Congress took note of the well-publicized NEH position, and in its next reauthorization budget, the endowment, now under Acting Chairman John Agresto, was actually required to provide goals and timetables to the EEOC. The White House, shying from controversy on this issue, made no effort to oppose the language in the reauthorization bill, which the President signed. NEH thus was forced by Congress to acquiesce in a policy it had objected to, for reasons it had believed were supported by the President; the agency had been orphaned. "We had no help from the White House," says Agresto.[26] And there was a further irony: When Bennett declared the NEH position in 1984, Clarence Thomas was working to persuade his fellow commissioners that goals and timetables should be "optional" and thus not obligatory upon federal agencies. Late in the second term, a majority of commissioners agreed with Thomas. Reporting goals and timetables thus became optional for everyone but the NEH. Had there been a White House civil rights office, this strange sequence of events might never have occurred.

Reagan's failure to govern effectively and coherently in respect to quotas also was measured in rhetorical terms. As was not the case with, say, taxes or communism, Reagan did not publicly articulate, on any regular basis and with the needed specificity, his administration's policies on civil rights. At times his appointees filled the rhetorical void: Pendleton and Reynolds in particular set the terms of public debate in ways they thought best. Reynolds became known for his remark that quotas are "morally wrong," Pendleton for his comment that quotas are "morally bankrupt." Neither Reynolds nor Pendleton used especially effective rhetoric, but even if they had, their words were no substitute for the President's. Only the President is positioned to comprehend policy across the departments and agencies, and it was a President who was needed to fashion the ends and means of his anti-quota policy and frame rhetoric suitable to its achievement.

This chapter has focused on how a President ought to govern administratively—in, that is, the execution of the laws by his subordinates. It has argued in particular the need for White House mechanisms that can assist the President in developing and implementing coherent policy in key areas throughout the executive branch. As events discussed in this and previous chapters make clear, Bob Jones perhaps especially, administrative governance cannot be pursued by itself, without attention to legislative needs or congressional responses (or court responses, for that matter.) That is why any White House group or council charged with addressing a particular issue must think about it comprehensively, in terms of all three branches. Thinking this way is no guarantee of an effective pursuit of policy, but it is an important first step.

# 13

# STRATEGIC LEADERSHIP

Reagan, the Fallacy of
"Cabinet Government," and
the NSC

I n his First Inaugural, Ronald Reagan uttered one of his most famous statements, cheered by conservatives: "Government is not the solution to our problem. Government is the problem." Reagan said that in specific reference to the government's negative impact upon the economy, then sputtering into recession. But government, while it can be and often is problematic (and was in 1981, hurting the economy), is not therefore to be despised. The teaching of the Declaration of Independence—equally available to conservatives and liberals alike—is that governments are instituted in order to secure rights. Government is in a fundamental sense the solution to a most basic problem, for without it the rights of individuals have no chance of being secured.[1] The choice is always between better and worse forms (and practices) of government; consider that the Articles of Confederation were a problem to which the *better* government of the Constitution was the solution.

The Constitution was superior in large part because of its provision for energy in government, which, as James Madison wrote in *Federalist No. 37*, "is essential to that security against external and internal danger . . . which enter[s] into the very definition of good government."[2] The framers understood the executive as the source of "energy in government," and they expected it especially in the context of national security. Alexander Hamilton said as much in *Federalist No. 70*: "The actual conduct of foreign negotiations, . . . the arrangement of the army and navy, the direction of the operations of war—these, and other matters of a like nature, constitute what seems to be most properly understood by the administration of government."[3] Today we would say that all of this constitutes national security leadership.

Notwithstanding the unnuanced rhetoric of his First Inaugural, Reagan at a general but quite important level supplied such leadership for the nation, thereby affirming the importance of government and of his own office in particular. In fact, in retrospect, Reagan can be said to have assumed the mantle of national security leadership at the outset of his presidency. As Martin Anderson has pointed out in *Revolution*, Reagan's *first* priority was to rebuild America's military strength, the *second* to rebuild its economic strength.[4] The first (which, by the way, meant *more* government in terms of government expenditures) could not be pursued, however, until the second was—hence Reagan's early effort to revive the economy. And for Reagan, as he took office, rebuilding America's military strength was not an end in itself but a strategic means—to the ends of averting nuclear war and even helping cause the demise of communism.

Reagan's leadership on this obviously critical score should be more recognized than it often has been in accounts of his tenure.[5] But it is a mistake to credit Reagan in this vital respect without also recognizing and learning from his failure to provide, from the very beginning of his presidency onwards, leadership of a more systematic and institutional kind, that is, within the executive branch. Carnes Lord, author of *The*

*President and the Management of National Security*, defines this kind of leadership in terms of "the conceptualization of strategy in a form that is practically useful, and a sustained effort at giving it operational reality through monitoring its implementation and imposing penalties for failure."[6] "Strategic leadership," as Lord puts it, requires an interest in government, indeed a commitment to government in an institutional sense, that Reagan often lacked.[7]

Writing in the wake of the Iran-contra affair, Lord, who served on the National Security Council from 1981 to 1984, surveyed the problems that were symptomatic of Reagan's failure to grasp the reins of the national security bureaucracy and provide the necessary leadership. These included the persisting difficultly in coping effectively with international terrorism or its sponsors despite the administration's early, publicly stated commitment to do so; the bureaucratic delays in providing U.S. assistance in the form of anti-air missiles and other munitions to the Mujahideen in Afghanistan; the uncertain approach to the political-military situation in Lebanon, which led to the bombing of the Marine contingent in Beirut that killed 211 U.S. soldiers; the misguided arms-for-hostages initiative that became the first half of the Iran-contra affair; the policy toward Nicaragua that vacillated between containment of the Sandinistas and confrontation; weaknesses in U.S. intelligence and counterintelligence that were exposed in, for example, the Moscow embassy scandal; bureaucratic disarray (seen in the constant quarreling between State and Defense) in the development of arms control policy, which ultimately created the conditions in which the highest officials made spasmodic, ad hoc decisions; the inadequate preparation for the Reykjavik summit in late 1986 (the Joint Chiefs of Staff did not have an opportunity to review the military implications of the President's proposal to eliminate all U.S. and Soviet nuclear-armed ballistic missiles within ten years); and systematic weaknesses in the U.S. defense establishment—even the successful Grenada operation suffered from interservice competition, command and communications failures, and inept planning.[8]

Reagan was by no means the first President to offer weak institutional leadership. As Lord observes, the problem has existed, to one degree or another, since the United States assumed its central role in world events a half century ago. Yet writing in the *Washington Post* in late 1986, Zbigniew Brzezinski, President Carter's National Security Adviser, concluded that under Reagan "the decision-making process at the very top is institutionally more fragmented than at any point since World War II." Brzezinski's observation that Reagan "has not imposed a top-down decision-making system" remained accurate for the balance of his tenure.[9] While it applied most emphatically to the national security bureaucracy, it also applied, to one degree or another, to the rest of the executive branch.

Reagan's approach to managing the executive branch has not lacked for publicity. The President himself summarized it in an interview with *Fortune* two months before the public disclosure in 1986 of the Iran arms deal: "Surround yourself with the best people you can find, delegate authority, and don't interfere as long as the policy you've decided upon is being carried out."[10] Drawing upon his experience in California as Governor, Reagan saw himself as the chairman of the board—his cabinet. Fixated by the idea of "cabinet government," Reagan thought he could appoint "the best people" to head the departments and agencies, bring them to the White House in cabinet sessions where he would make decisions after seeking their advice and counsel, and then send them out to do his bidding.

But "cabinet government" was for Reagan and will be for any President a will-o-the-wisp. The reasons are evident to anyone who has spent much time in Washington. Forces opposing the President's views—in the bureaucracy, Congress, and the press, and among the various interest groups—pull on even those department heads who share the President's views, undermining efforts to achieve policy unity in the executive. Understandably a President will try to retain control over the choices for subcabinet positions. But the same forces work on subcabinet executives as on their superiors. This is not to deny the imperative of making a concerted effort to pick the best "instruments of execution," a subject discussed in Chapter 9. But no President should forgo the effort to establish close to him an institutional counterbalance. Needed, within the White House, are strong mechanisms by which the President can translate his views into coherent policies and then superintend their implementation throughout the executive branch—by those well-chosen (he must hope) instruments of execution.

It became clear early in the Reagan administration that the President's "cabinet government" philosophy could not work and needed institutional supplements. Chief among other things, five subcabinet groups called cabinet councils were created (a sixth was added later). Each focused on a specific area involving the economy or domestic policy. But the councils, which Reagan nominally chaired but seldom attended, proved almost as ineffectual as the formal cabinet meetings and were discontinued in the second term. So it was that, for the most part, the huge task of helping Reagan manage the executive branch fell, in the first term, to the triumvirate of James Baker, Michael Deaver, and Edwin Meese and, in the second, to Don Regan (the Chief of Staff). Thus, Reagan never established the strong White House systems that his idea of cabinet government implicitly rejected but which his own experience had counseled the need for.

In regard to national security, Reagan did have a White House system in place when he took office—the National Security Council, created by statute in 1947. But in keeping with his belief in "cabinet government," Reagan, who like many of his predecessors knew less about foreign affairs than domestic issues, purposely downgraded the NSC apparatus, criticized during the 1970s for taking on too much authority. Reagan's first National Security Adviser, Richard Allen, was amenable to a deemphasis of the NSC and its staff, and even recommended it. In a dubious departure from past practice but a sign of the new dispensation, Allen did not report directly to the President but through Edwin Meese III, and he could never be sure whether his memos were passed by Meese to the President.[11] Allen was the first of several weak appointees to a weakened position, including Bud McFarlane, who claims that on one occasion Reagan could not even remember his name, and John Poindexter, who would testify after leaving office that he decided not to seek presidential approval for diverting funds to the contras from the arms sales to Iran, that he took this action on his own.

Reagan's notorious preference for policy-making by consensus and his dislike of conflict only contributed to the weak national security presidency that his misguided belief in "cabinet government" and in a reduced role for the NSC would have produced in any event. As it happened, Reagan typically did not get agreement but just the opposite from cabinet heads holding national security portfolios. George Shultz at State and Caspar Weinberger at Defense often were at odds—on arms control and the Soviet Union, on Lebanon, on Central America. Hoping for harmony, Reagan was inclined, as Lou Cannon has put it, "to please all the principal players on his team, even when their objectives were incompatible."[12] Thus he often would split the differences, even when this resulted in ill-defined policy. Lebanon is a case in point. Reagan's two secretaries of state—first Alexander M. Haig, Jr., and then Shultz—constantly disagreed with Defense Secretary Weinberger on both the ends and means of U.S. policy, and Reagan typically sought a middle ground that was dubious policy but nonetheless satisfied him because it seemed to soften the differences among subordinates.[13] Reagan's wish to avoid disharmony also led him to leave to contending subordinates what he thought were mere "details" but which were often the essence of policy. Reagan thus ensured further conflict not only at the cabinet level but down below, in the bureaucracies themselves. Often, too, Reagan simply neglected to oversee the implementation of policy. "What was missing," says Jeane Kirkpatrick, who served during Reagan's first term as U.S. Ambassador to the United States, "was follow-through. . . . What was missing was the President saying, 'Now do it, or do it this way. Cut it out. Don't do that.' "[14]

Leaving to Reagan biographers to explore why he so disliked conflict and so wanted to please others, it is obvious this President's approach to managing national security issues (if one may say he "managed" them at all) cannot be recommended. Disagreement among top officials is not to be avoided; it can be productive, provided that the President disciplines himself enough to reason his way to the best possible policy. Beyond this, however, there is the critical institutional point: No President should deny himself, as Reagan did, a strong White House system for managing national security. Indeed, given the President's constitutional responsibility in this area, such a system is imperative.

In his book, *The Presidency and the Management of National Security*, Carnes Lord has usefully articulated the steps the President should take to strengthen his control over the national security agencies and to lend greater strategic coherence to national security policy.[15] The National Security Council is key. Its staff is presidential staff but should not be regarded as *personal* staff that does what the President wants independently of the State and Defense departments, and other parts of the national security bureaucracy. Neither should it be seen as just another national security agency, with no distinctive role in interagency policy deliberations. Nor should it be viewed, as it most often has been, as a unit that simply coordinates what the various agencies do; that is a prescription for letting the bureaucracy do whatever it wants to do.

As Lord argues, the right way to conceive the role of the NSC is in terms of how it can help the President in carrying out his constitutional responsibilities. The nation's security may be threatened by forces within or without; national security is a term that most broadly signifies the President's responsibility under the Constitution. Still, much of what we mean by national security encompasses foreign affairs, which, together with defense and intelligence, are what Lord calls the "core areas." The agencies with primary responsibility for each are, respectively, the State Department, the Defense Department, and the Central Intelligence Agency. Like the Secretaries of State and Defense, the U.S Ambassador to the United Nations is a member of the cabinet, although the ambassador's staff is part of State. The Agency for International Development (whose focus is economic assistance) and the Arms Control and Disarmament Agency work closely with State. The Energy Department has responsibilities related to the development of nuclear weapons. In addition to its principal responsibility for defense, the Pentagon has important intelligence duties. The Federal Bureau of Investigation has obligations for domestic security and counterintelligence. Beyond the core areas, on the periphery of national security, lie certain scientific and technological issues, mobilization and emergency planning, and space policy. A variety of other cabinet departments and subcabinet agencies are engaged in these tasks.

The various departments and agencies each have their own missions, and they are surrounded by unique communities of interest. The advice each offers the President may therefore be limited. But the President needs strategic thinking that transcends the perspectives of the departments and agencies. Because his policy, as ultimately formulated, may be in conflict with what a department or agency might have preferred, oversight of the bureaucracy in its execution of policy is necessary.

These, then, are the two main tasks of the NSC: strategic planning and ensuring the implementation of policy. The President must give the NSC the authority to do these tasks, and the President must communicate the fact of that authority to cabinet officers and other top officials. The President must establish clear ground rules by which his national security apparatus will work, and he must be willing to enforce them.

The President's management of national security issues—like his management of other parts of the executive branch—depends in the final analysis upon him. But that is as it should be under a Constitution in which the executive power is vested in a single person.

The temptation for those Presidents who regard themselves as especially capable in national security affairs is that they will effectively dispense with the NSC and rely instead on their own contacts and skills. George Bush is an example. His NSC staff is a relatively weak one, and Brent Scowcroft, his National Security Adviser, is more a personal adviser than an institutional manager or strategic thinker. Instead of relying on a strong NSA and NSC staff, Bush has worked informally with Secretary of State James Baker and his aides, and whomever else they recruit. While the Bush approach facilitates "secrecy and dispatch," qualities Hamilton prized in a President, its manifest weakness is institutional; for if no one in this group is aware of an issue, it is probably being left to the permanent bureaucracy to manage as it sees best. So it happened in the months leading up to Iraq's invasion of Kuwait. As reported by the *Wall Street Journal*'s Paul Gigot, writing in *The National Interest*, while there was some sentiment within the State Department to harden U.S. policy towards an increasingly menacing Saddam Hussein, that message never made it to the informal group managing Bush's foreign policy.[16] Had Bush been served by a strong NSC able to see the entire radar screen of foreign policy—had he disciplined himself enough to insist upon one—he might have been advised in a way that would have resulted in a shift in U.S. policy towards containment of Saddam's bellicose intentions in the Middle East. In that event, the U.S. government might have communicated a different message to Saddam than the tragically laconic one April Glaspie delivered on the eve of his invasion of Kuwait: "We have no opinion on the Arab-Arab conflicts, like your border disagreement with Kuwait."

Liberals and conservatives alike often tend to think of a strong presidency in terms of the President's charisma and skills. And certainly the personal qualities an individual brings to the job will affect his tenure, for better or worse. It is, however, an office to which every President is elected, and he must attend to its institutional aspects if he is to provide the leadership the Constitution uniquely expects of him.

# 14

# EXECUTIVE ETHICS
## A Presidential Responsibility

I return now to the fact that while the government is administered by others—not directly by the President—it is nonetheless the President who under the Constitution is responsible for what those others do.[1] They are *his* instruments of execution. The President is responsible for not only their actual job performance but also their behavior in office. Both for the sake of the office he swears to execute and the laws he swears to uphold, he must address allegations of malfeasance. This is not his only or highest duty, of course. Demands of national security may conflict with the duty to enforce the criminal law. But most cases of alleged misconduct do not implicate national security or other important considerations. That is why charges of malfeasance usually demand resolution on their own terms. Most of the time, the issue for a

President is, or should be: "How should I respond on the merits to this allegation?" The answer is, it depends. It depends on many things, beginning with the specificity, credibility, and seriousness of the charge. But the one invariable is the President's responsibility for responding to the allegation.

In light of the large body of law developed over two centuries, the Take Care Clause has especially important implications for the President and his responsibility to address allegations of wrongdoing made against his subordinates. Today there are three kinds of law the President is responsible for enforcing upon executive officials: law applying to all citizens; law applying to all government officials; and law applying only to the executive branch (or only to certain parts of it). Presidential subordinates handle most allegations of misconduct made against executive officials, pursuant to the relevant law, whether civil or criminal. While only the exceptional case comes or should come to the President for any decision, he nonetheless is responsible for the faithful execution of the relevant laws throughout the executive branch.

The Constitution does not leave executive-branch ethics to the President alone. Congress exclusively possesses the impeachment power, and through its use and other means it can attempt to expose malfeasance and prod Presidents and cabinet members to do their duties under relevant law. (Of course, as the full stretch of our political history shows, Congress can also take unjustified "ethics" aim, often for purely partisan reasons, at a President or a cabinet member.) Still, it is the President who has the immediate responsibility for executive ethics. When President Washington confronted his Secretary of State with charges of treasonous behavior and fired him (unjustifiably, as it turned out), he was acting in accord with this understanding of presidential duty. So was President Garfield, almost a century later, when he insisted that his Attorney General investigate criminal charges against his presidential campaign manager (who was indicted and ultimately acquitted). So was his successor, President Cleveland, when he demanded a conflict-of-interest investigation of his Attorney General (who was not charged with any wrongdoing).[2] There are many examples, just as there are many examples on the other side, as consider Presidents

Buchanan, Grant, and Harding, who were generally lax when it came to responding to alleged misconduct on the part of top-ranking aides.

The Nixon presidency wrote a new chapter in the history of executive-branch malfeasance. No administration prior to Nixon's had escaped charges of misconduct as defined by contemporaneous ethics norms. But scandal had not dominated political life. In *Responses of the Presidents to Charges of Misconduct*, C. Vann Woodward compared allegations of malfeasance to "a slight cold or passing headache."[3] Nixon, of course, did not have a "cold" or a "headache"; he became the first President ever to resign from office. Since then, the political environment in which Presidents must take responsibility for their subordinates has changed so dramatically as to be almost qualitatively different. When President Bush said in a speech on ethics during his first week in office that "we are in a new era," he was guilty of understatement.

How we arrived in the new era is a story in itself—too long for these pages.[4] Suffice to say that from the mid-1960s on the presidency itself came to be more and more distrusted, thanks in large part to Vietnam and Watergate.[5] The balance of the 1970s was devoted to institutional reforms largely directed at the so-called "imperial presidency."[6] Of increasing concern to many reformers were executive-branch conflicts of interest, real and apparent.

Such concern proceeds from unassailable principle, namely that public office is a public trust.[7] Regulation against conflict of interest thus is regulation before the event. It is an effort to prevent the actual crime of violating the public trust; more precisely, it is an effort to prevent the temptation that might lead to such crime.[8] Concern about conflict of interest dates back to the original Constitution itself.[9] And the first Congress passed a law forbidding the Treasury Secretary from investing in government securities, thus foreclosing any possible conflict of interest that might arise between the official's public and personal financial interests. Not until 1853, however, in response to the then prevailing "spoils system" did Congress enact the first major conflict-of-interest law, one of five passed over the next twenty years. Most of the provisions, all of which apply to members of the executive branch but only a few to Congress, impose criminal penalties. After World War II, public concern about conflict of interest intensified, thanks in large part to the growth of government and its expanding reach into the American economy. (The bigger the government, it seems, the more scandal we are likely to have.) In 1951 a Senate subcommittee recommended a tightening of conflict of interest restraints. And in 1953 the Senate Armed Services Committee forced Charles Wilson, president of General Motors whom President Eisenhower had nominated as Secretary of Defense, to dispose of his GM holdings as a price for confirmation.[10]

In 1965 President Johnson issued Executive Order 11222, which in critical ways defines the new era Bush referred to. The order covers a broader range of conduct than the criminal law and applies throughout (and only to) the executive branch. Executive officials are instructed to "avoid any action, whether or not specifically prohibited . . . which might result in, or create"—and here is the important phrase—"the appearance" of "using public office for private gain"; "giving preferential treatment to any organization or person"; "impeding government efficiency or economy"; "losing complete independence or impartiality of action"; "making a government decision outside of official channels"; or "affecting adversely the confidence of the public in the integrity of the government." Because the order officially ratifies "appearances"—and especially the appearance of a conflict of interest—as a matter of official concern, the perception of a situation has often become more important than the facts, both to formally designated ethics authorities and also to the press.

In the wake of Watergate, President Carter took additional steps to eliminate conflicts of interest and their appearance from the executive branch. Vowing to "restore the confidence of the American people in their own government," Carter laid down strict conflict-of-interest guidelines for top appointees, covering public disclosure of financial assets, divestiture of assets that could create conflicts of interest, and restrictions on post-government employment.[11] Congress codified the Carter guidelines in the Ethics in Government Act of 1978. This statute contained the new special prosecutor law. Empowering attorneys as no ordinary prosecutor ever has been, the statute has required investigation of allegations that in ordinary circumstances would not have been pursued.[12] Thanks in large part to this law, finding and prosecuting executive vice has come to be regarded as an almost absolute good in our political culture.[13]

The impulse to exhaustive investigation and prosecution characterizes the "new era" in executive-branch ethics. What assists the pursuit of alleged wrongdoing are requirements that officials disclose unprecedented amounts of personal and financial information.[14] The Watergate-educated press is eager to convey and investigate further this information.[15]

While Congress has become the subject of increasing ethics concern—what with the forced resignations of House Speaker Jim Wright and Majority Whip Tony Coelho, the "Keating Five," and the House bank and Post Office scandals—this fact does not eliminate the need a President has for intelligently coping in this new era. Ronald Reagan provides a case study of a President whose ethics strategy was plainly inadequate. In his history of the first two Reagan years, Laurence Barrett of *Time* magazine wrote that "if you judged only by headlines, the Reagan administration supplied as much grist as the scandal mills of Washington could handle."[16] For example, a $1,000 gratuity intended for the First Lady was intercepted by the President's first National Security Adviser, Richard Allen, placed in a safe, and then apparently forgotten; a small amount of money, and no apparent evil, but the administration had an "appearance" problem. Another example involved Attorney General Smith, who accepted a $50,000 severance bonus from a steel company. Smith had served on its board of directors, but he took the money soon *after* becoming Attorney General—an act of jaywalking in the new era. Smith quickly returned the money once the stories cascaded in upon him, explaining that he wished to "dispel all of the concerns raised in the press." Also, an independent counsel was named—the first in the Reagan years—to review corruption charges against Labor Secretary Ray Donovan (relating to matters occurring before he took office). Still, as Barrett put it, the first Reagan years contained no "red-meat scandal," no Watergate.[17]

In 1984, the new ethics era began manifesting a more partisan side as congressional Democrats used charges of malfeasance against the Reagan executive. Edwin Meese, Reagan's choice to succeed Smith as Attorney General, had his 1984 confirmation hearings effectively postponed for a year because of allegations of wrongdoing first made by Senate Judiciary Committee Democrats. An independent counsel reviewed some eleven charges involving Meese's financial affairs and his financial disclosure forms, finding no basis for prosecution. In 1985, the Democratic majority on the House Judiciary Committee composed a 1,200-page report on congressional testimony given by the Justice Department's Theodore B. Olson that led to an independent counsel investigation (but no prosecution).

The administration endured much rougher ethics weather in the second term. In 1986, Michael Deaver and Lyn Nofziger, both now in the private sector, were accused of violating the 1978 addition to the criminal code that prohibited lobbying within a year after leaving the government; independent counsels were duly appointed, and Deaver was eventually convicted of perjury. Nofziger was convicted of violating the lobbying ban. (On appeal, his conviction was overturned: the law was said to be vague.) In the final years of the Reagan administration, there was the independent counsel investigation of Iran-contra and a second independent counsel investigation of Ed Meese. The partisan criticism of Reagan increased. In 1987 Senator Dale Bumpers, the Arkansas Democrat, declared, "I doubt seriously whether any administration has had more people leave under disgrace or indictment." In 1988 Representative Patricia Schroeder, a Democrat from Colorado, publicized a list of 242 "individuals appointed by or serving in the Reagan administration who have been the subject of charges of unethical conduct."[18] Finally, in 1989, details of criminal wrongdoing involving political as well as career officials at Housing and Urban Development became public, leading to an independent counsel investigation.

Had Reagan known beforehand about his own tenure what Bush had been able to observe, he might have administered the office in regard to ethics as his successor did, announcing early on an "ethics week," giving a major public speech, insisting on the most ethical conduct from his top aides, and emphasizing that they should insist on the same from their subordinates. Leadership of this kind would not have prevented the special prosecutor investigation (commenced in late 1981) of Labor Secretary Raymond Donovan, because the conduct at issue occurred *before* Donovan entered the government. On the other hand, the kind of concerns that would have led Reagan to adopt such an ethics strategy might have led him to appoint someone other than Donovan. In any event, it is probable that such a strategy would have worked a preventive effect.

Putting to one side the Iran-contra affair, whose complicated roots include presidential failure to administer foreign policy and bitter political division between Congress and the executive over Central America (and which is discussed in Chapters 6 and 16), whether all of the other "ethics" problems would have been avoided is obviously doubtful. One reason is human nature. Another is that the ethics culture in the 1980s was such that almost all the precautions imaginable would not have prevented certain "scandals" from happening. The obvious example is the independent counsel investigation of Theodore Olson, who served as one of Reagan's top legal advisers from 1981 through 1984. Olson was investigated solely as a result of congressional testimony he gave regarding an assertion of executive privilege; there was never a hint of any personal corruption on Olson's part. Congressional Democrats effectively compelled a criminal inquiry that but for the political use of the independent counsel statute would never have occurred.

Still, had Reagan exerted leadership, he would almost surely have prevented some of the ethics problems his administration later encountered, which weakened his ability to govern. A Reagan gospel on executive ethics could have fostered a different atmosphere within the administration. Consider the difference Reagan might have made had he said, in enough speeches to drive home his points, that executive branch officials have a responsibility to behave in a way that brings credit rather than disrepute upon the office; that perceptions matter because faith in government is often a matter of perception as much as reality; and that he expects his officials always to act in ways that are above suspicion. Consider, too, had he said that he expected the heads of departments and agencies to enforce the highest standards upon both political and career officials. And consider, finally, had Reagan made his gospel on executive ethics a fundamental of *conservative* political faith. The virtues necessary to avoid ethics violations, as defined in the "new era," probably would have been in greater supply. There would have been more awareness of the ethics rules, more caution about actions subject to unfriendly interpretation, more prudence in the way relationships were carried on with private friends and associates. It is hard to believe there would not have been more displays of common sense, more instances of good judgment, more executive ethics, as the rules and regulations define it. Reagan thus could have taken better care of the presidential office and the execution of the laws. And had he done so, he would have been better positioned, politically, to defend "the constitutional rights" of the executive in the legislative battle over reauthorization of the independent counsel law. Thus, the proper administration of office could have assisted the President in a case of legislative governance—and self-defense.

To say that Reagan should have properly administered the office in respect to ethics is probably to ask for a different President. Ethics, for Reagan, suggested the problem of big government. In speech after speech, over three decades, Reagan had observed that big government resulted in waste, fraud, and abuse. Reagan had a point, but he was unable to admit the possibility of malfeasance or even of poor judgment on the part of those who worked for him. Reagan biographer Lou Cannon observes that Reagan "assumed that everyone who worked for him was of the highest caliber."[19] That explains why Reagan felt he did not need to remind them to behave ethically or act wisely. It also explains why—to cite perhaps the most egregious ethics lapse during the Reagan years—the Department of Housing and Urban Development, ostensibly managed by people of the highest caliber, could produce Republican forms of waste, fraud, and abuse, leading Jack Kemp, newly arrived at HUD to clean up after Sam Pierce, to say that "those who criticized big government only to make money off of it are guilty of hypocrisy."[20]

Having failed to provide a gospel on ethics, Reagan also

failed to discharge his duty under the Constitution in taking responsibility when charges of malfeasance were leveled at his aides. On those occasions, Reagan typically defended them by saying that the allegations constituted an attack on him. This defense was often used by conservatives during the 1980s. But while it is sometimes true that ethics charges are simply politics by other means, conservatives and others who mount such a defense must be willing to apply autonomous critical standards. Otherwise, they will have no basis for ethics other than partisan politics, and they will cede the moral high ground to their opponents.

An important reason for having a strategy that will prevent or at least reduce the kind of ethics problems that can arise in the new era is that they drain energy from the executive, weakening the presidency both institutionally and politically. This, and the critical importance of good judgment, are the main lessons to be drawn from the two ethics cases involving one of Reagan's closest aides, Edwin Meese III.[21]

Consider the first investigation of Meese, in 1984. Had Meese not been nominated to succeed Smith, he would not have come under formal ethics scrutiny; his political opponents in Congress would not have been motivated to call for one. At the same time, Meese's own actions, when measured by the new standards, created an opening his opponents were quick to exploit. Meese's wife had borrowed $15,000, interest-free, to buy stock. Meese had failed to report the loan on his financial disclosure forms. Meese also had offered the man who lent the money a job as one of his White House assistants. The independent counsel found no evidence that this and other loans the Meeses received from various people who later got federal jobs were bribes for the positions. Meese meanwhile indicated he had drawn lessons for himself. This experience, he said in a public statement, "has taught me a great deal about the special circumstances of official life in Washington and the need for constant vigilance and sensitivity, not only to actual conduct but also to how conduct may be perceived." During the confirmation hearing in early 1985, Meese sounded the same themes as he told the Senate Judiciary Committee that he had learned a great deal "about how people view things, or how people might view things."

And I can assure you [Meese continued] that I have a much higher level of sensitivity to these matters now than I did when I arrived in Washington. And I can assure you that I would take great pains to avoid any kind of a situation or circumstance that might give rise to a misunderstanding or misinterpretation of my acts or what I intended.

Meese had been inattentive to ethics rules and, by his own admission, insensitive to "appearances." He had offered a job to someone to whom he and his wife were in debt, an offer that could be construed by others in a negative light. Obviously, the better judgment would have been to avoid a relationship subject to harsh assessment.[22] Meese had been sloppy; he had, in effect, left a shirt-tail hanging out—where it was easily reached by political opponents.

Before Meese spoke his repentant words before the Judiciary Committee, he already had behaved in a way that would in time attract the attention of a second independent counsel. While White House Counselor in 1981, Meese was approached by his close friend, E. Robert Wallach, who asked him to help a private corporation, the Welbilt Electronic Die Corporation (later called Wedtech), obtain a government contract. Meese agreed to help, and through aides, assisted Welbilt in procuring the contract. In early 1987 company officials who had pleaded guilty to certain crimes tried to implicate Meese in the scandal then enveloping Wedtech. In May 1987 independent counsel James McKay began an investigation into whether Meese had violated federal conflict of interest laws. By late fall McKay had substantially concluded his inquiry. Still, consistent with the post-Watergate impulse to investigate exhaustively, as would not have been done in ordinary circumstances, McKay broadened his inquiry into other aspects of Meese's public and private life, most of them involving his friend Bob Wallach, who in 1989 was convicted and sentenced to six years in federal prison for Wedtech-related activities. (On appeal Wallach's conviction was reversed on grounds that the government's main witness had perjured himself.) Various new questions were probed over the winter of 1987 and the spring of 1988; media leaks became routine.

Finally, in July 1988, when McKay filed his sealed report with the special court, Meese held a press conference to announce both his complete "vindication" and intention to resign. When the McKay report was unsealed, however, the public learned its conclusion that Meese had "probably" committed crimes (notably, and characteristically of the new era, the putative crimes were *not* related to the original Wedtech inquiry) but that prosecution was not warranted.[23] Soon thereafter a former Meese aide, William Weld, who headed Justice's Criminal Division until early 1988 (and in 1990 was elected Governor of Massachusetts), told a Senate panel that had *he* been the prosecutor, he would have presented the case to the grand jury for indictment. In early September, the Office of Government Ethics, apparently infuriated by Meese's use of the word "vindication," issued a lengthy statement drawing on Executive Order 11222. OGE faulted Meese for, among other things, "inattention" to new ethics rules and a failure to take "care" that "acts are not misinterpreted." "A major purpose of this memorandum," said OGE, "is to remind and inform that simply avoiding criminal conduct is not the mark of public service. The duties imposed by non-criminal standards are far harder to discharge. They may even be strange and seem overly restrictive . . . [but] they must not be ignored." Finally, Meese's successor, Richard Thornburgh, issued the Justice Department's own internal ethics agency's report, which concluded that Meese violated both Executive Order 11222 and the Department's own Standards of Conduct.

Had Meese exercised better judgment in his relationships with Bob Wallach, the second independent counsel probably would not have been triggered, and there would have been no piling on Meese by Weld, the OGE, or Thornburgh. The supplication of a close friend is often the most easily acted upon and the least easily resisted. In the new era, however, one must beware even, or especially, a friend's entreaties. Again, good judgment is essential.

There are costs to staying in office while under investigation, as Meese did.[24] One is to personal reputation, since everything written about the investigation receives more publicity than it would otherwise. A second cost—and, from the standpoint of the presidency, a more important one—is institutional. On December 1, 1987, when McKay had basically concluded his inquiry into the Wedtech matter, Meese's attorneys asked that he announce the end of the investigation. They argued that it was "in the national interest that public speculation over the prospects of the person occupying this office be laid to rest promptly. The Attorney Generalship and the Department of Justice would be improvidently harmed if public speculation is permitted to endure any longer than is absolutely necessary." This statement recognized that the person cannot be separated from the position, that investigation of the leader of a cabinet agency can damage the institution. That happened in this case. The harmful impact of the investigation and of the speculation about Meese was felt less in the department's routine work than in its ability to advance initiatives—to govern. "Meese's own clout, as a result of his troubles, is, if possible, even lower than the rest of the Administration," wrote *National Review* in June 1988. "The Meese Justice Department has been one of the vanguards of conservatism in Reagan's Washington . . . consistently advancing good people and good causes. Its ability to do this down the homestretch, while Meese is focused on his personal battle royale, is nil."[25]

A third cost is political. Meese's presence in office became an increasing political liability to the President, and the liability effectively transferred to George Bush in his bid for the presidency. Meese's resignation came on the eve of the Republican Convention.[26] Future Presidents will surely want aides who leave office at least when Meese did. But future Presidents also must rethink the Reagan policy—basically that no official should resign unless indicted—under which Meese stayed in office. The better course for a President would be to indicate, at the start of an administration, that heads of departments (if not also White House aides) under independent counsel investigation must take a leave of absence for the sake of energetic government.

The cost to energetic government of the two investigations of Meese can be measured in the sands of time. Meese could have served fifty-eight months as Attorney General, from March 1984 to January 1989. He lost the first eleven months because of the first independent counsel investigation. He spent some fourteen months of his actual tenure under the cloud of the second investigation. And he left office five months before the end of the administration—probably earlier than he would have but for the investigation. Meese served only twenty-eight months free of criminal investigation; twenty-eight out of a possible total of fifty-eight in office, less than half.

If better judgment on Meese's part could have prevented the investigations that interrupted and diminished his public service, better ethics management on the President's part might have produced from Meese the necessary prudence and, in consequence, a stronger presidency. As is true with other matters, so with executive ethics: The ultimate responsibility lies with the President.

# 15

# BAD BEHAVIOR REWARDED
## The Stockman Story

The President is responsible for behavior on the part of his aides that compromises the conditions of energetic government. Incompetence on the job, malfeasance as defined by the ethics laws, and bad judgment can do that. But other kinds of behavior also drain away energy—for example, presidential aides who speak against a President's policies to Congress or the press. David Stockman provides a case in point.

Stockman was the child prodigy of the Reagan administration. Only thirty-four and already a two-term congressman when President Reagan appointed him in 1981 to head the Office of Management and Budget, Stockman managed within his first weeks on the job to conduct a comprehensive review of the fiscal year 1982 budget and to secure approval for much of it on Capitol Hill. Drawing on his enormous knowledge of

the budget and huge reserves of energy, Stockman, a libertarian conservative, rapidly became the President's central
economic policymaker and was widely seen as one of the administration's most able figures. *Newsweek*, in a typical acco-
lade, marveled at his "buzz-saw intellect." By year's end,
however, Stockman had become a different story. It transpired
that from December 1980 through September 1981 Stockman
had periodically eaten breakfast with the *Washington Post*'s
William Greider at the Hay Adams Hotel, a block from the
White House. Over eggs and bacon Stockman shared with
Greider his private thoughts about the effort to enact the President's tax and spending policies. The result was an article in
the December 1981 *Atlantic Monthly* that revealed Stockman's concerns and doubts about Reaganomics and his frus-
trations with the political process.[1] "None of us really
understands what's going on with all these numbers," he told
Greider at one point. "Kemp-Roth [the 1981 legislation that
cut marginal tax rates by 25%] was always a Trojan horse to
bring down the top [marginal income tax] rate," he also said.
And: "It's kind of hard to sell 'trickle down' . . . so the supply-
side formula was the only way to get a tax policy that was
really 'trickle down.' Supply side is 'trickle down' theory."[2]
"The Education of David Stockman," as the article was headlined, was Stockman's statement—some would say confession—that the very economic program he had worked to
establish was flawed. A gleeful Gary Hart read the entire
article into the *Congressional Record* as soon as it became
public in early November. The piece stunned Stockman's administration colleagues, but he was not asked to leave. Stockman grew obsessed with the mounting budget deficits, issuing
apocalyptic warnings about their impact upon the economy.
He became the administration's leading exponent of tax increases to close the widening gap between outlays and receipts. Finally leaving office in 1985, he published the
following year *The Triumph of Politics*, a deeply pessimistic
memoir in which he undertook to explain, as the subtitle had
it, *Why the Reagan Revolution Failed.*[3] By "the triumph of
politics," Stockman meant that the ordinary politics of our
system had blocked necessary spending cuts and stopped necessary revenue increases, letting the deficits grow and grow.

Stockman concluded that politicians of all stripes were unprincipled and self-interested but nonetheless accurate barometers of the electorate who protect the nation from zealots like himself. Stockman got an advance in excess of two million dollars and heavy gunfire from former colleagues—"a masterpiece of distortion" was how Martin Anderson described it.[4]

Stockman did not like government. He was an economic libertarian who saw government and the institutions of government, including the presidency and its bully pulpit, as things to be manipulated in order to further his ideology, his "Grand Doctrine," as he called it. "When his appointment as budget director first seemed likely," wrote William Greider in the *Atlantic*,

> he had agreed to meet with me from time to time and relate, off the record, his private account of the great political struggle ahead. The particulars of these conversations were not to be reported until later, after the season's battles were over, but a cynic familiar with how Washington works would understand that the arrangement had obvious symbiotic value. . . . I benefited from an informed view of policy discussions of the new administration; Stockman, a student of history, was contributing to history's record and perhaps influencing its conclusions. For him, our meetings were another channel—among many he used—to the press. The older generation of orthodox Republicans distrusted the press; Stockman was one of the younger "new" conservatives who cultivated contacts with columnists and reporters, who saw the news media as another useful tool in political combat. "We believe our ideas have intellectual respectability, and we think the press will recognize that," he said. "The traditional Republicans probably sensed, even if they didn't know it, that their ideas lacked intellectual respectability."[5]

In *The Triumph of Politics*, Stockman wrote that he used Greider, "a friend and a committed liberal" who had "an open mind," as a "sounding board week in and week out in order to test 'our' arguments and learn 'their' objections." He clearly wanted a story to be written, and it is clear that Greider had him pegged, correctly, as someone who wanted to use the press to advance his views. "We were engaged in a battle of ideas," wrote Stockman. "The Reagan Revolution could never be won unless the establishment, politicians and opinion makers gave our ideas a fair hearing. They had to be convinced. . . . Which was why I had been talking to Bill Greider." Stockman said he had a different understanding of the ground rules, actually a nonunderstanding. "[W]e had gotten so absorbed in the argument between our side and theirs that we hadn't clarified the ground rules about quotations." Stockman said he was "furious" at Greider for using the quotes, especially the one describing Kemp-Roth as a "trojan horse."[6] After the story broke, Greider told a reporter that in September Stockman had advised him that he could publish the article.

It is elementary that an executive officer should not only know the ground rules for engaging the media but also demonstrate prudence in talking to reporters, even on background or off the record. And it is elementary that such an officer be consistent in what he says. Stockman also ate breakfast in the first months of 1981 (and at the Hay Adams, evidently a Stockman hangout) with columnist Robert Novak. In 1986 Novak wrote that Stockman "had been telling William Greider almost exactly the opposite of what he had told me." "I could not tell," said Novak, "when David was or was not telling the truth."[7]

But the issues raised by Stockman's discussions with Greider go beyond these relatively simple matters. Should Stockman have been talking with Greider at all? There is a dark view of Stockman's intentions which holds that through publication of the article he wanted to "replace the President's [economic] program" with "a new one that had himself at the center."[8] Thus, when Stockman told Greider to publish, he did so because he thought he had won the internal administration fight over economic policy and that the President soon would propose cutting back substantially the tax-rate cut Congress had approved in the summer. Stockman thought the article, appearing at a time when he had prevailed within, would solidify the victory and repudiate once and for all the "crackpot theories" that had found "their way [Stockman told Greider] into the legislative channels."[9] Some who hold this view even have speculated that the ambitious Stockman was trying, through these means, to tout himself as someone of presidential material. As it happened, the President decided not to repudiate the Kemp-Roth tax cut. So when the article appeared in November, Stockman's comments about the tax cut came at a time when it was still intact, as it would in fact remain.

If the dark view of Stockman is true, if Stockman was that scheming, then he should have been relieved of his duties as soon as the article appeared. Yet even on a more benign reading of his breakfasting with Greider, on a reading that accepts as true his explanation of his purposes, he should have been dismissed. Granting that Stockman wanted to engage the battle of ideas through the media, he apparently never contemplated the risks involved. Quite apart from whether he might be misquoted, or quoted when he did not want to be— both important considerations—there was the President to consider, specifically whether what he, Stockman, might say would damage the President's ability to govern. After all, the President *is* his top aides. While achieving practical unity in the executive is always hard, the difficulty does not relieve the President or his aides of the duty at least to try.

In his memoir, Stockman shows no sign of having matured in his understanding of the kind of issue presented by his discussions with William Greider. There he excoriates fellow government officials for "leaking" to the press.[10] But he offers no principle by which one might define a leak or when it might be justified. For Stockman, the propriety of leaking evidently turns upon who does it, and whether the person's ideology is the correct one, not on any set of considerations that factor in the presidency itself. Stockman did not take the presidency seriously as an institution to be protected and preserved.

Seldom does experience so conclusively teach a lesson as do the Stockman breakfasts with William Greider. No one exercising the executive power should behave as Stockman did.[11] Nor should a President, faced with a Stockman-like situation, indulge such an aide, as Reagan did.

By all accounts, Reagan's top aides, with one exception,

wanted Stockman fired. The exception was Chief of Staff James Baker, who thought it would be harder for Reagan to run the government without Stockman, and who also believed firing Stockman would give credibility to what the budget director had told Greider, and perhaps even motivate him to become a leading outside critic of the administration.[12] Baker won out; Stockman stayed.

Lore has it that an angry President took the young Stockman to the "woodshed." But as we know from Stockman's memoir, among other sources, no such thing happened. Stockman had lunch with Reagan. The President did not flog but sympathized with Stockman, telling him he had been "a victim of sabotage by the press." He asked him to stay on, adding that "the fellas think this is getting out of control. They want you to write up a statement explaining all this and go before the press this afternoon."[13] Following Baker's instruction, Stockman simply made up the woodshed story, thus shifting media attention from the substance of what he had said to his loyalty. There was now the human story, that of the young aide who had been reprimanded but not fired by the kindly President he had embarrassed. And the colorful "woodshed" metaphor ensured that it would play in this way, as for example, it did in *Time*, whose headline was, "A Visit to the Woodshed." "I played out the script that the White House public relations men had designed," Stockman explained in his memoir. "And the *Atlantic* scandal soon faded away."[14]

Journalistic accounts of this episode written after 1986, and thus after Stockman had explained what really happened, typically include admiration for the administration's public relations skill. Consider the treatment by Hedrick Smith in *The Power Game*. "The way the Reagan White House handled those damaging revelations [Stockman's] is a classic lesson in snuffing out bad news before it damages the president."[15]

But that is not the lesson for those who wish faithfully to execute the presidential office. For one thing, there is the matter of honesty. Stockman lied, but his lie did not protect a life; by no stretch of the executive imagination could it have been justified. And James Baker was an accomplice in the deceit. No good purpose was served by their behavior. To the contrary, it damaged the presidency. While working in the near term to divert attention away from the substance of what Stockman had said, the woodshed story in the long run only encouraged disrespect for the President on the part of his top aides—as well as more anti-Reagan talk by those aides, to the press. Had the President dismissed Stockman, that would have sent a clear message throughout the administration that talk out of school, against the President and his programs, would not have been tolerated. It would have tightened up an administration that by the end of 1981 was splintering into factions that competed against each other through the press. This continued throughout Reagan's two terms, weakening the conditions of energetic government. Reagan's leaky vessel of state became so much a part of the Washington scene that an astounded Mark Shields, a liberal columnist, wrote in the January 14, 1983 *Washington Post* a piece titled, "Leak, Leak, Sink, Sink." "[T]he Democrats would love to take credit for the job done on Reagan. But they cannot. The unfavorable picture of Ronald Reagan has been created and developed by Ronald Reagan's own advisors." Shields observed that the unceasing attack upon the President from within his own ranks was "no tribute to the President's managerial duties." Or to his understanding of the office he held.

James David Barber's *The Presidential Character*, first published in 1972, has encouraged professional and lay observers alike to see Presidents in terms of certain personality "types" ("active-active, active-passive, passive-active, passive-passive").[16] One unfortunate consequence of his work is that it directs attention away from the institutional nature of the office and the behavior it demands on the part of both the President and his aides—whoever the President is, liberal or conservative, Democrat or Republican, and whoever his aides are. The original purpose of the presidency was in large part to provide the American government with the energy it lacked under the Articles of Confederation. An energetic independent executive was needed both to administer the government and to serve as a countervailing political force against Congress.[17] Energy was unquestionably the precious commodity in the new political order, and the issue that faces every strong President is how energy is most wisely used and most effectively protected under the Constitution.

Presidential aides must take care not to engage in behavior that damages unity in the presidency and compromises the conditions of energetic government. But it is the President who is ultimately responsible for such behavior. A President who comprehends this responsibility will be prepared to deal with aides whose behavior drains away energy. Self-defense is a presidential duty not just when bills usurping his powers are presented to him, and not just in the litigation of his constitutional rights, but also in the administration of his subordinates. Had Reagan seen his responsibility in November 1981, he would have disallowed the "woodshed" hoax and dismissed David Stockman.

Reagan's predisposition to see his aides as "victims" (recall that he thought Stockman a victim of the media) and to dismiss any ethics charges against them as politically motivated, cannot be recommended. A President must be willing to address the merits and, unless there are good reasons to the contrary, let the chips fall where they may. His reputation, his political effectiveness, and his faithfulness to the office are at stake.

# 16

# NON-ENERGY AND IRRESPONSIBILITY

## Iran-Contra

No book focused mainly on the Reagan and Bush administrations can omit the hyphenated scandal that emerged in public view in November 1986. I treat Iran-contra at this stage of the book (and briefly, for those exhausted by other analyses of the subject) because it usefully illustrates several points developed in Parts One and Two.

Let us begin by describing some basic facts, beginning with the Iran half of Iran-contra. It was President Reagan who wanted the release of the American hostages held in Beirut by Iranian terrorists. But when his State Department was unwilling to provide a strategy for achieving their release, he turned to his National Security Adviser, Robert McFarlane, who obliged him with a dubious scheme begun when the President agreed to authorize a dialogue with ostensibly moderate Iranian officials likely to contend for power in the event of the death of the Ayatollah Khomeini; these officials had contacts with the terrorists in Beirut. As a show of U.S. good faith, and on the advice of the Israelis, Iran, then fighting Iraq, was to get weapons. Thus, in 1985 Israel sold arms to Iran (on the understanding that the United States would replenish its stock), and then in 1986 the United States sold weapons directly. The hope was that the Iranian officials would persuade the terrorists in Beirut to release the American hostages. Three American hostages eventually were freed as a result of this covert operation, although new hostages were also taken.

As for the contra half, it was the NSC staff that came up with what its principal originator, Oliver North, called "the neat idea" of overcharging for the arms sales in order to divert this "profit" to the contras at a time when Congress was cutting off U.S. aid. Through this means (as well as others), North and those working with him covertly tried to keep the contras alive—a goal they knew was the President's, although Reagan always denied knowledge of the funds diversion.

The Iran half of Iran-contra was bound to have been controversial. It contradicted publicly stated administration policy that the United States would not make any concessions for the release of hostages on grounds that to do so would encourage even more hostage taking. It also conflicted with official rhetoric, as the administration had encouraged other nations to observe the American arms embargo against Iran, in place since 1979, and generally to punish terrorism and refuse to negotiate with terrorists. In 1984 Secretary of State George Shultz had designated Iran a sponsor of international terrorism, and in June 1985, just before the United States commenced its involvement in the arms sales, the President himself, commenting on the hijacking of a TWA airliner by Shiite terrorists, said: "The United States gives terrorists no rewards and makes no prisoners. We make no concessions. We make no deals." Once the story of the Iran arms sales broke, in early November 1986, Congress and the news media pursued the various contradictions, with the President himself maintaining that there had been no swapping of arms for hostages.

The funds diversion was bound to have been even more controversial, as it touched the volatile politics of U.S. foreign policy in Central America. As discussed in Chapter 6, Congress was sharply divided on the issue of contra aid, expressing itself in the various Boland amendments. When the Reagan administration revealed the funds diversion in late November, the Iran story graduated into the Iran-contra scandal. Neither half of Iran-contra would not have occurred under a strong President.

While it was the National Security Council staff that hatched both the Iran initiative and the funds diversion to the contras, it was the President himself who created the circumstances in which the agency rose to such dubious prominence. The President intentionally weakened the NSC, assigning principal responsibility for developing foreign policy to the State Department. But Reagan did not insist that State and the rest of the national security apparatus provide a better way of getting the hostages released than the NSC staff advised. So Reagan wound up effectively ceding the matter to this agency.[1] The various formal investigations of the Iran initiative concluded that it was badly executed, a result that could have been predicted given the downgrading of the NSC staff.[2] Reagan himself had only a hazy understanding of the Iran initiative and was unaware of many aspects of its implementation or their potential consequences. He did not demand a review of the progress of the initiative; he did not hold those engaged in the effort accountable, nor did he demand more involvement from his Secretaries of State and Defense. "I may not have asked enough questions about how the Iranian initiative was being conducted," Reagan has observed, indicting his national security leadership.[3] Meanwhile, having signed into law without protest the third Boland amendment (as discussed in Chapter 6), yet also wanting to sustain the contras, Reagan effectively produced a situation in which a subordinate like Oliver North could believe that diverting funds from the arms sales to the contras was indeed a "neat idea."

The problem at the root of the Iran-contra affair was not so much the existence of some "rogue government" operating beyond the law, but an absence of the kind of government that only a strong President can provide. In this instance, such a President would have made clear his differences with Congress when the Continuing Appropriations Act for 1985 was sent to him (and indeed far before then). Administratively, such a President would have established and empowered a strong NSC staff to help him think strategically and oversee the implementation of his policies. Such a staff would not have indulged Reagan's weaknesses for those held hostage in Beirut by obliging him with the hair-brained scheme of selling arms to Iran; nor would it have decided on its own authority simply to shift some of the profits from those sales to the beleaguered freedom-fighters in Central America.

The weakness of the Reagan presidency extended down through the ranks. National Security Adviser John Poindexter (McFarlane's successor) should have understood the Iran initiative's potential for controversy and that diverting funds from the arms sales to help the contras would only add to it. Poindexter was a technician, not a strategist, and he had little political savvy. He should have recognized that the President should have been given the chance to judge for himself whether or not to undertake such an execution of office. Poindexter's apparently unilateral decision to approve the transfer of profits from the arms sales to the contras demonstrated more than anything else his unfitness for the position to which Reagan had appointed him. A presidential aide should not act as Poindexter did in approving the funds diversion; to do so is effectively to usurp the executive power that the Constitution vests only in the President. Such acts violate the political ethic for which there is no criminal penalty, but which lies at the heart of any serious understanding of the presidency.

Poindexter is an easy choice for a whipping, as are North and McFarlane. But the heads of the two main executive departments—George Shultz, the Secretary of State, and Caspar Weinberger, the Secretary of Defense—added to the weakness of Reagan's national security presidency by distancing themselves from the Iran initiative. Both men had an obligation to monitor the implementation of a policy they had disagreed with and to seek changes in it as they saw fit—or else consider resigning. They did not do that, choosing instead to remain in the state of relative ignorance that the NSC staff preferred for them. The minority report of the Iran-contra congressional committees aptly observed:

> If a top official cannot honestly serve his President
> ... raising questions about implementation even
> when disagreeing with the underlying policy deci-
> sion, then it is time to think about resigning. Presi-
> dents need the judgment and support, even if it is
> honestly skeptical support, of their top appointees. If
> the appointees find the policy so repugnant that they
> can only distance themselves from it, then they are
> not doing their best to serve.[4]

Had Shultz and Weinberger "raised questions," the administration might well have handled in a more prudent manner
the requirement imposed by the National Security Act that
the President notify the intelligence committees of Congress
of any covert operation on a "timely" basis. Timeliness is not
spelled out in the statute and in the final analysis must remain a matter of executive discretion, but it was imprudent
for the administration to go so long without notifying Congress, which learned about the initiative from the news accounts in early November. (As one congressman, Henry Hyde,
observed, Reagan could have bought some political "risk assurance" had he notified Congress at some earlier point.[5]) A
more involved Shultz and Weinberger might have forced the
President to confront the reporting issue, and it is not incon-
ceivable that their better judgment about the policy might at
some point have prevailed—perhaps before North and Poindexter began diverting funds to the contras.

If both halves of Iran-contra revealed a weak national
security presidency, Reagan's response to it was also anemic,
appearances notwithstanding. Reagan did make public the
funds diversion, reported to him by Attorney General Edwin
Meese III, who discovered it during a weekend inquiry into
the implementation of the Iran initiative.[6] He did fire Poindexter and North. He did empanel an outside commission (led
by former Senator John Tower) to investigate Iran-contra.
Through his Justice Department he did seek the appointment
of an independent counsel to investigate any criminal wrongdoing. And eventually he did admit that, in the parlance so
favored by Presidents, mistakes were made.

Yet these actions and others, as well, can be construed in

a different and more persuasive manner. The conclusion is hard to avoid that Reagan was less interested in taking responsibility for what had happened on his watch as President and dealing with it in a manner that would best serve the office and the Constitution than in getting rid of a "problem" soiling his reputation by whichever expedients seemed most conducive toward that end.

Once Meese uncovered the funds diversion, the President and his advisers wanted the fact made public immediately. Fearing charges of cover-up and ultimately an impeachment effort, they wanted to be seen as taking quick, decisive action. While those fears were understandable given the post-Watergate political culture, they did not call for the kind of almost condemnatory disclosure the administration made on November 25, 1986—one day after Meese had reported his findings to the President. The administration should have announced the fact of the funds diversion—that much was the right call—but generally proceeded in a different way. The presidency would have been the better for it had Reagan done his duty by the Constitution, even if in the short run Reagan himself might have suffered even more criticism, if that seems possible.

At the outset, and consistent with what the office requires of its occupant, Reagan should have accepted political responsibility for what happened under him, even if, in the case of the funds diversion, he had never authorized it. Taking responsibility would have meant summoning Poindexter and North and questioning them; after all, they are supposed to answer to him. In his memoir, Reagan concedes that this is what he should have done: "If I could do it over again, I would bring both of them into the Oval Office and say, 'Okay, John and Ollie, level with me. Tell me what really happened and what it is you have been hiding from me.' "[7] Taking responsibility also would have meant publicly discussing the contra half of the scandal in a way designed to defend the presidency; toward this end Reagan could have explained the political context created by the Boland amendments in which some members of his administration had undertaken to aid the contras, and he could have emphasized the constitutional authority of the President to conduct foreign policy, while admitting that the diversion of funds was an unwise means to the end sought in Central America.[8]

Finally, taking responsibility also would have meant appropriately addressing any real misconduct on the part of his aides. In this respect, Reagan could have insisted that there was no merit in prosecuting government officials for attempting to carry out a President's policies (even those that lack his authorization), so long as they don't profit privately or violate criminal statutes of obvious applicability. The Justice Department, in its submission to the special court for an independent counsel, could have asked for a much more limited jurisdiction. As it happened, the Justice Department made a submission giving whomever the special court appointed virtual carte blanche to proceed as he wished. The administration got the independent counsel it deserved, Lawrence Walsh, who proved the kind of counsel that the statute allows: one that sees his authority as higher than the President's, one willing to expand existing criminal statutes beyond their original terms and previous applications, one willing to investigate as though nothing else mattered but pinning a crime on someone, anyone.

Walsh moved to enforce criminal statutes rarely applied against executive branch officials in their representations to Congress over substantive political differences. "I may be preoccupied with establishing a legal principle," said Walsh after a jury found John Poindexter guilty of, in effect, lying to Congress, "but when [District] Judge [Gerhart] Gesell held that it was a crime to lie under these circumstances, he established a rule of law and a legal precedent. And when the juries have found that this was done, that confirms the charges that we made." On appeal, those charges didn't stick, for reasons that would have persuaded an ordinary prosecutor, forced to pick and choose among many cases and not obligated to focus on just one, to quit the hunt much earlier.[9]

Whatever one may think of North, Poindexter, McFarlane, and others investigated by Walsh, it was Reagan who set in motion the criminal process that unfairly picked on these men and which indeed established a legal precedent for prosecution of executive officials accused of misleading Congress. While executive branch officials should not mislead or lie to

226

Congress, the fact that such conduct may now be subject to criminal prosecution raises important policy questions that have not been adequately addressed by Congress or the President through the formal legislative process. These questions include ones of context (such as whether the laws purportedly violated by North and Poindexter cover both sworn and unsworn statements) as well as motive (such as whether protection of national security, as opposed to corrupt motive, qualifies as a criminal motive). One of the more astonishing facts about the Poindexter prosecution is that Walsh was able to maintain that protecting the President from political damage, through false or misleading congressional testimony, is not just bad judgment but a federal crime. (Never was the stoic Poindexter accused of corrupt motive, such as private gain from the arms sales.) However attractive the precedent established by Walsh and the federal judiciary may seem, under the principle it expresses a host of executive officials from past administrations—including a President or two— would have been candidates for prosecution.[10]

Reagan also failed to defend the presidential office when he complied with the congressional request, unprecedented in its reach, for NSC and even presidential records of matters not involving allegations of executive malfeasance. Reagan refused to assert executive privilege—the power of a President to withhold certain information from Congress—thus setting an unfortunate precedent for the future. The responsible course of action, one concerned for the presidency, would have been to protect the records at issue. It is striking that during Poindexter's 1990 trial, Reagan in fact asserted executive privilege in response to a request for certain presidential materials. Possibly, Reagan now wanted to protect the office. More plausibly, the same unstated rationale was present here as before: that ultimately Reagan wanted to protect only himself. Thus, self-protection meant waiving executive privilege in the first instance, because otherwise he would look "bad" publicly; it meant asserting it in the second instance, because otherwise the materials in question might make the former President look "bad."

It is unrealistic to say that the Reagan who had failed to resist the independent counsel reauthorization, who had failed to publicly oppose the Boland amendments, and who had created for himself a weak national security presidency—it is unrealistic to say that this Reagan could have responded to Iran-contra in November 1986 and thereafter in ways that would have prevented further damage to the presidential office. Yet Reagan cannot be excused responsibility for the latter any more than he can for the former. His irresponsibility thus compounded left a legacy of scandal in which the presidency, and our form of government, was the loser. This was not the scandal of Iran-contra routinely remarked.[11] But those who aspire to be President, and to serve Presidents, should learn from it.

# PART THREE

# THE PRESIDENT AND THE APPOINTMENT OF JUDGES

The scholarly literature on the presidency is silent about the President's role in selecting and appointing federal judges, including Justices of the Supreme Court. In none of its editions does Richard Neustadt's *Presidential Power* speak to the subject. Almost as quiet is Richard M. Pious's *The American Presidency*, published two decades later.[1] The subject has been treated by specialists, such as Henry J. Abraham, whose *Justices and Presidents* remains the essential work for those interested in the history of Supreme Court appointments.[2] Abraham ought to be ready more widely: The President's exercise of his constitutional power to nominate and, subject to Senate confirmation, appoint both Justices and judges deserves treatment by generalists. This power is especially significant today, because an ever larger federal judiciary addresses issues involving more and more matters of concern to ordinary Americans. It is a striking but little known fact that, as a result of vacancies and the creation of additional judgeships, a judge today is nominated and appointed, on average, once every eight days. And it is the President who initiates and, more than anyone else, affects this process. From the perspective of the Constitution, judges, as James Madison once put it, are "shoots from the executive stock."[3]

The Constitutional Convention debated judicial selection. Those who feared power tended to favor appointment of judges by the branch closest to the people, the legislature. They were opposed by those who thought legislatures tended toward irresponsibility and even tyranny and who argued that legislative excesses should be checked by the executive.[4] The framers eventually decided to locate the responsibility for nominating judges in the executive. They did so for two reasons: The people could more easily hold the President—a single person—accountable for judicial selection than it could a multitude of legislators; and the President would be far less likely than the legislature to select judges for parochial reasons. In this regard, the unique position of the President in the constitutional order—as the only national officer, "acting for and sympathizing with every part of the United States," as James Madison put it—proved a compelling consideration.[5] It is worth recalling that during the ratification debates, a criticism of the new Constitution was not that it shifted too much power to the executive in judicial selection, but that it did not give the executive enough, since Senate approval of nominees was required for appointment to occur.

The actual text of the Constitution provides that the President "shall nominate, and by and with the advice and consent of the Senate, shall appoint . . . judges of the Supreme Court." As with treaties, the Constitution here provides for, in effect, a one-house (the Senate) veto over a decision by the President. Madison captured the essence of the constitutional design when he wrote that it "would unite the advantage of responsibility in the Executive with the security afforded in the second branch against any incautious or corrupt nomination by the Executive."

His colleague Hamilton, who in fact first suggested during the Convention the method of nomination and appointment that the Constitution sets forth, explained the design more fully in *The Federalist* when he wrote that "one man of discernment"

> is better fitted to analyze and estimate the peculiar qualities adapted to particular offices than a body of men of equal or perhaps even superior discernment.
> The sole and undivided responsibility of one man will naturally beget a livelier sense of duty and a more exact regard to reputation. He will, on this account, feel himself under stronger obligations, and more interested to investigate with care . . . and to prefer with impartiality the persons who may have the fairest pretensions to them. He will have fewer personal attachments to gratify than a body of men. . . .

In an "assembly of men," Hamilton continued, "we must expect to see a full display of all the private and party likings and dislikes, partialities and antipathies, attachments and animosities, which are felt by those who compose the assembly." Hamilton envisioned bargaining among legislatures— "Give us the man we wish for this office, and you shall have the one you wish for that"—and concluded that the public interest would not be advanced by congressional appointment of judges.[7]

Hamilton also thought that presidential nomination of judges would be tantamount to their appointment, that the Senate would stop the appointment only of "unfit characters from State prejudice, from family connection, from personal attachment, or from a view to popularity."[8] As a forecaster Hamilton has been proved wrong. The Constitution left open the possibility that the Senate may reject a nominee for any reason. The framers did not anticipate the rise of political parties, much less the sharp differences over judicial philosophy in our own time, and down through the years the Senate had refused to confirm nominees especially at the Supreme Court level for reasons that go beyond those Hamilton enumerated in *The Federalist*. Henry Abraham has described the principal ones: opposition to the nominating President, not necessarily the nominee; the nominee's involvement with a visible or contentious issue of public policy or opposition to his perceived political views; opposition to the record of the incumbent Supreme Court, which the nominee has presumably supported (or would add to); senatorial courtesy; and a concerted, sustained opposition by interest or pressure groups.[9] Since 1789, 28 of the 146 nominations to the High Court—the most recent being that of Robert H. Bork—have been rejected by the Senate. The history of presidencies past, not to mention that of Ronald Reagan's, teaches that a judicial nomination is by no means a judicial appointment.

In placing judges on the federal bench, the President is faced, first of all, with the administrative task of selecting the person, and then with the legislative job of getting the nominee confirmed.[10] Chapter 17 treats certain basics relevant to the first labor. Chapter 18 discusses the Bork confirmation process, which teaches important lessons both for the selection of Justices in the "post-Bork era"—as now qualified by the battle over the Thomas nomination in 1991—and for their Senate confirmation. Chapter 19 addresses the vital work of selecting the *lower* federal judiciary. As the Carter presidency shows, a President may not get the chance to choose a Supreme Court Justice but he will get many chances to name judges to the district courts and circuit courts of appeals. Chapter 20 examines the potentially enormous impact a President can have upon the federal judiciary by observing the difference in particular cases that Reagan and Bush appointees have made. In the jurisprudential direction of the federal courts, as in other areas, it is up to the energetic executive to pursue effectively what the Constitution positions and empowers him to establish.

# 17

# HOW (AND HOW NOT) TO SELECT A JUSTICE

## Scalia, Ginsburg, and O'Connor

The Constitution is silent as to the criteria that should guide Presidents in choosing a judge. This is a matter clearly within the President's discretion. Since the time of George Washington the considerations that have decisively influenced Presidents in judicial selection have included political patronage, geographical balance, judicial philosophy, and—especially in recent years—race and gender. Of these, judicial philosophy should be decisive, assuming, of course, that the nominee under consideration satisfies the basic standards of character, judicial temperament, and legal experience and competence. This is also because the most important legacy the President can seek through judicial selection is jurisprudential in nature. The business of the Supreme Court is the adjudication of cases and controversies. The Court renders judgments that make the evening news, but it is the doctrine the Court creates for those judgments that augurs the future. Whatever the composition of the Court in terms of race, gender, religious affiliation, and political party, it *does* jurisprudence, and the President can influence its jurisprudence through his Supreme Court choices. FDR did. Indeed, FDR is perhaps the greatest example of a President who by design influenced the path of the law through judicial selection. He used three criteria in choosing his nine Justices: absolute loyalty to the principles of the New Deal; firm adherence to a civil libertarian and egalitarian philosophy of government under law; and sympathy for executive power in the foreign policy context.[1]

FDR's intentional work on judicial selection stands in sharp contrast to that of some other recent Presidents, who paid less attention to judicial philosophy, if any. To his later regret, Dwight Eisenhower selected Earl Warren and William Brennan for the Court; Ike could have influenced the Court's substantive direction had he chosen more wisely. And Lyndon Johnson selected Justices for the worst reason—what Henry Abraham has called "sheer cronyism."[2]

Ronald Reagan took office with the stated intention of selecting Justices who shared his judicial philosophy. As a presidential candidate in 1980, Reagan said he wanted judges who "would interpret the laws, not make them." On May 6, 1980 he told the *Wall Street Journal*: "I think for a long time we've had a number of Supreme Court Justices who, given any chance, invade the prerogative of the legislature; they legislate rather than make judgments, and some try to rewrite the Constitution instead of interpreting it. I would want a constitutionalist." This was a statement of Reagan's view of how Justices (and, by implication, all federal judges) should interpret and apply the Constitution. But Reagan was also concerned about the exercise of judicial power in general. Thus, the GOP Platform in 1980 included a pledge that Reagan would select judges (at every level) "who share our commitment to judicial restraint."[3]

Reagan's judicial philosophy related to his overall philosophy of government. When Reagan said in his inaugural speech that "government is the problem," his statement may fairly be interpreted as including in his critique the third branch of government. Few students of the Supreme Court would deny that the Warren Court had an expansive view of judicial power. Arguably, it was the most activist ever; not only did it proscribe, without clear constitutional warrant, numerous legislative acts, but—what was new in the history of the Court—it also prescribed what various governmental bodies should do.[4] The Warren Court provoked a strong popular reaction. When Chief Justice Warren himself decided to step down in the spring of 1968—a presidential campaign year—President Johnson designated Associate Justice Abe Fortas, a political and judicial liberal, as his successor. The Senate Judiciary Committee approved the nomination, but conservative senators, believing a Fortas Court would be an extension of the Warren Court, prevented his nomination from coming to a vote, thus forcing Warren to stay on the Court another year. Richard Nixon ran in part against the Warren Court, vowing to name "strict constitutionalists." In 1969, he appointed a federal appeals court judge, Warren Burger, to take Earl Warren's place. But the Burger Court, which included three other Nixon appointees, continued many of the Warren Court innovations and broke startling new ground. It was the Burger Court, for example, that in *Roe* v. *Wade* said that the unenumerated privacy right announced by the Warren Court in 1965 encompassed a woman's right to an abortion; the hugely controversial decision displaced abortion policies in the states.[5] So when Reagan campaigned for office in 1980, the excessive exercise of judicial power remained an issue, although it was not so sharply focused as it had been in 1968, when the Court was still the Warren Court and Warren himself was about to resign.

Now, it is axiomatic that Presidents who aspire to leave their jurisprudential mark upon the Court through judicial selection must at least aim for that goal, as Reagan did. But having that intention is not enough. Nixon had hoped to end the Warren Court activism with his four appointments to the Court, but in general he did a poor job choosing nominees. His first nominee—Burger—was easily confirmed, and over his tenure, which ended with his resignation in 1986, Burger provided much (though by no means all) of the conservative jurisprudence Nixon had sought. Nixon quickly had a second opportunity to fill a vacancy, when Justice Fortas, under intense public and private pressure as a result of his relationship with convicted financier Louis E. Wolfson, resigned. But Nixon's choice, southern appeals court judge Clement F. Haynsworth, Jr., was rejected by the Senate; the charge against him was insensitivity to conflicts of interest—an especially potent charge since Haynsworth was to take Fortas's seat. Even such anti-Fortas, "strict constructionist" Republican Senators as Robert Griffin of Michigan and Jack Miller of Iowa voted against Haynsworth. An irate Nixon then committed what Henry Abraham has described as "an act of vengeance" intended "to teach the Senate a lesson and to downgrade the Court."[6] He picked another Southerner, a district judge, G. Harrold Carswell of Florida, who provoked opposition on grounds of ethics and judicial temperament. It was Carswell who drew one of the most unwittingly memorable comments in support of a Supreme Court nominee: "Even if he is mediocre there are a lot of mediocre judges and people and lawyers. They are entitled to a little representation aren't they, and a little chance? We can't have all Brandeises, Cardozos, and Frankfurters, and stuff like that there."[7] (The speaker was Senator Roman Hruska of Nebraska.) Carswell went down, the vote 51-to-45 against. Nixon blasted the Senate, making statements that simply could not withstand scrutiny. He claimed that the Senate had denied him the right to see his nominees confirmed (there is no such right) and that this right had been accorded all Presidents before him (not true, as Haynsworth and Carswell were the twenty-sixth and twenty-seventh nominees to experience Senate defeat). Nixon then nominated federal appeals court judge Harry Blackmun of Minnesota, whom the Senate easily confirmed. But Blackmun did not fulfill Nixon's hopes. Nixon had said he would not pick as a justice a "super-legislator with a free hand to impose social and political viewpoints upon the American people," but it was Justice Blackmun who wrote the "super-legislating" opinion of the Court in *Roe* v. *Wade*. Only William Rehnquist, Nixon's fourth appointee, fully lived up to his expectations, and ironically this choice, like some of the others, was not made with great care.[8]

Having good intentions, then, is not enough. The President who wants to put his jurisprudential stamp on the Court cannot afford to do other things with his nominating power, much less use it to try "to teach the Senate a lesson"; he must keep his eye firmly on his target. And to ensure that he most effectively pursues his goal he must have a process in place that can provide good advice; as argued elsewhere in this book, having an appropriate institutional mechanism is critical. There is probably no better example of how a presidency should work in an institutional sense in choosing a nominee than the Reagan administration process that resulted in the Scalia selection in 1986. It was Antonin Scalia, of course, who filled the seat left vacant when Reagan elevated Associate Justice William Rehnquist to replace Chief Justice Burger. The two nominations were paired and announced at the same time, and their hearings and confirmations followed in train.[9] Scalia thus was the new addition to the Court.

The administrative effort that led to the Scalia selection began in 1985, long before anyone knew a vacancy might occur, when Attorney General Edwin Meese III asked Assistant Attorney General William Bradford Reynolds to advise him just in case. Reynolds assembled a team of Justice Department officials (about twenty in all) who examined about twenty prospects, most of them sitting federal judges, many appointed by Reagan. The group reviewed everything known about the candidates. And it focused especially on judicial philosophy. Each candidate's published writings, including judicial opinions, and speeches were collected and placed in notebooks, and then read and assessed by three-person units assigned by Reynolds.[10] Reynolds set aside a large office as a reading room where all of the written assessments, together with the notebooks containing the candidate's writings, were available for study by group members. As the final leg of the process, Reynolds convened sessions during which the group debated the relative merits of the candidates. The Reynolds team concluded by giving equal priority to two individuals: Bork and Scalia. Neither was ranked over the other; both were regarded as the best available, most well-qualified exponents of Reagan's judicial philosophy. Moreover, both men were seen as giants in the law, men who could someday rank among the few greats who have served on the Court. When Burger indicated his intention to resign, Reynolds was able to advise Meese without delay, recommending that the President pick Bork or Scalia as part of a two-step approach in which Rehnquist would be named to take Burger's place, with Scalia or Bork simultaneously named to replace him. Agreeing, Meese forwarded the advice to Reagan, who ultimately made the only remaining decision when, after interviewing both candidates, he chose Scalia.

Future Presidents will find it useful to study the Reagan effort with respect to the Scalia choice. A President who wants to ensure that he makes the best possible choice, for the sake of jurisprudential impact, should strive to nominate as quickly after the vacancy occurs as possible; the longer he waits, the more likely it is that he will be pressured by interest groups and the media into selecting someone who is less than ideal, from the perspective of his judicial philosophy. To be able to nominate as soon as possible—within hours and not more than a few days after a vacancy occurs—the President needs help. Given his other duties, no President today can expect to do more than interview the finalists for a Supreme Court seat. His aides must do most of the work. So it happened in the choice of Scalia; the Reynolds team provided the needed administrative help by creating a pool of candidates and reviewing the substantive merits of each. When Reagan selected Scalia, he could be confident that he was picking someone who shared his judicial philosophy. Even more, Reagan was naming someone whose potential contribution to the Court seemed enormous; Reagan was picking, as a President should do, for the future.

The Scalia-selection process stands in sharp contrast to the process which resulted in the Ginsburg choice a year later. Reagan, one recalls, named Douglas Ginsburg after the Senate had rejected Robert Bork's nomination to fill the seat vacated by Justice Lewis Powell. Ginsburg, then forty-one, a former Harvard Law professor, had served one year on the U.S. Court of Appeals for the District of Columbia. Before that he had served in the Reagan administration, in the Office of Management and Budget and also the Justice Department. Reagan tapped Ginsburg on October 29, 1987, but ten days later his nomination had to be withdrawn.

Ginsburg shared the President's judicial philosophy. But that is not enough in today's political climate. A nominee must also be free of the kind of controversy attending personal and professional life that can, and in this instance did, destroy the individual's prospects for the Court. In quick order, the press reported aspects of Ginsburg's life that the administration had not known. His wife, an obstetrician, had once performed abortions. That dulled enthusiasm for the nomination on the political right, although by itself it would not have caused its demise. More serious was the report of a possible criminal conflict of interest. While serving at Justice, Ginsburg, at the same time as he had an investment in a cable television company, also contributed to the development of the Department's position in a Supreme Court case addressing whether First Amendment rights extend to cable television. The question of "government ethics" this posed would possibly have postponed if not undermined the Ginsburg nomination, because it required lengthy investigation by the Criminal Division of the Justice Department.[11] Finally, the matter that sealed his fate was his admission, occasioned by press inquiries, that he had smoked pot on several occasions in the past, including while a law professor.[12] This was the proverbial straw that broke the camel's back. Republican Senators expressed public doubts about the viability of the nomination, as did members of the Reagan cabinet.[13] Ginsburg had little choice but to ask the President to withdraw his nomination.

The Reagan administration could and should have known more about Ginsburg beforehand. The fundamental reason it did not is that it did not take the time needed to conduct a thorough review. Caught unprepared by the Bork rejection, the Justice Department hastily turned to Ginsburg, who had not been among those screened by the Reynolds team in 1986, or later.[14] Those parts of the government with special responsibility for examining the personal life of a candidate—the White House Counsel's Office and the Federal Bureau of Investigation—did not do the job. The latter's background investigation turned up nothing about past drug usage. Somehow the press found out about it quite easily. The White House Counsel's office, which is supposed to be curious about a potential nominee's personal life, was not curious enough.

It is elementary, then, that in selecting a Justice a President should not rush forward with a nomination—however much it might satisfy his judicial-philosophy standard—that has not adequately been reviewed for the kind of controversy that can immediately overwhelm it. Some controversies are worth having; the kind kicked up by the Ginsburg nomination was not. Presidents should know in every vital respect just who they are considering for the High Court. This is especially important today, given the power of the press and its often intense investigation of Supreme Court nominees.

The age of a nominee is a fact—not one anyone has to dig for—that should interest the President who wishes to maximize his jurisprudential impact. Here the Scalia choice is also instructive. Reagan chose Scalia over Bork in part because of age; Scalia, at fifty, was nine years Bork's junior.[15] All other things being equal, age ought to be a consideration because Justices may serve as long as they like. Obviously, the longer a Justice serves, the more influence he can wield. Joseph Storey, thirty-two when James Madison put him on the Court in 1811, served thirty-four years. John M. Harlan, forty-four at the time of his appointment by Rutherford Hayes in 1877, also served thirty-four years. William O. Douglas was forty-one when FDR appointed him in 1939, and he served thirty-six years, longer than anyone in the twentieth century. William Brennan, forty-nine when named by Eisenhower in 1956, served thirty-three years. There are other examples. Indeed, of the dozen Justices who have served thirty or more years on the Court, only one (Justice Oliver Wendell Holmes) was above sixty when he was appointed, and nine were under fifty. In picking Scalia over Bork, the President was hoping to take advantage of the difference in their ages.

The Douglas example, by the way, was on the minds of Justice Department officials who advised the President to select Ginsburg, then forty-one. President Bush's choice of Clarence Thomas, forty-three, also sought to capitalize on youth. That degree of youth has obvious risk: a young (as Supreme Court picks go) nominee may not have a well-formed legal mind and could chart a course sharply divergent from what his sponsor wished.

The Scalia choice was a home run for Reagan, from the standpoint of judicial philosophy. But a President is not always positioned to do that well. Unique political circumstances may force him to compromise and nominate less than the best exemplar of his judicial philosophy. Still, the energetic executive will make sure that in any compromise he gives away as little as possible.

In 1981, Reagan gave away more than necessary when he selected Sandra Day O'Connor, an Arizona court of appeals judge, to replace Justice Potter Stewart. In O'Connor, Reagan picked a judicial conservative, but not the best available.[16] The President passed over Utah supreme court judge Dallin H. Oaks, federal appeals court judge J. Clifford Wallace, and Robert Bork. All three were better qualified than O'Connor according to the traditional measures of ability and experience. And—the critical point—all three were markedly superior exemplars of Reagan's judicial philosophy.

The President selected O'Connor because he thought he had promised the nation he would name a woman. On October 14, 1980, Reagan, then the Republican nominee, stated at a press conference in Los Angeles that he would name a woman to "one of the first Supreme Court vacancies in my administration." The specific words—"one of the first"—seemed so carefully chosen as not to be a promise, but Reagan considered it a solemn vow, which had been made after advice that his campaign was dragging and that women were less likely than men to support him.[17] So it was that Reagan wound up choosing O'Connor. "Gender," Henry J. Abraham has observed, "was *the* primary concern of the Reagan Administration in choosing Judge O'Connor."[18] Judicial philosophy was a subordinate concern.[19]

It should not have been. While it was foolish of Reagan to make the promise he did, the vow was vaguely worded, hardly on the order of George Bush's "no-new-taxes" promise. Reagan reasonably could have selected Oaks or Bork or Wallace in 1981 while maintaining that he would still name a woman, inasmuch as there would probably be additional opportunities to nominate. That would not have been an unreasonable statement, given that vacancies occur once every two years, on average, and that the 1981 vacancy had been the first since 1975. A nomination of Oaks or Bork or Wallace in 1981 would have sailed through the Senate, then controlled by Republicans, and Reagan's jurisprudential legacy would probably be stronger.

While the lessons taught by the Scalia, Ginsburg, and O'Connor nominations remain in force today, no President—and certainly no Republican President—who hopes to do his best in terms of jurisprudential impact can fail to learn from the Bork confirmation battle and the new era in the politics of judicial selection it commenced. This is the subject of the next chapter.

# 18

# CONFIRMATION LESSONS
## Bork, Souter, Thomas

In selecting Robert H. Bork in 1987 to fill the vacancy created by Justice Lewis Powell's retirement, President Reagan could not have found a better qualified exponent of his judicial philosophy than this former Yale law professor and Solicitor General who had served six years on the U.S. Court of Appeals for the District of Columbia Circuit.[1] Like Antonin Scalia, Bork had earned high distinction for his contributions to the law, having, among other things, written an influential book on antitrust law.[2] Bork probably would have been easily confirmed had he been nominated to succeed Justice Potter Stewart or to take Associate Justice William Rehnquist's seat in 1986. By 1987 the Senate had changed hands, as Democratic success in the 1986 elections gave that party a majority. With the end nearing of the Reagan presidency, now weakened by the Iran-contra scandal, and with Democrats hoping for the presidential victory in 1988, the stage was thus set for the Democratic Senate, providing it could find an effective way to do so, to oppose a Reagan nominee who precisely because of his intellect and judicial philosophy was more threatening to liberals than someone of lesser ability and paler judicial philosophy would have been.

Mere hours after Reagan announced the nomination Senator Edward Kennedy delivered a short speech about what he called "Robert Bork's America":

> [W]omen would be forced into back alley abortions, blacks would sit at segregated lunch counters, rogue police could break down citizens' doors in midnight raids, school children could not be taught about evolution, writers and artists could be censored at the whim of government, and the doors of the federal courts would be shut on the fingers of millions of citizens for whom the judiciary is—and is often the only—protector of the individual rights that are the heart of our democracy.... President Reagan ... should not be able to reach out from the muck of Irangate, reach into the muck of Watergate [Bork, as Solicitor General, had carried out the order to fire Special Prosecutor Archibald Cox in 1973], and impose his reactionary vision of the Constitution on the Supreme Court and the next generation of Americans. No justice would be better than this injustice.[3]

Some observers thought Kennedy had made a mistake by speaking so harshly and so quickly about Bork. But his speech inspired Washington-based liberal groups to unite in opposition. Six of these in particular (including the Leadership Conference on Civil Rights, the NAACP Legal Defense Fund, the Mexican-American Legal Defense and Educational Fund, and the People for the American Way) plotted strategy on July 8, a week after the nomination was announced. At their meeting was Senate Judiciary Committee Chairman Joseph Biden, a declared presidential candidate; Biden told the group he opposed the nomination. Biden also put off the confirmation hearings until after the August recess, thus putting Bork on hold for longer than any nominee in history—seventy-seven days. (The past average had been a mere fourteen.[4]) The time enabled the groups to wage against the nominee what proved to be a modern political campaign, but their work was by no means disconnected from the labors of Biden and his fellow Democrats on the Judiciary Committee. As pointed out by Ethan Bronner, author of *Battle for Justice: How the Bork Nomination Shook America*, Biden "went to work hand in hand with the liberal groups that had declared war on Bork. Sub rosa, his staff met weekly with group representatives and stayed in constant telephone contact with them." After each meeting a Biden aide told the representatives, "Remember, this was all off the record."[5] Thus did the anti-Bork effort go forward outside the Senate, but with the advice and consent of the senators who mattered.

The outside effort against Bork sought to undermine the traditional presumption favoring confirmation and to create an atmosphere in which the Senate could far more easily reject the nomination. This meant that the deliberative nature of the process had to be upset; it had to be conformed to ordinary, which is to say elective, politics. Ann Lewis, sister of Democratic Representative Barney Frank and a leader of the forces opposed to Bork, said as much after Bork had been defeated: "This had to be fought beyond the walls of the Senate. If this were carried out as an internal Senate battle, we would have deep and thoughtful discussions about the Constitution, and then we would lose."[6]

Fighting beyond the walls of the Senate meant creating a public image of Bork that would be politically unpopular. Taking Bork's voluminous writings, his briefs as Solicitor General, and his opinions while a federal judge for six years, and paring away all subtleties, complications, and shadings—butchering them, in sum—the nominee's opponents raised, as Bronner put it, "the specter of birth-control police, poll taxes, and literacy tests."[7] Of course, this specter had no prospect; these issues had been long settled as political and legal matters. But by raising it, the anti-Bork coalition thus avoided such current issues as abortion and affirmative action. They portrayed Bork as a man who on the Court would "turn back the clock," thus threatening already achieved progress. In sum, Bork was presented as far outside the mainstream.

The campaign against Bork included "actualities," radio

spots that sounded like newscasts and that stations slipped in to fill up air time. It included video news releases, and editorial memos to an eventual total of 1,700 newspaper editorial boards and individual reporters. And it included a concentrated lobbying effort of the national news organs of greatest impact, such as the *New York Times*, and of course the television networks. In reference to the anti-Bork liberal message framing that came her way over fax and via the phone, Linda Greenhouse, who covers the Supreme Court for the *Times*, told Bronner that "[n]ever before" had she seen such a concerted effort to shape coverage.[8] Finally, the campaign also included paid television advertising. Its lone national television ad, sponsored by the People for the American Way, became quite well-known; it featured actor Gregory Peck on the steps of the Supreme Court, gravely commenting as to how Bork threatened privacy, civil rights, and free speech. The press ran stories about this ad, thus giving it free publicity.

The campaign also made use of polls, some of which were skewed in such a way as to produce predictable anti-Bork results. These, in turn, were reported by the press.[9] The polls provided an "objective" basis for senators to cast their vote.

By Labor Day the campaign outside the walls of the Senate, which was largely unopposed, had its intended effect, as the traditional presumption favoring confirmation had been destroyed. The burden was now on Bork to prove himself worthy of a Supreme Court seat.

There has long been an argument over whether Bork's own testimony could have saved him at this late stage. Perhaps it could have, had he played it differently, with more attention to the politics of the situation, although he could not in good conscience have compromised substantive positions he truly believed in. But the evidence strongly suggests that the deck had been stacked against the nominee. Knowing the hearings would be televised, for example, the Senate Judiciary Committee positioned the table at which Bork sat in such a way as to create for him the least favorable television shots. And it is known that key moderates who did not sit on the committee already had made up their minds. The balance of confirmation power lay in the South, where Democratic senators who might well have voted for Bork decided not to.

Before the hearings Senator Bennett Johnston of Louisiana told his Alabama colleague, John Shelby, that Shelby would have to vote against Bork "because you're not going to turn your back on 91 percent of the black voters in Alabama who got you here." Shelby later told Ethan Bronner of the *Boston Globe* that by the start of the hearings "[t]hings were set in concrete politically."[10]

As the hearings took place, the anti-Bork groups that had campaigned against Bork shrewdly continued their effort. Their leaders convened in a "War Room" located near the hearing room; there they watched the proceedings and wrote statements they issued to the press on a timely basis (that is, in time for news deadlines, including those of the networks). There was no comparable effort on Bork's behalf. The groups also disappeared at just the right moment. Whereas in the past representatives of some of the groups, such as the National Organization for Women, had proved quite willing to testify formally before the committee regarding whatever legislative issue was at hand, this time the organizations decided that testimony would be too risky. Senate Democrats would not allow their political agenda—a quite radical one—to be exposed on national television, and Bork's chief sponsor, the President, did not hold that agenda up for public inspection.

Thus Bork himself—or rather the picture of him drawn by his opponents both outside and in the Senate—remained the issue. The vote against him was 58 to 42.

Bork, of course, was not the first nominee to be rejected by the Senate. Nixon nominees Carswell and Haynsworth had been defeated in the early 1970s, and since 1789 there have been twenty-eight in all who have been formally denied confirmation. And Bork was not the first nomination successfully opposed on political grounds or by interest groups. Yet the battle over Bork was unprecedented in a key respect: For the first time a confirmation process had been subjected to the mass-communication techniques typically used in electoral campaigns.

The lesson for the future is that, especially when the party opposite the President controls the Senate, the confirmation of a nominee, no matter how superbly qualified in conventional terms, as Bork was, cannot be assumed. Indeed, when the Senate is Democratic, the assumption of a conservative Republican President can only be that confirmation is a battle to be won. Moreover, the President must be willing personally to enter the battle. Not only must he lobby individual senators, as Reagan failed to do effectively, waiting until late September before he made even his first phone call to Capitol Hill in Bork's behalf. But he must also be willing to take on senators who publicly oppose the nominee. Reagan did not respond to Kennedy's first-day broadside against Bork. Kennedy's rhetoric violated the norms for deliberative democracy; it was popular speech of the most demagogic kind. Reagan should have used rhetoric to counter Kennedy; his speech should and need not have been demagogic, however. Reagan could have attacked Kennedy's speech precisely as demagoguery, arguing that such language, in addition to being untruthful and unfair, should have no place in the advice-and-consent process. Even more, Reagan could have decided to use popular rhetoric in strategic terms, framing the debate over the Bork nomination. (As it happened, Reagan did give one speech in Bork's behalf, but it was so obviously anticlimactic—coming after the hearings finished—that Reagan wound up giving his speech in midafternoon, with only CNN carrying it.[11]) Through speeches and press conferences the President could have defined the issue before the Senate. This would have required a President willing to stand by his own judicial philosophy, shared by the nominee, but as it happened Reagan fled from Bork, foolishly acquiescing in the strategy of his legislative assistants that the White House should portray the nominee not as a judicial conservative but, improbably, a moderate, a move that handed Bork's opponents a tactical victory.

As we saw in Part One, Presidents may use popular speech—properly, of course—in behalf of legislation. There is no good reason a President may not use it—again, properly—in behalf of Supreme Court nominees. And in the Bork instance, Reagan could have used rhetoric not only to challenge comments by a senator like Kennedy and generally to frame the debate over the nomination, but also to take on the groups campaigning viciously against his nominee. Indeed, Reagan's failure to do the latter also hurt the cause of deliberative democracy. No one exposed the legal and political agenda of those opposing Bork, and yet this surely was relevant to the substantive debate over the nomination.

Stated in legal terms, Bork's shortcoming was that he did not believe in the judicial enforcement of so-called unenumerated rights—that is, rights that are not specifically mentioned in the Constitution, or at least inferable from relevant constitutional history. Bork's Constitution was thus said to be cramped, limited, not "spacious" enough to protect the liberties of the American people. The battle over Bork's substantive views centered around a 1965 case, *Griswold* v. *Connecticut*, in which the Supreme Court struck down a Connecticut law forbidding the use of contraceptives.[12] The law was dubious public policy, as Bork pointed out. But the problem from his perspective (as well as the dissenters' in the case) was that it seemed at odds with precisely nothing in the Constitution. Some members of the Court's majority referred to a right of privacy that the law violated, although none of them offered an unambiguous textual source for such a right. Like Justice Hugo Black, who dissented in *Griswold*, Bork steadfastly refused to agree that judges should declare and enforce rights not found in the text or history of the Constitution. The outside groups and some senators pounded on Bork so as to make him out as a nominee opposed to any constitutional protection of "privacy." Bork protested, noting that the Fourth Amendment, because it protects against unreasonable searches and seizures, does secure a degree of privacy. But Bork had been pushed on the defensive and he was kept there, through caricature. And meanwhile the real agenda of those opposing him did not enjoy equal presence in the public debate. There was purpose in this. Consider how Morton Halperin of the American Civil Liberties Union persuaded its president not to testify:

> [Y]ou think you're going to . . . talk about the Bill of Rights and how important the Court's role is, but let me tell you what the first question is. The first question is going to be me . . . you say that Judge Bork doesn't understand the meaning of privacy in the Constitution. Is that right? Yes! You believe that pri-

251

vacy in the Constitution means that gays have to have the right to marry? Yes! . . . He said, "I understand; I understand."[13]

The views of Bork's opponents were never forced into public view. The judicial agenda of the most radical includes (among other things) the extension of the right of privacy to encompass rights to engage in homosexuality and prostitution, and to take illegal drugs.[14] Had the President directed public attention to this agenda, the nature of the issue would have been clearer, and probably in his favor, politically: More votes might well have come Bork's way. Equally importantly, Bork's view of constitutional interpretation, which has a long, honorable place in American law, would have enjoyed an important political defense. One of the consequences of the Bork defeat is that, so long as Democrats control the Senate, no Republican President will nominate a lawyer who does not pledge allegiance to judicial enforcement of at least some unenumerated rights. (And none has; by their confirmation testimony, Anthony Kennedy, David Souter, and Clarence Thomas agreed with unenumerated rights; each embraced the Court's 1965 discovery in *Griswold* of an unenumerated right of privacy.[15]) The irony is that Hugo Black, FDR's first appointee in 1937, a Justice widely regarded as the dean of the Court's mid-century civil libertarians, could not today be confirmed by a Democratic Senate, because Black is Bork, on unenumerated rights.

In sum, a President who selects the best for the Court and then finds his nominee under the kind of attack Bork endured must do better than Reagan did. But the great temptation in the wake of the Bork experience is that Presidents will choose less with the future in mind than the present, less with an eye toward the jurisprudential contribution his jurist might over time make than with an eye toward the confirmation process soon to occur. Of course, this is not just temptation, but unfortunate reality.

Consider President Bush's 1990 choice of Judge David Souter to replace Justice William Brennan. Where Bork had spent six years on the bench, Souter had been a federal appeals court judge for less than a year. He had written few judicial opinions, and none implicated the controversial issues of the day, such as the right of privacy, affirmative action, or church-and-state. Unlike Bork, moreover, Souter had not published books about the law or written law review articles attempting a sustained argument about significant legal issues. In consequence, Souter's substantive record could not easily be manipulated against him in a de facto political campaign; he could not be "borked"—the perfect word for what happened to Robert Bork—because there was little material for opponents to "bork" him with. Approved with little objection by the Senate, the Souter choice proved Bork a prophet. In his 1989 book, *The Tempting of America: The Political Seduction of the Law*, Bork predicted that a future President who wants "to avoid a battle like mine . . . is likely to nominate men and women who have not written much, and certainly nothing that could be regarded as controversial."[16]

The problem with nominating in such a risk averse manner is that a President eliminates from consideration those of already achieved intellectual distinction who are for that reason more likely to make a substantive impact upon the law. It is a formula for judicial mediocrity. Especially given in 1990 that his presidency was relatively young, and that the stiffest opposition to a nomination typically occurs in the third or fourth year of a term, President Bush should and could have made a bolder choice; all of the other candidates on the "short list" from which the President picked Souter had compiled a more formidable intellectual record in the law.

The following year, in selecting Judge Clarence Thomas to replace Justice Thurgood Marshall, President Bush appeared to follow the Souter formula. Like Souter, Thomas had been an appellate judge for about a year, writing only eighteen opinions, none of them controversial, and none involving the major issues of the day. And like Souter, Thomas had not written important law review articles or books. Like Souter, Thomas could not be opposed in the way Bork was. For these reasons, and one other, it is tempting to say that Bush again succumbed to the temptation of confirmability. The other reason is the one supplied by Thomas's early life, specifically the segregation he experienced while growing up poor in Pinpoint, Georgia. This worked publicly in Thomas's favor, precisely because the press is generally interested in human interest stories, and was in this case; no previous Court nominee had ever experienced what Thomas had as a child—not even the man he was to replace, Thurgood Marshall, a son of black middle-class parents in Baltimore. Ralph Neas, head of the Leadership Committee on Civil Rights, complained about the "fluff" stories on Thomas, as he called them; but the "Pinpoint" strategy pressed by the White House worked to create a political atmosphere during the late summer that favored Thomas's confirmation. More than one Senator was heard saying that if Thomas's hard-working grandfather, who had raised him, were up for confirmation, he'd have ninety-eight votes.

But plainly there was more work in the Thomas choice than considerations of confirmability. Indeed, Thomas arguably was less confirmable than some white judicial conservatives would have been—certainly far less confirmable than a David Souter clone. A black man who was also a political and judicial conservative, he was taking the place of the highest ranking black official in the federal government, a political and judicial liberal whose views approximated those of the civil rights establishment. For this reason, Thomas represented a threat to a certain group of political elites. Bush, hardly risk averse here, could not have chosen Thomas without knowing the confirmation battle that might ensue.

Bush may also be credited with political purpose in the choice, for a Justice Thomas would break the stereotypical mold of what a black lawyer is supposed to be—a Marshall twin, that is, a judicial liberal. Likewise, it speaks well of Bush as a tactician that in 1990 he placed Thomas on the court of appeals where he might acquire the judicial experience necessary to make him a more plausible candidate for the Supreme Court.

Still, when Bush tapped Thomas, the judge had yet to compile a record distinguishing him as one of the best exemplars of Bush's judicial philosophy; plainly there were others—all of them white, such as federal appeals court judges Frank Easterbrook and J. Harvie Wilkinson—ahead of him. While it can be said that Bush thus compromised on this critical standard, his selection of Thomas cannot be compared with President

Reagan's choice of Sandra Day O'Connor in 1981. As discussed in the previous chapter, the O'Connor choice, which had been made on the basis of a promise Reagan had made during the 1980 campaign to name a woman to the Court, represented an unnecessary compromise. Given the exceptional circumstances involved with filling the Marshall seat, the Thomas choice was not only a justifiable compromise in terms of demonstrated judicial philosophy but also a shrewd political act.

Because of the threat Thomas posed to liberal special interest groups, it is not surprising that well before the confirmation hearings were gavelled down, Patricia Ireland of the National Organization for Women in fact announced that her group (and others) intended to "bork" the nominee. The only outstanding question was the means they would employ. In the late 1980s, Thomas had made some comments here and there about natural law. These became the weapon of choice against him, but by the time Thomas was through testifying, it was clear that he could not successfully be attacked from this angle. The Judiciary Committee voted the nomination to the floor; at least sixty senators were expected to vote to confirm him. But then came one of the most infamous news leaks ever to issue from Capitol Hill. The sexual harassment charge by Anita Hill, a former employee of Thomas's, delayed the Senate vote by a week, as special (nationally televised) hearings were held. In the end Thomas was confirmed by the narrow margin of fifty-two to forty-eight.

Thomas's confirmation was a product of his courage. By refusing to be put on trial, and by aggressively taking on the Senate itself, he won a seat on the High Court.[17] Polls show that more Americans—large numbers of whom watched the nationally televised proceedings—believed Thomas than Hill, and that black Americans in particular overwhelmingly favored his nomination. The black laity thus disagreed with the black civil rights leaders. But it is the attitude of the rank-and-file voter that persuades senators, and as this was not the case with the Bork nomination, southern senators could not, in the face of the polling data from their states showing strong black support for Thomas, be persuaded to vote against the nominee.

Bush obviously could not have scripted how Thomas (or

anyone else in his position) would respond. But Bush at least did what a President who has studied Reagan's failure in respect to the Bork nomination must do: He strongly and quite publicly supported Thomas, not only before and during the September hearings but also during the bizarre period when the Hill accusation threatened to kill the nomination. Had the President waffled in his public support at any stage of this most unusual confirmation process, the nomination would not have become an appointment. Thomas today would not be on the Supreme Court.

In the wake of the Thomas confirmation battle, numerous senators—all Democrats—pleaded for more consultation between the President and the Senate before he selects a nominee; in other words, a summit of sorts to advise the President on his choice. The reason given for such a consultative summit—rare in the history of Supreme Court nominations—is that the confirmation process is broken and needs fixing. But no President should agree to this de facto sharing of his constitutional power to nominate judges of the Supreme Court unless the Senate absolutely forces him to do so; and there is not now a majority of senators who could compel such a sharing by refusing to approve the President's nominees, nor does one appear in sight. All there is, is a minority of senators—almost all of them liberal Democrats—who are steadfastly opposed to judicial conservatism.

They, indeed, are the reason the process is "broken." There is no serious question that the news leak came from a liberal Democratic senator, either from him personally or from his staff, or both. And whoever it came from may have had assistance in getting the "information" to the news media from the liberal special interest groups, such as People for the American Way, which have specialized in opposing such nominees as Bork and Thomas. The very fact that Thomas was opposed by means of a news leak, especially one that apparently did not have the blessing of Anita Hill herself, suggests a corruption of a constitutional process by a corrupted liberalism. Not content to abide by formal procedures—once a hallmark of liberalism—by which it was apparent that Thomas would be confirmed, liberals decided to publicize Hill's charge in hopes that it would undermine the nomination; evidently a

Ginsburg scenario, in which the nominee withdraws under public pressure, was envisioned. Senate Judiciary Committee Chairman Joseph Biden was right to wonder during the second set of hearings how "we could call ourselves civil libertarians any more" when leaks of this fashion occur.

It is this corrupt variety of liberalism that a Republican President must take into account today as he ponders his Supreme Court choices and the confirmation process. This corrupted liberalism was present in the vicious attack against Robert Bork that distorted his substantive record. The Thomas confirmation merely shows that it is fully capable of taking new, even more underhanded forms. The strong President will be ready for it, however it comes. And true readiness will lie in a President's willingness to argue publicly against it, early in his tenure, well before any vacancy occurs. The President who does so must recognize the essential point in the post-Thomas confirmation era: that it is the Senate Judiciary Committee which is on trial. Such a President should insist that members of the Senate and their aides not resort to illiberal tactics in opposing a Supreme Court nominee. And he should alert the American people to the possibility that outside groups might hijack the formal confirmation process. As the *Washington Post* reported in a front-page analysis during the Hill-Thomas hearings, there is today an "increasingly symbiotic relationship between committee staffers, liberal interest groups, and the news media" in "a role once played almost exclusively by the Senate."

As a general matter, when the same party controls both elective branches, there will be few if any significant confirmation battles. But that does not promise to be our usual condition; so-called divided government seems our destiny at least in the near future. In this circumstance, the tasks of nomination *and* confirmation are formidable labors deserving the time and energy of any President intending, as he should, to place his jurisprudential stamp on the Supreme Court.

# 19

# A New Judge Every Eight Days

## Selecting the Lower Judiciary

The Judiciary Act of 1789 created thirteen district courts and three circuit courts of appeal; the district judges and Supreme Court Justices sat on the latter. These three levels of the federal judiciary—trials are held in district court and appeals are made to the circuit courts and ultimately the Supreme Court—have endured to the present, with two major changes. Appeals court judges have replaced the original district judge/Supreme Court Justice combinations. And the number of district judges and appellate judges has grown dramatically. Today there are roughly a hundred times as many lower court judges as sit on the Supreme Court. These judges are also (to quote again from Madison) "shoots off the executive stock": Presidents nominate and appoint them, subject to Senate confirmation.

Selecting the lower judiciary is a task of presidential governance more important than ever before in our history. Of the thousands of cases in the federal court system in any given year, only about six score make it to the Supreme Court. This is not to suggest that what the High Court does is relatively unimportant; to the contrary, it is the most critical court, for what it says must be adhered to by the courts below. Call it trickle-down law: The Supreme Court's influence is disproportionate to the few cases it decides. Even so, the lower federal judiciary wields enormous power, thanks in large part to the federal caseload that has grown so enormously since 1960. The fact is, for most Americans who go to federal court, the justice they experience is the justice dispensed in the lower courts, at the district level and then the appellate, if the decision is reviewed there. And this a President can be sure of: whether or not he gets the opportunity to select even a single Supreme Court Justice, he will have many opportunities to nominate judges to the lower bench. Jimmy Carter is a case in point. He had no Supreme Court vacancies to fill, but thanks to retirements and the creation of new judgeships (in 1978 Congress increased the size of the judiciary by 30 percent), he was able to pack the lower bench as no President had since FDR. In just four years Carter managed to fill 42 percent of the seats on the appeals and district courts. Given that judges may serve as long as they like, Presidents can affect the direction of the courts for decades. As late as 1986 there was one Roosevelt appointee still available for judicial duty.

Here is an arresting fact: During his presidency, Ronald Reagan nominated and appointed a judge to a district court or a court of appeals once every eight days, on average. With Congress creating eighty-five new judgeships in 1990, George Bush has nominated and appointed judges even more often— about once every seven days. But White House reporters, like the other generalists—the presidential scholars—tend to neglect this exercise of formal presidential power. Few who cover the White House take the time to understand the importance of the President's power to nominate and appoint judges or to report in depth on how a particular President exercises these powers. Just how lower-court judges come off

259

"the executive stock" seems not to interest White House journalists.

Still, those who covered Ronald Reagan are at least vaguely aware that the judges he nominated and appointed may constitute an important legacy to which George Bush has added. The numbers themselves are staggering: During his two terms Ronald Reagan appointed 368 lower court judges, 78 to the courts of appeals and 290 to the district courts. In all, he appointed slightly more than half the Article III judiciary.[1] In absolute numbers, he appointed more judges than any President ever. In percentage terms, he appointed a larger share of the federal bench than any President since Franklin Roosevelt, who managed to name 80 percent of a much smaller judiciary, having a record thirteen years in which to do that. Through March 1992, George Bush appointed another 152 lower court judges. By the end of his term, he and Reagan together will have appointed three-quarters of the lower federal judiciary.

As with the Supreme Court, the President who aims to leave a jurisprudential stamp on the lower courts must first of all intend to do that. Reagan and Bush have understood that as their purpose. Not all Presidents have. David O'Brien of the University of Virginia notes that John F. Kennedy "named [lower court] judges who ran against his own legal-policy goals," and quotes Victor Navasky's judgment that there was in Kennedy "an absence of any deep, abiding and overriding Kennedy commitment" in this area.[2]

A President of the necessary commitment cannot, however, expect that his purpose will be realized on its own. To help himself, he must take care to retain his nominating power. Also, he must establish a process that enables him to choose individuals who share his judicial philosophy.

The President can expect challenges to his authority to select federal judges. Historically, Senators often have regarded themselves as little Presidents when it comes to picking district judges, and from time to time the Senate has decided, in effect, to select circuit judges. Predictably, when the Senators effectively select judges, they do so for parochial reasons, as foreseen by Hamilton long ago.[3] The American Bar Association has also become a threat to the President's freedom to choose whom he may wish.

The energetic executive will learn how to fight for his nominating power by studying the Reagan and Bush presidencies. During his first weeks in office, Reagan's first Attorney General, William French Smith, asked Senators to provide three to five names for every district court vacancy in their respective states. Previously, a Senator had simply provided the President a single name whenever a seat in his state had opened up. Usually, the Senator's choice became the President's nominee; the President's discretion had been so sharply limited as to make him virtually a clerk.

Reagan also worked to ensure that he had the fullest possible discretion in choosing circuit judges. Here Reagan encountered a perverse consequence of Watergate. Griffin Bell, Jimmy Carter's first Attorney General, recalls a meeting, prior to Carter's swearing-in, with Senator James O. Eastland, the late Mississippi Democrat. As chairman of the Senate Judiciary Committee, Eastland advised Bell that judgeships at both the circuit and district levels were matters of "senatorial patronage." Bell said that this had not been his understanding, that he thought it was true only for district judges. Eastland replied that that used to be the case, but that with the decline of the presidency during Watergate, "the Senators," as Bell recalls him saying, "had moved in on the circuit judgeships as well."[4] Bell persuaded Eastland and other senators to allow President Carter to implement a new judicial selection procedure, which would employ "merit selection" commissions in each circuit. During the Carter presidency these commissions made recommendations to the Attorney General, who in turn advised Carter, who ultimately made the nominations. Reagan agreed with Carter that the power to nominate belonged where the Constitution places it—with the President—but he disagreed with the idea of merit-selection commissions, which worked outside the executive branch. Reagan placed the judicial selection process clearly within the executive branch along a line of authority that ran from the White House into the Justice Department.

Reagan also sought to reduce the limits on executive discretion effectively imposed by the American Bar Association, a private entity. Since 1948 the ABA, through its Standing Committee on Federal Judiciary, has provided to the Senate Judiciary Committee its views on judicial nominees. Since

1952 the committee has screened judicial candidates at the request of the Justice Department; it has investigated them and evaluated their qualifications in order to advise Justice as to their suitability for positions on the federal bench. Prior to Reagan, if the committee deemed a candidate "not qualified," the person usually was dropped from further consideration at Justice; in most instances the Attorney General did not advise the President to pick a candidate found "not qualified" by the ABA. The reason is obvious: Confirmation would be most difficult. Once the President did nominate an individual, the ABA made public its rating when providing it to the Senate Judiciary Committee.

Historically the standing committee has professed to assess judicial candidates according to such basic criteria as education and legal experience, judicial temperament, and the like. When Reagan took office, the Justice Department doubted that the committee used only those measures; it found evidence that anti-Reagan politics influenced committee judgments. Also, Justice found that some members of the standing committee unjustifiably favored certain legal experiences over others; a lawyer who had spent much of his career teaching law was likely to receive lower ratings than a trial lawyer, for example. Maintaining that the standing committee's influence upon judicial selection might jeopardize the President's ability to nominate candidates who shared his judicial philosophy, the administration advised the ABA that it would no longer send several names to be evaluated for each seat, as had been the custom in the 1970s, but just one, and that it would send the single name only at the end of the selection process, not while the individual was still under Justice Department review.

These early moves, taken together, positioned Reagan to exert almost complete control over the circuit court choices and to have *more* control over the district court selections; that is, they positioned him to exercise his constitutional power to nominate in a much less fettered manner. These steps were crucial, for otherwise Reagan would not have been so able to nominate judges who shared his judicial philosophy.

The Bush administration has continued the effort to preserve presidential discretion. For example, it has continued to insist on being provided with three to five names for each district court vacancy. And Attorney General Richard Thornburgh extracted a commitment from the ABA that it will *not* use ideology in assessing Bush nominees—an issue arising especially from the standing committee's assessment of Robert Bork, in which four of its members voted the nominee "not qualified," doing so for apparently political reasons. While the challenges to the President's nominating power may come from different quarters, what must not change is the willingness on the part of the energetic executive to protect and preserve his power.

A President who wants to leave a jurisprudential mark upon the courts must not only maintain his ability to select judges but also have in place a process that enables him to pick intelligently. Reagan had one. In 1981 Attorney General Smith took advantage of a departmental reorganization plan to set up a new office with the chief duty of advising him on judicial selection at both the circuit and district levels. The Office of Legal Policy, employing about twenty lawyers, remained in operation throughout the Reagan years; under three different assistant attorneys general, it served as the focal point for Reagan judicial selection.

OLP sought out judicial candidates in all places and especially where Republican administrations often had not previously thought to look—in law schools, for example. The office collected a candidate's published writings, including judicial opinions if the person was or had been a judge. It conducted telephone interviews with those who knew the individual both on a personal basis and professionally. OLP reviewed a candidate's personal and educational background, legal qualifications and experience, and judicial temperament. Should a candidate cross those initial hurdles of acceptability, the office then invited the individual to Washington for a series of interviews conducted by OLP lawyers as well as others in the Department. This was an innovation; Sheldon Goldman, the leading student of federal judicial selection, reports that Reagan was the first President ever to bring every serious candidate for a judgeship to Washington for extensive interviewing. The total number of candidates interviewed exceeded 1,000. According to Goldman, the Reagan administration engaged in the most systematic judicial screening of candidates ever seen, surpassing even the one carried out by FDR. Typically, a candidate had three or four different interviews. And for each judgeship, three or four candidates were interviewed. The focus of the interviews was to determine how they thought and reasoned about the law.

OLP made written recommendations to Smith and, later, to his successors, Edwin Meese and Richard Thornburgh. These choices were debated within the Justice Department; then the Attorney General carried the name of the person Justice supported to a weekly White House meeting that made the final recommendation to the President. In addition to the Attorney General, the Deputy Attorney General, and the Assistant Attorney General for OLP, those present at the White House meeting included the President's Chief of Staff, his counsel, his legislative affairs officer, and his personnel chief.[5] Once the choice was made, the name was forwarded to the Federal Bureau of Investigation for an extensive background check and also to the ABA's Standing Committee on Federal Judiciary. If the investigations of the FBI and the ABA failed to reveal any information that might question the fitness of the candidate for office, the President announced the nomination.

The Reagan administration's selection process was designed to find individuals of the highest competence who shared the President's judicial philosophy. There is, of course, more than one way to design such a process, and the Bush administration has done it differently, but no less effectively. While the Office of Legal Policy no longer exists by name, its function is carried out jointly by Justice and the White House Counsel's Office. As under Reagan, multiple interviews are conducted of each candidate.

In finding the best exemplars of the President's judicial philosophy, those who administer the selection process must discern how each candidate thinks about the law. But they should *not* ask how a candidate might rule in a specific case. To answer such a question is to corrupt the judicial process; litigants have every right to think that their case will be decided on the merits, not according to some advance commitment. There is no good evidence that the Reagan administration asked questions of this kind. Stephen J. Markman, in charge of OLP from 1985 to 1989, has said of his own experience that if this kind of questioning had occurred, evidence should not have been hard to come by, given the large number of candidates interviewed over eight years.[6]

While the energetic executive must fight to retain his nominating power, realism counsels that he will not always win. Down through the years, district court seats in particular have been subject to political "deals." Reagan himself, for example, finally yielded to the request of Washington Senators Dan Evans and Slade Gorton that he nominate a liberal Democrat, William Dwyer, to the district court; Dwyer did not share the President's judicial philosophy and was a most unlikely Reagan nominee, yet the administration decided to nominate the Democrat in exchange for Gorton's support of Daniel Manion, who was confirmed by a 50-to-49 vote for a seat on the U.S. Court of Appeals for the Seventh Circuit.[7]

Nor should a President expect his selection process, however well organized it might be to give him what he wants, always to come through. The Manion nomination is a good case in point. Kenneth Ripple was better qualified than Manion in terms of conventional criteria as well as judicial philosophy. (Ripple later was picked to fill another vacancy on the Seventh Circuit.)

Nor, finally, should a President expect that every nomination he makes will result in actual appointment. Reagan's judge-picking effort sometimes encountered political difficulties on Capitol Hill. There were delays in filling some judgeships that resulted from interbranch differences and even some Republican Party fights. For the first time in forty-eight years, a district court nominee was rejected by the Senate Judiciary Committee—one controlled by Republicans.[8] In the last two years of the Reagan presidency, when Democrats controlled the Senate, several nominees actually withdrew when it was apparent that their candidacies would be rejected.[9] (Had Reagan faced the same Democratic Senate in earlier years, he would not have been able to name as many of the younger judicial conservatives he appointed during his first term.) Such difficulties, however, should not be considered a sign of presidential ineffectiveness. To the contrary, they suggest just the opposite. There is a lesson here: Any President who attempts to claim his constitutional prerogative to choose lower court judges and to exercise his power in behalf of a certain judicial philosophy can expect to arouse opposition, even to lose some nominations, by formal vote or withdrawal.

Of course, almost all nominees will be confirmed. There is a reason for this: While the presidency is able to examine and evaluate large numbers of judicial candidates, Congress is not. Notwithstanding the increase in its staff in recent years, the Senate Judiciary Committee cannot spend the same amount of time or resources on each nominee as the executive branch can. As a result, only a few candidates are likely to experience intense scrutiny. Consider 1985–86, for example. During that period the Senate Judiciary Committee voted on 136 nominees. Only six had more than one *pro forma* hearing, with only one (a district court nomination) failing to be approved by the committee. Of the six with more than one hearing, two district judges were later confirmed without a recorded vote. And the four others—two for the appeals courts and two for the district courts—endured controversy and bitter confirmation battles. Yet all four were confirmed.[10]

Future Presidents hoping to influence the direction of the lower judiciary will review Reagan's effort. Reagan's judicial selection drew this observation from David O'Brien of the University of Virginia: "The process of judicial selection has changed in such fundamental ways that future administrations, whether Democratic or Republican, are sure to follow Reagan's lead in vigorously pursuing their legal policy goals when picking judges."[11] Every serious student of the matter has concluded that Reagan largely succeeded in maintaining a large degree of discretion in selecting judges, and that his judicial selection process generally produced competent candidates who shared his view of judging. Indeed, there is general agreement that Reagan did better on his own terms at judicial selection than any President since FDR.

A President who aspires to do as well as Reagan did must be willing to assert his constitutional prerogatives. He must seek to protect and indeed enhance his discretion to choose. This will require that he draw lines with the Senate and the

ABA. He must also be willing to make judicial philosophy the chief factor in his selections; if judicial philosophy is routinely subordinated to other concerns, such as political patronage, a President cannot expect to make a substantive imprint upon the courts. A President also must have assistants who organize and run an effective system for actually selecting candidates who share his judicial philosophy.

To argue that a President should take selection of the lower judiciary seriously is to say that a President must take his oath of office seriously. The oath obligates a President not only to execute the office faithfully but also to "preserve, protect, and defend the Constitution." The presidential office is essential to the constitutional order, and to the degree that a President effectively divests himself of the nominating and appointing powers vested in the executive as part of the overall design, he is in violation of the oath. At stake in judicial nominations and appointments is not only the political power of the President but also the very integrity of the constitutional order.

# 20

# A MATTER OF OPINIONS
## Jurisprudential Legacy

A President can only control so much. He can control whom he nominates to the courts, but not how his appointees actually decide cases and controversies. Still, if a President carefully selects his nominees with judicial philosophy in mind, he can reasonably expect to see that philosophy applied in the way cases and controversies are decided. He can expect a jurisprudential legacy.

Day by day, Ronald Reagan and George Bush built (and are building) one, both in the Supreme Court and courts below. With respect to the High Court, a final judgment cannot be made until the careers of O'Connor, Rehnquist, Scalia, Kennedy, Souter, and Thomas are over.[1] But already it is clear that Reagan and Bush did a more careful job of selecting Justices from their shared philosophical perspective than, say,

Woodrow Wilson or Dwight Eisenhower did from theirs. Wilson chose not only Louis Brandeis and John H. Clerkes but also, before them, James C. McReynolds, who as a Justice confounded his sponsor's legal aims.[2] And Eisenhower chose not only Potter Stewart and John Marshall Harlan but also Earl Warren and William Brennan, both of whose appointments he later regretted making.

To move closer to our time, Reagan and Bush plainly were more careful in filling the vacancies on their watch than Richard Nixon and Gerald Ford, who also had five in all, and whose judicial philosophy approximated that of Reagan's and Bush's. None of the Reagan-Bush appointees has become, or shown any serious signs of becoming, a judicial liberal; none has found the career path of Nixon appointee Harry Blackmun, author of the Court's notorious opinion in *Roe* v. *Wade*, who in the 1989 Term voted most with Justice William Brennan (in 102 out of 139 cases) and least with Justice Antonin Scalia (in only 69 out of 139 cases).[3] To the contrary, O'Connor, Rehnquist (as Chief Justice), Scalia, and Kennedy have proved to be judicial conservatives, broadly defined, and the scant evidence in so far on Souter, who voted with Justice O'Connor in 93 percent of the cases during his first term, and Thomas, who early in his first term demonstrated a strong tendency to vote with Scalia, indicates that they fit that description as well.[4]

Justice Powell's 1987 departure from the Court proved the turning point liberals feared. With Kennedy taking Powell's seat, a conservative court emerged. Still, it was only barely a conservative court, with judicial liberals still able to muster seemingly improbable majorities in such cases as *Metro Broadcasting* v. *Federal Communications Commission*, in which Justice Brennan wrote a five-to-four decision upholding an FCC minority preference policy.[5] It is with the further addition of Souter and Thomas (and the subtraction of Brennan and Marshall, the Court's most liberal members) that a more emphatically conservative Court has emerged—a joint achievement of Reagan and Bush. While Souter's presence on the Court in 1990–91 did not make an enormous difference in actual outcomes—about ten or so cases (out of 112) would have gone the other way had Brennan still been sitting—it did increase the size, and thus the strength, of conservative majorities. Six-three decisions supplanted five-four ones as the most common split during the 1990 Term, and the most dominant six-member majority included Rehnquist, White, O'Connor, Scalia, Kennedy, and Souter. Thomas's presence beginning in the 1991 term promised to make the Court more conservative.

That Reagan and Bush succeeded in naming judicial conservatives to the Court has not meant that these Justices have always adopted the positions advocated by the Solicitor General. In 1988, the Court, with Rehnquist writing and O'Connor joining his opinion, and only Scalia in dissent, ruled against Reagan in sustaining the independent counsel statute against constitutional challenge (*Morrison v. Olson*).[6] And in 1989, and again in 1990, the Court, with Kennedy and Scalia in the majority, rejected the Bush administration's argument that a statutory ban against burning the American flag does not violate the First Amendment.[7] (On these occasions Rehnquist and O'Connor dissented.) The differences between advocacy and judging help account for these outcomes, as does the fact that judicial conservatives sometimes disagree among themselves.[8]

Still, the Reagan-Bush appointees have had, in general, the impact upon the law that their sponsors intended. Their presence has slowed the judicial activism of the left to the point where it appears mostly in dissent—in opinions by the other Justices. And for the future, their presence, as Reagan critic Herman Schwartz observed in 1988, ensures that "it will be very difficult to move the Court substantially to the left, even if future appointments are made by Democratic presidents."[9] Given the Souter and Thomas appointments, made after Schwartz commented, it will be very, *very* difficult to move the Court to the left.

One way to understand the impact of the Justices appointed since 1981 is to compare what has happened with what might have happened in the few cases of clear implication for the struggle between judicial activism and judicial restraint, had Jimmy Carter or Walter Mondale or Michael Dukakis held the Oval Office.

In *Bowers* v. *Hardwick*, a 1986 case, the Supreme Court declined by the narrowest of margins—five to four—to expand the privacy right to include homosexual sodomy.[10] Justice O'Connor, at that point the only Reagan appointee, joined the majority opinion written by Justice Byron White, a 1962 choice of President Kennedy's. In rejecting an invitation to declare unconstitutional a Georgia anti-sodomy law, White wrote: "The Court is most vulnerable and comes nearest to illegitimacy when it deals with judge-made constitutional law having little or no cognizable roots in the Constitution. . . . There should be, therefore, great resistance to expand the substantive reach of those Clauses, particularly if it requires redefining the category of rights deemed to be fundamental. Otherwise, the Judiciary necessarily takes to itself further authority to govern the country without express constitutional authority." The majority in this case was made possible because O'Connor was on the Court—and Reagan had been President. Had Carter been elected in 1981, he would likely have named a Justice inclined to vote the other way; in 1982, a Carter-appointed district judge held in favor of a constitutional right to homosexual sodomy.

In *United States* v. *Verdugo-Urquidez*, the Court in 1990 was asked to create a new constitutional right—the right of a foreigner who does not live in the United States to Fourth Amendment protection.[11] By a five-to-four vote, the Court declined the invitation. All of Reagan's appointees were in the majority. Had a Democrat been President from 1981 to 1989, the result very likely would have been the opposite. A new constitutional right, with no justification in the text or historical materials, might well have been the result.

A similar comparison is possible in regard to the death penalty. Justices William Brennan and Thurgood Marshall have argued for years—at least 1,441 times, according to the U.S. Reports—that the death penalty violates the Constitution, notwithstanding its mention in the document itself. Justices Harry Blackmun and John Paul Stevens often joined Brennan and Marshall in voting against the death penalty. The Reagan and Bush appointees have in most instances supported the state's power to apply this sanction. Had Carter and Mondale and Dukakis filled the five vacancies that occurred over the past 12 years, the Brennan-Marshall position might today be the law of the land, and the death penalty absolutely banned from state and federal codes. Short of that, many more capital punishments statutes would have been voided than sustained, and the death penalty would be a far more difficult punishment for a state to impose.

From the perspective of judicial restraint, the Reagan-Bush Justices have by no means been "perfect." Treating a matter of first impression, the majority opinion in *Cruzan* v. *Director, Missouri Department of Health*, written by Chief Justice Rehnquist, indicated that a competent person (the plaintiff was incompetent) would have a constitutional right to refuse treatment, and thus to die.[12] In his concurring opinion, Scalia could find no "right to suicide" deserving judicial protection and stated that he "would have preferred that [the Court] announce clearly and promptly, that the federal courts have no business in this field." But instances like this, in which Reagan-Bush Justices flirt with new rights creation or otherwise show activist tendencies, have been few. In general, the Reagan-Bush Justices have been generally loath to create new constitutional rights or in other ways to expand the reach of the federal judiciary. In those cases, usually a small portion of the Court's docket, where there is a clean line between "activism" and "restraint," the Reagan and Bush Justices far more often than not have come down on the side of restraint. And they have even voted to overrule some activist precedents. At the end of the 1990 term, in *Payne* v. *Tennessee*, all five of the Reagan-Bush appointees voted to overrule two previous decisions (from 1987 and 1989) holding that so-called victim-impact statements in capital cases (introduced by the prosecutor at the sentencing stage of a criminal trial) violate the Constitution.[13]

Another way of understanding the emergent conservative Court is to consider its manner of deciding cases. University of Texas Law School professor Gregory E. Maggs has written that this Court often focuses "on the specific language of the Constitution and statutes rather than on the more general policy considerations [previous Courts] had given importance to." Maggs observes, for example, that in interpreting the Fourth and Eighth Amendments in two cases from the 1990 Term, the

Court "conducted detailed inquiries into the meaning of the words 'seizure' and 'punishment' while eschewing questions of policy."[14] Likewise, in another 1990 case, the Court, with Chief Justice Rehnquist writing, could find no specific language in the Civil Rights Act of 1964 indicating a prohibition against employment discrimination by U.S. employers against American citizens abroad.[15] This interpretive approach has influenced the Court's nonconservative members, as Justice Stevens, for example, now pursues "plain-language" arguments. Consistent with the Court's conservative approach to constitutional and statutory interpretation, it also has tended to defer to the elective branches at both the federal and state level. In sum—and in keeping with the intentions of Reagan and Bush—the Court today is providing less judicial government, an outcome that will draw praise or condemnation, depending on one's judicial philosophy.[16]

Reagan and Bush could have done better in selecting their Justices. Had Bork been picked in 1981 instead of O'Connor, or if Reagan had offered a more vigorous fight for Bork in 1987, or had Bush chosen more boldly than he did when he tapped Souter in 1980, the Court today would be not only more conservative but also more capable. Kennedy and Souter do not promise to be intellectual stars in the judicial firmament.[17] Still, the point remains that Reagan and Bush did well by their own intentions in appointing Justices. One has to go back to Franklin Roosevelt to find a presidency more successful than Reagan-Bush (combining the two is valid, given the shared judicial philosophy) in using the powers of nomination and appointment to influence the jurisprudential direction of the Supreme Court. FDR's appointees effected a revolution in constitutional jurisprudence concerning not only the taxing, spending, and commerce powers of Congress and state powers under the Tenth Amendment, but also civil liberties. For various reasons, the Reagan-Bush appointees are unlikely to leave such a deep and wide jurisprudential mark, but the impression they are leaving is generally what their sponsors intended.

Regarding the lower courts, here, too, any assessment is necessarily incomplete, given that Reagan and Bush judges will be sitting years, even decades hence. And given the greater influence of the Senate upon district court appointments, it is realistic to expect more deviations at that level from the judicial philosophy espoused by both of these Presidents. And in fact some have occurred. Still, it is important to bear in mind that a President can endure "bad" appointments at the district level more easily than he can at the higher levels. After all, a district court decision has more limited scope and can be overruled on appeal to a court on which sits perhaps even a majority of the President's judges, who presumably are more imbued with his philosophy, given his greater discretion in their selection. For these reasons it is important to note that when Reagan left office, he had appointed a majority of the judges on six of the thirteen federal appeals courts—the critically important D.C. Circuit, the Second, Third, Sixth, Seventh, and Tenth. As of early 1992, only the Fourth, the Ninth, and the Eleventh Circuits did not have majorities appointed by Reagan and Bush.

In 1983, when there were sixty-two Reagan-appointed judges on the bench, attorney Craig Stern read all of their 700-plus opinions in order to determine whether judicial restraint or activism had been the rule.[18] Stern found that exactly half of the sixty-two judges exercised judicial restraint in all of their significant cases, and that sixteen others did so in nearly all of theirs. Only nine exercised restraint in no more than half of their significant cases. Concluded Stern: "[T]he Reagan judiciary, so far, has lived up to [Reagan's] expectations."[19]

The task Stern set for himself was huge then. It would be far beyond the capacity of a single person now.[20] The number of Reagan judges increased sixfold, and by March 1992 the number of Bush judges reached 150. The number of opinions these judges write has jumped by the thousands with every passing year, the pages numbering in the hundreds of thousands. Still, enough is known about the work of the Reagan and also the Bush appointees to suggest that what Stern concluded has continued to be the case. Moreover, the courts where judicial performance can be expected to most reflect the judicial philosophy of the President—the circuits where Reagan-Bush judges form the majority—are not regarded as hotbeds of new-rights creation or other activist adventures.

274

Lawyers especially in those circuits who used to press for enlargements of judicial power are not doing that. "I'm just not going to approve [the filing of] an aggressive case that is trying to expand the boundaries of some new right," says Robert Lehrer, of the Legal Assistance Foundation of Chicago, which is in the Seventh Circuit, where a Reagan-appointed majority controls. A measure of Reagan and Bush success is that litigants formerly in the federal courts have turned to the state courts, even to federal and state legislatures. The Reagan-Bush exercise of the powers to nominate and appoint judges has stimulated judicial federalism.

As with the Supreme Court, it is useful to ask what might have happened, had Jimmy Carter, Walter Mondale, and Michael Dukakis packed the lower federal judiciary. Instead of seeking *less* judicial government, those Presidents would have sought more of it. Their judges would likely have behaved as many of the Carter appointees from 1977 to 1981 have, embracing the jurisprudential approach of the Warren Court and expanding the reach of the judicial power still further into American life. In 1985, for example, Carter appointee Jack Tanner rewrote the Civil Rights Act of 1964 to impose "comparable worth" upon the State of Washington. Comparable worth is the theory which holds that not market forces but a centralized, typically governmental, entity should determine wages, and that it should do so according to its assessment of what one job is "worth" when compared to other jobs. For example, under comparable worth theory, a school teacher might be paid more highly than a truck driver, because the former is reckoned to have more societal value than the latter, even though, in a market economy, a short supply of truck drivers, owing to the conditions under which they work, and a high demand for them might dictate salaries higher than those for school teachers. (Judge Anthony Kennedy, later Justice Kennedy, wrote the opinion for the Ninth Circuit reversing Tanner.) In 1980, a Texas district judge, George Cire, appointed by Carter, announced a parent's fundamental constitutional right "to send a child to summer basketball camp," thus overturning a Texas high school athletic association rule to the contrary. (The Fifth Circuit reversed him.) And in 1982, as noted earlier, a Carter appointee held that the constitutional right to privacy encompasses a right to homosexual sodomy, a ruling that struck down a Texas statute outlawing such conduct. This judge also said that the statute violated the Equal Protection Clause.

Before it adjourned its legislative session in 1990, Congress created eighty-five judgeships. By the end of 1992 it is expected that more than 75 percent of the nation's 827 federal trial and appeals court judges will have been appointed by Reagan and Bush. Many of these judges will still be on the job well into the twenty-first century. They likely will prove a powerful testimony to the proposition that whoever has the powers to nominate and appoint judges, and uses those powers energetically, can expect to leave a jurisprudential legacy. In this area, now as perhaps never so critically before, the presidency matters.

# THE STRONG PRESIDENCY
# AND PRESIDENTIAL
# LEADERSHIP

W hat, then, *is* the strong presidency? We may begin the
answer by considering that the President needs the help
of others to meet his constitutional duties. The President personally will select only a few of his aides, so he must have the
assistance of a carefully staffed personnel office if the several
thousand political positions within the executive branch are
to be well appointed. Every candidate for a political position
in the executive branch—and it makes no difference whether
the position is appointed by the President or one of his subordinates (or one of their aides)—must be measured in terms
of personal integrity and belief in public service, competence
(for the position at issue), teamwork, toughness, commitment
to change, and—last but hardly least—politically compatibility with the President and dedication to his principles. The

strong President will not waste appointments—or at least he will waste as few as possible—by naming or allowing the naming of people of unknown or unremarkable political views. Whatever the task—devising a legislative recommendation, drafting a State of the Union or veto message, enforcing a law, selecting a judge, negotiating a treaty, mapping a foreign policy—those who execute it must share the President's political premises. Personnel *is* policy. But policy is not just personnel. The energetic executive will establish and authorize White House systems to develop his policies and superintend their implementation through political appointees in the departments and agencies. Such mechanisms have critical roles to play in not only the administration of law but also the formulation of legislative measures.

Nothing can more quickly dissipate executive energy than charges of malfeasance, and actually wrongdoing itself, on the part of presidential subordinates—or the President, for that matter; think of President Nixon and Watergate, and think what might have happened to President Kennedy had his reckless liaisons with women and mobsters, which his most recent biographer, Thomas C. Reeves, has called "irresponsible, dangerous, and demeaning to the office of the chief executive," been reported while he was President.[1] Self-interest as well as the office itself should motivate Presidents to act above suspicion. And the "new ethics era" as well as the Constitution, which requires the President to take care that the laws are faithfully executed, should lead every President, as soon as he is inaugurated, to take steps designed to prevent "ethics" problems or—human nature being what it is—reduce their number. President Reagan did not do that, but President Bush, in a demonstration of the strong presidency, did. One difference in the two administrations lies in the greater loss of energy Reagan suffered on the ethics front, best indicated by the number of months the effectiveness of Edwin Meese III was reduced on account of the two independent counsel investigations of alleged criminal misconduct on his part. Effective strategies against ethics problems will insist on law-abiding behavior, of course, but emphasize prudence. For whatever else Washington may be good at today, it is very good, thanks to new laws, new attitudes, and more journalists, at generating executive-branch scandals, many of which could have been prevented by good judgment. (Was it really necessary for John Sununu, Bush's first Chief of Staff, to have his government chauffeur drive him to New York for a stamp collection exhibition?) The strong President will work throughout his tenure to prevent ethics problems and thereby preserve his administration's political strength. He will remember Alexander Hamilton's wisdom, in *Federalist No. 70*: "A feeble executive is but another phrase for a bad execution; and a government ill-executed, whatever it may be in theory, must be, in practice, a bad government."[2]

Ethics problems, as defined by the ethics laws, are not the only threat to executive energy. Aides who act as David Stockman did in 1981 in talking publicly against his administration's economic program also can enfeeble the presidency. Reagan should have discharged Stockman. Bush did not make that mistake in September 1990, when he relieved his Air Force Chief of Staff, not for talking against an administration program but for talking publicly about possible military strategy against Saddam Hussein. The presidency is not well served by such behaviors as Stockman's or the Air Force Chief's. Presidential subordinates must remember that they work for the President, and that it is the President alone in whom the executive power is vested. If an appointee cannot in good conscience implement the President's policies, he should attempt to persuade the President of the merits of his views. Failing in that, he should resign. There is honor in that course of action, both moral and constitutional.

The strong presidency, then, is organized and staffed and managed in ways designed to ensure its energy in behalf of the President's policies, whether they are pursued legislatively, administratively, or in both ways at once.

In recommending legislation to Congress, the strong President will speak publicly in its behalf. Today he has no choice but to do that if he is to meet his constitutional duty—he cannot be silent in the manner of nineteenth century Presidents. (On the other hand, the strong presidency most emphatically is not found in the Wilsonian notion that presidential leadership depends not upon the President's place within the constitutional order but upon his contingent personal traits, especially his ability to read the thoughts of the American people and stir them to action through rhetoric.) The President may and should make his case to the American people. But he must conceive and execute his rhetorical strategies not with "winning" only in mind; he must speak in ways that at least do not undermine deliberative democracy. He will not ask his speechwriters for yet another "war" metaphor, not otherwise seek to induce some false crisis. He will not speak in one idiom to the people and a different one (a more nuanced one) to Congress. And he will not prefer words to action. Reagan's 1988 State of the Union message might have been a satisfying television event, but it was not good governance; if Reagan did not like the continuing resolution presented to him the previous fall, he should have vetoed it. Thus he could have forced through his action greater attention to how much federal spending we should tolerate.

Rhetoric can be ill-used and underused. In 1990 Bush cut a profile in weakness when he opted for a budget summit behind closed doors with congressional leaders, thus declining to use his office to frame a badly needed public debate over how much government we need and are willing to pay for. Tongue-tied for so long, Bush tried to save his negotiated budget accord with a last-minute, televised address to the nation, as though this were how to use the bully pulpit. The public did not rally to Bush's side but against him. Bush did not understand that rhetoric must be part of a comprehensive governing strategy. Ideally—as Reagan used it in behalf of tax reform—rhetoric is employed over time in a public effort that includes speeches, press conferences, and the like—all of which are aimed at arguing, not merely asserting, or sound-biting, the President's legislative case.

Reagan generally understood, as Bush in his budget summitry performance did not, that a modern President cannot "bargain" his way to consensus with legislators from both parties. Bush's approach—the style of leadership endorsed by Richard E. Neustadt in 1960—assumed a consensus in the electorate itself that was missing. Today a President must make a public legislative case. In doing that—through good arguments—he will build coalitions. With an electorate conflicted over major domestic policy questions, this is a demand of presidential leadership.[3]

The energetic executive will argue his legislative case publicly and well, but he will also use his veto power, which unlike a speech can force Congress to pay attention to what the President thinks. The use of the veto includes not only its casting but its threatening. The more effective the threat, the less likely the veto will be cast. Effective veto threats are meant, and the only way they are known by Congress to be meant is through their casting when legislation has not been revised to satisfy the President. While, through early 1992, Bush did not "return" a bill on grounds of excessive or wrong-headed spending, he was, within the limited range of his veto presidency, a credible veto executive. With only one or two possible exceptions, he had followed through with vetoes of bills that did not measure up to his announced standards. By contrast, Reagan lost credibility as a veto executive because he often signed bills he had threatened to return.

The strong President will have a complete veto strategy. He will use his veto to block a bill he absolutely disagrees with or to shape one he can accept. He will use the power for policy reasons or constitutional reasons or, against the same bill, for both reasons. He will not accept the nonsense that it is somehow unconstitutional for a President to use the policy veto often, that frequent policy vetoes amount to "systematic policy control over" Congress, as Charles L. Black, among others, has argued. Prudence may limit the number of policy vetoes cast, but neither the Constitution nor constitutional policy does. The veto power is the President's, and he will use it whenever he cannot accept the policy served up to him by Congress. Policy vetoes can raise for public debate issues that have sorely needed it; the veto is a means, or at least a possible means, toward the end of greater deliberation. President Bush's 1990 veto of the civil rights bill on grounds that it promoted quotas did encourage a somewhat greater measure of thought over the degree to which race and ethnicity should be a basis for the allocation of benefits and opportunities in our society—an issue that had suffered from lack of legislative debate, having been dealt with primarily by the bureaucracy and the courts for twenty years.

The energetic President also will bear in mind the original reason the framers accorded the President the veto: constitutional self-defense (and in that a means of preserving a government of separated powers). Twice did Reagan—a weak President in this ongoing battle with Congress—fail to veto legislation reauthorizing the independent counsel statute, which usurps what Hamilton called "the constitutional rights of the executive." By contrast, Bush has consistently acted in self-defense, casting his veto against presidentially offensive legislation.

A legislative tool and weapon, the veto is cast after measures having passed *both* houses of Congress (one constitutional requirement for a law) are *presented* to the President (the second). The President who vetoes is under a constitutional obligation to explain himself, to give reasons, for the sake of deliberative democracy. That is why Presidents should take great care with what they say when they veto—just as they should when they recommend legislation and make popular appeals for it. The strong President will also go beyond what the Constitution requires when bills are presented to him. Article I, Section 7 discusses how a bill becomes law (and doesn't become law). The President may approve or veto a bill—or do nothing. Any bill not returned by the President within ten days becomes a law, just as surely as if the President had signed it. There is a qualification, however: if Congress passes a bill but then adjourns during the ten-day period, thus preventing the President from casting a veto, it "shall not be a law." From this provision has come the so-called "pocket veto," which President Madison was the first President to execute, in 1812. Note carefully: The constitutional text does not require the President to give reasons for what the Constitution suggests would have been a veto. But the energetic and responsible President, in cases of important legislation, will do that anyway, and Presidents from Madison through Andrew Johnson did so, the practice lapsing from Grant through Hoover before it was recovered by Franklin Roosevelt.[4]

On this point, Bush provides a model. In the wake of Iran-contra, members of Congress wished to ensure that never again would a President wait as long as Reagan did to notify Congress about a special intelligence activity; a majority in the Senate formed as early as 1988 in favor of requiring the executive to notify Congress in advance of every single intelligence activity. (The relevant bill did not reach the House floor.) When the issue arose in 1989, as part of the intelligence reauthorization act, President Bush wrote the chairman and vice-chairman of the Senate Intelligence Committee, advising that while he intended to provide "prior notice" in "almost all instances," there would be "rare instances" in which notice could not be provided in advance but "within a few days." Bush explained: "Any withholding beyond this period would be based upon my assertion of the authorities granted this office by the Constitution." Bush thus stated his views for the record, and he threatened a veto. In 1990, Congress passed an intelligence authorization bill that included provisions encroaching on presidential authority, and then adjourned. Bush pocket-vetoed the bill. But he did not do so silently. He wrote a memorandum of disapproval and made it public. This way he let his reasons be publicly known, and there could be no confusion about where he stood—either within the administration or on Capitol Hill (or in the press).

When approving legislation, the strong President will append statements to the most important bills, and in this way speak to Congress (although it is under no obligation to listen) and the executive branch (which is). Laws must be interpreted before they can be enforced. Signing statements thus become for a President vehicles—formal, public ones—for communicating to his "instruments of execution" how a new law should be implemented. Here again the President must take great care in what he says. President Bush junked a proposed signing statement for the Civil Rights Act of 1991 when it appeared to commit him to interpretations of the new law that would have eliminated some forms of affirmative action he apparently approved.

Administering the laws of Congress forms the great bulk of the work of the executive branch. The strong President will seek an "administrative presidency" in the departments and agencies. Within a given department, the status quo can be changed. The means of change (not counting personnel) are a threesome: altering procedures, reorganizing offices, and coordinating activities. Any change must be done prudently, for good reasons, and consistent with the law and the Constitution. And whatever is done must have the President's influence and approval. Thus the need for strong White House systems, which will not simply monitor or coordinate what the agencies propose; working under the President's direction and with political appointees in the agencies, they will actively shape policy for the executive branch and oversee its implementation.

In 1990, Bush taught much of what there is to know—by way of negative example—about an administrative presidency. Not surprisingly, given the history of this matter in the Reagan administration, the issue concerned civil rights. In November 1990, the Fiesta Bowl, located in Arizona, fashioned a plan to award $100,000 to each of the two universities (Alabama and Louisville) scheduled to play in the New Year's Day game, earmarking the money to be used as scholarships based exclusively on race. Bush's assistant secretary of education for civil rights, Michael Williams, learned about the Fiesta Bowl plan from news accounts—and saw a law enforcement problem. As Williams read Title VI of the Civil Rights Act of 1964, universities receiving federal funds, as both Alabama and Louisville do, may not lawfully award scholarships solely on the basis of race, even if the money comes from a private source. Williams wrote the bowl officials, commending them for their efforts "at advancing minority opportunities" but advising them of the universities' "civil rights obligations." Williams suggested other ways Fiesta officials could design a scholarship program that would not complicate the legal lives of Alabama and Louisville but still benefit minority students. His action was part of a more general law enforcement effort he was simultaneously undertaking—an example of an altered procedure—against most race-exclusive scholarships. As he publicly explained it, the only lawful, race-exclusive scholarships administered by universities receiving federal funds are those required as a result of desegregation litigation or by a law of Congress.

As soon as the new policy had been announced, there was an outcry. College and university administrators, in addition to the civil rights lobbies, vehemently objected, whereupon White House sources informed reporters that the President disagreed with Williams and that neither Bush nor anyone close to him in the White House had been informed about the policy in advance. Bush's Chief of Staff John Sununu commenced a speedy review of the issue.

Williams had a law enforcement responsibility, and he was right to be concerned about the Fiesta Bowl scholarship plan and the validity of other race-exclusive scholarships; and it is true, as he said, that his office for civil rights had over the past decade administered an incoherent policy on this issue. But there was a palpable disconnect both within the Education Department and between Education and the President. The new law enforcement policy should have been reviewed by the Education Secretary, and then in turn by the White House, and then ultimately by Bush, not only because of the importance of civil rights issues to any presidency but also because of his own interest in minority higher education; Bush, who had campaigned as the "Education President," had for years contributed to the United Negro College Fund. Although Williams had made an effort to inform the White House, it apparently was not enough. He ended up appearing to have acted on his own, as though he had the executive power and thus the discretion to change a law enforcement procedure. Whatever the validity of his new policy as a matter of law, it lacked presidential approval, and for that reason could not have been sustained. The energetic and responsible executive cannot be found in administrative actions that are not his.

But Bush was more at fault for the weak presidency revealed in this instance than Williams. Bush inherited Education Secretary Lauro F. Cavazos, appointed by Reagan in 1988, and had not removed him. Cavazos was a notoriously weak department head, who lacked new ideas and was a nominal administrator of Education. Bush knew this, and had asked for Cavazo's resignation just before Williams's policy announcement; had he not waited so long to replace the Education Secretary, Williams's new policy might have been properly examined by Lamar Alexander, Cavazos's successor. Even with Cavazos still in office, however, a strong presidency would have had in place a White House system for shaping and implementing Bush's civil rights policy throughout the executive branch. An office or council charged with this responsibility would have established procedures for knowing about proposed enforcement policies and actions in the relevant departments and agencies. Bush should have learned about the need for White House policy systems from the Reagan presidency, specifically from the Bob Jones fiasco, if not Iran-contra.

We cannot leave this Bush administration episode just yet, for there was more to the story, and this last is also instructive. The review of Williams's policy ordered by Sununu led within a week to a revised policy.[5] Under it, universities receiving federal funds could now administer race-exclusive scholarships established and funded entirely by private parties; thus, the Fiesta Bowl could go ahead with its original scholarship plan. On the other hand, universities receiving federal monies could not lawfully use money from their own general operating budgets for race-exclusive scholarships. The Education Department would provide all affected universities "a four-year transition period" to permit them to review their programs under Title VI and to ensure that no student currently benefiting from a race-exclusive scholarship suffered. During this time, Education would not pursue "a broad compliance review with respect to minority scholarships but [would] fulfill its statutory obligation to investigate any complaints received."

The revised policy seemed driven by a desire to let the Fiesta Bowl scholarship program proceed apace and to tame the administration's civil rights critics. The first happened, the second did not, but the remarkable upshot was that under the revised policy a private group could establish not only a scholarship program named for Martin Luther King, Jr., and benefiting blacks, but also one named for David Duke, and helping whites. A more well considered assessment of policy—one not rushed through on Christmas eve in order to solve a public relations problem—could not have led to such an outcome, and it fell to the new Secretary of Education to review the revised policy and change it. Of special concern here, however, is not the soundness of the policy Sununu revised but what it represented, for, although unnoticed at the time, the new policy effectively rewrote a statute of Congress. Under civil rights legislation enacted in 1988, a university receiving federal funds is so broadly obligated to abide by the civil rights laws that even its administration of funds received from private sources is covered. The revised policy in effect said that the 1988 law is no longer law, at least in respect to the administration of funds from private sources that have been designated exclusively for minority scholarships. While the President must interpret law before he enforces it, he cannot in effect assume the legislative power and write law for Congress. The energetic and responsible President may not do that, not if he takes the Constitution seriously.

There is more. According to the revised policy, "[r]ace-exclusive scholarships funded by state and local governments are covered by the Supreme Court's decisions construing the Constitution and thus cannot be addressed administratively." They can't? The Bush presidency seemed to be saying that the judiciary is the only branch that may interpret the Constitution. The strong presidency will never say that but will assert its independent right to interpret and apply the Constitution in the course of its work, whatever it is. President Reagan did not have to abide by what the Supreme Court decided in order to assert, through a veto, his constitutional judgment of the independent counsel law. And President Bush did not have to exclude from Title VII law enforcement any consideration of the Fourteenth Amendment.

To enforce the law is often to litigate, and the strong presidency will be in the federal courts, especially the Supreme Court, as often as the cases require and the Court permits. The point of being there is not, of course, to add to the nation's litigation explosion, but to defend the laws (unless plainly unconstitutional) and enforcement actions pursuant to those laws, and to preserve, protect, and defend the Constitution. Here, too, the energetic executive will assert its independent right to interpret the Constitution, which is not always the same as the gloss placed upon it by the Supreme Court. As Justice Felix Frankfurter said, the "ultimate touchstone" of constitutionality is not "what we [Justices] have said about it" but what the Constitution says; or (since this is a book about the presidency), as Lincoln said in responding to the *Dred Scott* decision, a Supreme Court decision is not necessarily a "thus sayeth the Lord."

No President—whether liberal, conservative, or whatever—will appoint a so-called Tenth Justice as Solicitor General (or Attorney General) unless he wishes to cede his constitutional power to the third branch. The strong President will pursue in the Supreme Court (and the courts below) his policy agenda wherever it is lawful and prudent to do so. *Firefighters* v. *Stotts* (the case involving the authority of judges under Title VII to impose layoff quotas upon a public employer) is a splendid example of a prudent pursuit, while *Bob Jones* (the case involving the authority of the IRS to revoke tax exempt status from racially discriminatory private schools) remains the best example of just the opposite.

It is through the Justice Department, and the Solicitor General's office, that the strong President will litigate the constitutional rights of the executive. In this regard, the Reagan administration's efforts in *INS* v. *Chadha*, noted earlier in these pages, merits a closer look. For it stands out as an example of the hard work that may be necessary to litigate the rights of the executive.

Recall that in *Chadha*, the Supreme Court held unconstitutional the legislative veto. It was pursuant to this device that Congress had, since the early 1930s, passed law in general terms with the provision that if it disagreed with an enforcement decision by one of the departments or an independent agency, the action could be vetoed by a joint resolution of both houses, or one house, or action by a committee, or even a subcommittee. Thus, in cases of disagreement, Congress did not have to pass new law subject to the President's veto power but could express itself through less burdensome, i.e., unconstitutional, means. Because it deprived the executive of his power at presentment and thus was an affront to a government of separated powers, every President since FDR with the exception of Jimmy Carter had opposed the legislative veto, and Carter, after flirting with it early in his presidency, turned against it, becoming a strong opponent. But not until the early 1980s did a case challenging the constitutionality of a particular legislative veto rise to the Supreme Court, thus raising the question of whether the incumbent President would defend his rights in that forum. As it happened, Reagan, like many other conservatives, including David Stockman and Jack Kemp, had supported the legislative veto on the political ground that it provided a good means of checking liberal regulatory decisions. Reagan, in fact, had endorsed the veto in a 1979 newspaper column and in a 1980 speech during the presidential campaign; so had the 1980 Republican platform. The government had to file in *Chadha* by May 1, 1981, so Reagan would have to change his mind if his administration were to oppose the veto; *Chadha* came to the Supreme Court on appeal from the U.S. Court of Appeals for the Ninth Circuit, which—with Judge Anthony Kennedy writing—had ruled against the device. "A review in depth of this issue," wrote Reagan's first Attorney General, William French Smith, in his memoir, "convinced me that we had no other course than to deal with the veto head on."[6] Smith did so, making an unusual, direct appeal to the President. It is in *Chadha* that American conservatism was forced to confront its instrumental view of the institutions of government, which had led it to side with Congress against liberal executives, and to think afresh about them from the standpoint of the Constitution. Smith, Solicitor General Rex Lee, who argued the case in the Supreme Court, and Theodore Olson, head of Justice's Office of Legal Counsel—Reagan appointees all three—deserve credit for understanding that the constitutional rights of the executive were at stake in *Chadha* and for aggressively pressing the President himself to see the interest of his office and his duty under the Constitution.[7] "I was ready to go home if the decision had gone the other way," says Olson. "The issues in the case were critical to the presidency."[8] The strong presidency is found not only in the President's willingness to defend the rights of the executive in the Supreme Court but also in the determination of his subordinates to help him do so, even, and especially, when the President himself is not minded to do so. The behavior of Smith and his Justice colleagues were models of executive character.

It is in the courts, of course, that the President's lawyers present their arguments. And it is in the exercise of his constitutional power to nominate and appoint judges that the strong President will seek a jurisprudential legacy, written in the thousands of opinions his judges will write. Presidents must choose their nominees with judicial philosophy centrally in mind, but to do that well they need help. The Justice Department and the White House Counsel's office are the places in which the energetic President will establish a reliable system for screening judicial candidates for the Supreme Court as well as the lower judiciary. The process by which the Reagan administration selected Antonin Scalia provides a worthy model for choosing a Supreme Court Justice; the system was established well in advance of any vacancy, and those who managed it focused intensively on the substantive views of potential nominees. The strong President will seek to avoid compromises on judicial philosophy especially in his Supreme Court choices; he should consider compromise only when a political situation clearly forces him to do so. This arguably occurred when Thurgood Marshall, the nation's first black Justice, stepped down, but plainly did not when, in filling the Potter Stewart vacancy in 1981, Reagan chose mainly on the basis of gender by naming Sandra Day O'Connor.

Of critical importance since the watershed battle over the Bork nomination is the need for the President's engagement in getting his nominee confirmed. No President can afford to sit passively, as Reagan did while Bork's opponents waged political war against him. Presidential rhetoric may be necessary in confirmation battles—rhetoric that backs the nominee while seeking to elevate the public discourse. The memory of what happened to Bork should not lead Presidents to make confirmability the central criterion of selection, as unfortunately clearly did happen when President Bush chose David Souter for the Court in 1990. Finally, the truly energetic executive will be constant in his attention to lower court nominations, there being so many, so often. He will fight for his powers to select judges, and he will select with judicial philosophy in mind, aware that he is creating a minor league of sorts from which he—and his party successors—may have the opportunity to promote to the big league of the Supreme Court. Scalia, Kennedy, Souter, and Thomas all put in time on benches below.

This book has been organized into its three parts—the President and Congress, the President and the Executive Branch, and the President and the Appointment of Judges. But the discussions in numerous chapters of this book make plain that the President must think about his work across the branches, in the sum of his powers and duties. To meet his duty to recommend measures he judges "necessary and expedient," for example, he may need administrative help in framing such measures, as was the case when President Reagan in 1984 asked Treasury Secretary Don Regan to devise a tax reform plan. This, however, is a relatively uncomplicated example. Consider the kind of thinking across the branches a President today must do: The altered procedure the President may order in discharging his administrative duty to execute the laws may be challenged in court and, if upheld by the Supreme Court, it may be amended by Congress. If a bill changing the new enforcement procedure passes both houses and is presented to the President, he may use his veto power to protect his administrative governance, providing he has veto strength—at least one third of one chamber, plus one vote, on his side of the issue. (Bush had veto strength in opposing the bill overturning the new Title X regulations governing federal funding of family planning clinics, which had been unsuccessfully challenged by Planned Parenthood in 1991 in *Rust* v. *Sullivan*.) Or consider this example: The agenda victory the President wins in the Supreme Court provokes congressional challenge. If a bill contrary to his views is in due course presented to the President, he may use his veto to foster needed public debate on the kind of new law needed, if any is. (Bush successfully used his veto to this end, in opposing the civil rights bill sent to him in 1990.)

The strategic governance of the strong President thus will take into account what may be achieved through the administrative presidency and what may need to be done through a legislative presidency, just as it will attend to what lawfully may be accomplished administratively in the implementation of new legislation. Not only the President but also his subordinates, in the White House and the departments and agencies, must think both administratively and legislatively. And so must the White House systems the President establishes to help him govern.

The latter can prove especially useful in ensuring consistency between administrative and legislative parts of a presidency that are related in subject matter if not directly in law. Bush needed a strong White House system to help him govern on civil rights (so did Reagan, as we saw in Chapter 12). Not only could such a system have helped Bush make whatever minority scholarship policy *he* regarded as desirable; also, it could have produced coherence between that policy and the one Bush was pursuing in his opposition to the civil rights legislation. As it happened, Bush wrapped up 1990 in contradiction. In sanctioning some race-exclusive scholarships (like the Fiesta Bowl's) in the week before Christmas, Bush endorsed judgments made entirely on the basis of race, at least in some contexts. This could not be squared with his opposition throughout the year to what he had called, accurately enough, a "quota bill." The strong presidency is not found in such incoherence.

The President who thinks both administratively and legislatively will seize the opportunity to govern. An example of a missed opportunity teaches just how a President might. In early 1992 Justice Clarence Thomas, taking care of some leftover business from his days as an appeals court judge, issued an opinion in *Lamprecht* v. *Federal Communications Commission* in which he struck down an FCC affirmative action program that, as its counsel admitted in oral argument, "doesn't have any basis in fact."[9] This case invites us to ask a question of presidential governance, for how is it that presidencies seemingly opposed to preferential policies on the basis of race and gender could have allowed them to flourish at the FCC?

While it is true that the FCC's preferential policies began well before Reagan took office, he did not have to preside over their perpetuation. In his second term, the agency did commence a review of the policies, whereupon Congress intervened to make sure the FCC would not reverse the status quo. In 1987, in a rider to an appropriations bill, Congress told the FCC that none of its funds could be used to repeal or even to study the preferential policies, unless the outcome of such a study recommended their retention. In 1988, and then again after Bush became President in 1989 and 1990, Congress continued so to instruct the FCC, each time in riders to appropriations bills. The FCC obeyed, and in due course revealed that it agreed with Congress, not the President. In 1990 litigation challenging the racial preference policy, and then again in the *Lamprecht* case, which concerned the gender preference policy, FCC lawyers defended them. If Reagan had not stirred himself to govern the FCC in behalf of race- and gender-neutral policies, neither did Bush, who, like Reagan, accepted the riders without protest at presentment.

What could Reagan, or Bush, have done? Better use of the appointment power would have helped; that the FCC is a so-called independent agency does not mean that philosophically compatible appointments dedicated to change could not have altered the status quo at the agency. Yet even the best appointees (from a President's point of view) also need the kind of support only a President can provide. In this instance Reagan could have vetoed the appropriations bill, objecting to the rider, and doing so on constitutional grounds. Alternatively, he could have approved the bill but employed a signing statement to explicitly disapprove the rider on constitutional grounds. The rider's infirmity lay in the fact that it represented a congressional effort to do what under the Constitution only the executive is authorized to do—enforce the laws. Administration of a law necessarily requires its interpretation, and under the Communications Act of 1934, the FCC is given broad policy-making discretion. Yet through the appropriations rider (an anti-deliberative maneuver indeed: it evades committee scrutiny and amendments, specifically focused recorded votes, and other risks, burdens, and incentives for compromise that the normal legislative process imposes on controversial policies) the Congress sought to impose upon the FCC a particular discretionary choice. Reagan—or Bush, who had his chances, too—could have added that the rider was doubly unconstitutional, since it required the executive to violate his understanding of the Equal Protection Clause of the Fourteenth Amendment, which guarantees to all citizens the equal protection of the laws.

Thus battling legislatively, Reagan, or Bush, also could have battled administratively, by using his explicit constitutional authority to order opinions in writing from executive officers (found in Article II). Either could have asked the FCC chairman to reexamine the agency's preferential policies, even to quit them, and *not* to defend them in litigation. No doubt controversy would have ensued, but a strong President would have been prepared for it.

Thinking both administratively and legislatively, one cannot leave the subject without noting the opportunity and even the duty the strong President has in the extraordinary circumstance of a possible war. Alexander Hamilton saw clearly how the President, in exercising his constitutional powers, might create "an antecedent state of things" that might influence the legislative decision to authorize war. Bush, the strong President in this regard, exercised his powers—freezing assets, deploying troops, negotiating through the United Nations and around the world—and in so doing created the circumstance in which Congress, on January 12, 1991, voted to support the war effort that commenced four days later. In embarking upon the plainly "arduous" and "extensive" enterprise of extracting Saddam Hussein from Kuwait, Bush was indeed the energetic executive, providing the leadership that could only have come, in our system of government, from the office he held.

The leadership of the constitutional officer who is the strong President thus has many definitions: in legislative contexts, in administrative ones, and in both, and in the selection and appointment of judges. His leadership not only will pursue substantive political goals, even "extensive and arduous enterprises" for the public good, but also seek to defend the office from which such pursuits—whether by him or his successors—are uniquely possible.

In 1861, after the attack on Fort Sumter, South Carolina, President Lincoln, among other actions extending executive power beyond their traditional limits, suspended the writ of habeas corpus. Against the charge that he had exercised a power that the Constitution appears to give to Congress, Lincoln said that if he had done that (he would not concede that he had), his act would have been justified both by his constitutional duty to faithfully execute the laws, including the supreme law of the Constitution, and also by his oath to preserve the government.[10] When a President takes emergency action as Lincoln did, we may be taught something important about the inherent limits of law—namely, that it is incapable of fully realizing the public good. Only a Constitution large enough to allow actions against the law for the public good is, ironically, law adequate to democratic government; as Lincoln understood, the Constitution "is different *in its application* in cases of Rebellion or Invasion, involving the Public Safety, from what it is in times of profound peace and public security."[11] Moreover, the genius of the Constitution is that such power as Lincoln exercised does not exist apart from the constitutional order, which provides means for checking exercises of the power. While the judgments of others typically come after the fact of presidential action, when its consequences can be most accurately assessed, the Constitution facilitates those judgments; the presidency, after all, is part of a government of separated powers, and it is an elected office. Thus, Congress can hold hearings and even commence impeachment proceedings. Courts can disagree with Presidents, as occurred in Lincoln's case, in *Ex parte Milligan*.[12] Public opinion, influenced by the press, has an informal but not inconsiderable role to play, and on Election Day, of course, the people can make their voices heard at the ballot box. These are not the only constraints. The very structure of the presidential office is such as to encourage energy *and* responsibility. A President who knows that he exists within a constitutional order designed to hold him accountable has an incentive to act more responsibly.

The strong President will know the Lincoln example and endeavor to rise to the occasion in such an extraordinary circumstance as Lincoln faced. He will not try, as Richard Nixon did, to lay claim to the Lincoln tradition of acting in the national interest as a defense for actions that may be deemed illegal. Suffice to say, Nixon did not face a clearly discernible crisis, as Lincoln manifestly had.[13]

One must hope that rebellion or invasion, or other genuine threat to the nation, will not be our lot. In general, the strong President will find routine "the application," as Lincoln would put it, of the Constitution. He will resist the temptation to cross constitutional lines. President Bush would have crossed such a line had he commanded the war in the Persian Gulf without congressional authorization; there had to be a law for him to proceed as he did. Likewise, he would have

295

crossed a line had he claimed that the Presentment Clause conferred upon him a "line-item" veto.

Constitutional line crossings may occur in informal ways. Consider, for example, the Johnson-Fortas connection. Having named his long-time friend and adviser Abe Fortas to the Supreme Court in 1965, Johnson continued to seek the lawyer's counsel on executive-branch matters. In 1968, for example, even after Johnson had named him to replace Chief Justice Earl Warren—a time when one would think the President might not be so imprudent or arrogant—Johnson asked Fortas to review a draft of his signing statement for the Safe Streets Act—controversial legislation bound to be the subject of litigation. This was typical of the kind of advice Johnson had sought from the Justice he still regarded as *his* lawyer. Writes Joseph Califano, Johnson's domestic policy adviser, Associate Justice Fortas

> had advised Johnson on the constitutionality of limits on the President's authority to close military bases and of the 1966 D.C. crime bill. He had helped assess the Supreme Court's likely response should the President unilaterally impose wage and price controls. He had been deeply engaged in shaping Vietnam and economic policies and in advising the President on a variety of crises, ranging from the Detroit riots to the 1967 railroad strike. Worst of all, he had advised the President on the Penn-Central case when it was pending before the Supreme Court and then written the Court's final opinion.[14]

Fortas, says Califano, "became part of the [White House] staff." But the strong President who must also be responsible does not thus informally mix the branches of government but is content with the executive branch, and with the powers the Constitution has confided in him. They are enough to do the job.

Too often have the Presidents of the past twelve years underused (or not well used) these adequate powers, whether in pursuing their substantive political goals or in defending the presidential office and the constitutional order in which it is found. Although neither did as well as they could, Reagan did better than Bush in pursuing substantive goals, and Bush did better than Reagan in defending the constitutional rights of the executive. Reagan's greater political success was a consequence of his much greater willingness (than Bush's) to articulate his substantive principles early on and often, throughout his presidency; indeed, the most severe mark against Bush is the familiar—and for the most part accurate—charge that he has no principles. Bush's deficit in this respect was seldom more clearly revealed than in the winter and spring of 1992 as he scrambled to take positions on a number of domestic and economic policy matters (welfare reform, student aid for higher education, excessive regulation, among others) that he had largely neglected. "If you are so concerned with [welfare reform]," a reporter asked the President at his press conference on the subject, "why haven't you been closely involved with it for the last three years?" "The politics drives some things," Bush replied, adding, damningly, "A lot of the issues we're talking about . . . they get much more clearly in focus every four years, and then you go ahead and try to follow through and do something about them." Reagan never seemed so lacking in conviction, or so driven by which way the political winds are blowing, as Bush. Reagan understood that the occupant of the presidential office must have a substantive political identity if he is to achieve anything, and that this identity cannot be established, and certainly cannot be preserved, except through frequent, at least rhetorical effort. Still, Reagan often substituted words for action—he, too, failed "to follow through"—and sometimes his words were woefully inadequate. Reagan was successful in pushing broad themes (democracy abroad, judicial restraint, making America strong again) but much less so in pushing particular ends (budget cuts, SDI funding and deployment, contra aid, the Bork nomination), often because he shied from making the specific, sometimes detailed arguments that would have been necessary.

Bush's greater success at self-defense was a consequence of his more consistent willingness (than Reagan) to assert his rights, although Bush, too, made compromises, most notably his Central American accord with Congress, which included an unconstitutional legislative veto. As indicated by his speeches, signing statements, and veto messages, Bush had a better grasp on the nature of the presidential office and its special place within the constitutional order. It is possible to learn from both presidencies, and to improve on them, for the strongest presidency will be equally interested in pursuing its policy goals and protecting its constitutional powers.

Among other strategies such a presidency might pursue, one in particular is worth noting here. To judge by certain pieces of legislation in recent years (the Boland amendments especially), Congress likes to force the President to concern himself with the merits of particular policies at the expense of his own powers. One way out of this bind might be for the President, early in his presidency, to state the political principles that will guide him and shape his policies in office. At the same time he would indicate in clear terms his determination to oppose encroachments by Congress upon the power of the office he holds. The reason for stating such intentions well in advance of their presence in any bill is that otherwise the President will not have laid down a marker to which he can refer once the legislation begins to move through Congress and toward his desk; the merits of what is in the legislation—or other political considerations—will dominate public discussion, and the President will more easily be forced to weigh policies that may not reflect his ideas against institutional power. It is very early on, for example, that the President could state clearly his intention to veto any legislation that contains a rider on some unrelated subject, any reauthorization of the independent counsel law, and any bill containing a legislative veto. It should go without saying that a President who takes such an unambiguous, institutional position should not himself undermine it by seeking legislation that proposes to compromise his authority. Whatever the political pressures might be, the strong President will resist, for the sake of his powers and therefore the cause of good government.

The original version of Richard Neustadt's *Presidential Power,* published in 1960, was not only a seminal study of the presidency but a book that expressed certain normative ideas about the presidency shared by most academics at the time.

Neustadt believed in a strong presidency, and he found his model of presidential leadership in Franklin Roosevelt.[15] For Neustadt, as for other political scientists and historians, his strong presidency went hand in hand with bigger, more powerful central government. Writing during the Eisenhower years, a down time for American liberals, Neustadt expressed their frustration with the incumbent administration and their hope that the 1960s would witness the advent of their kind of strong presidency. Offering governing strategies for such a President, Neustadt wrote, "We are confronted by an evident necessity for government more energetic, politics more viable, than we have been enjoying in the fifties."[16]

The first half of the 1960s, and the presidencies of John Kennedy and Lyndon Johnson, gave American liberals what they wanted. Who then could have guessed, however, that this period of liberal dynamism would also have been the final one in the progressive era opened by Theodore Roosevelt.[17] With Vietnam, and then Watergate, literature on the presidency—dominated by liberals—focused on the limitations of the office and the need for presidential accountability. Few writers, however, rejected the need for a strong presidency, even if they did not call it that. Nor did they relinquish their view that a strong presidency was necessary to effect the larger, more powerful government that, in their judgment, domestic circumstances, if no longer foreign ones, required. By the early 1980s, few writers on the presidency were prepared, however, to empathize with a presidency committed to a smaller, less intrusive domestic government, a goal that in itself was regarded by the conservatives who ascended to power as a necessary means toward a more vibrant America.

How to classify such a presidency? Among liberals and conservatives alike, it had been conventional to regard as "weak" any presidency favoring less central government, notwithstanding the contrary example of Andrew Jackson.[18] But in advancing his program for economic recovery in 1981, Ronald Reagan showed that, as a practical matter, a strong presidency was necessary to effect the conservative end of less government, defined in terms of lowered tax rates, slower rates of spending growth, fewer regulations of the private economy, and less judicial activism. At the same time, both

299

Reagan, in pushing for the defense spending that helped cause the demise of the Soviet Union, and later George Bush, in evicting Saddam Hussein from Kuwait, demonstrated the enduring need for a strong presidency in foreign affairs. In these efforts, both Reagan and Bush had far more in common with the liberal Presidents of decades past than did recent liberal aspirants to the office, such as Walter Mondale and Michael Dukakis.

On balance, Reagan was a stronger President than Bush. But from the perspective of this book, he does not suffice as a model for the strong presidency today. For such a model, in fact, one has to construct a composite of sorts by picking and choosing certain features from Presidents both recent and past, both Democratic and Republican, both liberal (or progressive) and conservative.

Both Roosevelts were determined to govern, and did govern, legislatively and administratively, just as, at least in 1981–82, in behalf of his economic program, President Reagan did. Understanding the jurisprudential legacy a President can achieve, both Roosevelts, like Reagan and Bush, took care to make judicial appointments at all levels on the basis of their judicial philosophies. Both Roosevelts, like Reagan and Bush, tried as strong Presidents should to litigate their agendas. And Theodore Roosevelt may stand out as the strongest President in respect to taking responsibility for his subordinates. "More than once while I was President my officials were attacked by Congress, generally because those officials did their duty well and fearlessly," he wrote in his autobiography. "In every such case I stood by the official and refused to recognize the right of Congress to interfere with me excepting by impeachment or in other constitutional manner. On the other hand, wherever I found the officer unfit for his position, I promptly removed him. . . ." Roosevelt added: "My secretaries and their subordinates were responsible to me, and I accepted the responsibility for all their deeds."[19] Would that every former President could say that; would that every President would act well upon that understanding.

Franklin Roosevelt, like his cousin before him, and Reagan, in 1981–82, did not shrink from tackling the issues of their time. And in doing so they helped change the terms of fundamental political debate. In *Franklin D. Roosevelt and the New Deal*, William E. Leuchtenburg observed that, at least in part because of FDR's leadership, "men of acumen" moved from debating, in 1932, prohibition, war debts, and law enforcement, to debating, by 1936, social security, the Wagner Act, and public housing.[20] Likewise, in part because of Reagan, political discussion in the early 1980s was directed away from economic redistribution toward economic growth (a reversal, by the way, of New Deal priorities; Roosevelt seemed confident that the problem of "supply" had been solved and that henceforth all government needed to be concerned with was equitable distribution[21]). Whatever one thinks about their policies, Roosevelt and Reagan alike took on "extensive, arduous enterprises" that were aimed at overcoming negative economic conditions (depression and recession, respectively) and which, in their different estimates of the matter, they thought would benefit the public.

Where Reagan (and also Bush) differed from Roosevelt was in his understanding of the relationship of the presidency to the nation. This difference goes to the heart of the idea of the strong presidency presented in these pages. Theodore Roosevelt not only engaged the issues of his time, as he surely should have, from the perspective of this book, but he also saw himself as *personally* responsible for the safety, prosperity, and happiness of all Americans.[22] Franklin Roosevelt shared that same attitude; he presented himself, in Leuchtenburg's phrase, "as the father to all the people."[23] While many of the measures successfully advocated by the Roosevelts and other liberal Presidents may be regarded and even justified in terms other than what might be called "Political Fatherhood," it is this understanding of the presidency that Lyndon Johnson also shared, and which led him and other liberals to plunge government into more and more areas with less and less good effect. It is this understanding, too, which can encourage Presidents to ignore constitutional limits or run roughshod over them by trying to mass the powers of government in order to take care, as they define appropriate care, of the American people.[24] Suffice to say, those who would be strong and responsible Presidents must resist the potentially dangerous call to fatherhood. The strong presidency is essential to good government, but good government cannot do everything constitutionally or effectively.

It is a standard liberal critique of the 1980s to call them a decade of private greed and excuses, caused by Reagan economic and domestic policies and symbolized by today's enduring, and large, budget deficits. Among other problems with this indictment, it ignores the seemingly contrary evidence of an explosion in charitable giving.[25] Be that as it may, most of these critics want higher taxes to close the deficit and to finance new programs to ameliorate various social problems; they want a return to the status quo ante Reagan, as though this were the central task of politics today. Ironically, what the critics typically fail to grasp is that the argument by which conservatives came to power in the 1980s was in fact aimed at reducing excess—a broadly defined excess.[26]

The rights explosion in the middle decades of the century had helped contribute to higher levels of crime and especially the violent crime often associated with drug trafficking; to greater levels, and even societal tolerance, of illicit drug use; to more abortions and indeed to acceptance, in many communities, of abortion on demand; and to the reduced ability of states and localities to govern themselves.[27] Federal courts often exceeded proper constitutional bounds as they sided with many of the new rights' claimants. The result was not only cultural disorder but also more federal judicial government than ever before, as courts effectively ran schools, hospitals, and other public institutions. Meanwhile, the actual government evolved over the decades in Washington had become too large, too ambitious, and too intrusive, venturing ineffectively into new areas. And with a loss of budget discipline, it had come to cost too much, not only in terms of appropriated dollars but also in terms of what the states and private entities had to pay out of their own pockets to fulfill congressional mandates (not accompanied by federal funds) and new regulations.

Reagan and Bush enjoyed more success against this multidimensional excess than their critics have typically granted. Both of them were notably successful in saying no, through their appointments to the federal judiciary, to excessive judicial government. And in a virtually unnoticed achievement, Reagan and Bush were able to inter the quite excessive idea of the President as some omniprovident, omnipowerful father of all Americans; this idea was itself a source of some of the cultural and governmental (in the form of laws and bureaucracies) excess against which Reagan rose to power (even as it was also a source of presidential enervation). Still, Reagan and Bush failed in a most significant respect, for they did not succeed in reforming the excessive government in Washington. Indeed, in some respects, the problem is worse now than when Reagan first took office. While Reagan managed to reduce the regulatory excesses of the federal government, Bush presided over their increase; his administration pumped out 17 percent more rules in its first two years than were promulgated during Reagan's eight years. And while Reagan managed to slow the average annual growth of domestic spending to $2.82 billion, in constant 1987 dollars, down from $15.3 under Jimmy Carter, Bush allowed it to grow at the amazing rate of $43.4 billion a year.[28] Meanwhile, throughout the Reagan and Bush years, federal mandates—state and local spending required by Washington—increased without much, and certainly not much effective, presidential protest. Medicaid, the medical care program for the poor established in 1965, is perhaps the best case in point. In 1970 the states spent 4 percent of their resources on Medicaid; in 1991, the figure was 14 percent, leading Florida Governor Lawton Chiles, a former U.S. Senator, to remark, "We're dealing with a federal partner who has a printing press and therefore does not have to respond to the crisis."[29]

For the foreseeable future, the main task for Presidents, liberal or conservative, and whether they will accept the task or not, will be that of saying no—or saying some variant of no, such as less. This is true in regard to not only domestic but also foreign spending, because now that the Cold War and the Soviet Union are no more, it is possible, and desirable, to cut the defense budget, an endeavor that will require telling community after community in state after state, and therefore one member of Congress after another, no. And in regard to domestic spending, future Presidents are going to have to face squarely middle- and upper-income earners, especially those who are retired or nearing retirement, a segment of the population that more reliably than any other turns out on Election Day.

Long ago Reagan posed the right question, even if he did

not press it as President. In 1964, in his celebrated campaign speech in behalf of Barry Goldwater, he asked: "Will you resist the temptation to get a government handout for your community?" Today "entitlements"—direct benefit payments to individuals—account for almost half of all federal spending and are twice as large as the defense budget. Because their rates of increase are fixed by statutory formula, most entitlement programs are growing by amounts that exceed both the inflation rate and the growth in federal revenues. While some entitlements aim to ameliorate the lot of our poorest citizens, the most costly, such as Social Security and Medicare, do not. In 1991, as reported by Neil Howe and Phillip Longman, the Social Security system paid more than $55 billion, and Medicare nearly $19 billion, to households with incomes above $50,000 a year.[30] Entitlement programs available to all without regard to income are chiefly responsible for our persistent budget deficits, but they are not the only kind of non-poor subsidies that are part of the budget excess. The small part of the budget containing "discretionary" spending—that which is voted year to year—includes many items that primarily benefit middle- and upper-income earners. Consider that the 1930s effort that began as an effort to prop up agriculture has become a subsidy of agribusinesses making more than $100,000 a year; according to Howe and Longman, some $50,000, on average, in direct federal payments goes to each of the 30,000 biggest grossing farmers in America.[31] Other programs requiring annual appropriations help the up-scale more than anyone else, and some of these lend assistance on matters that ideologically divide Americans. These include the arts endowment and the Corporation for Public Broadcasting. (There is no good reason that artists—including the wealthiest in Hollywood—could not create a private fund for the arts, free of government regulation, or that, in the new world of cable and narrowcasting, the CPB could not be sold to a private bidder.) And consider even such tiny but symbolic appropriations as the $500,000 subsidy received by a one-plane commercial airline to fly affluent business travelers to expense-account meetings at the posh Homestead resort in Hot Springs, Virginia. Taxpayers from Maine to Hawaii thus pay more than $150 per passenger to subsidize the travel of those in the higher-income categories. Essential Air Service is the name of this program; Entitlement Air Services would be better, for it perfectly expresses the tendency on the part of so many Americans today to regard themselves as entitled to some federal subsidy or other. This government works, in the view of those who benefit from it. But in a larger sense it does not work, for it is part of the government we have long since quit paying for but continue to run the tab on—leaving it to future generations to pay by one means or another.

The elective branch better positioned to say "no" or "less" especially to middle- and upper-income earners who benefit from government is the presidency. The executive power is vested in a single person, elected by all the people, whereas Congress has 535 members whose chief concern is the district or state they represent. Only the President, as Jefferson said in his Inaugural Address, can see the "whole ground." Today, with Congress encircled by interest groups left and right that are both cause and consequence of the excessive and bankrupting government, it is in most cases *only* the President who stands much of a chance of changing the status quo.

If they are going to contribute to good government, future Presidents, whether liberal or conservative, must, to one degree or another, undertake to reform entitlements, reduce or eliminate middle- to upper-income subsidies voted annually, ensure coherence and efficiency in executive rule-making, and stop Congress from telling the states and localities to carry out certain programs unless it also provides adequate funding. To have success, they will have to engage Congress on most of these matters, in speeches and vetoes. For Congress by itself is unlikely to reform entitlement spending or take away middle- or upper-income subsidies, or quit the practice of piling unfunded obligations upon states and localities; and Congress is likely to go beyond effective oversight of executive functions to politically motivated arm-twisting in an effort to prevent coherent and cost effective rule-making. Future Presidents also are going to have to say no and its variants to the American people. In regard to fiscal policy, this effort will be required even if taxes are increased, because, politically speaking, it is highly unlikely that taxes can be raised to cover the deficits the government now runs. Even in that event, many of the programs that are bursting the budget are ill designed from the perspectives of efficiency and equity and if left unchanged will probably create substantial budgetary imbalances in the future.

The President who undertakes what will clearly be an extensive arduous effort for the public benefit—one within his constitutional authority to attempt—will definitely risk his political future. But the strong presidency is not one that hoards popularity for the sake of reelection. Opinion polls, and reelection, are not the measures of the strong presidency, or, for that matter, a Prime Minister. In 1990, in Great Britain, Margaret Thatcher was turned out of office, her approval rating at a historically low 29 percent. When Ronald Reagan left office, his approval ratings were the highest of any President since World War II. "Like dying rich," as Charles Krauthammer has written, "this is a great moral failure."[30] The strong President may be defeated after a single term. The strong but thus defeated President may nonetheless qualify as a great one—great because of his service to the nation. This is the paradox, and the promise, of the American presidency.

# APPENDIX

# THE CONSTITUTION OF THE UNITED STATES OF AMERICA

PREAMBLE

We, the people of the United States, in order to form a more perfect union, establish justice, insure domestic tranquillity, provide for the common defense, promote the general welfare, and secure the blessings of liberty to ourselves and our posterity, do ordain and establish this Constitution for the United States of America.

ARTICLE I

SECTION I

All legislative powers herein granted shall be vested in a Congress of the United States, which shall consist of a Senate and House of Representatives.

SECTION II

[1] The House of Representatives shall be composed of members chosen every second year by the people of the several States, and the electors in each State shall have the qualifications requisite for electors of the most numerous branch of the State legislature.

[2] No person shall be a Representative who shall not have attained to the age of twenty-five years, and been seven years a citizen of the United States, and who shall not, when elected, be an inhabitant of that State in which he shall be chosen.

[3] Representatives and direct taxes shall be apportioned among the several States which may be included within this Union, according to their respective numbers, which shall be determined by adding to the whole number of free persons, including those bound to service for a term of years, and excluding Indians not taxed, three-fifths of all other persons. The actual enumeration shall be made within three years after the first meeting of the Congress of the United States, and within every subsequent term of ten years, in such manner as they shall by law direct. The number of Representatives shall not exceed one for every thirty thousand, but each State shall have at least one Representative; and until such enumeration shall be made, the State of New Hampshire shall be entitled to choose three; Massachusetts, eight; Rhode Island and Providence Plantations, one; Connecticut, five; New York, six; New Jersey, four; Pennsylvania, eight; Dela-

---

* Modern usage in spelling, punctuation, and capitalization has been employed.

307

ware, one; Maryland, six; Virginia, ten; North Carolina, five; South Carolina, five; and Georgia, three.

[4] When vacancies happen in the representation from any State, the executive authority thereof shall issue writs of election to fill such vacancies.

[5] The House of Representatives shall choose their Speaker and other officers, and shall have the sole power of impeachment.

## SECTION III

[1] The Senate of the United States shall be composed of two Senators from each State, chosen by the legislature thereof for six years; and each Senator shall have one vote.

[2] Immediately after they shall be assembled in consequence of the first election, they shall be divided as equally as may be into three classes. The seats of the Senators of the first class shall be vacated at the expiration of the second year, of the second class at the expiration of the fourth year, and of the third class at the expiration of the sixth year, so that one-third may be chosen every second year; and if vacancies happen by resignation or otherwise during the recess of the legislature of any State, the executive thereof may make temporary appointments until the next meeting of the legislature, which shall then fill such vacancies.

[3] No person shall be a Senator who shall not have attained to the age of thirty years, and been nine years a citizen of the United States, and who shall not, when elected, be an inhabitant of that State for which he shall be chosen.

[4] The Vice-President of the United States shall be President of the Senate, but shall have no vote, unless they be equally divided.

[5] The Senate shall choose their other officers and also a President pro tempore in the absence of the Vice-President, or when he shall exercise the office of President of the United States.

[6] The Senate shall have the sole power to try all impeachments. When sitting for that purpose, they shall be on oath or affirmation. When the President of the United States is tried, the Chief Justice shall preside; and no person shall be convicted without the concurrence of two-thirds of the members present.

[7] Judgment in cases of impeachment shall not extend further than to removal from office, and disqualification to hold and enjoy any office of honor, trust, or profit under the United States; but the party convicted shall, nevertheless, be liable and subject to indictment, trial, judgment, and punishment, according to law.

## SECTION IV

[1] The times, places, and manner of holding elections for Senators and Representatives shall be prescribed in each State by the legislature thereof; but the Congress may at any time by law make or alter such regulations, except as to the places of choosing Senators.

[2] The Congress shall assemble at least once in every year, and such meeting shall be on the first Monday in December, unless they shall by law appoint a different day.

## SECTION V

[1] Each House shall be the judge of the elections, returns, and qualifications of its own members, and a majority of each shall constitute a quorum to do business;

but a smaller number may adjourn from day to day, and may be authorized to compel the attendance of absent members, in such manner, and under such penalties, as each House may provide.

[2] Each House may determine the rules of its proceedings, punish its members for disorderly behavior, and with the concurrence of two-thirds, expel a member.

[3] Each House shall keep a journal of its proceedings, and from time to time publish the same, excepting such parts as may in their judgment require secrecy, and the yeas and nays of the members of either House on any question shall, at the desire of one-fifth of those present, be entered on the journal.

[4] Neither House, during the session of Congress, shall, without the consent of the other adjourn for more than three days, nor to any other place than that in which the two Houses shall be sitting.

## SECTION VI

[1] The Senators and Representatives shall receive a compensation for their services, to be ascertained by law and paid out of the Treasury of the United States. They shall, in all cases except treason, felony, and breach of the peace, be privileged from arrest during their attendance at the session of their respective Houses, and in going to and returning from the same; and for any speech or debate in either House they shall not be questioned in any other place.

[2] No Senator or Representative shall, during the time for which he was elected, be appointed to any civil office under the authority of the United States, which shall have been created, or the emoluments whereof shall have been increased during such time; and no person holding any office under the United States shall be a member of either House during his continuance in office.

## SECTION VII

[1] All bills for raising revenue shall originate in the House of Representatives; but the Senate may propose or concur with amendments as on other bills.

[2] Every bill which shall have passed the House of Representatives and the Senate shall, before it become a law, be presented to the President of the United States; if he approve he shall sign it, but if not he shall return it, with his objections, to that House in which it shall have originated, who shall enter the objections at large on their journal and proceed to reconsider it. If after such reconsideration two-thirds of that House shall agree to pass the bill, it shall be sent, together with the objections, to the other House, by which it shall likewise be reconsidered, and if approved by two-thirds of that House it shall become a law. But in all such cases the vote of both Houses shall be determined by yeas and nays, and the names of the persons voting for and against the bill shall be entered on the journal of each House respectively. If any bill shall not be returned by the President within ten days (Sundays excepted) after it shall have been presented to him, the same shall be a law, in like manner as if he had signed it, unless the Congress by their adjournment prevent its return, in which case it shall not be a law.

[3] Every order, resolution or vote to which the concurrence of the Senate and House of Representatives may be necessary (except on a question of adjournment) shall be presented to the President of the United States; and before the same shall take effect shall be approved by him, or being disapproved by him, shall be repassed by two-thirds of the Senate and House of Representatives, according to the rules and limitations prescribed in the case of a bill.

SECTION VIII

[1] The Congress shall have power to lay and collect taxes, duties, imposts and excises, to pay the debts and provide for the common defense and general welfare of the United States; but all duties, imposts and excises shall be uniform throughout the United States;

[2] To borrow money on the credit of the United States;

[3] To regulate commerce with foreign nations, and among the several States, and with the Indian tribes;

[4] To establish an uniform rule of naturalization, and uniform laws on the subject of bankruptcies throughout the United States;

[5] To coin money, regulate the value thereof, and of foreign coin, and fix the standard of weights and measures;

[6] To provide for the punishment of counterfeiting the securities and current coin of the United States;

[7] To establish post offices and post roads;

[8] To promote the progress of science and useful arts by securing for limited times to authors and inventors the exclusive right to their respective writings and discoveries;

[9] To constitute tribunals inferior to the Supreme Court;

[10] To define and punish piracies and felonies committed on the high seas and offenses against the law of nations;

[11] To declare war, grant letters of marque and reprisal, and make rules concerning captures on land and water;

[12] To raise and support armies, but no appropriation of money to that use shall be for a longer term than two years;

[13] To provide and maintain a navy;

[14] To make rules for the government and regulation of the land and naval forces;

[15] To provide for calling forth the militia to execute the laws of the Union, suppress insurrections, and repel invasions;

[16] To provide for organizing, arming and disciplining the militia, and for governing such part of them as may be employed in the service of the United States, reserving to the States respectively the appointment of the officers, and the authority of training the militia according to the discipline prescribed by Congress;

[17] To exercise exclusive legislation in all cases whatsoever over such district (not exceeding ten miles square) as may, by cession of particular States and the acceptance of Congress, become the seat of the Government of the United States, and to exercise like authority over all places purchased by the consent of the legislature of the State in which the same shall be, for the erection of forts, magazines, arsenals, dockyards, and other needful buildings;

[18] To make all laws which shall be necessary and proper for carrying into execution the foregoing powers, and all other powers vested by this Constitution in the Government of the United States, or in any department or officer thereof.

SECTION IX

[1] The migration or importation of such persons as any of the States now existing shall think proper to admit shall not be prohibited by the Congress prior to the year one thousand eight hundred and eight, but a tax or duty may be imposed on such importation, not exceeding ten dollars for each person.

[2] The privilege of the writ of habeas corpus shall not be suspended, unless when in cases of rebellion or invasion the public safety may require it.

[3] No bill of attainder or ex post facto law shall be passed.

[4] No capitation or other direct tax shall be laid, unless in proportion to the census or enumeration hereinbefore directed to be taken.

[5] No tax or duty shall be laid on articles exported from any State.

[6] No preference shall be given by any regulation of commerce or revenue to the ports of one State over those of another; nor shall vessels bound to or from one State be obliged to enter, clear or pay duties in another.

[7] No money shall be drawn from the Treasury but in consequence of appropriations made by law; and a regular statement and account of the receipts and expenditures of all public money shall be published from time to time.

[8] No title of nobility shall be granted by the United States; and no person holding any office of profit or trust under them shall, without the consent of the Congress, accept of any present, emolument, office, or title of any kind whatever from any king, prince, or foreign state.

## SECTION X

[1] No State shall enter into any treaty, alliance, or confederation; grant letters of marque and reprisal; coin money; emit bills of credit; make anything but gold and silver coin a tender in payment of debts; pass any bill of attainder, ex post facto law or law impairing the obligation of contracts, or grant any title of nobility.

[2] No State shall, without the consent of the Congress, lay any imposts or duties on imports or exports, except what may be absolutely necessary for executing its inspection laws; and the net produce of all duties and imposts, laid by any State on imports or exports, shall be for the use of the Treasury of the United States; and all such laws shall be subject to the revision and control of the Congress.

[3] No State shall, without the consent of Congress, lay any duty of tonnage, keep troops and ships of war in time of peace, enter into any agreement or compact with another State or with a foreign power, or engage in war, unless actually invaded or in such imminent danger as will not admit of delay.

## ARTICLE II

### SECTION I

[1] The executive power shall be vested in a President of the United States of America. He shall hold his office during the term of four years, and together with the Vice-President, chosen for the same term, be elected as follows:

[2] Each State shall appoint, in such manner as the legislature thereof may direct, a number of Electors, equal to the whole number of Senators and Representatives to which the State may be entitled in the Congress; but no Senator or Representative, or person holding an office of trust or profit under the United States, shall be appointed an Elector.

[3] The Electors shall meet in their respective States and vote by ballot for two persons, of whom one at least shall not be an inhabitant of the same State with themselves. And they shall make a list of all the persons voted for, and of the number of votes for each; which list they shall sign and certify, and transmit sealed to the seat of government of the United States, directed to the President of the Senate. The President of the Senate shall, in the presence of the Senate and House of Representatives, open all the certificates, and the votes shall then be counted. The person having the greatest number of votes shall be the President, if

such number be a majority of the whole number of Electors appointed; and if there be more than one who have such majority, and have an equal number of votes, then the House of Representatives shall immediately choose by ballot one of them for President; and if no person have a majority, then from the five highest on the list the said House shall in like manner choose the President. But in choosing the President the votes shall be taken by States, the representation from each State having one vote; a quorum for this purpose shall consist of a member or members from two-thirds of the States, and a majority of all the States shall be necessary to a choice. In every case, after the choice of the President, the person having the greatest number of votes of the Electors shall be the Vice-President. But if there should remain two or more who have equal votes, the Senate shall choose from them by ballot the Vice-President.

[4] The Congress may determine the time of choosing the Electors and the day on which they shall give their votes, which day shall be the same throughout the United States.

[5] No person except a natural-born citizen, or citizen of the United States at the time of the adoption of this Constitution, shall be eligible to the office of President; neither shall any person be eligible to that office who shall not have attained to the age of thirty-five years, and been fourteen years a resident within the United States.

[6] In case of the removal of the President from office, or of his death, resignation, or inability to discharge the powers and duties of the said office, the same shall devolve on the Vice-President, and the Congress may by law provide for the case of removal, death, resignation, or inability, both of the President and Vice-President, declaring what officer shall then act as President, and such officer shall act accordingly until the disability be removed or a President shall be elected.

[7] The President shall, at stated times, receive for his services a compensation, which shall neither be increased nor diminished during the period for which he shall have been elected, and he shall not receive within that period any other emolument from the United States or any of them.

[8] Before he enter on the execution of his office he shall take the following oath or affirmation:

"I do solemnly swear (or affirm) that I will faithfully execute the office of President of the United States, and will to the best of my ability preserve, protect, and defend the Constitution of the United States."

## SECTION II

[1] The President shall be Commander-in-Chief of the Army and Navy of the United States, and of the militia of the several States when called into the actual service of the United States; he may require the opinion, in writing, of the principal officer in each of the executive departments, upon any subject relating to the duties of their respective offices, and he shall have power to grant reprieves and pardons for offenses against the United States, except in cases of impeachment.

[2] He shall have power, by and with the advice and consent of the Senate, to make treaties, provided two-thirds of the Senators present concur; and he shall nominate, and, by and with the advice and consent of the Senate, shall appoint ambassadors, other public ministers and consuls, judges of the Supreme Court, and all other officers of the United States whose appointments are not herein otherwise provided for, and which shall be established by law; but the Congress may by law vest the appointment of such inferior officers, as they think proper, in the President alone, in the courts of law, or in the heads of departments.

[3] The President shall have power to fill up all vacancies that may happen

during the recess of the Senate, by granting commissions which shall expire at the end of their next session.

## SECTION III

He shall from time to time give to the Congress information of the state of the Union, and recommend to their consideration such measures as he shall judge necessary and expedient; he may, on extraordinary occasions, convene both Houses, or either of them, and in case of disagreement between them with respect to the time of adjournment, he may adjourn them to such time as he shall think proper; he shall receive ambassadors and other public ministers; he shall take care that the laws be faithfully executed, and shall commission all the officers of the United States.

## SECTION IV

The President, Vice-President and all civil officers of the United States shall be removed from office on impeachment for and conviction of treason, bribery, or other high crimes and misdemeanors.

## ARTICLE III

### SECTION I

The judicial power of the United States shall be vested in one Supreme Court, and in such inferior courts as the Congress may from time to time ordain and establish. The judges, both of the Supreme and inferior courts, shall hold their offices during good behavior, and shall, at stated times, receive for their services a compensation which shall not be diminished during their continuance in office.

### SECTION II

[1] The judicial power shall extend to all cases, in law and equity, arising under this Constitution, the laws of the United States, and treaties made, or which shall be made, under their authority; to all cases affecting ambassadors, other public ministers, and consuls; to all cases of admiralty and maritime jurisdiction; to controversies to which the United States shall be a party; to controversies between two or more States; between a State and citizens of another State; between citizens of different States; between citizens of the same State claiming lands under grants of different States, and between a State, or the citizens thereof, and foreign states, citizens, or subjects.

[2] In all cases affecting ambassadors, other public ministers and consuls, and those in which a State shall be party, the Supreme Court shall have original jurisdiction. In all the other cases before mentioned the Supreme Court shall have appellate jurisdiction, both as to law and fact, with such exceptions and under such regulations as the Congress shall make.

[3] The trial of all crimes, except in cases of impeachment, shall be by jury; and such trial shall be held in the State where the said crimes shall have been committed; but when not committed within any State, the trial shall be at such place or places as the Congress may by law have directed.

313

## SECTION III

[1] Treason against the United States shall consist only in levying war against them, or in adhering to their enemies, giving them aid and comfort. No person shall be convicted of treason unless on the testimony of two witnesses to the same overt act, or on confession in open court.

[2] The Congress shall have power to declare the punishment of treason, but no attainder of treason shall work corruption of blood or forfeiture except during the life of the person attainted.

## ARTICLE IV

### SECTION I

Full faith and credit shall be given in each State to the public acts, records, and judicial proceedings of every other State. And the Congress may by general laws prescribe the manner in which such acts, records, and proceedings shall be proved, and the effect thereof.

### SECTION II

[1] The citizens of each State shall be entitled to all privileges and immunities of citizens in the several States.

[2] A person charged in any State with treason, felony, or other crime, who shall flee from justice, and be found in another State, shall, on demand of the executive authority of the State from which he fled, be delivered up, to be removed to the State having jurisdiction of the crime.

[3] No person held to service or labor in one State, under the laws thereof, escaping into another, shall, in consequence of any law or regulation therein, be discharged from such service or labor, but shall be delivered up on claim to the party to whom such service or labor may be due.

### SECTION III

[1] New States may be admitted by the Congress into this Union; but no new State shall be formed or erected within the jurisdiction of any other State; nor any State be formed by the junction of two or more States or parts of States, without the consent of the legislatures of the States concerned as well as of the Congress.

[2] The Congress shall have power to dispose of and make all needful rules and regulations respecting the territory or other property belonging to the United States; and nothing in this Constitution shall be so construed as to prejudice any claims of the United States or of any particular State.

### SECTION IV

The United States shall guarantee to every State in this Union a republican form of government, and shall protect each of them against invasion, and on application of the legislature, or of the executive (when the legislature cannot be convened), against domestic violence.

314

## ARTICLE V

The Congress, whenever two-thirds of both Houses shall deem it necessary, shall propose amendments to this Constitution, or, on the application of the legislatures of two-thirds of the several States, shall call a convention for proposing amendments, which in either case shall be valid to all intents and purposes as part of this Constitution, when ratified by the legislatures of three-fourths of the several States, or by conventions in three-fourths thereof, as the one or the other mode of ratification may be proposed by the Congress; provided that no amendment which may be made prior to the year one thousand eight hundred and eight shall in any manner affect the first and fourth clauses in the Ninth Section of the First Article; and that no State, without its consent shall be deprived of its equal suffrage in the Senate.

## ARTICLE VI

[1] All debts contracted and engagements entered into, before the adoption of this Constitution, shall be as valid against the United States under this Constitution as under the Confederation.

[2] This Constitution, and the laws of the United States which shall be made in pursuance thereof, and all treaties made, or which shall be made, under the authority of the United States, shall be the supreme law of the land; and the judges in every State shall be bound thereby, anything in the Constitution or laws of any State to the contrary notwithstanding.

[3] The Senators and Representatives before mentioned and the members of the several State legislatures, and all executive and judicial officers both of the United States and of the several States, shall be bound by oath or affirmation to support this Constitution; but no religious test shall ever be required as a qualification to any office or public trust under the United States.

## ARTICLE VII

The ratification of the conventions of nine States shall be sufficient for the establishment of this Constitution between the States so ratifying the same.

## AMENDMENT I

Congress shall make no law respecting an establishment of religion, or prohibiting the free exercise thereof; or abridging the freedom of speech or of the press; or the right of the people peaceably to assemble, and to petition the government for a redress of grievances.

## AMENDMENT II

A well-regulated militia being necessary to the security of a free State, the right of the people to keep and bear arms shall not be infringed.

# CONSTITUTION OF THE UNITED STATES

## AMENDMENT III

No soldier shall, in time of peace, be quartered in any house without the consent of the owner, nor in time of war, but in a manner to be prescribed by law.

## AMENDMENT IV

The right of the people to be secure in their persons, houses, papers, and effects, against unreasonable searches and seizures, shall not be violated, and no warrants shall issue but upon probable cause, supported by oath or affirmation, and particularly describing the place to be searched, and the persons or things to be seized.

## AMENDMENT V

No person shall be held to answer for a capital, or otherwise infamous crime, unless on a presentment or indictment of a grand jury, except in cases arising in the land or naval forces, or in the militia, when in actual service in time of war or public danger; nor shall any person be subject for the same offense to be twice put in jeopardy of life or limb; nor shall be compelled in any criminal case to be a witness against himself, nor be deprived of life, liberty or property, without due process of law; nor shall private property be taken for public use without just compensation.

## AMENDMENT VI

In all criminal prosecutions, the accused shall enjoy the right to a speedy and public trial, by an impartial jury of the State and district wherein the crime shall have been committed, which district shall have been previously ascertained by law, and to be informed of the nature and cause of the accusation; to be confronted with the witnesses against him; to have compulsory process for obtaining witnesses in his favor, and to have the assistance of counsel for his defense.

## AMENDMENT VII

In suits at common law, where the value in controversy shall exceed twenty dollars, the right of trial by jury shall be preserved, and no fact tried by a jury shall be otherwise re-examined in any court of the United States, than according to the rules of the common law.

## AMENDMENT VIII

Excessive bail shall not be required, nor excessive fines imposed, nor cruel and unusual punishments inflicted.

## AMENDMENT IX

The enumeration in the Constitution of certain rights shall not be construed to deny or disparage others retained by the people.

# AMENDMENT X

The powers not delegated to the United States by the Constitution, nor prohibited by it to the States, are reserved to the States respectively, or to the people.

# AMENDMENT XI

The judicial power of the United States shall not be construed to extend to any suit in law or equity, commenced or prosecuted against one of the United States by citizens of another State, or by citizens or subjects of any foreign state.

# AMENDMENT XII

[1] The Electors shall meet in their respective States and vote by ballot for President and Vice-President, one of whom, at least, shall not be an inhabitant of the same State with themselves; they shall name in their ballots the person voted for as President, and in distinct ballots the person voted for as Vice-President, and they shall make distinct lists of all persons voted for as President and of all persons voted for as Vice-President, and of the number of votes for each; which lists they shall sign and certify, and transmit sealed to the seat of the government of the United States, directed to the President of the Senate. The President of the Senate shall, in the presence of the Senate and House of Representatives, open all the certificates and the votes shall then be counted. The person having the greatest number of votes for President shall be the President, if such number be a majority of the whole number of Electors appointed; and if no person have such majority, then from the persons having the highest numbers not exceeding three on the list of those voted for as President, the House of Representatives shall choose immediately, by ballot, the President. But in choosing the President the votes shall be taken by States, the representation from each State having one vote; a quorum for this purpose shall consist of a member or members from two-thirds of the States, and a majority of all the States shall be necessary to a choice. And if the House of Representatives shall not choose a President whenever the right of choice shall devolve upon them, before the fourth day of March next following, then the Vice-President shall act as President, as in the case of the death or other constitutional disability of the President.

[2] The person having the greatest number of votes as Vice-President shall be the Vice-President, if such number be a majority of the whole number of Electors appointed; and if no person have a majority, then from the two highest numbers on the list the Senate shall choose the Vice-President; a quorum for the purpose shall consist of two-thirds of the whole number of Senators, and a majority of the whole number shall be necessary to a choice. But no person constitutionally ineligible to the office of President shall be eligible to that of Vice-President of the United States.

# AMENDMENT XIII

## SECTION I

Neither slavery nor involuntary servitude, except as a punishment for crime whereof the party shall have been duly convicted, shall exist within the United States, or any place subject to their jurisdiction.

317

SECTION II

Congress shall have power to enforce this article by appropriate legislation.

AMENDMENT XIV

SECTION I

All persons born or naturalized in the United States, and subject to the jurisdiction thereof, are citizens of the United States and of the State wherein they reside. No State shall make or enforce any law which shall abridge the privileges or immunities of citizens of the United States; nor shall any State deprive any person of life, liberty or property, without due process of law; nor deny to any person within its jurisdiction the equal protection of the laws.

SECTION II

Representatives shall be apportioned among the several States according to their respective numbers, counting the whole number of persons in each State, excluding Indians not taxed. But when the right to vote at any election for the choice of Electors for President and Vice-President of the United States, Representatives in Congress, the executive and judicial officers of a State, or the members of the legislature thereof, is denied to any of the male inhabitants of such State, being twenty-one years of age, and citizens of the United States, or in any way abridged except for participation in rebellion or other crime, the basis of representation therein shall be reduced in the proportion which the number of such male citizens shall bear to the whole number of male citizens twenty-one years of age in such State.

SECTION III

No person shall be a Senator or Representative in Congress, or elector of President and Vice-President, or hold any office, civil or military, under the United States or under any State, who, having previously taken an oath as a member of Congress, or as an officer of the United States, or as a member of any State legislature, or as an executive or judicial officer of any State, to support the Constitution of the United States, shall have engaged in insurrection or rebellion against the same, or given aid or comfort to the enemies thereof. But Congress may, by a vote of two-thirds of each House, remove such disability.

SECTION IV

The validity of the public debt of the United States, authorized by law, including debts incurred for payment of pensions and bounties for services in suppressing insurrection or rebellion, shall not be questioned. But neither the United States nor any State shall assume or pay any debt or obligation incurred in aid of insurrection or rebellion against the United States, or any claim for the loss or emancipation of any slave; but all such debts, obligations, and claims shall be held illegal and void.

SECTION V

The Congress shall have power to enforce, by appropriate legislation, the provisions of this article.

318

## AMENDMENT XV

### SECTION I

The right of citizens of the United States to vote shall not be denied or abridged by the United States or by any State on account of race, color, or previous condition of servitude.

### SECTION II

The Congress shall have power to enforce this article by appropriate legislation.

## AMENDMENT XVI

The Congress shall have power to lay and collect taxes on incomes, from whatever source derived, without apportionment among the several States, and without regard to any census or enumeration.

## AMENDMENT XVII

### SECTION I

The Senate of the United States shall be composed of two Senators from each State, elected by the people thereof, for six years; and each Senator shall have one vote. The electors in each State shall have the qualifications requisite for electors of the most numerous branch of the State legislatures.

### SECTION II

When vacancies happen in the representation of any State in the Senate, the executive authority of such State shall issue writs of election to fill such vacancies: Provided, that the legislature of any State may empower the executive thereof to make temporary appointments until the people fill the vacancies by election as the legislature may direct.

### SECTION III

This amendment shall not be so construed as to affect the election or term of any Senator chosen before it becomes valid as part of the Constitution.

## AMENDMENT XVIII

### SECTION I

After one year from the ratification of this article the manufacture, sale or transportation of intoxicating liquors within, the importation thereof into, or the exportation thereof from the United States and all territory subject to the jurisdiction thereof, for beverage purposes, is hereby prohibited.

### SECTION II

The Congress and the several States shall have concurrent power to enforce this article by appropriate legislation.

SECTION III

This article shall be inoperative unless it shall have been ratified as an amendment to the Constitution by the legislatures of the several States, as provided in the Constitution, within seven years from the date of the submission hereof to the States by the Congress.

AMENDMENT XIX

SECTION I

The right of citizens of the United States to vote shall not be denied or abridged by the United States or by any State on account of sex.

SECTION II

Congress shall have power to enforce this article by appropriate legislation.

AMENDMENT XX

SECTION I

The terms of the President and Vice-President shall end at noon on the 20th day of January, and the terms of Senators and Representatives at noon on the 3d day of January, of the years in which such terms would have ended if this article had not been ratified; and the terms of their successors shall then begin.

SECTION II

The Congress shall assemble at least once in every year, and such meeting shall begin at noon on the 3d day of January, unless they shall by law appoint a different day.

SECTION III

If, at the time fixed for the beginning of the term of the President, the President-elect shall have died, the Vice-President-elect shall become President. If a President shall not have been chosen before the time fixed for the beginning of his term or if the President-elect shall have failed to qualify, then the Vice-President-elect shall act as President until a President shall have qualified; and the Congress may by law provide for the case wherein neither a President-elect nor a Vice-President-elect shall have qualified, declaring who shall then act as President, or the manner in which one who is to act shall be selected, and such person shall act accordingly until a President or Vice-President shall have qualified.

SECTION IV

The Congress may by law provide for the case of the death of any of the persons from whom the House of Representatives may choose a President whenever the right of choice shall have devolved upon them, and for the case of death of any of the persons from whom the Senate may choose a Vice-President whenever the right of choice shall have devolved upon them.

## SECTION V

Sections I and II shall take effect on the 15th day of October following the ratification of this article.

## SECTION VI

This article shall be inoperative unless it shall have been ratified as an amendment to the Constitution by the legislatures of three-fourths of the several States within seven years from the date of its submission.

# AMENDMENT XXI

## SECTION I

The eighteenth article of amendment to the Constitution of the United States is hereby repealed.

## SECTION II

The transportation or importation into any State, territory, or possession of the United States for delivery or use therein of intoxicating liquors, in violation of the laws thereof, is hereby prohibited.

## SECTION III

This article shall be inoperative unless it shall have been ratified as an amendment to the Constitution by conventions in the several States, as provided in the Constitution, within seven years from the date of the submission hereof to the States by the Congress.

# AMENDMENT XXII

## SECTION I

No person shall be elected to the office of President more than twice, and no person who has held the office of President, or acted as President, for more than two years of a term to which some other person was elected President shall be elected to the office of President more than once. But this Article shall not apply to any person holding the office of President when this Article was proposed by the Congress, and shall not prevent any person who may be holding the office of President, or acting as President, during the term within which this Article becomes operative from holding the office of President or acting as President during the remainder of such term.

## SECTION II

This article shall be inoperative unless it shall have been ratified as an amendment to the Constitution by the legislatures of three-fourths of the several States within seven years from the date of its submission to the States by the Congress.

## AMENDMENT XXIII

### SECTION I

The District constituting the seat of Government of the United States shall appoint in such manner as the Congress may direct:

A number of electors of President and Vice-President equal to the whole number of Senators and Representatives in Congress to which the District would be entitled if it were a State, but in no event more than the least populous State; they shall be in addition to those appointed by the States, but they shall be considered, for the purposes of the election of President and Vice-President, to be electors appointed by a State; and they shall meet in the District and perform such duties as provided by the twelfth article of amendment.

### SECTION II

The Congress shall have power to enforce this article by appropriate legislation.

## AMENDMENT XXIV

### SECTION I

The right of citizens of the United States to vote in any primary or other election for President or Vice-President, for electors for President or Vice-President, or for Senator or Representative in Congress, shall not be denied or abridged by the United States or any State by reason of failure to pay any poll tax or other tax.

### SECTION II

The Congress shall have power to enforce this article by appropriate legislation.

## AMENDMENT XXV

### SECTION I

In case of the removal of the President from office or of his death or resignation, the Vice-President shall become President.

### SECTION II

Whenever there is a vacancy in the office of the Vice-President, the President shall nominate a Vice-President who shall take office upon confirmation by a majority vote of both Houses of Congress.

### SECTION III

Whenever the President transmits to the President pro tempore of the Senate and the Speaker of the House of Representatives his written declaration that he is unable to discharge the powers and duties of his office, and until he transmits to them a written declaration to the contrary, such powers and duties shall be discharged by the Vice-President as Acting President.

## SECTION IV

Whenever the Vice-President and a majority of either the principal officers of the executive departments or of such other body as Congress may by law provide, transmit to the President pro tempore of the Senate and the Speaker of the House of Representatives their written declaration that the President is unable to discharge the powers and duties of his office, the Vice-President shall immediately assume the powers and duties of the office as Acting President.

Thereafter, when the President transmits to the President pro tempore of the Senate and the Speaker of the House of Representatives his written declaration that no inability exists, he shall resume the powers and duties of his office unless the Vice-President and a majority of either the principal officers of the executive department or of such other body as Congress may by law provide, transmit within four days to the President pro tempore of the Senate and the Speaker of the House of Representatives their written declaration that the President is unable to discharge the powers and duties of his office. Thereupon Congress shall decide the issue, assembling within forty-eight hours for that purpose if not in session. If the Congress, within twenty-one days after receipt of the latter written declaration, or, if Congress is not in session, within twenty-one days after Congress is required to assemble, determines by two-thirds vote of both Houses that the President is unable to discharge the powers and duties of his office, the Vice-President shall continue to discharge the same as Acting President; otherwise, the President shall resume the powers and duties of his office.

## AMENDMENT XXVI

### SECTION I

The right of citizens of the United States, who are eighteen years of age or older, to vote shall not be denied or abridged by the United States or by any State on account of age.

### SECTION II

The Congress shall have power to enforce this article by appropriate legislation.

# NOTES

CONSERVATIVES IN POWER AND THE STRONG PRESIDENCY

1. James Burnham, *Congress and the American Tradition* (Chicago: Henry Regnery Co., 1959), p. 128.
2. George Nash, *The Conservative Intellectual Movement in America* (New York: Basic Books, 1976), p. 239. It is a striking irony that in 1961 political conservatism organized itself *not* for the sake of electing a conservative Congress but a conservative President. That choice may have reflected an economy of time and resources, but it implicitly recognized the need for at least some kind of presidential leadership—and presumably more than a weak or passive executive might offer.
3. See, for example, *The Imperial Congress: Crisis in the Separation of Powers,* Gordon S. Jones, and John A. Marini, eds. (New York: Pharos Books, 1988).
4. See, for example, *The Fettered Presidency: Legal Constraints on the Executive Branch,* L. Gordon Crovitz and Jeremy A. Rabkin, eds. (Washington: The American Enterprise Institute, 1988).
5. Some libertarian conservatives seem to equate the strong presidency with liberalism. Writing in the *Wall Street Journal* of September 12, 1991, Doug Bandow, a fellow at the Cato Institute who served in the Reagan White House in 1981–82, accuses "many conservatives" of wanting "their Presidents to be like the liberal activists of yore."
6. An important exception, in the field of national security, is Carnes Lord, *The Presidency and the Management of National Security* (New York: Free Press, 1988). Lord served from 1981 to 1984 on the staff of the National Security Council.
7. *The Federalist No. 70* (A. Hamilton) (New York: Mentor Books, 1961), p. 423.
8. Joseph Califano, *The Triumph and Tragedy of Lyndon Johnson: The White House Years* (New York: Simon and Schuster, 1991), p. 338.
9. Walter Mondale, *The Accountability of Power: Toward a Responsible Presidency* (New York: David McKay, 1976), p. xv. I am indebted to Gary Schmitt for the phrase "presidential nation." He distinguishes this concept from that of "presidential governance," the latter being consistent with what the Constitution envisions.
10. George F. Will, "Fly Me, Air Uncle Sam," *Newsweek,* December 2, 1991, p. 90.
11. There are, of course, some notable exceptions. Senator Al Gore, for

example, differed from his Democratic brethren by voting to support the administration's military effort against Saddam Hussein.

12. James Q. Wilson, *Bureaucracy: What Government Agencies Do and Why They Do It* (New York: Basic Books, 1989), p. 378.
13. See the discussion by James W. Ceaser in his comment on the paper given by Arthur M. Schlesinger, Jr., in the symposium, "The Constitution and Presidential Leadership," *Maryland Law Review,* vol. 47, no. 1 (1988): 112.
14. Richard E. Neustadt, *Presidential Power: The Politics of Leadership* (New York: John Wiley, 1960).
15. Ibid., p. vii.
16. Richard E. Neustadt, *Presidential Power and the Modern Presidents* (New York: Free Press, 1990), p. 29. This latest edition includes new chapters on Reagan.
17. Contrary to Neustadt, while under the Constitution some power obviously is not in the possession of one elective branch of government alone and thus can be said to be "shared," a great deal of power cannot be described that way. Neither the impeachment power (given to Congress) nor the pardon power (given to the President) is "shared," and the exercise of some powers held by the one branch can be blocked by the other only with great difficulty. As the Persian Gulf war showed, the President's authority as Commander in Chief of our military forces is just such a power. Bush deployed troops as he wished.
18. Hedrick Smith, *The Power Game: How Washington Works* (New York: Ballantine Books, 1989), p. 15.
19. *The Federalist No. 75* (A. Hamilton), p. 450.
20. Ibid.
21. Joseph M. Bessette and Jeffrey Tulis discuss Neustadt's view of the Constitution in "The Constitution, Politics, and the Presidency," in *The Presidency in the Constitutional Order,* Joseph M. Bessette and Jeffrey Tulis, eds. (Baton Rouge: Louisiana State University Press, 1981), pp. 3–4.
22. "Letter of Pacificus," *The Works of Alexander Hamilton,* Vol. 4, Henry Cabot Lodge, ed. (New York: G. P. Putnam, 1969), p. 438.
23. Hamilton's discussion of those powers and duties is found in *The Federalist Nos. 66–77.*
24. *The Federalist No. 73* (A. Hamilton), pp. 442, 445.
25. *The Federalist No. 70* (A. Hamilton), p. 423
26. *The Federalist No. 37* (J. Madison), p. 226.
27. Charles C. Thach, Jr., *The Creation of the Presidency 1775–1789: A Study in Constitutional History* (Baltimore: Johns Hopkins University Press, 1969), p. xi.
28. See generally Harvey C. Mansfield, Jr., *Taming the Prince: The Ambivalence of Modern Executive Power* (New York: Free Press, 1989).
29. *The Federalist No. 67* (A. Hamilton), p. 407.
30. *The Federalist No. 68* (A. Hamilton), p. 413.
31. Perhaps the best single volume on the creation of the presidency is Thach, *The Creation of the Presidency 1775–1789.*

32. *The Federalist No. 72* (A. Hamilton), p. 437.
33. In addition to the alterations by constitutional amendment (which have not changed the powers of the office), major changes include the development and institutionalization of a large White House staff, the growth of cabinet and subcabinet agencies, the rise of the administrative state, the democratization begun with the presidency of Andrew Jackson, and the advent of the bully pulpit in the presidency of Theodore Roosevelt.
34. Mansfield, *Taming the Prince,* p. 7. That latent teaching instructed both Jimmy Carter and Ronald Reagan against the legislative veto. Both Presidents were supportive of such a device; early in their presidencies both came to regard it as an invasion of their prerogative. In Reagan's case, his Attorney General, William French Smith, proved instrumental in turning him around, thus clearing the way for the administration's successful argument against the legislative veto in 1983 in *INS* v. *Chadha.*
35. The oath the President takes, spelled out in Article II, is: "I do solemnly swear (or affirm) that I will faithfully execute the Office of President of the United States, and will to the best of my ability, preserve, protect and defend the Constitution of the United States."

PART ONE
THE PRESIDENT AND CONGRESS

1. David A. Stockman, *The Triumph of Politics: Why the Reagan Revolution Failed* (New York: Harper & Row, 1986), p. 159.
2. Ibid., p. 12.
3. It is not even mentioned in the authoritative *Encyclopedia of the Constitution.* (4 vols.) Leonard W. Levy et al., eds. (New York: Macmillan, 1986).
4. See J. Gregory Sidak, "The Recommendation Clause," *The Georgetown Law Journal,* vol. 77, no. 6 (August 1989): 2079, 2082.
5. That the Recommendation Clause does not provide for the power to exercise the duty to recommend legislation is unimportant. If the President has a constitutional duty, he must have the power to exercise it, and he is vested at the beginning of Article II with "the executive power," which can be read as enabling the President to execute his various constitutional duties.
6. Sidak, "The Recommendation Clause," p. 2082, fn. 15.
7. Ibid., p. 2085.
8. Section 3 of Article II also includes the President's prerogatives to convene both houses of Congress or either of them on "extraordinary occasions," and to adjourn them when they disagree on the time of adjournment. The President has often exercised this first power, but never the second.
9. What is true of bills passed by both houses is also true of every order, or

resolution or vote "to which the concurrence of" both chambers is necessary. These, too, must be presented to the President for his approval or veto.

10. There is an interesting question here: What is the fundamental nature of the veto power—executive or legislative in character? That the veto power is provided for in Article I, the legislative article, suggests that the power is legislative. And the veto is designed to promote deliberation—which is the principle point of having a legislature; the veto is a revisionary tool. On the other hand, the veto is also designed to stop absolutely bad legislation and to enable the President to defend himself. In these respects, it seems to be energy. Hamilton himself called the veto "an ingredient" of energy. Perhaps the best way to understand the veto is as a legislative/executive mixture.

11. The Constitution also requires recorded votes when override efforts are made. Recorded votes are not required in other circumstances. The Constitution thus enables the public to know the precise nature of the political division on an issue.

12. Obviously, the two clauses do not define the totality of the relationship of the President to Congress. Congress has the power to confirm certain presidential nominees—including executive officers, judges, and ambassadors. And it must ratify treaties the President makes. I deal with judicial nomination and appointment in Part Three. My interest here in Part One is in the President's role in ordinary legislation—the central work of Congress. I do not discuss the legislative role of the Vice President, who is authorized to cast tie-breaking votes.

## Chapter 1
### Speaking from the Bully Pulpit

1. In thinking about presidential rhetoric, I have benefited substantially from a book and an essay on the subject. The book is *The Rhetorical Presidency* by Jeffrey K. Tulis (Princeton: Princeton University Press, 1987). The essay is "The Rise of the Rhetorical Presidency," by James W. Ceaser, Glen E. Thurow, Jeffrey Tulis, and Joseph M. Bessette, in *Presidential Studies Quarterly,* vol. 11 (Summer 1981). I agree with much of what these writers say, although I do not adopt their term, "the rhetorical presidency," which I take to be a pejorative. There is a place for rhetoric in a presidency, as Tulis et al. would agree. Presidential rhetoric, properly understood, must be distinguished from the rhetorical presidency.

2. Johnson went public in an effort to pressure Congress to adopt his reconstruction policies. His proper rhetoric was condemned in the press and by his political opponents and served as the basis for the tenth article of impeachment: "That said Andrew Johnson . . . mindful of the high duties of his office and the dignity and propriety thereof . . . did . . . make and deliver with a loud voice certain intemperate, inflamma-

tory, and scandalous harangues, and did therein utter loud threats and bitter menaces as well against Congress as the laws of the United States. . . . Which said utterances, declarations, threats, and harangues, highly censurable in any, are peculiarly indecent and unbecoming in the Chief Magistrate of the United States, by means whereof . . . Andrew Johnson has brought the high office of the President of the United States into contempt, ridicule, and disgrace, to the great scandal of all good citizens." Quoted in Tulis, *The Rhetorical Presidency,* pp. 90–91.

3. "Speech at Pittsburgh, Pa., February 15, 1861," in *The Collected Works of Abraham Lincoln* (9 vols.), Roy P. Basler, ed. (New Brunswick, N.J.: Rutgers University Press, 1953–55), vol. 4, p. 210.

4. *The Federalist No. 49* (J. Madison) (New York: Mentor Books, 1961), p. 317.

5. *The Federalist No. 71* (A. Hamilton), p. 432.

6. In 1801 President Jefferson discontinued the practice established by his two predecessors of presenting recommendations to Congress through speeches at the opening of each legislative session. J. Gregory Sidak observes that this commenced a decline of the President's legislative role under the Recommendation Clause. See J. Gregory Sidak, "The Recommendation Clause," *Georgetown Law Journal,* vol. 77, no. 6 (August 1989): 2092ff.

7. *The Federalist No. 72* (A. Hamilton), p. 437.

8. The legislation empowered the Interstate Commerce Commission to regulate railroad shipping rates and to enforce their compliance. See John Morton Blum, *The Progressive Presidents* (New York: Norton, 1982), pp. 40–42.

9. See Tulis, *The Rhetorical Presidency,* pp. 95–116.

10. Theodore Roosevelt, *The Autobiography of Theodore Roosevelt,* Wayne Andrews, ed. (New York: Scribner's, 1958), p. 197.

11. Quoted in Blum, *The Progressive Presidents,* p. 58. In this same letter, Roosevelt also said, "I believe in a strong executive; I believe in power. . . ."

12. See, for example, Blum, *The Progressive Presidents,* which treats the two Roosevelts, Wilson, and Johnson.

13. Woodrow Wilson, *Congressional Government: A Study in American Politics* (Baltimore: Johns Hopkins University Press, 1981; orig. ed., 1885). See the discussion of Wilson's effort to overcome separation of powers by Charles R. Kesler in "Separation of Powers and the Administrative State," in *The Imperial Congress: Crisis in the Separation of Powers,* Gordon S. Jones and John Marini, eds. (New York: Pharos Books, 1988), pp. 20–40.

14. Woodrow Wilson, *Constitutional Government in the United States* (New York: Columbia University Press, 1961; orig. ed. 1908).

15. Charles R. Kesler, "Woodrow Wilson and the Statesmanship of Progress," in *Natural Right and Political Right,* Thomas R. Silver and Peter W. Schramm, eds. (Durham, N.C.: Carolina Academic Press, 1984), p. 116.

16. Quoted in Ceaser et al., "The Rise of the Rhetorical Presidency," p. 162.
17. Tulis, *The Rhetorical Presidency*, p. 117.
18. Ibid., p. 129.
19. Wilson in fact intended that the President would be freed of administrative details so that he might concentrate on being a plebiscitary leader. For Wilson, the experts manning the administrative state would implement the policies determined by the legislative process, which the President would command by virtue of his visionary rhetoric.
20. Consider how Wilson regarded his relationship to the people. In his 1912 presidential campaign, Wilson said: "I have often thought that the only strength of a public man consisted in the number of persons who agreed with him; and that the only strength that any man can boast of and be proud of is that great bodies of his fellow citizens trust him and are ready to follow him. For the business of every leader of government is to hear what the nation is saying and to know what the nation is enduring. It is not his business to judge *for* the nation, but to judge *through* the nation as its spokesman and voice." Quoted in Kesler, "Woodrow Wilson and the Statesmanship of Progress," p. 123.
21. Garry Wills, "The Presbyterian Nietzsche," *The New York Review of Books,* January 16, 1992, p. 58.
22. Robert S. Hirschfield, ed., *The Power of the Presidency: Concepts and Controversy,* 3rd Edition (New York: Aldine De Gruyter, 1982), p. 49.
23. Blum, *The Progressive Presidents,* p. 18.
24. Ibid., p. 178.
25. Harry McPherson, *A Political Education* (Boston: Little, Brown, 1972), pp. 310–2.
26. Democratic pollster Patrick Cadell advised Carter at the start of his term that "governing with public approval requires a continuing political campaign." It is with the Carter presidency that governing and campaigning are finally theorized into a single activity.
27. After the Iranian hostage crisis, Carter quit his rhetorical effort and attempted to act presidential—as a constitutional officer. Ceaser et al., "The Rise of the Rhetorical Presidency," p. 158.
28. David A. Stockman, *The Triumph of Politics* (New York: Harper & Row, 1986), pp. 105–9.
29. See Tulis, *The Rhetorical Presidency,* pp. 197–202.
30. SDI served a critical role in arms control negotiations with the Soviet Union, and it may serve a future role in U.S. defense strategy. Indisputably, it was Reagan's idea; had he not been President, the project would not have been born. See Lou Cannon, *President Reagan: The Role of a Lifetime* (New York: Simon and Schuster, 1991), pp. 318–23.
31. Louis Fisher, "The Presidential Veto: Constitutional Development," in *Pork Barrels and Principles: The Politics of the Presidential Veto* (Washington: National Legal Center for the Public Interest, 1988), p. 23.
32. Presidents have had speech writers since Hamilton and Madison composed for Washington; not until this century, however, and especially since the Kennedy administration, did Presidents hire individuals

*only* to write speeches. The most well-known recent speechwriter is Peggy Noonan, who worked for Reagan and Bush. The distance in terms of governing ability between Alexander Hamilton and most modern speechwriters is galactic.

33. *The Fettered Presidency: Legal Constraints on the Executive Branch,* L. Gordon Crovitz and Jeremy A. Rabkin, eds. (Washington: American Enterprise Institute, 1989), p. 12.

34. In Reagan's memoir he talked about going around the legislative branch in order to get the people to see an issue his way. Reagan aimed to rally the people to compel Congress to act. See Ronald Reagan, *An American Life* (New York: Simon and Schuster, 1990), pp. 234, 288, 318.

35. See Tulis, *The Rhetorical Presidency,* pp. 10–13.

## CHAPTER 2
## TAX REFORM

1. Jeffrey Birnbaum and Alan Murray, *Showdown at Gucci Gulch: Lawmakers, Lobbyists & The Unlikely Triumph of Tax Reform* (New York: Random House, 1987), p. 108.

2. Don Regan, *For the Record: From Wall Street to Washington* (New York: Harcourt Brace Jovanovich, 1988), p. 204.

3. Jeffrey K. Tulis, *The Rhetorical Presidency* (Princeton: Princeton University Press, 1987), p. 194.

4. Birnbaum and Murray, *Showdown at Gucci Gulch,* p. 99.

5. Tulis, *The Rhetorical Presidency,* p. 195.

6. Birnbaum and Murray, *Showdown at Gucci Gulch,* p. xiv.

7. John Morton Blum, *The Progressive Presidents,* (New York: Norton, 1982), p. 68.

8. See Ronald Reagan, *An American Life* (New York: Simon and Schuster, 1990), p. 234.

9. Lou Cannon, *President Reagan: The Role of a Lifetime* (New York: Simon and Schuster, 1991), p. 554.

## CHAPTER 3
## "NO NEW TAXES"

1. My analysis of Bush's execution of office in this chapter primarily relies on news accounts in the *Washington Post,* the *New York Times,* and the *Wall Street Journal.* For a single account of the events from May through October 1990, see Alan Murray and Jackie Calmes, "How the Democrats, with Rare Cunning, Won the Budget War," *Wall Street Journal,* November 5, 1990.

2. Speechwriter Peggy Noonan crafted the lines on lips and taxes in George Bush's 1988 acceptance speech. Noonan gave this account of the

writing of the speech in her book, *What I Saw at the Revolution: A Political Life in the Reagan Era* (New York: Random House, 1990):

> Jack Kemp told me to hit hard on taxes, Bush will be pressured to raise them as soon as he's elected, and he has to make clear he won't budge. (This became, 'The Congress will push me to raise taxes, and I'll say no, and they'll push, and I'll say no, and they'll push again. And all I can say to them is read my lips: No New Taxes.' Aides to the vice president later took out 'read my lips' on the grounds, I believe, that lips are organs, there is no history of presidential candidates making personal-organ references in acceptance speeches, therefore . . . Anyway I kept putting it back in. Why? Because it's definite. It's not subject to misinterpretation. It means, I mean this.)

After the budget war of 1990 was over and Bush had agreed to some new taxes, Noonan told the *Wall Street Journal* that when she was writing Bush's 1988 convention speech, Richard Darman had advised her to strike the six words—"Read my lips: No new taxes"—on the grounds that it was "phony macho." The words stayed in. Bush warmed to them, especially as he saw their useful effect during his campaign.

3. The three-paragraph press release was actually composed during the breakfast. The week before Darman had offered a new plan of spending cuts with no additional taxes, which the Democrats rejected. Before the breakfast meeting, the Democratic leaders, Senator Majority Leader George J. Mitchell, House Speaker Thomas S. Foley, and House Majority Leader Richard A. Gephardt, had decided they would push the President to make a public statement on the need for new taxes as a way to get the talks moving again. At the breakfast, they pushed hard, with Mitchell asking, "Why don't you draft a statement right now?" Darman obliged. The Democrats were satisfied with the statement in all respects but one, its beginning. It consisted of a vague, passive introductory phrase: "It is clear that . . ." According to newspaper accounts, the Democrats succeeded in changing that to: "It is clear to me [meaning George Bush] that . . ." The breakfast group agreed that the White House would release the statement, that the Democratic leadership would hold a news conference on Capitol Hill, and that neither side would gloat over the apparent concessions made by the other. The release having been simply posted on the White House bulletin board, the President and his advisers naively believed that it did not commit him to higher tax rates and would leave him "wiggle room" on the tax issue.

4. Bush's strong preference for press conferences was revealed in a press conference (where else?) held in December 1989 at the Malta Summit. Asked how he was going to report to the American people on the summit, and whether he would do so in "an Oval Office speech," Bush responded, "Well, I just did one [a Thanksgiving evening address] just before going"—as though he often gave such speeches—"and I don't want to abuse the hospitality of the air waves." Bush added, "I think we can get the message out by responding to questions." For a discussion of

Bush's press conferences, see my article titled "Press Secretary Bush," *The American Spectator,* vol. 23, no. 2, (February 1990): 32–33.

5. Bush's aides told reporters that the point of his speech was to provide nervous congressmen "presidential cover" so that they could vote for the agreement. They said they "were swamped with calls, all against. The thing just turned on us." *Washington Post,* October 6, 1990.

6. *Congressional Quarterly,* October 13, 1990, p. 3393.

7. "Crossing the T in Taxes, Lawmakers' Eyes Turn to Votes on Deficit Deal," *New York Times,* October 26, 1990.

8. James W. Ceaser, Glen E. Thurow, Jeffrey Tulis, and Joseph M. Bessette point out that politicians often use rhetoric simply to win power, when they should see it as an instrument of responsible statesmanship. Bush's understanding of rhetoric in the campaign was one of what these authors would call "mere persuasion," nothing higher. "The Rise of the Rhetorical Presidency," *Presidential Studies Quarterly,* vol. 11 (Summer 1981): 168.

9. Paul G. Merski, "A Decade of Budget Summitry," published by the Tax Foundation, Washington, June 1990, p. 2.

CHAPTER 4
VETOES AND SIGNING STATEMENTS

1. Charles L. Black, Jr., "Some Thoughts on the Veto," *Law and Contemporary Problems,* vol. 40, no. 2 (Spring 1976): 101.

2. "Bush's Veto Strategy," *U.S. News & World Report,* July 2, 1990, pp. 18–20.

3. A second Presentment Clause follows the first. Article I, Section 7, clause 3 requires presentment of every "order, resolution or vote to which the concurrence of the Senate and House . . . may be necessary." This clause ensures that all legislative measures destined to become law will be subject to the President's veto power.

4. Robert J. Spitzer, "The President's Veto Power," in *Inventing the Presidency,* Thomas E. Cronin, ed. (Lawrence: University of Kansas Press, 1989), p. 168.

5. Alexis de Tocqueville, *Democracy in America* (Garden City, N.Y.: Anchor Books, 1969), p. 122.

6. This is not the case with the so-called "pocket veto," which is tantamount to an absolute veto. Under the Constitution, if the President fails to veto a bill within ten days (excepting Sundays), it becomes law "unless Congress by their adjournment prevent its return, in which case it shall not be a law." If the President keeps legislation in his "pocket" during the ten days Congress is in adjournment, he has in effect vetoed the bill. He may do so without sending an explanation of his veto to the house in which the bill originated. I do not treat the subject of the pocket veto except to say that some wish to milk more than it can yield. For a history of the pocket veto, see Louis Fisher, *Constitutional Con-*

*flicts Between Congress and the President* (Princeton: Princeton University Press, 1985), pp. 150–54.

7. Technically, two-thirds of a *quorum* is needed. See *Missouri Pacific Ry. Co.* v. *Kansas* 248 U.S. 276 (1919).

8. Peter M. Shane and Harold H. Bruff, *The Law of Presidential Power* (Durham, N.C.: Carolina Academic Press, 1988), p. 104.

9. *The Federalist No. 48* (J. Madison) (New York: Mentor Books, 1961), p. 308.

10. *The Federalist No. 51* (J. Madison), pp. 321–22.

11. *The Federalist No. 48* (J. Madison), p. 309.

12. *The Federalist No. 73* (A. Hamilton), pp. 443, 445.

13. Ibid., p. 442.

14. 462 U.S. 919 (1983).

15. In March 1989, Secretary of State James Baker announced an agreement between the two branches by which Congress would provide limited nonmilitary funding to the Nicaraguan opposition to the Sandinista government through February 28, 1990 (when elections were to be held). Part of the deal was that each of four congressional committees was given the unilateral power to stop the funding after November 30, 1989. The official statement announcing the accord contained no mention of this legislative veto. White House Counsel Boyden Gray told the President what the grant of power to the committees meant, arguing that the administration had unconstitutionally signed on to a legislative veto. For a powerful criticism of the Bush administration's action in this instance, see J. Gregory Sidak, "The President's Power of the Purse," *Duke Law Journal,* vol. 1989, no. 5 (1989): 1215–1217.

16. *The Federalist No. 73* (A. Hamilton), p. 443.

17. Ibid.

18. Ibid.

19. 4 Wheat. (17 U.S.) 316 (1819).

20. James Reichley, *Conservatives in an Age of Change: The Nixon and Ford Administrations* (Washington: Brookings Institution, 1981), p. 325.

21. Black, "Some Thoughts on the Veto," p. 90.

22. Ruti Teitel, "Bush, the Veto President," *New York Times,* December 9, 1990.

23. Robert J. Spitzer pointed out Teitel's constitutional errors in a letter to the *New York Times,* December 24, 1990.

24. *The Federalist No. 73* (A. Hamilton), p. 446

25. Quoted in Terry Eastland, "George Bush into the Breach," *National Review,* November 4, 1991, p. 42.

26. The audience for signing statements includes not only the executive branch and Congress, but also, in some instances, the federal courts. Whether a court consults a presidential signing statement in determining the meaning of a statute is, of course, up to the reviewing court and its members. The most logical consultation of a signing statement occurs in cases in which past interpretation of a provision by the execu-

tive branch is in dispute. Thus, in *INS* v. *Chadha* it was argued that the executive had acquiesced in the executive veto by signing and enforcing laws containing the device. Rejecting this argument, the Supreme Court observed that "eleven Presidents, from [Woodrow] Wilson through [Ronald] Reagan ... have gone on record at some point to challenge the congressional vetoes as constitutional." Many times the "at some point" was at presentment, in a signing statement.

27. Bush said certain management conferences authorized by the legislation were inconsistent with the Constitution. The legislation authorized governors and other state and local officials to appoint some of the conference membership. Bush said this was at odds with the Appointments Clause of the Constitution.

28. 478 U.S. 714 (1986).

29. It is a mistake to regard a signing statement that objects on constitutional grounds to a particular provision as a veto of any kind. The power of the President to make what has been called a "constitutional excision" does not come from the Presentment Clause but the President's duties to faithfully execute the laws and to defend the Constitution, both of which are Article II, executive powers.

30. For Glazier's argument as well as a useful compendium of essays on the subject, see L. Gordon Crovitz, ed., *Pork Barrels and Principles: The Politics of the Presidential Veto* (Washington: National Legal Center for the Public Interest, 1988). For Crovitz's treatment of the subject, see L. Gordon Crovitz, "The Line-Item Veto: The Best Response When Congress Passes One Spending 'Bill' a Year," *Pepperdine Law Review,* vol. 18, no. 1 (1990): 43–55. Other useful analyses include J. Gregory Sidak and Thomas A. Smith, "Four Faces of the Item Veto: A Reply to Tribe and Kurland," *Northwestern University Law Review,* vol. 84, no. 2 (1990): 437–449.

31. Before 1974, Presidents had "impounded" funds since the Washington presidency. (Impoundment occurred whenever the President spent less than Congress appropriated during a given period.) The 1974 budget act, responding to impoundments by President Nixon that Congress thought excessive, effectively ended the practice. One argument for the line-item veto is that it has in effect occurred since Washington's day—through impoundment—the budget act notwithstanding. But impoundment and the line-item veto differ, as J. Gregory Sidak and Tom Smith have pointed out, "in that impoundment permits the President to convert his veto of a line item from a discrete variable (limited solely to the choice between ratification and veto) to a continuous variable, whose magnitude in dollars the President can adjust at his discretion. The pure line-item veto, by contrast, simply permits the President to exercise, on a disaggregated basis, a discrete choice between ratification and veto. In this respect, the impoundment power appears greater than the line-item veto—though this appearance, of course, does not in itself imply that the President necessarily has the lesser line-item veto authority." "Four Faces of the Item Veto," p. 448. Whatever its constitutional

status, impoundment is not a power derived from the Presentment Clause, as the line-item veto purports to be.
32. Crovitz, "The Line-Item Veto," p. 43.

CHAPTER 5
SELF-DEFENSE, PLEASE

1. *The Federalist No. 73* (A. Hamilton) (New York: Mentor Books, 1961), p. 445.
2. 487 U.S. 654 (1988). For an account of the administration's litigating effort in *Morrison,* see Charles Fried, *Order and Law: Arguing the Reagan Revolution—A Firsthand Account* (New York: Simon and Schuster, 1991), pp. 132–71. Fried served as Solicitor General from 1985 to 1989. For a discussion of *Morrison* as well as a history of the independent counsel law, see Terry Eastland, *Ethics, Politics, and the Independent Counsel: Executive Power, Executive Vice 1789–1989* (Washington: National Legal Center for the Public Interest, 1989). The statute itself is codified at 28 U.S.C. §§ 591–599.
3. The "Saturday Night Massacre" led to a flurry of legislative proposals designed to ensure the independence of a Watergate prosecutor. Those gaining the strongest congressional support included provisions calling for the court appointment of the special prosecutor and denying presidential discretion to effect his removal. No legislation was passed, however. The immediate need for a politically independent prosecutor was effectively met with the administration's appointment of Leon Jaworski to succeed Cox and its assurances to Congress that his work would not be compromised.
4. The special court had this authority once the Attorney General made formal application for appointment of a special prosecutor. And the court had no discretion in whether or not it appointed a prosecutor; the Attorney General's application made appointment obligatory.
5. Section 546 of Title 28 vests in district courts the power to appoint *interim* U.S. attorneys. But this law does not deny the President the power to appoint U.S. attorneys; the President may remove a court-appointed U.S. attorney anytime he wishes and appoint the person of his choice.
6. The statute provided that everyone holding office with the advice and consent of the Senate was entitled to hold office until the President appointed a successor duly confirmed by the Senate. In addition, it provided that the Secretaries of State, Treasury, War, Navy, and Interior, the Postmaster General, and the Attorney General should hold office during the term of the President who had appointed them and for one month thereafter, "subject to removal by and with the advice and consent of the Senate." The Tenure of Office Act thus challenged the unconditional authority of the President to remove a department head for any reason he wished; this authority was understood to be contained within the executive power, as James Madison argued during the famous debate on the President's removal power in 1789. President An-

336

drew Johnson vetoed the Tenure of Office Act, as he should have, only to watch both houses vote to override. In 1887 Congress finally repealed the law following a confrontation over the executive's power to remove executive officers.

7. *The Federalist No. 69* (A. Hamilton), p. 416.

8. The world got a peek at Justice's view of the law when, in early 1981, Tim Kraft filed a lawsuit challenging the law on constitutional grounds. The House Counsel wrote Attorney General William French Smith, asking his view of the statute. On April 17, 1981, in a publicly released letter expressing his "serious reservations," Smith responded:

> In some or all of its applications, the Act appears fundamentally to contradict the principle of separation of powers erected by the Constitution. The power to enforce the law and to prosecute federal offenses is committed by the Constitution to the Executive branch. Indeed, the courts have generally recognized that the prosecution of federal offenses is an executive function within the exclusive prerogative of the Attorney General, and, ultimately, the President. For that reason federal prosecutors must be accountable [ultimately] to the President. The Special Prosecutor Act removes the responsibility for the enforcement of federal criminal laws from the Executive branch and lodges it in an officer who is not appointed by, accountable to, or save in extraordinary circumstances, removable by the Attorney General or the President.

Smith concluded by noting that if the Justice Department's view was sought in future litigation, it "would espouse views consistent with the above and addressed to the specific facts of the case." In the meantime, he added, unless Congress changed the law or the courts declared it unconstitutional, the Department would continue to comply with its requirements. In sum, the Department would enforce the law even thought it was prepared to argue in court against it.

9. A President works through the subordinates he appoints. The issue of appointments is an aspect of administration, discussed in Part Two. Suffice to say here that the government's top lawyer—the Attorney General—should have been the key figure in leading the administration's fight against the independent counsel law.

10. "Any statutory restriction on presidential removal of a federal prosecutor like the independent counsel," said John R. Bolton, the Department's legislative affairs chief in correspondence with Congress, "must yield to the explicit constitutional responsibility of the President to direct the prosecutor's execution of the laws."

11. In a memorandum drafted by the Office of Legal Counsel, Justice told Reagan that the bill was "fundamentally incompatible with the separation of powers mandated by the Constitution," that it directly usurped the President's "constitutional right and responsibility to execute the laws," and that in reducing the Attorney General's discretion it "effectively nullif[ied]" his role, and therefore the President's, in criminal law

enforcement. Justice also pointed out that a veto would have no impact on current independent counsel cases, inasmuch as the law required that any case begun during the life of the statute would run its natural course, with all the powers conferred upon existing independent counsels fully preserved. The Department recommended that the President say the following in a statement accompanying his veto: "This bill would enact a statute so fundamentally incompatible with the tripartite system of government established by our Constitution that I believe I have no responsible alternative. My objections to the present bill are rooted in the constitutional imperative that persons empowered to investigate and prosecute federal criminal offenses must be ultimately accountable to the President, the representative of all the people." The Justice brief in *Morrison* objected to the method of appointment under the statute, its limitation on the removal power, and its interference with the President's responsibility to execute the laws.

12. Reagan appointees wrote the only two opinions; Justice Kennedy was recused.

13. Paul W. Kahn, "Why Reagan Lost the Special Prosecutor Case," *Hartford Courant,* July 3, 1988.

14. As Kahn explained, "Without the appointment of a special prosecutor in the first place, it is difficult to imagine who might take the case to the Court." Ibid. Suppose the issue had been brought before a court. It would have been most unlikely that the federal judiciary would have ordered the President to enforce the law. See *Mississippi* v. *Johnson,* 4 Wall. (71 U.S.) 475 (1867). With the issue left to the elective branches, Congress could have decided to revise the law on the President's terms. On the other hand, talk of impeachment might have filled the Washington air. One can imagine the argument: that the President himself was doing something unconstitutional; that in refusing to execute a law of the United States, as the Constitution commands him to do, he was violating it in a most serious way. Articles of impeachment might have been drafted. A wise President would have avoided this controversy by relying upon a veto strategy instead.

15. I rely here on the recollections of Kenneth W. Starr, who assisted William French Smith in the transition and later served as his counselor, before President Reagan appointed him in 1983 to the U.S. Court of Appeals for the District of Columbia Circuit. In 1989 President Bush appointed Starr to succeed Charles Fried as Solicitor General.

16. 462 U.S. 919 (1983).

17. For a comprehensive treatment of legislative vetoes and the *Chadha* case, see Barbara H. Craig, *Chadha: The Story of the Epic Constitutional Struggle* (New York: Oxford University Press, 1987).

18. Writing for the Court, Chief Justice Warren Burger said that whenever congressional action has the "purpose and effect of altering the legal rights, duties, and relations of persons" outside the legislative branch, Congress must act through both Houses in a bill presented to the President.

19. William French Smith, *Law and Justice in the Reagan Administration:*

*Memoirs of an Attorney General* (Stanford: Hoover Institution Press, 1991), p. 222.

20. Seymour has proved the most eccentric of independent counsels to date. He drew his own office seal, featuring an eagle with its head turned defiantly in the opposite direction from the one of the Justice Department seal; the point, as he put it, was that his office had "total independence." And it was Seymour who, upon winning Deaver's conviction on perjury, told reporters how much "loose money" there was in Washington, before going out to advertise himself as someone willing to accept large fees to talk about government ethics.

21. Because I discuss only the conduct of independent counsels *before* Reagan was presented with the second reauthorization bill, I omit the unreasonable behavior of counsels since then, especially Walsh's. See my discussion of Walsh in "The Independent-Counsel Regime," *The Public Interest,* no. 100 (Summer 1990): 68–80; and in "Above the Constitution?" *Commentary,* May 1991, pp. 60–62.

22. After Reagan signed the reauthorization bill, it came to light that Morrison had committed another dubious act. With the applicable statute of limitations to expire on March 10, 1988, Morrison threatened Olson with a "sealed, protective indictment" if he did not waive his rights to the expiration of the statute of limitations. Olson agreed; Morrison got more time. But Olson had little choice. Had he been indicted, he could not, under the statute, have recovered legal fees, even if acquitted. With his expenses running close to one million dollars, Morrison's threat was tantamount to blackmail, made all the more outrageous by the fact that she not only had no reasonable assurance of winning a conviction but also had no evidence against Olson.

23. Meese, often more "pragmatic" than some conservatives believed, probably would not have opposed the law. My sense is that he probably would have been influenced by the same political considerations that led Reagan to sign the bill. See Chapter 12, note 12, for a discussion of another instance in which Meese was the Reaganite pragmatist—his decision *not* to change the pro-quota enforcement of Executive Order 11246.

24. First-term Treasury Secretary and second-term Chief of Staff Donald Regan writes in his memoir, "Of all the inherent duties of an American President, the duty to say no on matters of principle is among the most important. In the Reagan White House the word was seldom uttered, and then usually only at the last possible moment.' Donald T. Regan, *For the Record: From Wall Street to Washington* (New York: Harcourt Brace Jovanovich, 1988), p. 245. Charles J. Cooper, who served seven years in the Reagan Justice Department, the final three as Assistant Attorney General for the Office of Legal Counsel, dealt with all the issues involving the President's rights and responsibilities, including the independent counsel statute. Cooper faults Reagan's White House advisers: "Preserving presidential prerogatives, protecting the office itself, was not viewed as that important. Far more important was getting a good political result or avoiding a bad one." Interview with the author, June 2, 1990, Washington, D.C.

25. The Justice Department managed legislative strategy and the constitutional litigation—but with no guidance from the White House.
26. *The Federalist No. 71* (A. Hamilton), p. 432.
27. *The Federalist No. 48* (J. Madison), p. 310.
28. Fried, *Order and Law,* p. 144
29. *Morrison* provides a precedent for Congress to take the President's power to appoint an executive officer and vest it in the judiciary whenever it thinks it has a compelling reason to do so. The decision also is precedent for Congress to limit the President's power to remove an executive officer performing core duties unless the restriction "impede[s] the President's ability to perform his constitutional duty," as Rehnquist put it in his opinion for the Court. The Court neither defined what a sufficient reason for shifting the appointment power might be, nor what a restriction impeding the President's ability to perform his constitutional duty might look like. *Morrison* is precisely the kind of standardless decision that invites Congress to experiment. Significantly, in the wake of *Morrison,* legislation was introduced proposing a special environmental prosecutor who could be removed only for—familiar language—"good cause." And consider this: If Congress may limit the President's ability to control criminal law enforcement officers, if such a limitation does not prevent him from carrying out his constitutional duties, then Congress also, seemingly with more ease, could limit the President's ability to control or remove officers engaged in nonprosecutorial functions. (For example, it might create an independent arms control agency.)
30. 4 Wheat. (17 U.S.) 316 (1819).
31. James D. Richardson, ed., *A Compilation of the Messages & Papers of the Presidents: 1789–1897,* 10 vols. (Washington: U.S. Government Printing Office, 1895–1899), vol. 2: 576ff.
32. Joseph Bessette, "Guarding the Constitution: The Supreme Court and Legislative Tyranny," a paper delivered at a symposium on the Supreme Court sponsored by the American Enterprise Institute, May 24, 1991.
33. Equally perversely, the law encourages congressional irresponsibility. Congress doesn't have to investigate or commence impeachment proceedings when it has a system of court-appointed independent counsels it can activate.

### CHAPTER 6
### CONGRESS AGAINST THE PRESIDENT

1. Democrats disagreed with the President about the extent and even the existence of communist threat to Central America. Many believed that the Sandinistas would not export revolution to neighboring countries if the United States would simply butt out of its internal affairs; some thought democratic political reform inside Nicaragua would quickly follow an end to the civil war. The possibility of protracted civil war—a war the U.S. military might eventually be drawn into—was also worrisome.

2. See the *Report of the Congressional Committees Investigating the Iran-Contra Affair, with Supplemental, Minority, and Additional Views,* H. Rept. 100-433, S. Rept. 100-216 (Washington, 1987), pp. 489–90.

3. Boland IV, in effect from August 8, 1985 to March 31, 1986, provided $27 million in humanitarian aid only. And Boland V, in effect from the end of 1985 to October 17, 1986, permitted a classified amount of military and paramilitary aid to the Contras. The Boland era ended in October 1986 when Congress passed a $100 million contra-aid package that included $70 million in military aid.

4. The members of Congress who sat as the minority on the Iran-Contra investigating committees reminded the nation, and future occupants of the Oval Office: "The President's inherent constitutional powers are only as strong . . . as the President's willingness to defend them." *Report of the Congressional Committees Investigating the Iran-Contra Affair,* p. 445.

5. Ibid., p. 407.

6. Michael J. Malbin, "Legalism versus Political Checks and Balances: Legislative-Executive Relations in the Wake of Iran-Contra," L. Gordon Crovitz and Jeremy A. Rabkin, eds., *The Fettered Presidency* (Washington: American Enterprise Institute, 1989), pp. 286–89.

7. Ibid., p. 287.

8. Ibid., p. 288.

9. Ibid.

10. For discussion of what Reagan should have done, see Mark Falcoff, "Making Central America Safe for Communism," *Commentary,* vol. 85, no. 6 (June 1988), pp. 23–24.

11. Lou Cannon, *President Reagan: The Role of a Lifetime* (New York: Simon and Schuster, 1991), p. 358.

12. Ibid. p. 368.

13. For an excellent discussion of Hayes's action, which I adopt here in large part, see J. Gregory Sidak, "The President's Power of the Purse," *Duke Law Journal,* vol. 1989, no. 5 (1989): 1217–22.

14. Quoted in ibid., p. 1221.

## CHAPTER 7
### THE POLICY POWER OF THE VETO POWER

1. For discussion of the Reagan effort against quotas, including the litigation, see Part Two, Chapters 11 and 12.

2. 109 S.Ct. 2115 (1989).

3. The bill was returned to the house in which it originated, as provided for in the Constitution. With the Senate voting on the veto first, and failing to override, the legislative process came to a halt. Had the House voted, the strong likelihood is that the veto would have been sustained. Kennedy-Hawkins passed the House, but the vote was a dozen votes short of the margin needed for a two-thirds override.

4. Thus, in July remarks to the National Council of La Raza, Bush said, "I [want] to sign the civil rights bill of 1990 and not a quota bill of 1990. . . .

[W]e all know quotas aren't right. They are not fair. They divide society instead of bringing people together. And as leaders and representatives of the Hispanic-American community, I owe it to you to see that this legislation does not say to the young kids, you only fit in if you fit into a certain numbered quota. That is not the American dream. . . . I want desperately, I want very much, to sign a civil rights bill. . . . Talks are still going on. And we [will] renew the fight for a civil rights bill that I can sign . . . a bill that does not result in quotas."

5. "Indiscriminate Goal," *New Republic,* July 2, 1990, p. 7.
6. See Thomas Byrne Edsall and Mary D. Edsall, *Chain Reaction: The Impact of Race, Rights, and Taxes on American Politics* (New York: Norton, 1991) and Peter Brown, *Minority Party: Why Democrats Face Defeat in 1992 and Beyond* (Washington: Regnery Gateway, 1991).
7. For a compilation and analysis of these resources, see Terry Eastland and William J. Bennett, *Counting by Race: Equality from the Founding Fathers to Bakke and Weber* (New York: Basic Books, 1979).
8. I have elaborated these points in "George Bush's Quota Bill," *Policy Review,* no. 57 (Summer 1991): 45–49.
9. Quoted in Hugh Davis Graham, *The Civil Rights Era: Origins and Development of National Policy* (New York: Oxford University Press, 1990), p. 151.
10. 401 U.S. 424 (1971). As Hugh Graham observes, the EEOC's own *Administrative History* of 1969 acknowledged that Congress had defined discrimination as one of "intent in the state of mind of the actor," and that it did not consider professionally developed ability tests as discriminatory. The EEOC, though, had come to disregard "intent as crucial to the finding of an unlawful employment practice" and instead emphasized forms of employer behavior that "prove to have a demonstrable racial effect without clear and convincing business motive." The EEOC thought that either Congress would have to amend Title VII to embrace disparate impact theory or that the agency would have to change its policy to return to Congress's model of intentional discrimination. Graham, *The Civil Rights Era,* pp. 388–89.
11. Herman Belz, *Equality Transformed: A Quarter Century of Affirmative Action* (New Brunswick: Transaction, 1991), p. 54.
12. I have the E.F. Wonderlic memorandum in my files. It is undated but, on the basis of relevant Labor Department documents at the time, appears to have been sent to employers either in late 1972 or early 1973.
13. Stuart Taylor reported this example in *Legal Times,* May 13, 1991. Race-norming first came to widespread public attention in 1990. The civil rights legislation passed and approved by President Bush in late 1991 explicitly outlawed the practice.
14. Under *Wards Cove,* a plaintiff must isolate and identify the specific employment practices said to cause the statistical disparity; he cannot simply point to the disparity, even when properly drawn. Lower federal courts had held that plaintiffs in disparate impact cases do not have to specify the particular practice(s) responsible for the disparity. In cor-

recting those courts, the Supreme Court observed that every one of the Supreme Court's disparate impact cases focused on the impact of a *particular* employment practice.

15. Title VII cases fall into two categories: disparate treatment and disparate impact. Disparate treatment simply means different treatment that reflects an intention to discriminate and does not typically involve statistical proofs. Disparate treatment cases are obviously consistent with the original terms of Title VII. In these cases, the burden of proof lies with the plaintiff. By insisting that in disparate impact cases the burden of proof must lie with the plaintiff, the Court in *Wards Cove* might have been signaling an intention to bring the disparate impact approach in line with the disparate treatment approach, perhaps even someday to eliminate it altogether.

16. Bush could have proposed outlawing any arbitrarily imposed or irrational requirements that impede a minority group's progress in the work place. Under this rule, if an employer did not have a good reason for a challenged requirement, then a court could infer discriminatory intent, thus making a disparate impact case into a disparate treatment case. This should be the goal of any reform effort that seeks to honor the principle of nondiscrimination.

17. In *Lorance,* 190 S.Ct. 2261 (1989), the Court held that a lawsuit by three women alleging employment discrimination must fail because it was filed too late under the applicable limitations period in Title VII. In *Patterson,* 109 S.Ct. 2363 (1989), the Court held that the Civil Rights Act of 1866 is limited by its terms to prohibiting discrimination in making and enforcing contracts, and does not extend to [as the Court said] "problems that may arise later from the conditions of continuing employment." The Reagan administration had argued for different results in these two cases; the Bush administration's decision to support corrective legislation in these instances was not surprising.

18. Much of the compromise effort focused on the definition of business necessity. In the House the language requiring an employer to prove that an employment practice is "essential to effective job performance" was changed so that the employer would have to show "by objective evidence" that each employment practice "bears a substantial and demonstrable relationship to effective job performance." But Justice objected to the new language on grounds that it would impose standards "as difficult to understand as they are to meet." It maintained that employers would resort to quotas, and it reiterated its position that a veto would be recommended if the bill was not changed. Following the President's May 17 veto threat, the search for compromise was renewed. Kennedy proposed changing the definition of business necessity from a practice "essential to effective job performance" to one that bears a (as the House version had put it) "substantial and demonstrable relationship to effective job performance." The amendment also dropped the phrase, added in the House version, which required employers to prove business necessity by "objective evidence"—a phrase Justice had ob-

jected to. While Kennedy and his colleagues maintained that theirs was not a quota bill, Attorney General Richard Thornburgh disagreed. "The central problem," Thornburgh told the *Washington Post*, "is the notion that pure statistics, in and of themselves, can create a presumption which shifts the burden of proof to the employer." "Hiring-Quota Issue Snags Rights Bill," *Washington Post*, May 18, 1990.

19. Because the original administration position had been that only *Lorance* and *Patterson* should be revised legislatively, one may say that the administration wound up agreeing with supporters of Kennedy-Hawkins on the need to revise all of the other issues addressed in their bill. The administration and Kennedy-Hawkins supporters specifically agreed that an employer should be held liable for a discriminatory motive, even if the employer could show an action resulting from such a motive had an otherwise justifiable rationale. In the end there remained some differences over issues the administration agreed to revise, such as how much a victim of intentional discrimination can recover in damages. Still, the main sticking point between the administration and Kennedy-Hawkins supporters involved the issues in *Wards Cove*. See "Civil Rights Veto Stems from Dispute over Discrimination Ruling," *Washington Post*, October 24, 1990.

20. Bush also would have been in a stronger position to do battle with Congress over a reprise of Kennedy-Hawkins in the next legislative session.

21. John DiIulio of Princeton University makes a strong case that "the underclass problem," is "a crime problem." "The Impact of Inner-City Crime," *The Public Interest*, no. 96 (Summer 1989): 28–46. "More locks, cops, and corrections officers would make a more positive, tangible, and lasting difference in the lives of today's ghetto dwellers," p. 46.

22. Concerning the two *Wards Cove* issues still disputed from the 1990 legislative battle, the legislation as enacted sided with the Bush administration on one and in effect "punted" on the other. Under the new law, a plaintiff in a Title VII disparate impact case must identify which of the employer's practices is causing the disparate impact; the Bush administration had insisted on maintaining this element of *Wards Cove*. As for "business necessity," the new law says that employers must show their selection criteria are "job related for the position in question and consistent with business necessity"—a term that is not elsewhere defined in the statute. It is possible that the Supreme Court will interpret "business necessity" in much the same manner as it did in *Wards Cove*. I have discussed this detail and others in "Andrea's Abomination," *The American Spectator*, January 1992, pp. 57–59.

## CHAPTER 8
### THE POWERS OF PERSUASION

1. According to Bob Woodward's account in *The Commanders*, William Barr, then the deputy attorney general, advised the President both that

he had sufficient constitutional authority to act without congressional authorization and that he nonetheless, for reasons of prudence, should ask Congress for such law. Defense Secretary Richard B. Cheney agreed with the first but not the second, arguing that the President should not risk a politically devastating loss by asking Congress to vote for war. Bush could not accept Cheney's position, feeling that he "had to try" to get congressional approval. Bob Woodward, *The Commanders* (New York: Simon and Schuster, 1991), pp. 356–58.

2. Letter of "Pacificus," Vol. 4, *The Works of Alexander Hamilton,* Henry Cabot Lodge, ed. (New York: G. P. Putnam, 1969), p. 442. The specific issue was whether President Washington had the power to issue the Neutrality Proclamation without prior congressional approval. Hamilton said he did. The President had the duty to carry out the Treaty of 1778 with France, which created a perpetual alliance between the two nations. In doing so, the President had to decide how the treaty applied in the present situation and to act on that understanding, even if his action affected the power of Congress to declare war.

3. Other Presidents who have established "an antecedent state of things" that affected a congressional decision about the use of force include President Polk, in 1846. Polk intentionally placed the U.S. army where hostilities might ensue—in territory that had been claimed by both Texas (added to the Union in 1845) and Mexico. After fighting broke out, Polk asked Congress for a declaration of war, which he got. A century later President Roosevelt took steps pursuant to his powers that established "an antecedent state of things" which led him to consider a preemptive strike on Japan. Of course, Pearl Harbor settled the issue of the United States's entry into World War II.

4. In *The Federalist No. 69,* Hamilton noted that the authority of "the British king extends to the *declaring* of war and to the *raising* and *regulating* of fleets and armies." See *The Federalist No. 69* (A. Hamilton) (New York: Mentor Books, 1961), p. 422.

5. Often neglected in discussions of the framing of the War Clause is the framers' concern that an adventuristic President might launch a war of conquest; by denying the executive the power to declare war and vesting it in Congress, the body closest to the people, the framers hoped to prevent, or at least make more difficult, America's entry into a kind of war well-known to any student of politics or history at that time and proscribed in our time by the United Nations Charter. Article 2, Paragraph 4 of the U.N. Charter states that all member nations "shall refrain in their international relations from the threat or use of force against the territorial integrity or political independence of any state, or in any other manner inconsistent with the purposes of the United Nations." There are only two exceptions—the right of individual or collective self-defense against an armed attack, and collective action taken by the United Nations to deal with serious disturbances of the peace.

6. Louis Fisher, *Constitutional Conflicts Between Congress and the President* (Princeton, N.J.: Princeton University Press, 1985), p. 287.

7. *Report of the Congressional Committees Investigating the Iran-Contra Affair, with Supplemental, Minority, and Additional Views,* H. Rept. 100-433. S. Rept. 100-216 (Washington, 1987), p. 466.

8. Ibid., p. 466.

9. Some have argued that the change from "make" to "declare" war means that the President was given *only* the power to repel sudden attacks. But two delegates opposed this change because they understood it to mean that the President would now have the power "to commence war." The framing of the clause does not settle the scope of the President's power to make war or use military force.

10. Imagine North Carolina sending its state police to Wilmington to stop an invasion or threatened invasion by another country, while the President of the United States, accepting the advice of wrongheaded lawyers, sits on his hands, waiting for Congress to act. Because the President takes an oath that requires him to "preserve, protect, and defend" the Constitution, he also has authority sufficient for him to act even if, in the most wildly improbable case, Congress were to pass a resolution telling him *not* to send troops to Wilmington. The President is also required by the Take Care Clause of Article II to faithfully execute the laws, which include the Constitution, "the supreme law of the land," as it refers to itself in Article VI; some faithful execution it would be if a President were to do nothing while North Carolina, which is constitutionally guaranteed (in Article IV) a republican form of government *and* protection against invasion, was forcibly subtracted from the Union. Also worth noting in this connection is the Guarantee Clause, found in Article IV, which states: "The United States shall guarantee to every State in this Union a republican form of government, and shall protect each of them against invasion." The President thus is obligated by the Constitution to initiate military force to defend a state against invasion, regardless of what Congress might do legislatively.

11. Robert Scigliano, "The War Powers Resolution and the War Powers," in *The Presidency in the Constitutional Order,* Joseph M. Bessette and Jeffrey Tulis, eds. (Baton Rouge: Louisiana State University Press, 1981), p. 144.

12. Ibid., pp. 124–43.

13. Quoted in J. Gregory Sidak, "To Declare War," *Duke Law Journal,* vol. 41, no. 1 (1991): 60.

14. Quoted in ibid.

15. Should Congress have passed a formal declaration of war on the order of the five enacted over the nation's two-hundred year history? The Constitution does not prescribe just how Congress should exercise its power "to declare war." And by its own terms the Iraq Resolution itself may be construed as a declaration of war. It authorized the President "to use United States Armed Forces pursuant to United Nations Security Council Resolution 678 (1990) in order to achieve implementation" of eleven Security Council resolutions passed in response to Iraq's invasion of Kuwait. Resolution 678 in particular authorized member

346

states of the U.N. to "use all necessary means, after January 15, 1991, to uphold and implement all relevant Security Council resolutions and to restore international peace and security in the area." For a powerful statement of the view that Congress should have declared war in a formal sense, see Sidak, "To Declare War."

16. Woodward, *The Commanders,* p. 223.
17. Ibid., p. 285.
18. Ibid., p. 288.
19. Ibid.. pp. 288–89.
20. The military leadership was upset by the request; Army General H. Norman Schwarzkopf, the commander of the U.S. Central Command responsible for the Middle East and Southwest Asia, thought he needed another two months to prepare and position his troops for defense, and that to do the same for an offensive effort would take another eight to twelve months. Bush, the civilian, clearly was in control.
21. Woodward, *The Commanders,* p. 324.
22. Ibid., p. 338.
23. Ibid., p. 339.
24. One provision in the War Powers Resolution is unconstitutional when measured against *INS* v. *Chadha,* 103 S.Ct. 2764 (1983). Absent a declaration of war or specific statutory authorization, armed forces must be withdrawn by the President "if the Congress so directs by concurrent resolution." Under *Chadha,* which invalidated the legislative veto, this provision is unconstitutional because it does not satisfy the demands of the Presentment Clause.
25. Following the brief land war begun on February 24, President Bush announced the liberation of Kuwait and ordered a cease-fire on February 27. Iraq quickly indicated that it would comply with all of the U.N. Security Council resolutions. The Persian Gulf war lasted fewer than sixty days. That was a consequence of modern war technology, not some presidential desire to beat the deadline of the War Powers Resolution.
26. Charles Krauthammer, "Bush's March Through Washington," *Washington Post,* March 1, 1991.
27. Ibid. Krauthammer's observation about the bully pulpit especially applies in the context of foreign policy.
28. Harvey C. Mansfield, Jr., *Taming the Prince* (New York: Free Press, 1989), p. 6.
29. Bush was faulted after Iraq had been pushed from Kuwait on numerous grounds: for not taking the fight to Baghdad, for failing to inflict heavier losses upon the Iraqi military, for not militarily helping the anti-Saddam opposition within Iraq, for failing to make the removal of Saddam a clear war aim. Agree or disagree, all of these were choices within Bush's discretion to make, as they should have been.
30. For a discussion of U.S. policy toward Iraq in the 1980s, including that of Bush in 1989–90, see Paul Gigot, "Iraq: an American Screw-Up," *The National Interest,* no. 22 (Winter 1990–91): 3–10. For a discussion of what Bush did wrong before August 2, 1990 and after February 28,

1991, see George Weigel, "On the Road to Isolationism?" *Commentary,* vol. 93, no. 1 (January 1992): 36–42.

## PART TWO
### THE PRESIDENT AND THE EXECUTIVE BRANCH

1. Of the initial administrative effort by the Continental Congress, Charles C. Thach, Jr., wrote, "Everything was confusion." See Charles C. Thach, Jr., *The Creation of the Presidency 1775–1789: A Study in Constitutional History* (Baltimore: Johns Hopkins University Press, 1969), p. 61.
2. Ibid., p. 70.
3. Geoffrey P. Miller, "Independent Agencies," *The Supreme Court Review,* vol. 3 (1986): 41.
4. Quoted in Jeremy Rabkin, *Judicial Compulsions: How Public Law Distorts Public Policy* (New York: Basic Books, 1989), p. 102.
5. Rabkin, *Judicial Compulsions,* p. 68. In directing the executive branch, the President also has competition from the federal judiciary. Rabkin's book is an excellent treatment of this relatively recent and problematic development.
6. Quoted in Thach, *The Creation of the Presidency,* p. 64.
7. Richard P. Nathan, *The Administration Presidency* (New York: Macmillan, 1983).

## CHAPTER 9
### PICKING THE INSTRUMENTS OF EXECUTION

1. Representing Massachusetts in the First Congress, Fisher Ames observed that no President could "personally execute all the laws." Suffice to say, Ames's remark has proved all the more true with the passage of time—and more and more laws. Charles C. Thach, Jr., *The Creation of the Presidency 1775–1789: A Study in Constitutional History* (Baltimore: Johns Hopkins University Press, 1969), p. 147.
2. Ibid., pp. 152–53.
3. And, in recent years, in terms of race and gender.
4. Quoted in Richard P. Nathan, *The Administrative Presidency* (New York: Macmillan, 1983), p. 30 (my emphasis).
5. William Bennett, in an interview with the author, November 15, 1988, Washington, D.C.
6. Rowland Evans, Jr., and Robert D. Novak, *Nixon in the White House: The Frustration of Power* (New York: Random House, 1971), p. 70.
7. James Q. Wilson, *Bureaucracy: What Government Agencies Do and Why They Do It* (New York: Basic Books, 1989), pp. 198–99.
8. A related point can be made with respect to Edwin Meese III, who was probably the aide closest to Reagan politically but whose poor judg-

ments in private matters led to criminal investigations that reduced both the time he could serve as Attorney General and his effectiveness while in office.

9. William Kristol, "Can-Do Government," *Policy Review,* no. 31 (Winter 1985): 62.

10. For a discussion of Bennett's tenure at Education, see Chester E. Finn, Jr., "Education Policy and the Reagan Administration: A Large but Incomplete Success," *Education Policy,* vol. 2, no. 4 (1988): 351–59. Education is the only cabinet department in which the federal role is not only not central to the subject in the department's charge, but also not even particularly important. (This, by the way, is a good reason not to have a cabinet-level Department of Education.) Bennett proved that a cabinet secretary need not be limited by this fact. He did so by adopting rhetorical strategies in which he argued for certain ideas—such as the "Three C's" of "choice, content, and character." Because most of the decisions regarding school choice, curriculum content, and moral education are made in the states, he did not have to be as concerned, as other cabinet secretaries presiding over departments in which the federal role preempts all others (such as State or Defense) definitely must be, with ensuring consistency between rhetoric and governance. Ironically, then, the very nature of his department freed him to speak generally about its subject matter and to make more of his position than anyone thought possible. Suffice to say, rhetoric was central to Bennett's strategic governance model, as employed both at NEH and Education.

11. Carnes Lord, "Executive Power and Our Security," *The National Interest,* no. 7, Spring 1987, p. 12.

12. Obviously, no President can hope to direct the government with political appointees from the previous presidency. President Andrew Jackson initiated the practice of sweeping out the holdovers from the previous presidency, and that should be the practice of every energetic executive. Ronald Reagan swept out the Carter appointees in the first years of his presidency, as his subordinates followed the rule, as Edwin Meese put it, that "an empty office" is "better than . . . a holdover."

13. Bert A. Rockman, "The Style and Organization of the Reagan Presidency," in *The Reagan Legacy: Promise and Performance,* Charles O. Jones, ed. (Chatham, N.J.: Chatham House Publishers, 1988), p. 9.

14. Joel D. Aberbach and Bert A. Rockman, "From Nixon's Problem to Reagan's Achievement: The Federal Executive Reexamined," in *Looking Back on the Reagan Presidency,* Larry Berman, ed. (Baltimore: Johns Hopkins University Press, 1990), p. 183.

15. Becky Norton Dunlop, "The Role of the White House Office of Presidential Personnel," in *Steering the Elephant: How Washington Works,* Robert Rector and Michael Sanera, eds. (New York: Universe Books, 1987), p. 151.

16. Rockman, "The Style and Organization of the Reagan Presidency," p. 10.

17. Martin Anderson, *Revolution* (New York: Harcourt Brace Jovanovich, 1988), p. 195.
18. G. Calvin Mackenzie, "Cabinet and Subcabinet Personnel Selection in Reagan's First Year" (paper presented at the annual meeting of the American Political Science Association, 1981). Quoted in Jones, *The Reagan Legacy*, p. 107. See also Lou Cannon, *President Reagan: The Role of a Lifetime* (New York: Simon and Schuster, 1991), pp. 74–75, for an account of the personnel effect undertaken both before and prior to the election in 1980.
19. Richard P. Nathan, "The 'Administrative Presidency,' " *The Public Interest*, no. 44 (Summer 1976): 40. For Nathan's comprehensive treatment of the subject, see his book, *The Administrative Presidency*.
20. Nathan, "The 'Administrative Presidency,' " p. 53.
21. Quoted in Nathan, *The Administrative Presidency*, p. 5.

CHAPTER 10
CHANGING THE STATUS QUO

1. Discussing the struggle between Congress and the President over administration, James Q. Wilson writes, "The President brings to this struggle four main weapons: choosing people, altering procedures, reorganizing agencies, and coordinating activities." James Q. Wilson, *Bureaucracy: What Government Agencies Do and Why They Do It* (New York: Basic Books, 1989), p. 260. These *are* the President's four main weapons, and I use Wilson's terms in this chapter in discussing three of them.
2. When Reagan took office, crime levels had increased and criminal justice systems at all levels were straining to deal with the massive breakdown in law and order. Illegal drug use was taking a greater social toll, obscenity and child pornography were infecting communities across the nation, and terrorists increasingly threatened Americans both at home and abroad. Antitrust and civil rights law had become encrusted with legal excess, much of it encouraged by previous Justice Departments, but none of it required by relevant law and much of it conflicted with that law. The Reagan Justice Department sought administratively to address the legal, political, and cultural excess, and to strengthen the rule of law. To be sure, the Department also sought legislation, as certain statutory tools were thought necessary to the governing enterprise, and the Department played the key role (discussed in Part Three) in assisting the President in judicial selection. I focus in this chapter on efforts at Justice to change the administrative status quo.
3. William French Smith, *Law and Justice in the Reagan Administration: Memoirs of an Attorney General* (Stanford: Hoover Institution Press, 1991), p. 93.
4. Title VII of the Civil Rights Act of 1964 created a federal right to equal employment opportunity free of discrimination based on race or sex.

The Justice Department shares authority for enforcing Title VII with the Equal Employment Opportunity Commission. Justice enforces Title VII against public employers, the EEOC against private employers.

5. Justice's anti-terrorism policy was effective within U.S. borders, but the more complicated task of stemming terrorism abroad proved far more difficult.

6. Wilson, *Bureaucracy*, pp. 265–67.

7. 111 S.Ct. 1759 (1991).

8. Peter M. Shane and Harold H. Bruff, *The Law of Presidential Power* (Durham N.C.: Carolina Academic Press, 1988), pp. 88–89. In theory executive orders are directed to those who enforce the laws but often they have at least as much impact upon the governed as the governors. Executive Order 11246 is clearly of this kind.

9. Norman C. Amaker, *Civil Rights and the Reagan Administration* (Washington: Urban Institute Press, 1988), pp. 121–30.

10. As discussed in Chapter 5, a similar point can be made with respect to legislation presented to the President for his approval or disapproval. The President has an independent right to judge the constitutionality of the statute presented to him.

11. For a discussion of this effort, see Christopher C. DeMuth and Douglas H. Ginsburg, "White House Review of Agency Rulemaking," *Harvard Law Review*, vol. 99, no. 5 (1986): 1975–88.

12. Ibid., p. 1080.

13. Ibid., p. 1088.

14. See Christopher DeMuth's remarks on this turn of events in an interview conducted by Adam Meyerson, in "Captain of Enterprise," *Policy Review*, no. 60 (Spring 1992), pp. 16–17.

## CHAPTER 11
### LITIGATING THE AGENDA

1. 111 S.Ct. 1759 (1991).

2. 784 F. 2d 521 (4th Cir. 1986).

3. For a useful discussion of litigation as a policy tool, see Joseph A. Morris, "Clauswitz Updated: Litigation as the Continuation of Policy Making by Other Means," in *Steering the Elephant: How Washington Works,* Robert Rector and Michael Sanera, eds. (New York: Universe Books, 1987), pp. 73–86.

4. *Boston Firefighters Union* v. *Boston Chapter NAACP,* 461 U.S. 477 (1983).

5. 694 F. 2d 987 (5th Cir. 1982), *aff'd as modified,* 729 F. 2d 1554 (1984) (en banc).

6. *Bratton* v. *City of Detroit,* 704 F. 2d 878, *rehg denied,* 712 F. 2d. 222 (6th Cir. 1983), *cert. denied,* 465 U.S. 1040 (1984).

7. 467 U.S. 561 (1984).

8. 476 U.S. 267 (1986).

9. 478 U.S. 421 (1986).
10. 478 U.S. 501 (1986).
11. 480 U.S. 149 (1987).
12. 480 U.S. 616 (1987).
13. 488 U.S. 469 (1989).
14. 490 U.S. 642 (1989).
15. 109 S.Ct. 2180 (1989).
16. *Metro Broadcasting Inc.* v. *F.C.C.*, 110 S.Ct. 2997 (1990). Justice White's positions in the two cases may be explained by the fact that *Stotts* was a Title VII case while *Metro Broadcasting* was a Fourteenth Amendment case.
17. Congress did not disturb the holding in *Wards Cove* as to the proper statistical comparison in a disparate impact case. And it codified another part of the decision, requiring the plaintiff to identify the particular employment practice allegedly causing the disparate impact.
18. This was not the first time during the Reagan-Bush era that a victory in Court proved only the first half of a game that Congress ultimately won. In 1984 the Justice Department managed to succeed with its argument in *Grove City College* v. *Bell,* 465 U.S. 555 (1984)—to wit, that colleges or universities receiving federal funds are obligated to comply with civil rights laws only in the part of the institution receiving the funds, not in all its parts. But four years later Congress passed new law making the coverage institution-wide, doing so over a veto.
19. Theodore Olson, assistant attorney general for the Office of Legal Counsel, advised Smith in an internal memorandum: "[T]o permit the EEOC, an executive agency subject to the control of the President and the supervision of the Attorney General in litigation matters, to present to the court views contrary to those already presented by the Attorney General for the United States ... whether as an amicus or as a full party would seriously frustrate and undermine the constitutional unity and integrity of the Executive."
20. Lincoln Caplan, *The Tenth Justice: The Solicitor General and the Rule of Law* (New York: Alfred A. Knopf, 1987).
21. I draw upon arguments made by Roger Clegg in his review of Lincoln Caplan's book. See Roger Clegg, "The 35th Law Clerk," *Duke Law Journal,* no. 5 (November 1987): 964–75.
22. Of course, Caplan's seemingly procedural objections may well be masking partisan disagreement. In the summer of 1991, President Bush overruled his Solicitor General, Kenneth W. Starr, by ordering a reversal in his position in a higher education desegregation case. Lincoln Caplan and others of his persuasion did not publicly object—probably because they agreed with Bush.
23. *Graves* v. *New York,* 306 U.S. 466, 491–92 (1939) (Frankfurter, J., concurring).
24. For illuminating discussions of *stare decisis,* see Robert H. Bork, *The Tempting of America: The Political Seduction of the Law* (New York: Free Press, 1989), pp. 155–59; and Charles J. Cooper, "*Stare Decisis*:

Precedent and Principle in Constitutional Adjudication," *Cornell Law Review* 73 (1988): 401–10.

25. *Payne* v. *Tennessee,* 59 U.S.L.W. 4818 (1991), overruling *Booth* v. *Maryland,* 482 U.S. 496 (1987) and *South Carolina* v. *Gathers,* 490 U.S. 95 (1989).

26. Charles Fried, *Order and Law: Arguing the Reagan Revolution—A Firsthand Account* (New York: Simon and Schuster, 1991), p. 170.

CHAPTER 12
POLICY MUDDLE

1. In the context of Title VII enforcement, Reynolds told a House subcommittee that the Department "no longer will insist or in any respect support the use of quotas or any other numerical or statistical formula designed to provide to non-victims of discrimination preferential treatment based on race, sex, national origin or religion." Reynolds also explained that one set of numerical requirements, though arguably not preferential in nature, did remain in the enforcement policy. The Department would seek, as Reynolds put it, "percentage recruitment goals for monitoring purposes." That is, as part of the remedy in Title VII cases, the Department would ask employers to devise and file recruitment goals "related [as Reynolds described them] to the percentage of minority or female applicants that might be expected to result under a non-discriminatory employment policy." Justice would review these goals and the progress toward them in order to assess employer compliance with the law, but, according to Reynolds, it would not treat the goals "as inflexible standards which must be met by the employer without regard to qualification." The essence of the new Justice position was that there would be no "numerical requirements" of the kind Reagan complained about in the 1980 campaign—except, if one wishes to count them as such, at the recruitment level.

In explaining why the Department would no longer support quota relief, he went beyond Smith's practical argument, calling quotas "unsound as a matter of law and unwise as a matter of policy." Reynolds said that the text and history of Title VII mandated nondiscrimination, citing Senator Hubert Humphrey's remark during the congressional debate in which Humphrey rejected the notion that the new law would even permit racial quotas.

Over the next seven years Justice stuck to the Title VII enforcement policy announced by Reynolds, except in one respect: In Reagan's second term, it dropped the percentage goals at the recruitment level, making the Justice policy completely free of any numerical requirements. Meanwhile, throughout the Reagan years the Justice Department used power available to no other part of the executive branch, waging a strong litigating campaign against employment quotas and, indeed, racial preferences in general; color-blind law was the goal.

2. 443 U.S. 193 (1979).

3. "Civil Rights Division Head Will Seek Supreme Court Ban on Affirmative Action," *Wall Street Journal,* December 8, 1981.

4. Title VII of the Civil Rights Act of 1964 outlaws employment discrimination. Applying to employers of fifteen or more persons, it proscribes hiring, promoting, or firing on the basis of race, color, religion, sex, or national origin. When a judicial remedy is sought for a demonstrated violation of the law, whether by aggrieved parties or the relevant government agency, a court may not only forbid the employer from engaging in the discriminatory practice but also, as the law states, "order such affirmative action as may be appropriate, which may include, but is not limited to, reinstatement or hiring of employees, with or without back pay, . . . or any other equitable relief as the court deems appropriate." Under Title VII, responsibility for enforcing the law upon private employers falls to the Equal Employment Opportunity Commission, which may seek administrative and (as a result of 1972 amendments) judicial remedies. The EEOC also has the authority to enforce antidiscrimination laws within the federal government.

5. Summoned repeatedly by congressional Democrats to explain the new policy, Thomas rejected the view of the Carter administration that quotas were the only effective means of combating racial discrimination, arguing that employers too often hid behind the number of minorities hired instead of truly providing genuine equal opportunity for these individuals. Commissioners William Webb (appointed in 1982) and Rosalie Gaull Silberman (appointed in 1985) voiced similar views in congressional hearings.

6. After 1986 and 1987 Supreme Court rulings supporting the use of quotas in Title VII cases, the General Counsel for the EEOC, Charles Shanor, advised field attorneys for the agency that goals and timetables may be used "in appropriate cases." But he defined these cases so narrowly as to make quotas a remedy of last resort, observing that the EEOC "will not use goals and timetables as 'engines of discrimination' . . . nor . . . as a convenient way to avoid liability for past transgressions of the statutes we enforce." Thomas meanwhile successfully argued within the EEOC that even where goals might be lawful (according to the Supreme Court) as a remedy, there were generally tougher and more effective alternatives. See Clarence Thomas, "Affirmative Action Goals and Timetables: Too Tough? Not Tough Enough!" *Yale Law & Policy Review,* vol. 5, no. 2 (Spring/Summer 1987): 402–3.

7. The executive order states that a federal government contractor will agree "not [to] discriminate against any employee or applicant for employment because of race, color, religion, sex, or national origin. The contractor will take affirmative action to ensure that applicants are employed, and the employees are treated during employment, without regard to their race, color, religion, sex, or national origin."

8. Herman Belz, *Equality Transformed: A Quarter Century of Affirmative Action* (Rutgers: Transaction Books, 1991), p. 191.

9. For a more detailed description of the proposed changes, see Belz, *Equality Transformed,* pp. 192–94, and Normal C. Amaker, *Civil Rights and the Reagan Administration* (Washington, D.C.: Urban Institute Press, 1988), p. 119.
10. Belz, *Equality Transformed,* p. 192.
11. Both liberals and conservatives opposed the changes, for different reasons. See Belz, *Equality Transformed,* p. 194.
12. In the fall of 1985 Attorney General Edwin Meese III, in his capacity as head of the Domestic Policy Council within the Reagan Cabinet, proposed a new executive order to replace Executive Order 11246. It would have prohibited the Labor Department from requiring contractors to adopt [in the words of the proposal] "any numerical quota, goal, or ratio, or otherwise to discriminate against, or grant any preference to, any individual or group on the basis of race, color, religion, sex, or national origin with respect to any aspect of employment." William Bradford Reynolds, head of the Civil Rights Division within the Justice Department, was the source of this idea. In 1983 Reynolds had tried to persuade Attorney General Smith to challenge E.O. 11246. In January 1984, in an internal memorandum to Smith, Reynolds observed that

> the Federal Government under this Administration has consistently failed to adhere to the President's principles of color (and gender) blindness. Most, if not all, federal agencies continue to utilize the same invidious race and sex classifications of previous Administrations in both the programs they administer and their own employment practices. Under the rubric of "goals" or correcting "underutilization" of minorities and women, these agencies have established numerical selection classifications that inevitably result in preferential treatment for nonvictims of discrimination. This is, of course, precisely the practice which we have vigorously attacked in courts . . . as illegal, unconstitutional and inherently immoral.

Among other programs identified by Reynolds was the Labor Department's enforcement of the Executive Order 11246. "OFCCP," he wrote, "has refused to delete the offensive 'goals' and 'underutilization' requirements from their regulations."

Emboldened by the Supreme Court's decision in *Firefighters* v. *Stotts,* which voided a racial quota, Reynolds wrote Smith again in December of 1984:

> The President's reelection mandate provides a unique, albeit potentially short-lived, opportunity to conform . . . the Executive's actual practices with the policies and . . . legal mandates that it has consistently and strongly espoused. Any excuses for further delaying full implementation of the color-blind principle . . . have clearly lost all force in light of *Stotts.*

Reynolds wrote that "with a stroke of a pen" the President should "replace this executive order with one that makes clear that the federal government does not require, authorize or permit the use of 'goals,' or any other form of race or gender conscious preferential treatment by federal contractors." This, he said, "would not only immediately terminate the federal government's most pernicious discriminatory practices but also serve as a spur for implementing race and gender neutrality throughout the Executive Branch." Reynolds sent Smith a draft of suggested revisions to the executive order as well as a memorandum for the President outlining a program for conforming the government's civil rights programs to color-blind principle.

Smith was about to leave office, and Reynolds's executive order proposal languished until Edwin Meese III became Attorney General. Reynolds eventually persuaded Meese to take on the assignment. Labor Secretary William Brock adamantly and shrewdly opposed Meese. Brock publicly rejected the notion of adopting color-blind nonpreferential practices, stating that "we are beyond the emotion of the economic necessity of full participation of all minority groups in the work force." But he did not argue the merits with Meese so much as the politics. Sensing that practical arguments worked best with Meese, Brock maintained that revision of the executive order would cost the President politically. Meese came to believe that changing the executive order would be a largely symbolic act too costly in political terms to undertake. (Serving as Director of Public Affairs for the Justice Department during this period, I once heard Meese say that reforming the executive order was a symbolic crusade of the kind conservatives seemed especially inclined to undertake.) According to Gary McDowell's account, Meese thought any change might (1) provoke Congress to pass law requiring the executive order regime; (2) weaken political support in Congress for the President as a general matter; (3) hurt the President as a matter of perception generally; and (4) also hurt the Republican Party. See Gary L. McDowell, "Affirmative Inaction," *Policy Review,* no. 48 (Spring 1989): 32–37. (I brought McDowell to the Department of Justice as associate director of public affairs; for his article McDowell interviewed, among others, both Brock and Meese.) With Don Regan, then the White House Chief of Staff, not inclined to pursue reform either, the issue died in the Domestic Policy Council.

13. Clarence Thomas, in an interview with the author, October 18, 1989, Washington, D.C.

14. William Bradford Reynolds, in an interview with the author, October 31, 1989, Washington, D.C.

15. In his memoir, William French Smith observed that Edwin Meese III, then at the White House, had actually opposed Reynolds, on grounds that "we should have . . . someone with more experience in civil rights, and someone with a stronger political background." Smith, *Law and Justice in the Reagan Administration: Memoirs of an Attorney General* (Stanford: Hoover Institution Press, 1991), p. 25.

16. 461 U.S. 574 (1983).

17. David Whitman, "Ronald Reagan and Tax Exemptions for Discriminatory Schools," in *How the Press Affects Federal Policymaking: Six Case Studies* (New York: Norton, 1986), pp. 254–94. See also Smith, *Law and Justice,* pp. 100–105.

18. Their position is best explained by the fact that Reagan, during the campaign, had criticized the IRS for denying tax exemptions "by administrative fiat" to private schools like Bob Jones. Indeed, Reagan spoke at the university during the 1980 campaign. To have proposed legislation empowering the IRS against such schools as Bob Jones could hardly have struck White House aides as something this President wanted to do.

19. Charles J. Cooper, in an interview with the author, June 2, 1990, Washington, D.C. Cooper was an aide to Reynolds in the Civil Rights Division and later an assistant attorney general for the Office of Legal Counsel.

20. So did the administration's handling of the extension of the Voting Rights Act, originally enacted in 1965 and one of the most successful pieces of civil rights legislation. The act was scheduled to expire in 1982, so the question of its extension arose in 1981. Instead of coming out early for a simple extension of the act, the administration dawdled before siding with Southern legislators opposed to any extension. The President eventually agreed to legislation that encourages racial districting.

21. The person who probably best represented Reagan's views on race was Edwin Meese III. Like Reagan, Meese opposed quotas. And like Reagan, but unlike Reynolds, Meese supported minority set-asides. Appearing on a CBS edition of "Face the Nation" at the end of his second month as Attorney General and therefore Reynolds's supervisor, Meese endorsed government set-aside programs for black and other minority businessmen as "permissible," even as he assailed preferences for blacks and other minorities seeking jobs or promotions as "impermissible quotas." Reynolds, knowing the Department had opposed set-asides in a federal appeals court, put out a statement attempting to clarify Meese's comments in order to preserve the integrity of the Department's litigating position; such were the internal divisions over matters of basic importance. (An irony of Meese's position on set-asides was that his involvement in helping an ostensibly "minority"—fraudulently declared, as it turned out—firm get set-aside money led to his second independent counsel investigation.) It is not surprising that in 1986 Meese and Reynolds ultimately parted ways on the question of the executive order's revision, hotly contested within the Reagan Cabinet. Meese's refusal to push the reform reflected his own sense—probably correct—that Reagan would have agreed with him.

22. White House aides also invested their energies in activities that, however useful, were poor substitutes for presidential involvement in the anti-quota effort. The Civil Rights Commission, critical of Reagan civil rights policies, became the object of White House attention; aides sought

to recompose it through new appointments, especially those of Clarence Pendleton (as chairman) and Linda Chavez (as staff director). The White House aides got what they wanted: CRC criticism of Reagan subsided. In the second Reagan term, after Chavez's departure, the commission drifted into irrelevance.

23. Regarding Nixon, see Herman Belz, *Equality Transformed,* pp. 94–97. On Bush, see Chester E. Finn, "The Bush Administration and Quotas," *Commentary,* November 1991, pp. 17–23.

24. Policy need not be fixed within the first day or month or year of a presidency; it may and in most cases will develop. Of importance is the President's decisive involvement in the policy development.

25. In 1984 the Justice Department used *Stotts* as the rationale for commencing a review of some fifty-one state and local governments involved in consent decrees containing quotas. Despite language that seemed to justify Justice's reading of Title VII as prohibiting quotas in contexts other than layoffs, the post-*Stotts* effort drew little support in either those jurisdictions or the lower courts, and it eventually died when the Supreme Court approved the limited use of quotas in four cases in 1986 and 1987. As it happened, there were unions challenging some of these agreements in light of *Stotts,* and the United States was a party to those agreements; the Justice Department was obligated to be ready to take a position. Still, Justice did not have to announce a "review" of every consent decree. A more prudent course would have been simply to have filed in each case as it arose, abiding each event in the lower court until the Supreme Court finally did speak. Two years later, there was also the effort to use *Wygant,* a constitutional ruling, as the rationale for saying that the employment goals and timetables imposed by OFCCP upon federal contractors are unlawful. But *Wygant* could not be effectively used for this purpose. The *Wygant* plurality rejected a quota that was fashioned as a result of comparing the percentage of minorities employed with their percentage in society at large. But the goals imposed under the executive order are devised after a comparison is made between the percentage of minorities employed by a firm and their percentage in the available labor market—not the society at large. Justice's use of *Wygant* in the executive order battle counsels not against using Court decisions to leverage executive branch policy but against using decisions with legal doctrine that is ill-suited for the effort.

Justice's uses of *Stotts* and *Wygant* to leverage policy are the kind of administrations of office that a White House civil rights review office could have examined early on.

26. John Agresto, in an interview with the author, September 29, 1988.


CHAPTER 13
STRATEGIC LEADERSHIP

1. For a comprehensive treatment of individual rights and their relationship to government, see Walter Berns, "Judicial Review and the Rights

and Laws of Nature," *The Supreme Court Review,* vol. 3 (1982): 49–83.

2. *The Federalist No. 37* (J. Madison) (New York: Mentor Books, 1961), p. 226.

3. *The Federalist No. 72* (A. Hamilton), pp. 435–36.

4. Martin Anderson, *Revolution* (New York: Harcourt Brace Jovanovich, 1988), p. 57.

5. As I write, there is evidence that Reagan's leadership will be better recognized as time passes. For example, in *The Turn: From the Cold War to a New Era: The United States and the Soviet Union 1983–1990* (New York: Poseidon Press, 1991), Don Oberdorfer writes, "Ronald Reagan . . . made a crucial contribution to the developments of the late 1980s. Reagan's self-confidence and the confidence that he instilled in the American people, his surprising eagerness to negotiate with the leaders of the Soviet 'evil empire,' and his deep belief that nuclear weapons posed a deadly peril to his nation and mankind, all played a major part in what took place. It is unlikely that an American president who was considered a moderate or liberal in foreign policy could have accomplished such a dramatic improvement in U.S.–Soviet relations, so swiftly and with so little conservative opposition" (p. 438).

6. Carnes Lord, *The Presidency and the Management of National Security,* (New York: Free Press, 1988) p. 174. Lord's book is essential for anyone interested in this subject. I am indebted to Lord for his insights.

7. Ibid., p. 86. Lou Cannon's 1991 book provides abundant evidence of Reagan's indifference to the national security parts of the government that one might have expected a conservative President to pay close attention to, and to direct at least much more carefully than Reagan did. See *President Reagan: The Role of a Lifetime* (New York: Simon and Schuster, 1991), p. 339.

8. Carnes Lord, "Executive Power and Our Security," *National Interest,* no. 7 (Spring 1987): 4–5; and Lord, *The Presidency and the Management of National Security,* pp. 3–4.

9. Lord, *The Presidency and the Management of National Security,* p. 4.

10. Cannon, *President Reagan,* p. 182.

11. Ibid., p. 341.

12. Ibid., p. 308.

13. Ibid., p. 394.

14. Ibid., p. 373.

15. See Lord, *The Presidency and the Management of National Security,* especially pp. 147–75.

16. Paul Gigot, "A Great American Screw-Up: The U.S. and Iraq, 1980–1990," *The National Interest,* no. 22 (Winter 1990–91): 7–8.

CHAPTER 14

EXECUTIVE ETHICS

1. James Wilson, whose influence on the creation of the presidency was substantial, put it this way: The President is "responsible for every

nomination he makes." Quoted in Jonathan Elliott, *The Debates in the Several State Conventions on the Adoption of the Federal Constitution* (Philadelphia: J. P. Lippincott, 1896), p. 480.

2. So was President Theodore Roosevelt, when he forced the resignation of the commissioner of the General Land Office, upon learning that he had suppressed reports of a land-fraud ring. And so was President Coolidge, when he fired his Attorney General on grounds of misconduct.

3. *Responses of the President to Charges of Misconduct,* C. Vann Woodward, ed. (New York: Dell Publishers, 1974), p. ix.

4. Elsewhere I have discussed this subject. See my book, *Ethics, Politics and the Independent Counsel* (Washington, D.C.: National Legal Center for the Public Interest, 1989).

5. Wariness of executive power has been a feature of American political life since the creation of the presidency in 1787. But the depth of distrust in the late 1960s and 1970s was unprecedented. In part, the distrust grew from the general skepticism about authority that characterized the 1960s. In part, too, it was fueled by the great cleavage of opinion about the Vietnam War, which was registered in an unprecedented turn in White House press relations. By late 1967, according to James Deakin of the *St. Louis Post-Dispatch,* "the relationship between the President and the Washington press corps ha[d] settled into a pattern of chronic disbelief." Quoted in Paul Johnson, *Modern Times* (New York: Harper & Row, 1983), p. 646. This did not change with Nixon's election; indeed, because he was more conservative than Johnson, Nixon was especially despised in certain influential circles. Columnist David Broder perceptively wrote in 1969 that "the men and the movement that broke Lyndon Johnson's authority in 1968 are out to break Richard M. Nixon. . . . The likelihood is that they will succeed again, for breaking a President is, like most feats, easier to accomplish the second time around." Quoted in ibid., p. 647. Nixon's participation in the cover-up of the nation's most notorious "third-rate burglary" made the task even easier. Watergate came to stand not simply for small crime but an attack on constitutional liberties. It not only drove Nixon from office but fed the growing distrust of the presidency as an institution.

6. The three most important were: the Budget and Impoundment Control Act, the War Powers Resolution, and the Ethics in Government Act, which established the system of court-appointed special prosecutors discussed in Chapter 5.

7. Reflection on this principle leads initially not to conflict of interest concerns but more immediate ones, such as treason and bribery. These are the only crimes explicitly mentioned in the Constitution, and for good reason: in the dawn of a new government, lines must be drawn against the most serious threats. Acts of treason are obviously not in the public, that is, the American interest, and any government that tolerated treason would soon disintegrate. As for bribery, its essential element is a payment to influence official action. Bribery assumes a *quid* for a *quo*. A public official, upon receiving money (or value in kind) from a private party, is expected to take certain official action that

benefits his partner in crime. A government that did not outlaw bribery would soon find itself sold out to private interests.

In the scale of things, conflict of interest is a matter less serious than treason or bribery. Consider what is involved: A public official receives a large sum of money from a government contractor. But there is no agreement or discussion about the contractor's receiving a benefit, as occurs with bribery. The official may or may not give a contract to the donor, but suppose he does not. On what theory would receiving the money be wrong? It cannot be on a theory of bribery, obviously, or theft (which also violates the public trust but which depends solely on what a government official does with government property, not on any relationship with a private party). The only theory on which receiving the money would be wrong is that the gift creates a conflict of interest likely to warp the official's judgment or to create the appearance of improper influence.

8. One can go to exceptional lengths to prevent this kind of temptation; Plato forbade his philosopher kings from holding any personal economic interests whatsoever. But any society that focuses on conflict of interest is likely to be relatively healthy; a society worried about a coup d'etat might laugh at ethicists inveighing against conflicts of interest.

9. Article I of the Constitution, for example, forbids members of Congress from accepting government positions where the "emoluments" of office "shall have been increased" during a member's term, and from accepting "any present, emolument, office, or title . . . from any king, prince or foreign State." The former provision eliminates the possible conflict a member might have between his own financial interest and the public interest. The latter eliminates the possible conflict a member might have between the American interest and a foreign interest. Both provisions, in different ways, stand as sentinels protecting the interest of the United States.

10. Other Eisenhower officials were subjected to heightened ethics scrutiny by Congress and the media. The most famous (or infamous) of these was Eisenhower's chief of staff, Sherman Adams, who in 1958 eventually resigned office after months of questions about his relationships with a New England financier. A sign of the times, in 1960 Harvard University Press published *Conflict of Interest and Federal Service* and in 1961 a companion volume, *Federal Conflict of Interest*. The first was a comprehensive study of conflict of interest law, the second a digest of the same. The books, which remain the most important in their field, provided the learning essential to the 1962 recodification of the conflict of interest statutes.

11. Carter placed most of his financial holdings in a trust and leased his farmland and the family business, the point being, as Carter himself said, to ensure that "whatever happens here in Plains, based on my decisions concerning agriculture, will not affect my income one way or the other." Plato would have demanded more, but as it was Carter went further than any previous President ever had.

12. The independent counsel law reflected not just the deep distrust of the

presidency but also a belief that every last bit of executive malfeasance should be uncovered and punished, virtually without regard to other considerations.

13. The Carter administration had its own troubles in the new ethics culture. The Management and Budget Director, Bert Lance, had difficulty complying with Carter's ethics guidelines and eventually resigned from office following a congressional investigation into his finances. Two of Carter's closest aides—Chief of Staff Hamilton Jordan and 1980 campaign adviser Tim Kraft—became the first individuals to be investigated under the special prosecutor law (for allegedly using cocaine, changes that ordinarily would not have been pursued). In 1979, the Carter Justice Department appointed a special prosecutor to investigate the Carter Peanut Warehouse case, which involved the President's brother, Billy Carter. (There was no prosecution.) In an earlier day, Lance probably would have been confirmed, Jordan and Kraft would not have been investigated, and Billy Carter would have been left alone. Ironically, the new era in ethics actually created scandal.

14. The 1965 executive order required cabinet-level and other top advisers to file with the Civil Service confidential statements listing ownerships, stocks, and other sources of income. In 1971 the White House started requiring presidential appointees to submit confidential financial statements and information on future employment agreements. Meanwhile, some Senate committees began asking prospective appointees—the nominees they would have to pass on—to fill out financial questionnaires. Until 1978, however, the amount of disclosed information actually put into the public domain was small. The Ethics in Government Act not only required more information but also total disclosure. And not only presidential appointees but also other high-ranking executive officers were required to file. An officer now had to report, among other things, the source, type, and amount of earned income other than government salary, various facts about personal and even family finances (involving real estate holdings, stocks, bonds, or other securities), and any "gifts" of transportation, lobbying, food, or entertainment. The new law also defined the requirements of a qualified blind trust and created an Office of Government Ethics within the executive branch for the purpose of determining (among other things) whether proposed trusts of this kind were bona fide. Here the new law provided for various civil penalties, including fines for those who knowingly and willfully falsified a report or failed to file. The reports were to be reviewed by designated ethics authorities and corrected as necessary before, of course, being made available to the public through the news media.

15. Watergate occurred at a time in which the national news media, and television in particular, were experiencing a rise both in prestige and influence that had begun in the 1960s, with the Kennedy presidency. Watergate accelerated the media's rise, ratifying journalism's self-described role as the watchdog that exists to ferret out official wrongdoing. And after Watergate members of the Fourth Estate rarely

operated as some had in the past, as unacknowledged but proud extensions of the executive branch. Fred Graham, formerly of CBS, has observed that in 1965 there was "a close affinity" between the media and the presidency. Graham himself was a presidential appointee in the Kennedy-Johnson administrations; he served as speechwriter for Labor Secretary Willard Wurtz from 1963 to 1965. He left that job to become law correspondent for the *New York Times*. Today there is no such affinity between the prestige press and the executive branch.

16. Laurence I. Barrett, *Gambling with History: Reagan in the White House* (New York: Penguin Books, 1984), p. 456.

17. Ibid., p. 457.

18. Bumpers was wrong (consider the Grant and Nixon administrations, and note that changing political and legal standards make comparisons difficult, at best). And Schroeder was grossly misleading (she listed only those against whom allegations in media accounts had been made; no effort was made to find out what had become of the charges, and in many instances they came to nothing). Bumpers and Schroeder were representative types in the "ethics wars"—a form of politics by other means—that characterized the Reagan years. Bumpers and Schroeder sought partisan advantage as Democrats and an institutional edge for a Congress controlled by Democrats, a fact not lost on Republican Rep. Newt Gingrich, who filed the ethics charge that led to House Speaker Jim Wright's resignation in 1989.

19. Lou Cannon, in a telephone interview with the author, October 10, 1989. "Whenever I put the ethics question to him," Cannon told me, "Reagan responded in one of two ways. He either talked about the size of government and the need to cut it down. Or, as he did in the cases of Donovan and Meese, he dismissed the allegations as attacks upon him that are politically inspired."

20. Jack Kemp, in an interview with the author, October 30, 1989, Washington, D.C.

21. When Meese came to the Justice Department in 1985, he asked me to head the Office of Public Affairs. (I had been a special assistant to Attorney General William French Smith from 1983 to 1985.) I served under Meese as the Department's chief spokesman until May 1988, when he asked me to leave. (See note 25, below.) At this time Meese was under investigation by an independent counsel. Two months later, after the independent counsel closed his inquiry (he did not seek an indictment), Meese announced his resignation.

22. Quite apart from any "ethics" problem, there was the more serious managerial problem raised by such a job offer: Does a manager still have the necessary authority to manage an employee to whom he is in debt?

23. *Report of Independent Counsel in Re Edwin Meese III*, Spec. Div. No. 87-1 (D.C. Cir.), July 5, 1988: 27, 29. The "crimes" involved Meese's participation in telecommunications matters before the Justice Department and his failure to disclose the sale of securities on his 1985 federal income tax return.

24. Meese's experience raises the critical question for a President of whether a top aide should remain in office while under official investigation, especially by an independent counsel. At the outset of McKay's investigation Meese announced that he would stay in office during its pendency. This decision reflected Reagan's judgment that an official should not resign unless indicted. And this judgment in turn reflected a principled consideration: That no one should be driven out of office on the basis of mere allegation, that there is a due process that ought to be observed, and that to abort this process by premature resignation might be understood as an admission of guilt. Having taken the position he did, Meese could *not* have resigned before McKay concluded his work. The question for the future is not whether Meese should have resigned but whether the Reagan principle is sufficient for deciding future cases like Meese's. Staying in office, as Meese did during the fourteen months of the investigation, served the Reagan principle, but it also had negative consequences that future Presidents must weigh in the balance.

25. "Re: Meese," *National Review,* June 24, 1988, p. 15. Morale of political appointees at the highest levels inside the department declined. The Meese-Wallach relationship in particular was inexplicable to many senior officials, including me; Meese had even approached Wallach about becoming his counselor (if not actually offering him the job) in the spring of 1987. One morning in early spring, the second ranking official in the department, Arnold Burns, and Weld, the head of the Criminal Division, startled Washington with the abrupt announcement of their resignation. It was a protest, a silent one—no public explanation was offered—its purpose being to force the President to force Meese out of office. Given the President's long association with Meese, I did not see how that could have worked, and it did not. Yet the resignations of Reagan appointees, hand-picked Meese associates, indicated the disarray within the Department.

   On May 13, a Friday, I was surprised when Meese, in a brief conversation in his office, asked me to leave. He had concluded that I was not defending him well enough and could not be relied upon to defend him in the future. He asked me to leave within thirty days, and said that "of course" we'll "fete" you—give you a party. That was not for me. I left on Monday, with Meese justifying his action to the media on grounds that it makes sense to "change leadership" every now and then, just as the Baltimore Orioles had done in firing its manager, Cal Ripken, who had opened the 1988 season with thirteen straight losses. As a baseball fan, I took some consolation that Meese used a baseball analogy, although it was ill-considered. The Orioles had proceeded to lose six more games under Ripken's replacement.

   My story was but a footnote in the scheme of things. It is worth noting here because it illustrates the institutional consequences of remaining in a cabinet office while under formal investigation. Such an investigation is enormously self-preoccupying. My regret was that people who had joined together in causes larger than themselves had been divided over smaller matters.

26. McKay filed his report two weeks before the Democratic Convention; had McKay not done so, and had Meese still been in office through July, the Democrats would have made more of an issue of the Republican Attorney General.

CHAPTER 15
BAD BEHAVIOR REWARDED

1. William Greider, "The Education of David Stockman," *Atlantic Monthly,* December 1981, pp. 27–54.
2. Ibid., p. 38, 46, 47.
3. See David A. Stockman, *The Triumph of Politics: Why the Reagan Revolution Failed* (New York: Harper & Row, 1986).
4. Martin Anderson, *Revolution* (New York: Harcourt Brace Jovanovich, 1988), p. 237.
5. Greider, "The Education of David Stockman," pp. 30, 32.
6. Stockman, *The Triumph of Politics,* p. 5.
7. Robert Novak in a letter to the *New York Times Book Review,* June 22, 1986.
8. Paul Craig Roberts, *The Supply-Side Revolution: An Insiders Account of Policymaking in Washington* (Cambridge, Mass.: Harvard University Press, 1984), p. 192.
9. Greider, "The Education of David Stockman," p. 54.
10. Stockman, *The Triumph of Politics,* p. 319.
11. Charles Fried, Reagan's Solicitor General from 1985 to 1989, is far wide of the mark when he writes in his memoir, "David Stockman . . . was the model of the presidential appointee; by intelligence, knowledge, and hard work he was able to master the details of his task and thereby impose his will. There is, however, a limited supply of people like David Stockman." *Order and Law: Arguing the Reagan Revolution—A First-hand Account* (New York: Simon and Schuster, 1991), p. 155. Fried saw himself as the David Stockman of the legal side of the Reagan Revolution. Suffice to say, there are better role models for an executive officer.
12. Bob Schieffer and Gary Paul Gates, *The Acting President,* (New York: Dutton, 1989), p. 145.
13. Stockman, *The Triumph of Politics,* p. 3.
14. Ibid., p. 8.
15. Hedrick Smith, *The Power Game: How Washington Works* (New York: Ballantine Books, 1988), p. 359.
16. James David Barber, *The Presidential Character* (Englewood Cliffs, N.J.: Prentice-Hall, 1972), pp. 12–13.
17. See Herbert Storing's insightful introduction to Charles C. Thach, Jr. *The Creation of the Presidency 1775–1789: A Study in Constitutional History* (Baltimore: Johns Hopkins University Press, 1969), pp. v–xii.

## CHAPTER 16
### NON-ENERGY AND IRRESPONSIBILITY

1. How might Reagan have provided strategic leadership in regard to the hostages held in Beirut? Michael Malbin has suggested two different ways. The President could have presented "a less categorical, subtler public face that would have explained the importance of, and the hard choices involved in, protecting the lives of individual Americans abroad." Or, says Malbin, the President might have represented himself as open to negotiations with terrorists, but also able and willing to take punitive action against terrorists (an approach similar to Israel's). Either approach would have provided a context in which some kind of Iran initiative could have been made—preferably a better conceived and executed one, involving the State Department. But either approach also would have required presidential rhetoric of a kind that Reagan did not typically provide. Such rhetoric would have been not only far more nuanced than what Reagan did offer on this issue ("We make no concessions—we make no deals") but would have striven to achieve more consistency between what was publicly said and, as Malbin puts it, "the subtler arguments appropriate for deliberation" among those dealing with the issues, and between nations. Michael J. Malbin, "Legalism versus Political Checks and Balances: Legislative-Executive Relations in the Wake of Iran-Contra," in *The Fettered Presidency: Legal Constraints on the Executive Branch,* L. Gordon Crovitz and Jeremy A. Rabkin, eds. (Washington, D.C.: American Enterprise Institute, 1988), pp. 280–81.

2. President Reagan asked former Senator John Tower to study NSC staff and operations, with particular focus on Iran-contra. The special review board, also known as the Tower Commission, found that the Iranian initiative "was handled too informally, without adequate written records of what had been considered, discussed, and decided." Certain legal issues were casually handled, and there was never any review of the progress of the initiative once it was underway. Neither was Congress notified, as required by the National Security Act.

3. Ronald Reagan, *An American Life* (New York: Simon and Schuster, 1990), pp. 540–41.

4. *Report of the Congressional Committees Investigating the Iran-Contra Affair, with Supplemental, Minority, and Additional Views,* H. Rept. 100-433, S. Rept. 100-216 (Washington, 1987), p. 536.

5. Ibid., p. 545.

6. Reagan was fortunate that he had better staff than the NSC's to assist him in finding out what his administration had been doing. In a November 20 meeting during which upcoming administration testimony in Congress was reviewed, Abraham Sofaer of the State Department challenged a version of the arms sales advanced in that testimony, and Charles J. Cooper of the Justice Department was sufficiently alert to understand the issues—new to him, in November of

1986—and to advise Attorney General Meese that something was seriously awry with the Iran initiative and merited his personal review. Had Cooper not acted, had he not insisted to Meese that the facts of the Iran operation be gathered, it is conceivable if not probable that news about the diversion would have been uncovered by journalism or Congress. That would have placed the presidency even more on the defensive.

Meese, for his part, moved quickly to tell the President of the conflicting accounts and advise him of the need to gather those facts. It is worth emphasizing that Meese was under no compulsion to ask for this task, which ordinarily would have fallen to the White House Chief of Staff. But Meese might have regarded Don Regan as limited in his ability to investigate and reasoned that there was a void to be filled. In any event, Meese effectively traded his hat of Attorney General for that of a White House Chief of Staff, in the process exposing himself to the kind of criticism that later ensued (namely, that he should have conducted not a civil but a criminal inquiry, since an Attorney General has criminal investigative authority). Someone of high position within the administration had to sort out what had happened with regard to the Iran initiative; Meese could have distanced himself from the scandal, much as Weinberger and Shultz had distanced themselves from the Iran initiative. It is to his credit that he did not. While certain aspects of Meese's inquiry can reasonably be questioned on procedural grounds, its integrity cannot be; no evidence has ever been produced suggesting that Meese or his aides skewed their inquiry for political reasons.

7. Reagan, *An American Life,* p. 543.
8. As a matter of constitutional policy, it was also questionable. The funds received from arms sales should have gone to the U.S. Treasury. Congress had decided that the contras should not receive any appropriated funds for military purposes, which means any Treasury funds.
9. Poindexter was indicted and convicted on five counts, including conspiracy to obstruct congressional inquiries by using false chronologies, making false statements to congressional committees, and destroying documents in connection with the Iran-contra initiatives. Not only his but also Oliver North's convictions were nullified by the federal appeals court in the District of Columbia. Congress had given North and Poindexter immunity in exchange for testimony. Not only could Walsh not use their immunized testimony against them in criminal proceedings, but he also had the burden of proving that his office in no way had relied upon that testimony. In the view of the appeals court, the trial judge had not held enough hearings to determine whether Walsh had met this burden.
10. Gideon Rose, "When the President Breaks the Law," *National Interest,* no. 9 (Fall 1987): 50–63.
11. One who did see the irresponsibility of Reagan was L. Gordon Crovitz, "How Ronald Reagan Weakened the Presidency," *Commentary,* September 1988, pp. 25–29.

PART THREE
THE PRESIDENCY AND THE APPOINTMENT OF JUDGES

1. Arthur Schlesinger's well-known *The Imperial Presidency,* published in 1973 (Boston: Houghton Mifflin), also neglects the subject.
2. Henry J. Abraham, *Justices and Presidents: A Political History of Appointments to the Supreme Court,* 2nd Edition (New York: Oxford University Press, 1985).
3. *The Federalist No. 47* (J. Madison), (New York: Mentor Books, 1961), p. 303.
4. For a concise discussion of the framing of the method of nomination and appointment, see Eugene W. Hickok, Jr., "Judicial Selection: The Political Roots of Advice and Consent," in *Judicial Selection: Merit, Ideology, and Politics* (Washington: National Legal Center for the Public Interest, 1990), pp. 3–14.
5. Quoted in ibid., p. 8.
6. *The Federalist No. 76* (A. Hamilton), pp. 455–56.
7. Ibid., p. 456.
8. Ibid., p. 457.
9. Abraham, *Justices and Presidents,* p. 39.
10. Presidents may unilaterally appoint a Justice or judge when the Senate is recessed and thus unable to pass on a nomination. But during the next session of Congress, the President must submit the appointed jurist for confirmation or else make a new nomination.

CHAPTER 17
HOW (AND HOW NOT) TO SELECT A JUSTICE

1. Henry J. Abraham, *Justices and Presidents: A Political History of Appointments to the Supreme Court,* 2nd Edition (New York: Oxford University Press, 1985), p. 210.
2. Ibid., p. 281. Johnson made four nominations, two of which were approved by the Senate. Abraham says the nomination of Thurgood Marshall was the only exception to the pattern of cronyism.
3. The "judicial restraint" philosophy, articulated by Reagan at a high level of generality and supplemented at times in more detail by his three Attorneys General, calls for a more restricted exercise of the judicial power. Generally speaking, a judge committed to judicial restraint would be disinclined to protect asserted rights not found in the Constitution or its history; likely to defer to government action unless it clearly violates the Constitution; and interested in making sure that cases and controversies have been properly raised and are ripe for judicial decision. I say "generally speaking," because a Justice committed to judicial restraint and a judge likewise committed might have different views, reflecting their different stations, about overturning a Supreme Court precedent. Lower court judges generally abide by Supreme

Court decisions, even if they think them erroneous. The Supreme Court is under no such obligation.

Also, it is worth noting here that "judicial restraint" has been defined in much more precise ways than Presidents Reagan and Bush have done; and scholars (and jurists) committed to judicial restraint have differed among themselves as to both the result and the reasoning in particular cases. But on balance they believe the exercise of judicial power should be more restricted than it has been in recent decades.

4. The literature on the Warren Court and judicial activism generally is large and growing. Useful works include Alexander Bickel, *The Supreme Court and the Idea of Progress* (New Haven: Yale University Press, 1978); Donald Horowitz, *The Courts and Social Policy* (Washington: Brookings Institution, 1977); Raoul Berger, *Government by Judiciary: The Transformation of the Fourteenth Amendment* (Boston: Harvard University Press, 1977); and Christopher Wolfe, *The Rise of Modern Judicial Review: From Constitutional Interpretation to Judge-Made Law* (New York: Basic Books, 1986).

5. 410 U.S. 113 (1973).

6. Abraham, *Justices and Presidents,* pp. 15–16.

7. Ibid., pp. 16–17.

8. Nixon's third appointee was Lewis Powell of Richmond, Va. Had Nixon completed his second term, he would have had the opportunity to fill the vacancy created by Justice William O. Douglas's resignation. As it happened, President Ford appointed federal appeals court judge John Paul Stevens, whose votes place him on the left side of the Court.

9. The decision to turn one vacancy into two proved a brilliant stroke, a shrewd use of the President's constitutional power to nominate. Scalia was not seen as a candidate for Chief Justice (nor, for that matter, was Bork), yet he, like Bork, was the best advocate of the President's judicial philosophy, all other things being equal. Meanwhile, Associate Justice Rehnquist, who also measured up well in terms of Reagan's judicial philosophy, was well-liked within the Court and seemed administratively able, as ideally a Chief Justice should be. He could assume the Chief's administrative duties without having to get acclimated to the Court, as someone entirely new would. With the two-for-one move, Reagan thus was able to appoint a Chief Justice capable of the administrative side of the job whose commitment to judicial restraint was already well demonstrated while also placing on the Court one of the two best available exponents of the same philosophy, who would not have to bother with nonjudicial business. Reagan's exercise of his power to nominate is one that a later President, in similar circumstances, would do well to consider.

10. Part of the Reynolds team, I reviewed Scalia.

11. The Criminal Division's preliminary investigation, lasting many weeks, did not lead to an independent counsel investigation.

12. Ginsburg issued this statement (through me): "I was asked whether I

had ever used drugs. To the best of my recollection, once as a college student in the Sixties, and then on a few occasions in the Seventies, I used marijuana. That was the only drug I ever used. I have not used it since. It was a mistake and I regret it."

13. William J. Bennett, the Education Secretary, effectively killed the nomination by advising Ginsburg to withdraw. For Bennett, there was a moral issue at stake. Ginsburg had smoked marijuana as a law professor, and for Bennett such activity taught indifference if not defiance of the law (marijuana use being against Massachusetts law). Bennett also saw a political problem arising from the juxtaposition of the Ginsburg nomination next to the administration's highly visible anti-drug effort. After conveying his views by phone to Ginsburg, Bennett became a news story; the Education Department proceeded to publicize his action, with White House encouragement, and White House aides who saw the Ginsburg nomination as Bennett did anonymously told reporters what the Secretary had done. The press stories placed additional pressure on Ginsburg, who the day after the Bennett phone call found himself on national television reading his withdrawal statement.

This was one of the stranger episodes in the Reagan presidency, and I happened to be involved in it. Bennett, who did not know Ginsburg, phoned me on Friday, the day after the nominee's admission of pot smoking; Bennett wanted to talk with Meese, who was out of town, giving a speech. I suggested to Bennett that he convey his views to White House Chief of Staff Howard Baker. Two hours later William Kristol, Bennett's chief of staff, called me to advise that Bennett had called not only Baker but also Reagan, who [Kristol said] had told Bennett to do what he thought he had to do. Bennett took this as a call to action, proceeding to call Ginsburg and advising him to withdraw. This shocked Ginsburg, who had heard this from no one else in the administration. That evening, Brad Reynolds, upset with Bennett's intervention, also decided Ginsburg should withdraw. So he did—the next day. However one assesses Bennett's action, a strong President would not effectively cede the fate of a Supreme Court nomination to a cabinet secretary not involved in judicial selection.

14. By the end of August it had become clear to me and several others in the Department (including John Bolton, head of legislative affairs) that the Bork nomination was in serious trouble. I thought this on the basis of my experience fielding reporters' questions and feeling the momentum shift against Bork, no thanks to the fact that Reagan and senior White House aides had idly spent the month in California. During the daily senior staff meeting on the Tuesday after Labor Day—when many were returning from vacations and other trips out of town, including the Attorney General, who had led a delegation of lawyers to China—I sounded the alarm of a possible Bork defeat and suggested we should begin now to search for a new nominee, just in case. Meese seemed uninterested in such a contingency plan; so far as I know, none was undertaken.

15. Another reason for the Scalia choice was the anticipated confirmation politics; in the event Rehnquist were strongly opposed (as it happened, he was, with thirty-three Senators voting against him), the paired nomination, it was thought, would need some extra political "lift." Scalia, of Italian ancestry, would be the first with that background on the Court, and it was thought that this fact might attract support from senators in other circumstances opposed to a judicial conservative. Scalia was confirmed without a single dissenting vote.

16. For the background on the O'Connor selection, I have relied primarily upon Abraham, *Justices and Presidents,* pp. 331–32.

17. Lou Cannon, *Reagan* (New York: Putnam, 1982), p. 290.

18. Abraham, *Justices and Presidents,* p. 333.

19. So was competence, in the view of some; as University of Virginia Law Professor G. Edward White put it, "a man with O'Connor's background would probably not have been nominated to the Supreme Court." Abraham, *Justices and Presidents,* p. 335. O'Connor was probably the best exemplar of Reagan's judicial philosophy within the then small pool of Republican women Reagan could have considered for the Court. This pool increased throughout the 1980s.

CHAPTER 18
CONFIRMATION LESSONS

1. The literature on the Bork confirmation battle includes a journalistic account by the *Boston Globe*'s Ethan Bronner, *Battle for Justice: How the Bork Nomination Shook America* (New York: Norton, 1989); a treatment in Bork's own book about constitutional interpretation, *The Tempting of America: The Political Seduction of the Law* (New York: Free Press, 1989); an account of the battle as told from the perspective of Bork's opponents, *The People Rising: The Campaign Against the Bork Nomination,* by Michael Pertschuk and Wendy Schaetzel (New York: Thunder's Mouth Press, 1989); and a book by Bork's supporters, *Ninth Justice: The Fight for Bork,* by Patrick B. McGuigan and Dawn M. Weyrich (Lanham, Md.: University Press of America, 1990).

2. See Robert H. Bork, *The Antitrust Paradox: A Policy at War with Itself* (New York: Basic Books, 1978).

3. Bronner, *Battle for Justice,* pp. 98–99.

4. Bork was not the first nominee to have hearings delayed for a lengthy period. Sandra Day O'Connor's confirmation hearings did not begin until two months after she had been nominated.

5. Bronner, *Battle for Justice,* p. 214.

6. Pertschuk and Schaetzel, *The People Rising,* pp. 122–23.

7. Bronner, *Battle for Justice,* p. 159.

8. Ibid., p. 149.

9. Ibid., pp. 151–52.

10. Ibid., p. 292.

11. As the Director of Public Affairs at the Justice Department during Reagan's second term, upon request I wrote several draft speeches for the President; these were duly transmitted to the White House, as were others written by other Justice officials. But Reagan did not give a major speech until the one described here. I recall what a senior Reagan adviser told me when I reiterated the need for the President to speak: "We know when it's best to use the President in that way."
12. 381 U.S. 479 (1965).
13. Pertschuk and Schaetzel, *The People Rising,* p. 229.
14. See Terry Eastland, "Bork Vote: Just a Battle in a 50-Year War," *Wall Street Journal,* October 27, 1987.
15. While the question of judicial enforcement of unenumerated rights is important in a theoretical sense, it is not a litmus test for who is and is not a judicial conservative, at least as that term has been used by the Reagan and Bush administrations. Moreover, so long as a nominee confines his acceptance of the right of privacy to the marital context, he (or she) has embraced something noncontroversial and unlikely to be litigated. The reason unenumerated rights theory is politically important is that the abortion right—which the Court said was part of the unenumerated right of privacy—is a subject of continuing litigation in the federal courts.
16. Bork, *The Tempting of America,* p. 332.
17. At one point Thomas rebuked Senator Howard Metzenbaum of Ohio, one of the most liberal committee members, by observing that "you, Senator" are not "my judge," that only God is. Suffice to say, such a remark could not have been composed by White House handlers but had to have come from within the nominee.

CHAPTER 19
A NEW JUDGE EVERY EIGHT DAYS

1. Reagan filled 372 of 736 Article III positions. Eighteen of his appointments were elevations to the appeals courts of district judges he had previously named. One Supreme Court appointment was an elevation, from an Associate Justice to Chief Justice (in the case of William Rehnquist). Two Reagan judges resigned during his tenure, three retired, and two others died. As a result, when Reagan left office in 1989, there were 346 of his appointees in active service, some 47 percent of the judiciary.
2. *Judicial Roulette: Report of the Twentieth Century Fund Task Force on Judicial Selection* (New York: Priority Press, 1988), p. 53.
3. During the Reagan years, for example, one senator recommended his wife; a House member, seeking influence, recommended his son. This, in practice, is typically what judicial selection means when members of Congress attempt it.
4. Griffin Bell, "Federal Judicial Selection: The Carter Years," in *Judicial Selection: Merit, Ideology, and Politics* (Washington: National Legal Center for the Public Interest, 1990), p. 26.

5. The White House Judicial Selection Committee was the institutional means of linking the work of the Justice Department to the Oval Office; it was an instrument of unity in the Reagan judge-picking executive.
6. Stephen J. Markman, "Judicial Selection: The Reagan Years," in *Judicial Selection,* p. 40, fn. 11. On this subject consider, too, Sheldon Goldman, a student of judicial selection, who wrote in 1987 that "there is no objective evidence that a 'litmus test' in terms of specific policy views has been employed [by the Reagan administration] to accept or reject candidates."
7. Had there been a tie, Vice President Bush would have cast the deciding vote.
8. Jefferson B. Sessions, U.S. Attorney from Mobile, Al., was the rejected nominee.
9. Law professor Bernard Siegan, nominated to the U.S. Court of Appeals for the Ninth Circuit, was perhaps the most publicized withdrawal.
10. David M. O'Brien, "The Reagan Judges: His Most Enduring Legacy," in *The Reagan Legacy: Promise and Performance,* Charles O. Jones, ed. (Chatham, N.J.: Chatham House Publishers, 1988), p. 72.
11. Ibid., p. 63.

CHAPTER 20
A MATTER OF OPINIONS

1. Assessment at any point in a judicial career is difficult. In general, judicial restraint is demonstrated not by the result in a particular case but the reasoning employed. Thus, a Justice may write an opinion that sustains a politically liberal statute, but the opinion itself may satisfy the obligations of judicial restraint. Any analysis of a particular Justice requires painstaking research of a kind that has not been done in regard to the opinions of the Justices in question.
2. See John Morton Blum, *The Progressive Presidents* (New York: Norton, 1982), pp. 76–78.
3. For a discussion of the Rehnquist Court and the Reagan-Bush Justices (not including Souter and Thomas), see Robert J. Guiffra, Jr., "The 1989 Supreme Court Term: Review and Outlook," in *The Public Interest Law Review 1992,* Terry Eastland, ed. (Durham, N.C.: Carolina Academic Press, 1992), pp. 163–185.
4. For an analysis of Souter's first year on the Court, see Gregory E. Maggs, "The 1990 Supreme Court Term: Review and Outlook," in *The Public Interest Law Review 1992,* Terry Eastland, ed. (Durham, N.C.: Carolina Academic Press, 1992), pp. 90–92.
5. 110 S.Ct. 2997 (1990).
6. 487 U.S. 654 (1988).
7. *Texas* v. *Johnson,* 491 U.S. 397 (1989); *U.S.* v. *Eichman,* 110 S.Ct. 2404 (1990).
8. Already the more important differences include: the degree to which

history should be used in substantive due process analysis; the degree to which the First Amendment protects free speech and religious liberty; whether separation of powers should be understood in terms of constitutional text only or also structure; and the circumstances under which clearly erroneous precedent may be jettisoned. A more obvious debate (than has taken place so far) over the extent to which the Constitution protects economic rights may be in the offing. In this debate, a Justice willing to revive the old substantive due process—and thus the activism—of the *Lochner* era would, in my judgment, find himself taking leave of the family of judicial conservatism.

9. Herman Schwartz, *Packing the Courts: The Conservative Campaign to Rewrite the Constitution* (New York: Scribner's, 1988), p. 151.
10. 478 U.S. 186 (1986).
11. 494 U.S. 259 (1990).
12. 110 S.Ct. 2841 (1990).
13. 59 U.S.L.W. 4814 (1991), overruling *Booth* v. *Maryland,* 482 U.S. 496 (1987), and *South Carolina* v. *Gathers,* 490 U.S. 95 (1989). As for overruling *Roe* v. *Wade,* in which the Court declared a constitutional right to an abortion, Justice Scalia has said explicitly that he would vote to reverse it while two other Reagan-Bush Justices (Rehnquist and Kennedy) are clearly inclined that way. A fourth, Justice O'Connor, has expressed skepticism about the validity of *Roe,* although it is unclear whether she will vote for its reversal. As of early 1992, neither Souter nor Thomas had written opinions indicating their views of *Roe.* Justice White, appointed by President Kennedy in 1962, dissented in *Roe* and is prepared to vote to overrule.
14. Maggs, "The 1990 Supreme Court Term," p. 76.
15. *EEOC* v. *Arabian American Oil Company,* 59 U.S.L.W. 4225.
16. The reduced level of judicial government is to some extent indicated by the declining number of cases the Court decides. In the 1990 Term, it issued 112 opinions, seventeen fewer than the year before and 21 fewer than in the 1988 Term.
17. For a penetrating analysis of Kennedy's and Souter's writings, see Bruce Fein, "It's Been All Downhill Since Bork," *The American Bar Journal,* October 1991, pp. 75–79.
18. Craig Stern, "Judging the Judges: The First Two Years of the Reagan Bench," *Benchmark,* vol. I, nos. 4 & 5 (July–October 1984). Political scientists have produced studies classifying judges by the outcomes of cases, disregarding their reasoning. This reflects the "quantitative" or "behavioralist" approach favored in academe and often accepted by journalism. Accordingly, decisions in which criminal defendants "win" are regarded as "liberal," while holdings for the prosecution are seen as "conservative." A similar "liberal" or "conservative" label is applied in cases involving the environment and civil rights. This kind of study is as easy as counting, because it *is* counting. Virtually all of the behavioral studies to date indicate that Reagan is getting what he wanted, because Reagan appointees have been more "conservative" than "liberal." Whatever the merit of these studies, they are beside the point,

because the outcome in a particular case is not what Reagan intended through judicial selection. It is quite possible for a judge committed to judicial restraint to interpret and apply the law correctly (in terms of judicial restraint) and a "liberal" plaintiff to win. The only study of merit so far is Stern's.

19. Ibid., p. 5.
20. This is a project some law school ought to undertake.

## THE STRONG PRESIDENCY AND PRESIDENTIAL LEADERSHIP

1. Thomas C. Reeves, *A Question of Character: A Life of John F. Kennedy* (New York: Free Press, 1991), p. 418.
2. *The Federalist No. 70* (A. Hamilton) (New York: Mentor Books, 1961), p. 423.
3. In her syndicated column of November 19, 1990, Jeane Kirkpatrick shrewdly observed that in his budget summit work Bush was "the very model of" the bargaining President endorsed by Neustadt, who wrote in *Presidential Power* that "the power to persuade is the power to bargain." This model does not promise to work when the electorate is as conflicted over major issues as it is today. Reviewing the 1990 edition of *Presidential Power* as the budget summit process of 1990 was taking place, Thomas B. Edsall observed that "there is a substantial dissonance between the problems of executive leadership as defined by Neustadt and the real difficulties facing Bush." *Washington Post Book World,* November 11, 1990.
4. Louis Fisher, *Constitutional Conflicts Between Congress and the President* (Princeton, N.J.: Princeton University Press, 1985), p. 150.
5. The revision was then later revised, a year later under new Education Secretary Lamar Alexander. This third edition of law enforcement change was approved by Bush. As policy, it made slightly more sense.
6. William French Smith, *Law and Justice in the Reagan Administration* (Stanford, Calif.: Hoover Institution Press, 1991), p. 220.
7. Credit also goes to OLC career attorney Larry Simms, who had fought the legislative veto during the Carter presidency as well. See Barbara H. Craig, *Chadha: The Story of an Epic Constitutional Struggle* (New York: Oxford University Press, 1987).
8. Theodore Olson, in an interview with the author, January 10, 1992, Washington, D.C.
9. No 88-1394 (slip op.), D.C. Cir., February 19, 1992.
10. For a discussion of Lincoln's use of prerogative power and the power generally, see Robert Scigliano, "The President's 'Prerogative Power,' " in *Inventing the Presidency,* Thomas E. Cronin, ed. (Lawrence: University of Kansas Press, 1989), pp. 236–56.
11. Letter to Matthew Birchard and others, June 19, 1863, in *The Collected Works of Abraham Lincoln* (9 vols.), Roy B. Basler, ed. (New Brunswick, N.J.: Rutgers University Press, 1953), vol. 7, p. 281.
12. 4 Wall. (71 U.S.) 2 (1866). The issue in the case was whether a civilian

citizen could be lawfully executed for treasonous activities by order of a military tribunal acting under authority of the President after the cessation of hostilities. The Supreme Court issued a writ of habeas corpus for Milligan's release from custody.

13. As Robert S. Hirschfield has observed, Nixon also did not "make candid public statements such as those in which Lincoln explained his extraordinary exertions of authority." *The Power of the Presidency: Concepts and Controversy* (New York: Aldine D. Gruyter, 1982), pp. 51–52.

14. Joseph Califano, *The Triumph and Tragedy of Lyndon Baines Johnson: The White House Years* (New York: Simon and Schuster, 1991) p. 315.

15. Of FDR, Neustadt wrote, "No President in this century has had a sharper sense of personal power, a sense of what it is and where it comes from; none has had more hunger for it, few have had more use for it, and only one or two could match his faith in his own competence to use it. Perception and desire and self-confidence, combined, produced their own record. No modern President has been more nearly master in the White House." *Presidential Power: The Politics of Leadership* (New York: John Wiley, 1960), p. 161. In his 1990 edition, Neustadt continued to regard Roosevelt as the best leadership model. See *Presidential Power and the Modern Presidents: The Politics of Leadership* (New York: Free Press, 1990), pp. 316–17.

16. Neustadt, *Presidential Power: The Politics of Leadership,* p. 192.

17. For a discussion of the liberal frustration and the liberal hope in the late 1950s and early 1960s, as well as reassessment of Neustadt's view of presidential power see John Hart, "Presidential Power Revisited," *Political Studies,* vol. 25, no. 1 (March 1977): 48–49.

18. Thus, Robert S. Hirschfield wrote in 1982 that "Reagan's ideological commitments . . . include such 'weak' presidency concepts as circumscribing the authority of the national government, respecting the principles of federalism and separation of powers, and returning resources to localities, enterprises, and individuals." Hirschfield did observe the paradoxical need Reagan had for a strong presidency to achieve these ends. *The Power of the Presidency,* p. 52.

19. Quoted in ibid., pp. 86–87.

20. William E. Leuchtenburg, *Franklin D. Roosevelt and the New Deal: 1932–1940* (New York: Harper Torchbooks, 1963), p. 326.

21. FDR's most philosophical speech is widely regarded to be his address on "Progressive Government," delivered to the Commonwealth Club in San Francisco on September 2, 1932. There Roosevelt said it was time "for a reappraisal of values." "Our task is not discovery or exploitation of natural resources, or necessarily producing more goods," he said. "It is the soberer, less dramatic business of administering resources and plants already in hand, of seeking to reestablish foreign markets for our surplus production, of meeting the problem of underconsumption, of adjusting production to consumption, of distributing wealth and products more equitably, of adapting existing economic organizations to the service of the people. The day of enlightened ad-

ministration has come." Franklin Delano Roosevelt, *Public Papers and Addresses,* Samuel I. Rosenman, ed., 13 vols. (New York: Random House, 1938–50), vol. 1: 751–52. Reagan, on the other hand, saw the paramount economic need as that of more production. The 1981 tax rate cuts were designed to increase the economy's supply of goods and services.

22. See Alfred H. Kelly, Winfred A. Harbison, and Herman Belz, *The American Constitution: Its Origins and Development,* 7th Edition (New York: Norton, 1991), p. 410.

23. Leuchtenburg, *Franklin D. Roosevelt and the New Deal,* p. 84.

24. FDR sought in effect to mass the powers of government with his court-packing scheme in 1937. Frustrated with decisions that had blocked certain New Deal measures, Roosevelt sent a message to Congress that called for the appointment of an extra Justice for each sitting Justice past the age of seventy. Roosevelt said the Court was behind in its work—an argument that was inaccurate and plainly disingenuous, given his desire to appoint a majority of Justices who sided with him. Roosevelt did not succeed, as the size of the Court remained the same. Eventually, of course, he was able to nominate and appoint Justices when routine vacancies occurred, and through those appointments he changed the direction of the Court.

25. See Richard B. McKenzie, "Was It a Decade of Greed?" *The Public Interest,* no. 106 (Winter 1992), pp. 91–96.

26. See James Q. Wilson, "Reagan and the Republican Revival," *Commentary,* October 1980, p. 26.

27. See Richard E. Morgan, *Disabling America: The "Rights Industry" in Our Time* (New York: Basic Books, 1984).

28. The source for these figures is Daniel J. Mitchell, John M. Olin Senior Fellow at the Heritage Foundation, in a letter to the *New York Times,* April 5, 1992.

29. Quoted in "Medicaid Malpractice," *Wall Street Journal,* January 6, 1992.

30. Neil Howe and Phillip Longman, "The Next New Deal," *The Atlantic Monthly,* April 1992, pp. 88–89.

31. Ibid., p. 93.

32. Charles Krauthammer, "In the Casino," *Washington Post,* May 3, 1991.

# SELECTED BIBLIOGRAPHY

## BOOKS

Abraham, Henry J., *Justices and Presidents: A Political History of Appointments to the Supreme Court,* 2nd Edition (New York: Oxford University Press, 1985).

Adams, James Ring, *The Big Fix: Inside the S&L Scandal* (New York: John Wiley, 1990).

Amaker, Norman C., *Civil Rights and the Reagan Administration* (Washington: Urban Institute Press, 1988).

Anderson, Martin, *Revolution* (New York: Harcourt Brace Jovanovich, 1988).

Barber, James David, *The Presidential Character* (Englewood Cliffs, N.J.: Prentice-Hall, 1972).

Barrett, Laurence I., *Gambling with History: Reagan in the White House* (New York: Penguin Books, 1984).

Belz, Herman, *Equality Transformed: A Quarter Century of Affirmative Action* (New Brunswick, N.J.: Transaction Books, 1991).

Bessette, Joseph M., and Jeffrey Tulis, eds., *The Presidency in the Constitution Order* (Baton Rouge: Louisiana State University Press, 1981).

Birnbaum, Jeffrey and Allan Murray, *Showdown at Gucci Gulch: Lawmakers, Lobbyists and the Unlikely Triumph of Tax Reform* (New York: Random House, 1987).

Blum, John Morton, *The Progressive Presidents* (New York: Norton, 1982).

Bork, Robert, *The Tempting of America: The Political Seduction of the Law* (New York: Free Press, 1989).

Bronner, Ethan, *Battle for Justice: How the Bork Nomination Shook America* (New York: Norton, 1989).

Buckley, William F., and Charles R. Kesler, eds., *Keeping the Tablets: Modern American Conservative Thought* (New York: Harper & Row, 1988).

Califano, Joseph, *The Triumph and Tragedy of Lyndon Johnson: The White House Years* (New York: Simon and Schuster,1991).

Cannon, Lou, *President Reagan: The Role of a Lifetime* (New York: Simon and Schuster, 1991).

———, *Reagan* (New York: Putnam, 1982).

Caplan, Lincoln, *The Tenth Justice: The Solicitor General and the Rule of Law* (New York: Knopf, 1987).

Cronin, Thomas E., ed., *Inventing the American Presidency* (Lawrence: University of Kansas Press, 1989).

Crovitz, L. Gordon, and Jeremy A. Rabkin, eds., *The Fettered Presidency* (Washington: American Enterprise Institute, 1988).

Eastland, Terry, *Ethics, Politics, and the Independent Counsel: Executive Power, Executive Vice 1789–1989* (Washington: National Legal Center for the Public Interest, 1989).

Eden, Robert, ed., *The New Deal and Its Legacy: Critique and Reappraisal* (Westport, Conn.: Greenwood Press, 1989).

*Federalist, The* (A. Hamilton, J. Madison, and J. Jay) (New York: Mentor Books, 1961).

Fisher, Louis, *Constitutional Conflicts Between Congress and the President* (Princeton, N.J.: Princeton University Press, 1985).

———, *Presidential Spending Power* (Princeton, N.J.: Princeton University Press, 1975).

Fried, Charles, *Order and Law: Arguing the Reagan Revolution—A Firsthand Account* (New York: Simon and Schuster, 1991).

Gottfried, Paul, and Thomas Fleming, *The Conservative Movement* (Boston: Twayne Publishers, 1988).

Graham, Hugh Davis, *The Civil Rights Era: Origins and Development of National Policy 1960–1972* (New York: Oxford University Press, 1990).

Hirschfield, Robert S., ed., *The Power of the Presidency: Concepts and Controversy*, 3rd Edition (New York: Adline De Gruyter, 1982).

Jones, Charles O., ed., *The Reagan Legacy: Promise and Performance* (Chatham, N.J.: Chatham House Publishers, 1988).

Jones, Gordon S., and John A. Marini, eds., *The Imperial Congress: Crisis in the Separation of Powers* (New York: Pharos Books, 1988).

*Judicial Roulette: Report of the Twentieth Century Fund Task Force on Judicial Selection* (New York: Priority Press, 1988).

Kelly, Alfred H., Winfred A. Harbison, and Herman Belz, *The American Constitution : Its Origins and Development*, 7th Edition (New York: Norton, 1991).

Leuchtenburg, William E., *Franklin D. Roosevelt and the New Deal 1932–1940* (New York: Harper & Row, 1963).

Linsky, Barton, Jonathan Moore, Windy O'Donnell, and David Whitman, *How the Press Affects Federal Policymaking: Six Case Studies* (New York: Norton, 1986).

Lodge, Henry Cabot, ed., *The Works of Alexander Hamilton* (New York: G. P. Putnam, 1969).

Lord, Carnes, *The Presidency and the Management of National Security* (New York: Free Press, 1988).

Mansfield, Harvey C., Jr., *Taming the Prince: The Ambivalence of Modern Executive Power* (New York: Free Press, 1989).

Nash, George, *The Conservative Intellectual Movement in America* (New York: Basic Books, 1976).

Nathan, Richard P., *The Administrative Presidency* (New York: Macmillan, 1983).

Nelson, Michael, ed., *The Presidency and the Political System,* 2nd Edition (Washington: Congressional Quarterly, 1988).

Neustadt, Richard E., *Presidential Power: The Politics of Leadership* (New York: John Wiley, 1960).

——, *Presidential Power and the Modern Presidents: The Politics of Leadership* (New York: Free Press, 1990).

Niskanen, William A., *Reaganomics: An Insider's Account of the Policies and the People* (New York: Oxford University Press, 1988).

Noonan, Peggy, *What I Saw at the Revolution: A Political Life in the Reagan Era* (New York: Random House, 1990).

Oberdorfer, Don, *The Turn: From the Cold War to a New Era: The United States and the Soviet Union 1983–1990* (New York: Poseidon Press, 1991).

Pertschuk, Michael, and Wendy Schaetzel, *The People Rising: The Campaign Against the Bork Nomination* (New York: Thunder's Mouth Press, 1989).

Pious, Richard, *The American Presidency* (New York: Basic Books, 1979).

*Pork Barrels and Principles: The Politics of the Presidential Veto* (Washington: National Legal Center for the Public Interest, 1988).

Rabkin, Jeremy, *Judicial Compulsions: How Public Law Distorts Public Policy* (New York: Basic Books, 1989).

Reagan, Ronald, *An American Life* (New York: Simon and Schuster, 1990).

Regan, Donald, *For the Record: From Wall Street to Washington* (New York: Harcourt Brace Jovanovich, 1988).

Reichley, James, *Conservatives in an Age of Change: The Nixon and Ford Administrations* (Washington: Brookings Institution, 1981).

Schlesinger, Arthur M., Jr., *The Imperial Presidency* (Boston: Houghton Mifflin, 1973).

Shane, Peter M., and Harold H. Bruff, *The Law of Presidential Power* (Durham, N.C.: Carolina Academic Press, 1988).

Smith, Hendrick, *The Power Game: How Washington Works* (New York: Ballantine Books, 1989).

Smith, William French, *Law and Justice in the Reagan Administration: Memoirs of an Attorney General* (Stanford: Hoover Institute Press, 1991).

Stockman, David A., *The Triumph of Politics: Why the Reagan Revolution Failed* (New York: Harper & Row, 1986).

Thach, Charles C., Jr., *The Creation of the Presidency 1775–1789: A Study in Constitutional History* (Baltimore: Johns Hopkins University Press: 1969).

Tulis, Jeffrey K., *The Rhetorical Presidency* (Princeton, N.J.: Princeton University Press, 1987).

Wilson, James Q., *Bureaucracy: What Government Agencies Do and Why They Do It* (New York: Basic Books, 1989).

Wilson, Woodrow, *Congressional Government: A Study in American Politics* (Baltimore: Johns Hopkins University Press, 1981; orig. ed., 1885).

Wilson, Woodrow, *Constitutional Government in the UnitedStates* (New York: Columbia University Press, 1961; orig. ed., 1908).

Woodward, Bob, *The Commanders* (New York: Simon and Schuster, 1991).

Woodward, C. Vann, ed., *Responses of the Presidents to Charges of Misconduct* (New York: Dell Publishers, 1974).


ARTICLES


Black, Charles L., Jr., "Some Thoughts on the Veto," *Law & Contemporary Problems,* vol. 40, no. 2 (Spring 1976): 87–101.

Ceasar, James W., Glen E. Thurow, Jeffrey Tulis, and Joseph M. Bessette, "The Rise of the Rhetorical Presidency," *Presidential Studies Quarterly,* vol. 11 (Summer 1981): 158–171.

Clegg, Roger, "The 35th Law Clerk," *Duke Law Journal,* no. 5 (November 1987): 964–975.

Crovitz, L. Gordon, "The Line-Item Veto: The Best Response When Congress Passes One Spending 'Bill' a Year," *Pepperdine Law Review,* vol. 18, no. 1 (1990): 43–55.

———, "How Ronald Reagan Weakened the Presidency," *Commentary* (September 1988): 25–29.

Dahl, Robert A., "Myth of the Presidential Mandate," *Political Science Quarterly,* vol. 105, no. 3 (1990): 355–372.

DeMuth, Christopher C., and Douglas H. Ginsburg, "White House Review of Agency Rulemaking," *Harvard Law Review,* vol. 99, no. 5 (March 1986): 1075–1088.

Devins, Neil, "The Civil Rights Hydra," *Michigan Law Review,* vol. 89, no. 6 (May 1991): 1723–1765.

Eastland, Terry, "George Bush's Quota Bill," *Policy Review,* no. 57 (Summer 1991): 45–49.

———, "The Independent-Counsel Regime," *The Public Interest,* no. 100 (Summer 1990): 68–80.

———, "Reagan Justice," *Policy Review,* no. 46 (Fall 1988): 16–23.

Falcoff, Mark, "Making Central America Safe for Communism," *Commentary,* vol. 85, no. 6 (June 1988): 17–24.

Fein, Bruce, "It's Been All Downhill Since Bork," *The American Bar Journal* (October 1991): 75–79.

Finn, Chester E., Jr., "Quotas and the Bush Administration," *Commentary* (November 1991): 17–23.

———, "Education Policy and the Reagan Administration: A Large but Incomplete Success," *Education Policy,* vol. 2, no. 4 (1988): 344–360.

Fisher, Louis, "The Curious Belief in Judicial Supremacy," *Suffolk University Law Review,* vol. 25, no. 1 (Spring 1991): 85–116.

Frisch, Morton J., "Executive Power and Republican Government— 1787," *Presidential Studies Quarterly,* vol. 17, no. 2 (Spring 1987): 281–291.

Gigot, Paul, "Iraq: An American Screw-Up," *The National Interest,* no. 22 (Winter 1990–91): 3–10.

Greider, William, "The Education of David Stockman," *Atlantic Monthly*, vol. 248, no. 6 (December 1981): 27–54.

Harrison, John, "The Role of the Legislative and Executive Branches in Interpreting the Constitution," *Cornell Law Review*, vol. 73, no. 2 (January 1988): 371–374.

Hart, John, "Presidential Power Revisited," *Political Studies*, vol. 25, no. 1 (March 1977): 48–61.

Howe, Neil, and Phillip Longman, "The Next New Deal," *Atlantic Monthly* (April 1992): 88–99.

Kristol, William, "Can-Do Government," *Policy Review*, no. 31 (Summer 1985): 62–66.

Lord, Carnes, "Executive Power and Our Security," *National Interest*, no. 7 (Spring 1987): 3–13.

McDowell, Gary L., "Affirmative Inaction," *Policy Review*, no. 48 (Spring 1989): 32–37.

Miller, Geoffrey P., "Independent Agencies," *Supreme Court Review*, vol. 3 (1986): 41–97.

Nathan, Richard, "The 'Administrative Presidency,' " *The Public Interest*, no. 44 (Summer 1976): 40–55.

"Presidency and Congress: Constitutionally Separated and Shared Powers," Federalist Society Symposium, *Washington University Law Quarterly*, vol. 68, no. 3 (1990): 485–705.

Rose, Gideon, "When the President Breaks the Law," *The National Interest*, no. 9 (Fall 1987): 50–63.

Schambra, William A., "Progressive Liberalism and American 'Community,' " *Public Interest*, no. 80 (Summer 1985): 31–48.

———, "The Roots of the American Public Philosophy," *Public Interest*, no. 67 (Spring 1982): 36–48.

Schlesinger, Arthur M., Jr., "The Constitution and Presidential Leadership," with comments by Phillip Kurland, Charles J. Cooper, Linda Greene, and James Ceaser, *Maryland Law Review*, vol. 47, no. 1 (1988): 52–114.

Sidak, Gregory J., "To Declare War," *Duke Law Journal*, vol. 41, no. 1 (1991): 27–121.

———, "The President's Power of the Purse," *Duke Law Journal*, vol. 1989, no. 5 (1989): 1162–1253.

———, "The Recommendation Clause," *Georgetown Law Journal*, vol. 77, no. 6 (August 1989): 2079–2135.

Sidak, Gregory J., and Thomas A. Smith, "Four Faces of the Item Veto: A Reply to Tribe and Kurland," *Northwestern University Law Review*, vol. 84, no. 2 (1990): 437–479.

Stern, Craig, "Judging the Judges: The First Two Years of the Reagan Bench," *Benchmark*, vol. 1, nos. 4 & 5 (July–October 1984).

Wildavsky, Aaron, "The Triumph of Ronald Reagan," *The National Interest*, no. 14 (Winter 1988–89): 3–9.

Wilson, James Q., "Reagan and the Republican Revival," *Commentary* (October 1980): 25–32.

# ACKNOWLEDGMENTS

From March 1983 to May 1988, I served in the U.S. Justice Department, an experience that led me to write this book. In doing so, I benefited from the works of predecessors, especially Charles Thach, Jr. (*The Creation of the Presidency 1775–1789: A Study in Constitutional History*), Jeffrey K. Tulis (*The Rhetorical Presidency*), Harvey C. Mansfield, Jr. (*Taming the Prince: The Ambivalence of Modern Executive Power*), and, while I find myself in disagreement with him, Richard E. Neustadt (*Presidential Power*).

I have also benefited from the insights of many individuals in academe and in journalism who observe presidencies and those who have served in the Reagan and Bush administrations. Some were generous enough with their time to read and comment on portions of the manuscript; all seemed al-

383

ways available for conversation. I am especially grateful to Herman Belz, Joseph M. Bessette, Steven G. Calebresi, Lou Cannon, Michael Carvin, Roger Clegg, Charles J. Cooper, Gordon Crovitz, E. J. Dionne, Chester Finn, Louis Fisher, Paul Gigot, John Harrison, Eugene Hickok, William Kristol, Carnes Lord, Nelson Lund, Michael Malbin, Gary L. McDowell, Adam Meyerson, Theodore B. Olson, Wladyslaw Pleszczynski, Gary Schmitt, J. Gregory Sidak, Tony Snow, Kenneth W. Starr, Charles Trueheart, R. Emmett Tyrrell, Jr., and George Weigel. Not incidentally, my friends Tyrrell and Pleszczynski, the editor-in-chief and managing editor, respectively, of *The American Spectator,* encouraged the gestation of this book by allowing me room in the magazine to write about the presidency.

Thanks are also due to those whose research or other work made this a better book: Hunter Boyd, Raymond Voegeli, Sarah Birmingham, Lawrence Florio, Ethan Reedy, Derek Mogck, and Robert Palladino.

And special thanks are in order for Dan Maclellan, who was a tremendous help especially during the final stages of this book and with the index.

My agent, Rafe Sagalyn, helped unite me with a superb publisher, The Free Press, whose president, Erwin Glikes, proved a terrific editor, knowledgeable about the subject of the book and wise in his comments and suggestions. His assistant editor, John Urda, proved of great assistance to me, and Edith Lewis skillfully supervised the copy editing and production.

I began this book while a fellow at the National Legal center for the Public Interest and finished it while in residence at the Ethics and Public Policy Center. A writer can find no more hospitable quarters than these, and I am grateful to both institutions. I am also grateful to the Harry Lynde Bradley Foundation and the John M. Olin Foundation, which have supported me in writing this book.

Love is patient, wrote Paul the Apostle, and my family, to whom I dedicate this book, has been more loving in that regard than I deserve. My wife Jill and my daughter Katie now have me back from the mental attic to which writer sometimes repair when composing at length. They know that I am glad to be back.

# INDEX

385